# WILEY

# Audit and Assurance Essentials for Professional Accountancy Exams

# WILEY

# Audit and Assurance Essentials for Professional Accountancy Exams

Katharine Bagshaw

## WILEY

*Registered office*

John Wiley & Sons Ltd, The Atrium, Southern Gate, Chichester, West Sussex, PO19 8SQ, United Kingdom

For details of our global editorial offices, for customer services and for information about how to apply for permission to reuse the copyright material in this book please see our website at www.wiley.com

*Library of Congress Cataloging-in-Publication Data*

Bagshaw, Katharine.
    Audit and assurance : essentials for professional accountancy exams / Katharine Bagshaw.
  1 online resource.
      Includes index.
    Description based on print version record and CIP data provided by publisher; resource not viewed.
    ISBN 978-1-118-45416-9 (ebk)—ISBN 978-1-118-45417-6 (ebk)—
    ISBN 978-1-118-45418-3 (ebk)—ISBN 978-1-119-96879-5 (pbk.)
      1. Auditing—Examinations, questions, etc.  2. Accounting—Examinations, questions, etc.  I. Title.
  HF5667
  657'.45—dc23

                                                                          2012050741

A catalogue record for this book is available from the British Library.

ISBN 978-1-119-96879-5 (pbk)        ISBN 978-1-118-45416-9 (ebk)
ISBN 978-1-118-45417-6 (ebk)        ISBN 978-1-118-45418-3 (ebk)

Set in 10/11pt Sabon LT Std by MPS Limited, Chennai, India.

Printed in Great Britain by TJ International Ltd, Padstow, Cornwall

# CONTENTS

For VB, DB and HLB

With many thanks indeed to David Chopping
and Gill Spaul for reading and making helpful
observations on this text

# INTRODUCTION

Accountancy qualifications matter. Good accountants help economies grow. Accountancy qualifications provide many people with important opportunities and the possibility of financial security. Doors that might otherwise have remained closed, open for qualified accountants. Auditing and assurance exams are an integral part of many accountancy qualifications and the purpose of this text is to help accountancy students pass auditing and assurance papers.

*This text seeks to explain the requirements of professional standards in just enough detail to give students the confidence to apply them to the questions that come up in exams.*

It is for:

- students taking auditing and assurance exams for accountancy qualifications. It covers both international and UK variants;
- undergraduate students pursuing degrees and other courses with an auditing and assurance element.

Auditing and assurance exams should not be difficult to pass but pass rates, particularly for lower level papers, are often poor, certainly by comparison with other papers. This is sometimes because students underestimate the paper which often results in inadequate preparation, but there are many students who do work hard and still fail to pass, often by one or two marks. This is a shame. It is often the result of inefficient study methods and exam techniques, both of which can be significantly improved provided students are prepared to do things *differently*. The first section of this text deals with these issues.

Each section begins with an explanation of why the student needs to read the section, what is important in it, what sort of questions come up and how to stand out from the crowd in exams. The end of each section sets out the essentials, what students need to remember, and questions that give students an idea of areas that often come up in exams.

*More questions and answers, updates and discussions of current issues appear at the web-site accompanying this text www.wiley.com/go/bagshaw_essentials*

This text is directed at students taking both lower- and higher-level papers, with an emphasis on the elements essential to both. It covers in detail the core elements of the major syllabuses, which are:

- professional ethics;
- international standards on auditing, review, assurance and related services engagements;[1]

---

[1] ISAs, ISREs, ISAEs and ISRSs.

- regulation, professional liability, money laundering and forensic auditing;
- corporate governance and internal audit.

Some verbatim quotes from auditing and ethical standards are provided. They are included with the relevant reference in the main body of the text. However, examiners tend to ask students to explain, describe or discuss matters rather than define them. Demonstrating an understanding is more important than remembering definitions. Detailed references to auditing and ethical standards are provided in footnotes for those who need or want to refer to sources, but no distinction is made between mandatory requirements, indicated in standards by the use of the word 'shall', and non-mandatory application material. The distinction is critical to standard-setters, regulators and developers of audit methodologies and software but it is generally less important in auditing and assurance exams.

This text is directed at students studying for the audit and assurance elements of syllabuses including the main ACCA qualification, its Certified Accounting Technician (CAT) qualification and its CertIA programme. It is also relevant to the main ICAEW qualification and its online ISAs programme. It may serve as a guide to up-to-date standards for experienced practitioners.

The author taught auditing and assurance to ACCA and ICAEW students for over a decade in the UK, Eastern Europe, Africa and Asia. She was examiner for ACCA's lower-level auditing paper for three years and since then has been closely involved in the development and implementation of auditing standards for practitioners in the UK and internationally. She currently works part-time for ICAEW's Audit and Assurance Faculty, sits on IFAC's Small and Medium Practitioner Committee, and writes and presents technical material on auditing standards. The views expressed in this text are the author's own and not those of ICAEW or ACCA.

# 1 AUDITORS, AUDITS AND OTHER TYPES OF ASSURANCE AND PASSING THE EXAM FIRST TIME

**Covering:** *The Role of Audit and Other Types of Assurance in the Economy, Accountability, Stewardship and Agency Theory, the Relationship between Auditors, Management and Shareholders, Overview of the Assurance Process from Planning to Reporting, the Style and Content of Auditing and Assurance Exams, Study Technique and Exam Technique.*

**Why do I need to read this section?**

*Because:*

- *questions on the nature and purpose of audit and assurance engagements are set regularly;*
- *of rising levels of audit exemption, particularly in Europe;*
- *of the important differences between audits, other forms of assurance, and non-assurance engagements;*
- *there are many misconceptions about audit and assurance which this short section will help you eliminate at the outset;*
- *there are many misconceptions about effective study, how examiners set papers and exam technique. This section should help you make the best use of the limited time you have to study for this paper.*

*With the exception of the material on study, exams and technique, all of the information in this section is covered in more detail in subsequent sections.*

**What is important in this section?**

*Understanding:*

- *that audit is a sub-set of assurance and that all assurance engagements are characterised by an assessment of the risk of material misstatement;*
- *the limitations of an audit as well as its benefits;*
- *that compilation and agreed-upon procedures engagements in which practitioners do not obtain any assurance at all are very different to assurance engagements such as audits and reviews.*

**What sort of questions come up in this area?**

*Questions regularly set in this area cover:*

- *the nature, purpose, advantages and disadvantages of an audit;*
- *the difference between audit and other forms of assurance such as reviews;*

- *the difference between assurance and non-assurance engagements, and what type of engagement is appropriate in a given set of circumstances.*

**How do I stand out from the crowd?**

- *Distinguish clearly between audits, reviews, other types of assurance, and non-assurance engagements.*

- *Give examples of non-audit assurance to demonstrate your appreciation of its growing importance.*

- *Use terminology accurately.*

## 1.1   THE NEED FOR AUDIT AND OTHER TYPES OF ASSURANCE

Like it or not, most of us have little choice about letting others manage our assets for us. We hand over our money to companies, banks, pension funds and governments in the hope that they will look after it and use it properly. We need auditors because we want some assurance about this. We want to be confident that the companies we invest in, the banks that look after our cash, the pension funds we hope will provide for our retirement and the governments that spend our taxes, will use the money we give them the way they ought to, the way they say they will. We also want to know that the money we donate for the education of poor people, for example, goes mostly towards school buildings rather than on the salaries of administrators, and we look to auditors for assurance about that, too.

*Audit* is a type of *assurance*. All large-scale operations need auditors because their directors need assurance that the assets and resources for which they are responsible are well-managed. Directors cannot always rely on what they are told by the employees who report to them. Employees make mistakes. Even where there are few mistakes, employees naturally seek to present their own performance in a favourable light. An *independent* view is likely to be more objective, accurate and critical. Many large bodies such as universities, hospitals and health authorities as well as companies, banks, government departments and pension funds, have *internal audit* functions for these reasons. Many of these entities are also subject to independent regulatory oversight and have *external auditors*, because the people needing assurance are not just their directors, but the people to whom the directors are directly or indirectly accountable. Companies, including banks, are accountable to their shareholders. Banks are also accountable to their depositors to some extent but the position of depositors is generally akin to that of creditors, rather than shareholders. Pension funds are accountable to the trustees who act on behalf of pensioners and governments are accountable to taxpayers and electorates. We are all at different times in our lives shareholders, depositors, taxpayers and pensioners. This means that the entities that manage our assets are accountable to us. The external auditors we appoint to them, directly or indirectly, report to us on the financial statements that their directors prepare.

**Auditors, Management and Shareholders: Fiduciary Duties, Accountability, Stewardship and Agency**

> External audits of companies are performed because of the *separation of the ownership and management* of company assets.

Companies belong to their shareholders.[1] Shareholders pay for their shares in the hope that the company will be well-managed, pay dividends from profits and that the value of their shares will increase. They need some confidence in what the company's managers, i.e. its directors or those charged with its governance, to whom they have entrusted their money, tell them about the company's performance and position.

> Company managers are *accountable* to shareholders for their *stewardship* of the company's assets. They have a *fiduciary relationship* with shareholders which means that *they must act in good faith*, for the benefit of the company and all of its shareholders, rather than running the company for their own benefit, or for the benefit of just a few shareholders.

Management accounts to shareholders by preparing financial statements showing the company's *performance*, i.e. a profit and loss account, its *position*, i.e. a balance sheet, and its *cash flows*.[2] If shareholders are dissatisfied with how management has performed, they can sell their shares or, if enough of them are dissatisfied, replace management.

> Companies employ external auditors to report to the shareholders on the financial statements prepared by management.
>
> *Auditors report to shareholders on whether the financial statements give a true and fair view of, or present fairly in all material respects, the financial position and performance of the company.* The audit report adds *credibility* to the financial statements.[3]

Management, not auditors, are responsible for the preparation of financial statements. If the financial statements do not give a true and fair view or present fairly the financial position and performance of a company (the two phrases are deemed to be equivalent), auditors qualify their audit opinion.

Auditors are the *agents*[4] of the shareholders who appoint them, but shareholders rarely disagree with the recommendation of management who also negotiate the auditors' terms, conditions and remuneration. The payment of auditors by the people they are reporting on creates a potential conflict of interest. For this reason, professional bodies and independent audit regulators monitor the conduct of audits.

In many jurisdictions, until fairly recently, there were statutory audit requirements[5] for all incorporated entities.[6] Audit exemption has changed this, particularly in the EU

---

[1]  'Stockholders' in some jurisdictions.
[2]  Financial statements also usually include a statement of changes in equity.
[3]  In some jurisdictions, auditors report to directors as well as, or instead of, shareholders. The phrase 'true and fair' is used in the UK. 'Present fairly' is used in the USA.
[4]  Directors are also the agents of shareholders, appointed to manage the company's assets.
[5]  Statutory requirements are requirements created by legislation (law).
[6]  In some jurisdictions a large number of incorporated entities such as companies were created because of an advantageous tax regime. In others, businesses are more likely to be constituted as partnerships or other unincorporated associations for the same reason. There is now a level of uniformity within the EU because of European company law. It provides for two basic

where the vast majority of companies are exempt from audit requirements based on their size.[7] However, audits of smaller entities continue for several reasons. In family-owned companies, most of the shareholders may also be directors who are actively involved in the day-to-day running of the business. Owner-managers do not need auditors to report to them on their own performance. Other shareholders, however, who are not involved in the business, may want an audit. Some smaller companies are required to have an audit despite the fact that they fulfil the size criteria for exemption, because of the public interest considerations arising from the fact that they operate in the banking, insurance or other financial services sectors, to which special requirements always apply.

The position described above is the UK position. It is similar to the position elsewhere in Europe because all EU Member States are subject to EU audit legislation.

The position in the USA is somewhat different. In the UK and Europe, company audit requirements are in legislation. There are no statutory audit requirements in the USA. Audits are required by the Securities and Exchange Commission (the SEC), a securities regulator, for entities whose securities are listed on the exchanges it regulates, such as NASDAQ and the New York Stock Exchange (NYSE). Auditors in the USA generally report to directors as well as stockholders and the purpose of assurance is to promote the orderly and efficient running of the capital markets.

### Assurance and Risk

Audits of historical financial information benefit existing and potential owners of companies by reducing the risk they take when they invest in companies. Audits also provide assurance to employees, tax authorities, customers and suppliers, lenders, trade unions and governments, all of whom need to know that the company they are dealing with is what it appears to be on paper. For tax authorities, audits reduce the risk of collecting the wrong amount of tax. For employees, audits reduce the risk that they will be employed by an entity that cannot pay them. For customers and suppliers, audits reduce the risk that orders will not be despatched and that invoices will not be paid. For lenders, audits reduce the risk that loans will not be repaid. Audits help

---

categories of company: private and public. The basic distinction between the two is that private companies may not offer their shares or debt securities for sale to the public. In France a Société Anonyme or SA is a public company, a *Société à Responsabilité Limitée* or SARL is a private company. In Germany and other German-speaking jurisdictions, an *Aktiengesellschaft* or AG is a public company, a *Gesellschaft mit beschränkter Haftung* or GmbH is a private company. In the UK, a Public Limited Company (Plc) is a public company, a Limited Company (Ltd) is a private company.

[7]  Size criteria for audit and accounting purposes in many jurisdictions are based on turnover, assets and number of employees. While the criteria for turnover and assets have changed, the criterion for the number of employees has not, and in the EU that number has been 50 employees for a small company for many years. These limits are dealt with in more detail in section 9.

maintain the quality of financial information on the public record used by government and trade unions in collective negotiations between employer, employees and government representatives. In these ways, the assurance provided by audits contributes to the proper functioning of the economy and society as a whole, as well as benefiting shareholders.

### Different Types of Assurance

Audit is only one type of assurance, but it remains the most widely recognised. For exam purposes, the most important distinctions are between:

- *reasonable assurance engagements,* such as *audits* of historical financial information in which the practitioners' (auditors') conclusion is in the form of a positive audit opinion;

- *limited assurance engagements,* such as *reviews* of historical financial information which consist primarily of inquiries and analytical procedures, in which the practitioners' conclusion is expressed in negative terms, on whether anything has come to their attention to indicate that the financial statements may be materially misstated;

- *engagements which do not involve assurance,* such as *compilation engagements,* in which practitioners compile financial information from information supplied, often referred to as accounts preparation engagements, and *agreed-upon procedures* engagements in which practitioners report on the factual findings of procedures they have agreed to perform.

It is important to note that the core work of practitioners in many jurisdictions continues to be accounts preparation, tax and audit work, despite the fact that much of this work is now automated. Changes in recent years mean that firms are no longer restricted to this type of work though, and an increasing number of smaller firms now specialise in providing business and systems advice. Nevertheless, all businesses, especially small businesses, are likely to continue to need professional help to comply with regulatory requirements for the foreseeable future.

In both compilation engagements and audit engagements, the financial statements, including the underlying assumptions and significant judgements made, remain the responsibility of the client.

The proprietors of many businesses assume, perhaps understandably, albeit mistakenly, that good quality accounts preparation software means that they can dispense with the services of a professional accountant. Professional accountants sometimes lose clients who decide either to prepare their own accounts, or to employ cheaper accountants without professional qualifications, only to have the client return after a few years when things have gone wrong. Rightly or wrongly, the level of technical expertise and professional judgement required to prepare even a simple set of financial statements in many jurisdictions is greater than is often expected.

The benefits of employing a professional accountant to prepare accounts or perform an audit include the fact that professional ethics require practitioners to avoid being associated with misleading information. Professional ethics also require that practitioners be objective in the case of accounts preparation engagements, and independent in the case of audit engagements. Professional accountants are subject to regulation and disciplinary arrangements and are accountable for the quality of their work not just to the client, but to a professional body and in some cases an independent regulator.

Assurance can be obtained on non-financial information such as the effectiveness of internal controls and greenhouse gas statements, and on forward-looking information such as profit forecasts and projections, as well as on historical financial information. Different types of assurance are discussed further in section 8.

### The Purposes, Benefits and Limitations of Audit

The purpose of an audit is to *enhance the confidence of intended users* in the financial statements.[8]

The *objectives of auditors* are *to obtain reasonable assurance* about whether the financial statements are free from material misstatement and have been prepared in accordance with the financial reporting framework.[9]

The *benefits* of an audit include:

- reducing the risk of management bias, fraud and error;
- enhancing the credibility of financial information through auditor independence and expertise so that:
  - customers and suppliers can confidently do business with the audited entity and banks and others can lend to it;[10]
  - markets can allocate capital efficiently;
- the recommendations auditors can make for improvements to internal control;
- the financial discipline imposed by an audit which helps companies grow.

The inherent *limitations* of an audit include:

- the fact that 100% testing cannot be performed;
- human error in the selection, performance and evaluation of audit procedures;
- time and cost constraints which mean that audit evidence is persuasive rather than conclusive;

---

[8]  ISA 200 on overall objectives, paragraph 3.
[9]  ISA 200 on overall objectives, paragraph 11.
[10]  For very small businesses, audited financial statements are less important to banks lending to them than the security provided by attaching charges to personal and business assets, such as directors' homes, land and buildings, inventory and receivables.

- the inherent limitations of internal controls, which include the possibility of management override of controls, and fraudulent collusion in which employees collude to misappropriate assets and falsify the related records to cover it up;

- the inherent limitations of financial reporting, which include subjectivity and the need to exercise judgement in calculating estimates such as depreciation and allowances for bad debts.

An audit is not always in the best interests of a company, or even possible. Audits are not cheap. A compilation engagement may suffice if the association of a well-regarded practitioner with the financial statements is all that is required. Certain conditions must be met for any assurance to be obtained and, if they are not, audits and reviews cannot be performed. The criteria for assurance engagements are further discussed in section 8.

### The Assurance Process

Audits, reviews and other reasonable and limited assurance engagements all broadly follow the same overall process.

#### *Acceptance and planning*

Before accepting any assurance engagement, practitioners must ensure that they have complied with ethical and quality control requirements. Ethical requirements demand that they **independent** of the entities on which they report and **competent** to perform the engagement. There must be no conflict of interests with existing clients and management must not lack integrity. **Quality control** requirements demand that the firm has in place procedures to ensure that assurance engagements are conducted in accordance with professional standards, by having proper methodologies, human resources procedures and training, for example. They also require the supervision and review of work on individual engagements. If the engagement is a new one, the firm must complete the protocols for changes in professional appointment and make inquiries of the previous practitioner about whether there is any reason the engagement should not be accepted.

Administrative requirements include the need to issue an **engagement letter** and **liaise with third parties** involved in the engagement such as internal auditors, firms appointed to other group companies, and any experts. Timetabling and allocation of staff are substantial exercises for large engagements, particularly where there are tight reporting deadlines for large listed entities.

Commercial considerations are always relevant. Has a reasonable *fee* been negotiated? Is the client *able to pay*? Firms may perform credit checks using credit rating agencies, like any other business extending credit to a new customer.

#### *Risk assessment by understanding the business*

All assurance engagements involve risk assessment. Risk assessments for reasonable assurance engagements involve extensive analysis of the risks associated with internal control, where appropriate. They go further than assessments for limited assurance engagements in which the risk analysis will only extend to determining the risks of material misstatement.

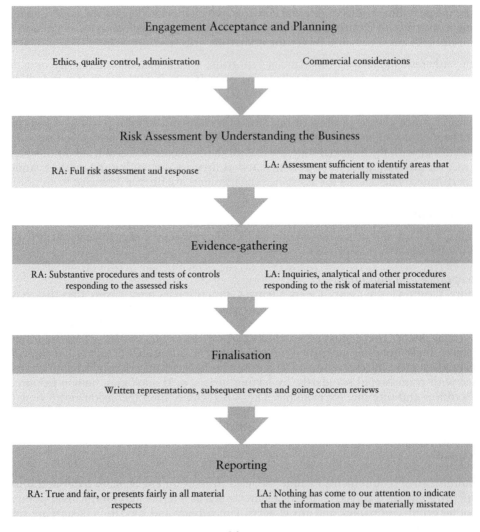

RA = *reasonable assurance engagements*

LA = *limited assurance engagements*

**Figure 1.1**   Overview of the assurance process

### Evidence-gathering

For reasonable assurance engagements, evidence-gathering involves responding to the assessed risks with tests of control and substantive procedures. Substantive procedures consist of tests of details and analytical procedures.[11]

---

[11] Tests of details involve checking individual transactions such as invoices, and balances such as receivables. Analytical procedures involve the analysis of aggregated data, such as review of expenditure on a monthly basis.

In limited assurance engagements, evidence-gathering involves addressing the risks of material misstatement with inquiries, analytical and other procedures as appropriate. There is much less emphasis on internal control and practitioners do not seek to verify or substantiate responses to queries in the way that they do for reasonable assurance engagements.

### Finalisation

The areas covered when finalising an assurance engagement include:

- *written representations* which are required to confirm that management acknowledges its responsibility for the information reported on and for the systems underlying it. Representations also confirm that all relevant information has been provided to practitioners. They confirm management assertions and support other evidence in material areas such as the key assumptions on which significant estimates are based;

- *subsequent events* reviews which are performed after the period-end. Some subsequent events, such as a significant bad debt or the acquisition of a significant new business shortly after the period-end, may require adjustment or disclosure in the information reported on.

### Assurance Reports

Assurance reports generally include:

- *a title and addressee* such as, 'Independent auditors' report to the shareholders of XYZCO;

- *an introductory paragraph* identifying the information reported on, such as the financial statements prepared in accordance with IFRS, often referring to page numbers;

- *the responsibilities of management* for the information and the assumptions on which it is based;

- *the practitioners' responsibilities* to conduct the engagement in accordance with ethical and quality control requirements, auditing or other relevant standards and a summary of the work performed;

- *a conclusion* in the form of either *an opinion on truth and fairness/fair presentation* in a reasonable assurance engagement, or, in a limited assurance engagement, *a conclusion on whether anything has come to the practitioners' attention to indicate that the information is materially misstated*;

- *a signature, date* and *location*.

In the UK, the requirement that all financial statements give a 'true and fair view' was first introduced in the Companies Act 1947 and amended the former phrase 'true and correct'. The phrase 'presents fairly in all material respects' is more commonly used in the USA.

The 'true and fair view' is enshrined in the European Community's Fourth Directive which sets out the form and content of company accounts.

**What an Audit is Not: Common Myths about Auditing and Financial Reporting**

An audit is not a guarantee that the financial statements are not materially misstated. The audit opinion is just that, an opinion.

Auditing standards recognise that a properly performed audit may not detect a material misstatement, because of the inherent limitations of an audit, internal controls and financial reporting. Audit risk is the risk that an unmodified audit opinion is issued where a modified one is appropriate. That risk can be reduced to a quantifiable and acceptable level, but it cannot be eliminated altogether.

Some corporate collapses are the result of management fraud, but most arise from some combination of a lack of profitability, an inability to manage cash flows or excessive debt. They are rarely, if ever, *caused* by auditors.

**A Short History**

Audits and auditors have been around for a long time. An auditor is someone who hears or listens. The Latin root of the word auditor is *auditus,* meaning 'a hearing'. Historically, senior estate staff were said to hear accounts of the management of medieval estate assets and report back to landowners. Modern auditors came into being when companies and corporations started to proliferate in the UK, USA and elsewhere in the 19th century.

Modern companies in the UK and corporations in the USA and elsewhere are artificial legal persons. They exist in their own right independently of their directors and owners (their shareholders or stockholders). Companies and corporations have rights such as limited liability and obligations such as the requirement to prepare financial statements and, in some cases, to have them audited.

In the UK, the Joint Stock Companies Act 1844 and the Limited Liability Act 1855 facilitated collective investments in the risky, diverse and large-scale projects of the industrial revolution such as mines and railways, often overseas. The propensity of some promoters of such projects to overstate their prospects to impressionable investors, together with the need for stocks and shares[12] in such entities to be properly priced and traded in well-ordered markets, led to the development of the stock markets, securities legislation and companies legislation. The basic system of company registration introduced in the mid-1800s is still in place in the UK. The forbears of the professional accountancy bodies and firms were founded in the late 19th and early 20th centuries in the UK and the USA.

---

[12] In the UK, investors in companies hold shares. In the USA, investors in corporations hold stocks. There is little now to distinguish between the terms 'stocks' and 'shares'. US business terminology is more conservative than its UK equivalent and the term 'company' in the USA can refer to a partnership or other unincorporated association, as it once did in the UK. Shares in the UK are traded not on London's Share Exchange but on its Stock Exchange.

Prior to the 1844 Act, corporate bodies such as companies and corporations could only be formed by Act of Parliament or Royal Charter or other mechanisms designed for large institutions and groupings such as ecclesiastical institutions, universities, hospitals, cities, guilds and professions. The British East India Company was granted a Royal Charter in 1600. The Dutch East India Company was chartered in 1602 by the States-General of the Netherlands. Both were granted trading monopolies and administrative powers. Much general trade in goods and services in the UK and elsewhere in the world was transacted by individuals and unincorporated associations until the mid-19th century. This was administratively cumbersome because any legal or other action by the association had to be conducted in the joint names of all those involved.

Industrialisation and the development of company law in the UK and securities legislation in the USA in the late 19th and early 20th centuries changed all of this. Modern audit requirements vary enormously from jurisdiction to jurisdiction. We have seen that in the USA there is no statutory requirement for the audit of any entity and that only those with debt or equity securities listed on a US exchange are required to have an audit. By contrast, in some European countries all incorporated entities, regardless of size, are still subject to a statutory audit requirement under company law. Some jurisdictions, including some in the former Soviet Union, have introduced audit requirements conducted under international standards for the first time only fairly recently.[13] Some former European colonies in Africa and Asia still follow the practices of the old colonial power, but this is changing.

## 1.2   PASSING THE EXAM FIRST TIME

**Auditing and Assurance Exams and Study Technique**

Auditing and assurance present nothing like the intellectual challenge of accounting for deferred tax, fair values, or complex financial instruments, but some very bright people struggle with auditing and assurance exams. There are four ways to avoid this struggle:

- *respect the paper:* auditing and assurance exams usually have more words than numbers. Some students leave revision for the paper until the last minute, spending more time on other papers that are genuinely more difficult. Auditing is not rocket science but it does require time and effort and it cannot be picked up overnight, ***don't underestimate it;***

- *question practice and more question practice:* many students overdo rote learning at the expense of question practice. We learn how to sail by messing around in boats. To become a better mountaineer, it is necessary to climb a few mountains. Reading books about sailing and climbing will help, but they are no substitute for the real thing. To pass auditing and assurance exams, it is necessary to practice questions. Most students who struggle with auditing and assurance exams are not lazy, but their efforts are sometimes misdirected and ***altering the learning/question practice ratio in favour of the latter always helps;***

- *better exam technique:* poor exam technique is probably the least common reason for failing auditing and assurance exams, but it can be important. No matter how

---

[13] Tax audits are still required in many jurisdictions.

well you answer questions 1 and 2, in almost all cases, it is virtually impossible to pass the paper if you do not attempt questions 3 to 5. A very small minority of students have handwriting that is so poor as to be illegible where handwritten papers are submitted but many students irritate markers with untidy handwriting, and it is generally better not to irritate your marker if you can avoid it.

- '*. . . my English lets me down*', is a common worry among students whose first language is not English. It is almost always nonsense. If students make it as far as taking the exam, the quality of their written English is rarely, if ever, the problem. It is important to note that the correlation between oral and written skills is not always as close as might be expected. Some students who do not speak English particularly fluently are very articulate in writing. The fact that you cannot speak English as well as you would like does not mean that you cannot pass an auditing and assurance exam.

  Markers rarely see truly incomprehensible exam scripts and those that are, are usually written by students whose first language *is* English. It is much more common for exam scripts simply not to have enough in them for a pass, and this is true regardless of whether the student's first language is English.

  Some accountancy students with a business, scientific or technical background find it difficult to articulate their thoughts and written papers can present a significant challenge. It is no exaggeration to say that some of the brightest students have problems in this area. It is often less the result of an inability to write well, and more a lack of confidence and practice. Students appearing to struggle with a question, when asked to express the answer verbally, are sometimes very well able to do so but have a mental block when it comes to writing it down. The appropriate advice in such cases may simply be to 'write down what you are thinking', or 'write down what you have just said'. Such students need to be strongly encouraged to write things down, because question practice is not just 'helpful', it really is essential to passing the exam first time;

- *good material and good teachers:* there is a small amount of very poor study material around, a great deal of indifferent material and some very good material. It all claims to be the best. Give yourself a chance and use the best you can find and trust your own judgement. Read a bit of it and see. Does it make sense? Is it hard to read? Time spent trying to learn from excessively detailed materials that cover the syllabus but do not explain it, is time lost. If the study materials you have been using have not worked for you, use different material. The same considerations apply to tuition providers.

Some students fail auditing and assurance exams repeatedly, by just a few marks. The cause is almost always some combination of the factors listed above. Re-sitting auditing and assurance exams *is* avoidable.

### Practising questions
It is always a great deal easier to read the book than it is to try a question but *the key to passing auditing and assurance exams is practising questions, in full, under exam conditions.* There are two reasons for this. Firstly, it makes neurons fire and

establishes good thinking habits. Secondly, you learn from the answer. It does not matter how badly you do, provided you *try the question without looking at the answer,* giving it a decent amount of time, and then *underline the elements of the answer you missed, and write or paste them into your own answer.* The fact that you may never look at the question again is of no importance. The action of writing or pasting the missed material into your own answer means that when you next encounter something similar, you are much more likely to remember what you missed.

No study material can cover all of the material in every possible exam. Learn from the answers to questions, particularly past exam questions, as well as the study material. There are many past papers together with answers freely available on the examining bodies' web-sites; use them.

*Different types of question*
Questions come in many shapes and sizes.

*Short form questions* generally need answers in note form only; no marks are awarded for writing in full sentences. This type of question does need practice though because short form answers can degenerate. Markers sometimes have to decide whether the student really understands the point and deserves a mark, but has simply failed to articulate it clearly, in which case half a mark may be appropriate, or whether the student simply doesn't understand and is perhaps trying to hide the fact by being cryptic.

Consider the following part response to the question, '. . . give examples of requirements relating to long service applicable to key audit partners':

(a) ethical prohibitions on engagement partners serving PIE audit clients for over 7 years;

   *or*

(b) professional ethical requirements force staff on audit clients to change so as to avoid long service

The latter point is long on form but has little content. Despite its length, it will probably attract fewer marks than the former. The former is more specific in that it refers to engagement partners rather than staff, and does not simply repeat information in the question. It gives a time period rather than simply referring to long service and it refers to PIEs rather than audit clients generally. Even if the figure given in the first point was wrong, more credit might be given for this than for simply referring to long service. The second point uses three words in referring to professional ethical requirements and uses the term 'change', which is correct, but the term 'rotate' would be better because that is the term used in IESBA's *Code*.

*Letters, reports and briefing notes:* if letters, reports or briefing notes are asked for, the format alone will often attract marks. Students sometimes waste an extraordinary amount of time trying to think of amusing names for companies or individuals which, unfortunately, can irritate markers. It is much better, albeit not as much fun, to stick with an established format and a set of names and addresses for where they are not provided in the question.

*Letters* need to look something like this:

---

Benco Inc                                                Vinco Partners
1, High Street                                            2, High Street
Upton                                                            Upton
Midshire 67467                                          Midshire 67767

5 March 20XX

Dear Mr X/John [Salutation appropriate to the relationship – if in doubt, be formal]

**Proposed Services for Benco Inc [Subject matter]**

Thank you for coming into the office last week to discuss your requirements. I have great pleasure in setting out below the different types of services we are able to offer. I also suggest below which of those service might be appropriate to your specific circumstances. [Brief, polite formalities]

*[Brief summary and conclusions/recommendations if appropriate]*

Details of the *[subject matter]* are included in appendix 1 to this letter

### Appendix 1

---

*Reports* need to look something like this:

---

**Title: Vinco Partners – Developing Criteria for Engagement Quality Control Reviews**

**Report to:** the Partners of Vinco

**Partners' meeting date:** XX/YY/20XX

**Prepared by:** D Fraser, K Smith

### Principal Conclusions and Recommendations

The firm is required to develop a policy for the performance of Engagement Quality Control Reviews (EQCRs) for audit clients other than listed entity audit engagements.

We *recommend* that EQCRs be conducted for the following audit clients *[Main headings of report]*

- *all entities in the financial services sector;*

- *entities with not-for-profit status where revenue exceeds $XXX;*

*Time and cost budgets* for the performance of EQCRs in the first year are expected to be. . . .

### Detailed Recommendations/Findings/Methodology

**Background**

We are a growing firm. . . .

    1. **Entities in the financial services sector**

We currently have 16 clients in this sector ranging from. . . .

    2. **Not-for-profit entities**

We currently have a large number of smaller not-for-profit entities but very few are audit clients. . . .

**Time and cost budgets**

The principal assumptions underlying the calculations set out in appendix 1 are as follows. . . .

### Appendix 1

*Briefing notes* need to look something like this:

**Title:** Briefing Notes for Audit Team Members Not Present at the XX/YY/20XX Planning Meeting for the Audit of Timco for the period-ended. . . .

**Subject:** Discussion of the susceptibility of the financial statements to material misstatement arising from fraud and error

**Date:** XX/YY/20XX

**Prepared by:** T Evans

Summary of conclusions: the initial assessment of the risk of material misstatement due to fraud in prior years has been LOW, due to the high quality of the control environment and despite some significant high risk areas. In the current year . . .

**Considerations relevant to the assessment**

- The *financial statements* consist of a balance sheet, statement of comprehensive income, cash flow statement and statement of changes in equity. An unmodified audit opinion was issued . . .

- *Significant risk areas* in prior years have included: poorly controlled overseas subsidiaries, complex financial instruments . . .

- The overall control environment has been assessed as good in the past but there have been significant changes in management during the year . . .

- Etc.

*What do I do if . . .?*

- *The question seems to want the same information twice:* it is acceptable to repeat yourself across two different questions, but it is not acceptable within one question. If in doubt as to where within a question to include material, include it at the first possible point and then refer to it the next time it seems to be relevant. The mark allocation might give some indication as to where the material fits best.

- *The question has something in it that I can't find a use for in the answer:* tutors spend a lot of time persuading students to answer the question that is set, rather than the question the student thinks should have been set, but sometimes it seems impossible to use what appears to be background information. If you really cannot find a use for it, maybe it is just background information. For example, the introduction to some questions refers to the name of the relevant ISA. Generally, this is genuine background information. It does, of course, mean that no credit will be given for mentioning the name of the ISA in the answer. If a question does not mention the name of an ISA, it might be appropriate to refer to it in an answer but it is unlikely that much credit will ever be given for doing so.

- *I seem to be stating something really obvious:* some questions seem to want you to make some very simple observations, such as the fact that profits have risen in analytical procedures questions. If the question asks you to comment on profits, you do need to make the observation, but you also need to explain its significance. It is perfectly acceptable to guess what the significance might be, but if you really have no idea, you should still make the observation.

- *The question asks for three examples and I've got four:* ask yourself whether you really have four, or whether two are just different aspects of the same point, and whether you can make them together as one point.

- *The question asks for three examples but I've only got two:* have you really only got two? Are there perhaps two elements of one example that can be separated out? If you really only have two, don't say the same thing twice just to make three points because it is usually very obvious and, once again, it irritates markers.

### Syllabus coverage: there is far too much to learn!

All of the professional bodies revise their syllabuses regularly. Standard-setters are in the business of setting and revising standards. These revisions are often described as radical, but real change is slow. Basic questions on the audit of income, expenditure, property, plant and equipment, inventories, receivables, cash, bank, payables and long-term liabilities have been set in much the same way for many years, and continue to be set, because they remain relevant.

Examiners cannot cover the entire syllabus in one paper, but most attempt to cover it over a series of papers. This means that if an area that is not often examined came up last time, it is less likely to come up this time. If an area that is often examined has not come up for some time, it is more likely to come up next time. It really is worthwhile looking at past papers on the examining body's web-site to form your own opinion on what might come up. Examiners occasionally examine the same obscure area in quick succession, in an attempt at raising awareness of something they think needs more attention because students did very badly in it the first time round. Many examiners also have their 'pet' subjects, which is another reason for looking at what has come up recently.

In a perfect world, with unlimited time to revise, students would go into an exam having thoroughly revised all areas for all papers. Working all areas in detail is ideal but most students simply will not do this. Some hard decisions have to be made about what to cover in detail, what to skim and what to leave out altogether.

Most students try to work the key areas in some detail and have an overview of the other areas. Working key areas in a lot of detail and ignoring other areas completely is another approach and it can work, but it is risky because it limits the number of questions students can attempt in the exam.

Students who choose unpopular questions stand out. Unlike many other exams, there is scope in marking auditing and assurance exams for the exercise of judgement, and for giving or withholding from the student the benefit of the doubt. Markers try not to reward students who attempt unpopular questions disproportionately, but there are fewer candidates to compare the student against, which may work in the student's favour. This is one reason for attempting such questions but if you really know very little about an obscure area, it is probably best avoided if possible. It is better to scrape a pass on a question that everyone tries, than to fail, marginally, an obscure one!

For a variety of reasons, not all auditing and assurance standards are clear. Occasionally an error has been made, but this is very rare. Sometimes a matter is deliberately left unclear when members of a standard-setting board cannot agree, and a standard needs to be issued. Everyone goes away thinking that their position has been accommodated. Examiners tend to avoid these areas.

### No more knowledge-based questions?

From time to time, professional bodies and the bodies that regulate them announce that there have been too many knowledge-based questions and not enough emphasis on higher-level skills, especially application skills. The rationale is that rote learning is not just lazy, but unnecessary because professional ethics and auditing standards are all available online, and many exams are conducted on an open-book basis. Students cannot apply what they do not know, though, and they cannot apply what they do not understand. Some basic knowledge is essential and it is still impossible to pass auditing and assurance exams without it.

### Terminology

On the face of it, much of the terminology used by auditors about audits and assurance seems to be straightforward, but it should be treated with care. Many of the words used, such as 'independence', 'review' and 'assurance' have one meaning in ordinary English as well as a technical meaning in the context of auditing and assurance. It is important to understand and use the technical meaning properly. This is one of the reasons that some students underestimate auditing and assurance papers.

*Having a life*

There is nothing mysterious about passing auditing and assurance exams. No magic wand is required. All that is required is a plan to get through the material in the time period allotted, and a modicum of discipline in sticking to the plan. Easier said than done, of course, but not that hard. Boredom is a problem and managing distractions can be important. Getting friends and family into the habit of leaving you alone for two hours three evenings a week may be hard, but it can be done. Harder still is getting yourself into the habit of staying away from Facebook, emails, texts and TV on a regular basis, but even that can be done. If you cannot face going back to the same room to study, do it somewhere else, but not somewhere with a TV. Try moving the furniture around. If your desk faces a window, turn it to the wall. The alternative is living in a permanent state of anxiety about how much work you have not done!

## Exam Technique

In the exam centre:

- if you can, *answer the questions on the paper in reverse order*. It means you are out of synch with everyone else and will not be distracted by what they are doing. Alternatively, just do the *easiest question first* to give yourself confidence, but be strict with the amount of time you spend on it;

- remember that if you are submitting a handwritten paper, *poor handwriting irritates markers* and you want to make the marker's life easy. Really clear handwriting is unusual and makes an exceptionally good impression;

- split answers up into *manageable chunks* that the marker can tick, but don't do so artificially because it is usually very obvious;

- highlighting and underlining can also irritate markers and are sometimes prohibited;

- *answer the question set*, not the question you think should have been set;

- *take the easy marks:* if the question asks for a letter, prepare a letter. If it asks for a report, include a title, an executive summary, a description of the work performed, etc. If brief notes are asked for, no marks will be available for anything more;

- *keep on writing:* exams are sometimes deliberately set so there is insufficient time to answer all questions on the basis that real life is like this, but there will always be questions you struggle to answer. Think about what the examiner is really looking for, but remember that if you do not write anything, you cannot earn marks. If you write something, it might earn marks.

In the vast majority of cases, examiners are looking for a very small amount of knowledge, but mostly for a lot of imagination in applying that knowledge to a given scenario.

It is impossible to memorise a complete list of tests of controls and substantive procedures, and all of the finalisation procedures for audits, reviews, compilation and agreed-upon procedures engagements, but students sometimes appear to believe that that is the right thing to do. Even the most experienced audit partners cannot do this, but what practice and experience does enable them to do is to come up with a lot of examples. Auditing and assurance exams are often the first stages of that experience and students should have confidence that what they invent, or make up in terms of tests, has value.

### Section essentials: what you need to remember

- *Why assurance is needed.*
- *The overall assurance process.*
- *The meaning of the terms stewardship, agency and accountability.*
- *The benefits and limitations of an audit, and alternatives to audit.*
- *The differences between audits and reviews.*
- *That you have bigger battles to fight than passing auditing and assurance exams! Make sure you get through them first time.*

# SECTION 1, QUESTION

Professional accountants can provide a wide range of assurance services including assurance on historical financial information, greenhouse gas statements and prospective financial information. They also provide non-assurance services such as compilation engagements, which are subject to different requirements.

Audits of historical financial information, together with compilation engagements, remain an important part of the service offering of many firms of all sizes.

**Required:**

**Outline briefly:**

(a) the nature of audit and compilation engagements and the
    differences and similarities between them.                    (7 marks)

(b) the benefits of an audit and its limitations.                 (6 marks)

(c) the main stages of the assurance process.                     (7 marks)

**Total**                                                         **(20 marks)**

# 2 TAKING ON PROFESSIONAL WORK AND MAINTAINING STANDARDS

**Covering:** *professional standards, changes in a professional appointment, professional ethics, the audit appointment process, ISA 210 Agreeing the Terms of Audit.*

### Why do I need to read this section?

*In many jurisdictions, anyone can call themselves an accountant, but not everyone can call themselves a Chartered Accountant or a Certified Public Accountant (CPA). Professional accountants and their work are regulated, particularly audit work. Laws and regulation, auditing and accounting standards, professional ethics and the requirements of professional bodies all govern what accountants and auditors may and may not do.*

*Under most syllabuses, on almost every paper at every level, there is a question on taking on a new engagement or changing an existing one. It is easy to examine ethical requirements and they are important in practice. They are even more important when professional bodies come under pressure from regulators to improve training and standards, as they do from time to time.*

### What is important in this section?

*Just about everything! Examiners set a very wide range of questions on ethics. In recent years, questions about whether a firm is able to accept a particular type of engagement have become more common. This is because of the increase in the range of services practitioners can offer, bringing with it questions about independence, competence and conflicts of interest. There is an increasing tendency among legislators to prohibit or restrict the provision of non-audit services by auditors to their audit clients, and to circumscribe the activities of those authorised to operate in regulated areas generally.*

### What sort of questions come up in this area?

*Many questions in this area ask whether a firm should take a new client or provide additional services to existing clients. Often, there is no specific discussion of the matter within ethical requirements. Students sometimes mistakenly think they have either misunderstood the question or have missed an area of study. They have not. Examiners are looking for arguments based on the fundamental principles in such cases.*

*Very difficult ethical questions are occasionally set but usually only as part of case studies. Consistent marking of answers to such questions can be hard to achieve, because a very wide range of answers has to be acceptable. Complex ethical issues do arise in practice and they can only be resolved with any degree of confidence by practitioners with substantial practical experience.*

*Questions often appear in lower-level papers on the need to agree engagement terms and the contents of engagement letters.*

**How do I stand out from the crowd?**

*Few students mention the importance of commercial considerations when answering questions about new engagements but in practice this is important! Fee negotiations and the ability of the client to pay are critical considerations.*

*Students often rightly note the fact that practitioners sometimes need to consider withdrawing from engagements in accordance with the requirements of ISAs and ethical requirements. Indicating that walking away from a client is in practice a last resort, and that it is better not to take on a client than to have to terminate the relationship later, demonstrates maturity.*

*A lack of management integrity is a serious consideration and practitioners must not be associated with misleading information, so it is important to note that in practice a lack of management integrity is rarely clear cut.*

## 2.1    INTRODUCTION TO PROFESSIONAL STANDARDS

In most jurisdictions, the law prohibits anyone calling themselves a 'doctor' unless they have gone through an approved, rigorous training regime, passed exams, are required to keep up to date and are subject to monitoring and disciplinary arrangements. In many jurisdictions, contrary to popular belief, the designation 'accountant' is not protected in this way and anyone can call themselves an accountant.[1]

In many jurisdictions, a simple distinction between a qualified and an unqualified accountant is the most important one but in others the position is not quite so clear. The International Federation of Accountants (IFAC) has considered describing a 'professional accountant' as one distinguished by requirements to:

• demonstrate competence;

• uphold high professional standards;

• comply with a code of ethics;

• submit to enforcement.

---

[1]  The same is not generally true of the terms 'Chartered Accountant' or 'Certified Public Accountant'. Such terms are usually restricted to those who have passed the relevant exams and are members of the relevant professional bodies.

Demonstrating competence and upholding high professional standards require education, training and continuing professional development (CPD). Professional bodies, governments and independent regulators usually undertake enforcement by investigating complaints and by actively monitoring firms.

The requirements with which professional accountants must comply include:

- technical standards, such as International Standards on Auditing (ISAs);[2] ethical and other standards governing behaviour set by professional bodies and national standard-setters such as the IESBA's *Code of Ethics for Professional Accountants* (IESBA's *Code*);[3]

- the requirements of accounting standards, company law and securities regulators.

Many developed jurisdictions now apply ISAs with additional requirements or guidance known in the UK as 'pluses'. These deal with local legal, regulatory and other requirements. Many jurisdictions also base their ethical standards on the IESBA's *Code*.[4] In the UK, for example, auditing and ethical standards for audit and assurance engagements performed in the public interest are developed by the *Audit and Assurance team within the Codes and Standards Division of the Financial Reporting Council*.[5] UK ethical standards are generally more stringent than the IESBA's *Code* and they have been adopted by ACCA and ICAEW.[6]

*This text highlights those areas in which UK standards are more restrictive than IESBA's Code.*

*The requirements below apply to all engagements except where the reference is to audit engagements. All references to audit engagements in this section also apply to review engagements. For other assurance engagements, similar but less restrictive provisions apply.*

---

[2] The International Auditing and Assurance Standards Board (IAASB) develops and promulgates ISAs and other standards such as International Standards on Quality Control (ISQCs) and International Standards on Review Engagements (ISREs).

[3] The International Ethics Standards Board for Accountants (IESBA) sets the *Code of Ethics for Professional Accountants*. The IAASB and IESBA are both independent standard-setting bodies operating under the auspices of IFAC.

[4] UK auditing standards are known as ISAs (UK and Ireland). Jurisdictions using ISAs in some way include the UK, South Africa, Canada and Australia. The American Institute of Certified Public Accountants (AICPA) sets standards for auditors of non-listed entities in the USA and bases its standards on ISAs, as do all of the Big 4 and many other larger firms. Chinese Standards on Auditing have 'achieved full convergence with ISAs', according to a joint statement of the IAASB and the Chinese Auditing Standards Board dated November 2010.

[5] The Audit and Assurance team within the Codes and Standards Division of the Financial Reporting Council was formerly known as the *Auditing Practices Board*.

[6] ACCA and ICAEW also have their own ethical standards that, like IESBA's *Code*, also cover non-assurance engagements.

*Inadvertent violations* of ethical requirements require prompt correction and the establishment or strengthening of safeguards. These requirements are being strengthened in line with those jurisdictions that have more stringent requirements. Inadvertent violations of independence requirements may be important, but they may be inconsequential. In some jurisdictions such as the UK, inadvertent violations of audit engagements should be reported to the engagement or ethics partner. Current proposals suggest that violations should be discussed with the audit committee.

## 2.2   FUNDAMENTAL PRINCIPLES, THREATS AND SAFEGUARDS

IESBA's *Code* notes that:

> *A distinguishing mark of the accountancy profession is its acceptance of the responsibility to act in the public interest. Therefore, a professional accountant's responsibility is not exclusively to satisfy the needs of an individual client or employer.*
>
> **IESBA's *Code*, section 100.1**

Professional bodies, standard-setters and independent regulators all state that their activities are in, or take account of, the *public interest* and while there is yet no generally accepted definition of the public interest, it means, among many other things, that taking on professional work amounts to more than a simple agreement to do the work for a fee. Ethical requirements mean that professional accountants must not allow their names to be associated with misleading information, to be associated with clients who lack integrity, or allow bias or conflicts of interest to override their judgement. Professional accountants must be objective. For assurance engagements, independence of mind and independence in appearance are also important.

> **Public Interest Entities (PIEs)**
>
> Accounting standards, laws, regulation and professional ethics often distinguish between public interest entities, to which enhanced requirements apply, and other entities. Definitions vary but most encompass *listed entities,* i.e. entities whose debt or equity securities are traded on a recognised or authorised exchange[7] and other entities defined by laws or regulation as public interest entities. These include *very large unlisted entities,* including those that employ large numbers of people, and entities with a *large number and wide range of stakeholders,* particularly where they hold assets in a fiduciary capacity, such as *banks, pension funds, insurance companies and others* in the financial services sector.

---

[7]   The distinction between listed and unlisted entities is not generally the same as the distinction between public and private companies. Within the EU, the essential difference between public and private companies, the minimum capital requirements aside, is that the securities (debt and equity) of a public company *may* be offered for sale to the public. Private companies may not do this. Many public companies are unlisted, but could be listed (i.e. their securities offered for sale to the public) if they chose to comply with the relevant requirements.

## 2.2.1 FUNDAMENTAL PRINCIPLES

Professional ethics consist of:

- *5 fundamental principles* applicable to all professional accountants;
- requirements applying to professional accountants in *public practice;*
- requirements applying to professional accountants in *business.*

The IESBA and most other ethical standard-setters take a *conceptual* approach to professional ethics. This identifies *fundamental principles, threats and safeguards* rather than covering every situation with detailed rules.

Professional accountants are required to *identify and evaluate the significance of threats* to compliance with the fundamental principles and *apply any necessary safeguards to eliminate* the threats or *reduce them to an acceptable level.*

*Safeguards* are necessary if the professional accountant cannot determine that a *reasonable and informed third party would be likely to conclude that compliance with the fundamental principles is not compromised.*

*Five fundamental principles*

The five fundamental principles are:

- *integrity*: being *straightforward and honest* in *all professional and business relationships,* which means not knowingly being associated with materially false or misleading statements or statements made recklessly;
- *objectivity*: not allowing *bias, conflicts of interest or undue influence* of others to override professional or business judgements. Objectivity is a state of mind and it is possible to be objective without being independent. Independence, which is important for assurance engagements such as audits and reviews, requires:
  - *independence of mind,* that enables the professional accountant to act with integrity, objectivity and professional scepticism;
  - *independence in appearance,* i.e. the avoidance of facts and circumstances that are likely to compromise integrity, objectivity, or professional scepticism in the eyes of reasonably well-informed third parties;
- *competence and due care*: maintaining professional knowledge and skill to provide clients or employers with services performed diligently[8] in accordance with technical and professional standards. Competence requires:
  - sound judgement in applying professional knowledge;
  - education and training to gain it;
  - maintenance through CPD to keep up with business, professional and technical developments;

---

[8]  Diligence implies care, thoroughness and timeliness.

– staff and partner training and supervision;
– making clients and employers aware of the limitations inherent in professional services.[9]

- *confidentiality:* not disclosing information acquired through professional or business relationships in the absence of the specific authority of the client,[10] unless there is a legal or professional right or duty to do so, and not using confidential information for personal advantage or the advantage of third parties, by not engaging in insider trading, for example. Confidentiality requirements apply to information disclosed by prospective clients and employers and continue to apply after the end of relationships with them. Confidentiality means being alert to the possibility of inadvertent disclosures to close business associates and family members and in a social context. *A professional right or duty to disclose may be*:

  – *required by law* where, for example, a professional accountant is subpoenaed by a court of law[11] or where he or she is required by legislation to report matters such as suspicions of terrorism or money laundering;
  – *to comply with the quality review requirements* of professional bodies or regulators or in responding to their inquiries or investigation;
  – *to protect the professional accountants' interests* in legal proceedings, when taking legal action to recover unpaid fees or in defending negligence claims, for example;
  – *to comply* with ethical or other technical requirements.

It is recognised that the decision to disclose is often less than straightforward, particularly where information is incomplete or unsubstantiated. Requirements to disclose suspicions of money laundering and terrorist activities, for example, are by definition disclosures of incomplete and unsubstantiated information.

- *professional behaviour:* complying with relevant laws and regulations and avoiding any action that discredits the profession. This means:

  – complying with relevant laws and regulations;
  – avoiding actions professional accountants know or should know may discredit the profession;
  – in marketing and promotion, being honest and truthful and not making exaggerated claims or disparaging references to the work of others.

### 2.2.2   THREATS

Professional accountants must *identify, evaluate and take action to reduce to an acceptable level*:

---

[9]   The inherent limitations of an audit, for example, include the fact that a properly performed audit may not detect all material misstatements because audit evidence is persuasive and not conclusive, and because it is not possible to test every transaction and balance.
[10]   Any client-authorised disclosure must be permitted by law. Data protection legislation in many jurisdictions now prevents the disclosure of a great deal of information about private individuals without their specific consent.
[11]   Subpoenas can require an individual to testify in court or to provide evidence.

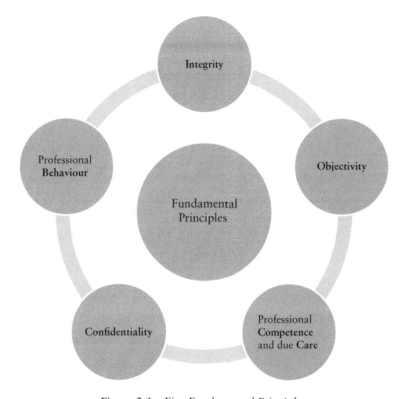

**Figure 2.1**    Five Fundamental Principles

- *self-interest threats*: that financial or other interests will inappropriately influence them;
- *self-review threats*: that they will effectively review their own work or that of colleagues within the same firm or employer;
- *advocacy threats*: that they will promote a client's or employer's position to the point that their objectivity is compromised;
- *familiarity threats*: that an excessively long or close relationship with a client or employer results in excessive sympathy to their interests or readiness to accept their work;
- *intimidation threats*: that they will be deterred from acting objectively because of actual or perceived pressures.

### 2.2.3  SAFEGUARDS

Safeguards can be:

- implemented by the profession, legislation and regulation;
- firm-wide or engagement-specific;
- created by clients.

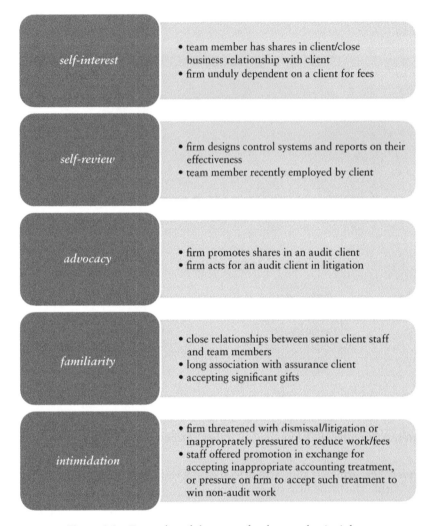

| | |
|---|---|
| *self-interest* | • team member has shares in client/close business relationship with client<br>• firm unduly dependent on a client for fees |
| *self-review* | • firm designs control systems and reports on their effectiveness<br>• team member recently employed by client |
| *advocacy* | • firm promotes shares in an audit client<br>• firm acts for an audit client in litigation |
| *familiarity* | • close relationships between senior client staff and team members<br>• long association with assurance client<br>• accepting significant gifts |
| *intimidation* | • firm threatened with dismissal/litigation or inappropriately pressured to reduce work/fees<br>• staff offered promotion in exchange for accepting inappropriate accounting treatment, or pressure on firm to accept such treatment to win non-audit work |

**Figure 2.2**    Examples of threats to fundamental principles

*Safeguards created by the profession, legislation or regulation* for all professional accountants include:

- educational requirements for entry into the profession, training and CPD requirements, professional standards and monitoring and disciplinary arrangements;

- specific duties to report breaches of ethical requirements;

- corporate governance requirements which require discussion with or approval of audit and non-audit services by those charged with governance;

- 'whistle-blowing' arrangements that enable anyone to draw attention to unethical conduct.

Many *firm-wide and engagement-specific safeguards in the work environment* to eliminate or reduce threats to an acceptable level are already required by International Standard on Quality Control No 1 (ISQC 1) and ISA 220[12]. They include:

- a firm's leadership stressing compliance with professional ethics and the public interest;

- policies managing interests or relationships between the firm, team members and clients and the revenues received from a single client;

- using different partners and staff for the provision of non-assurance services to an assurance client and rotating senior team members;

- external independent reviews of a firm's work.

---

*In the UK, ES 1[13] requires firms* to appoint an *ethics partner* to:

- *take responsibility* for the firm's ethical policies and procedures and their effective communication;

- *issue guidance* to individual partners to ensure consistency;

- *receive reports* from staff and engagement partners where threats to ethical standards arise.

It also requires the firm or its leadership to establish:

- a control environment that places adherence to ethics above commercial considerations;

- policies and procedures to prevent employees from taking management decisions;

- threats to its objectivity and relevant safeguards.

There are also many references in UK ethical standards to 'persons in a position to influence the conduct and outcome of the audit' which is a potentially broader category than 'members of the audit team'.

---

*Safeguards implemented by the client* cannot by themselves reduce threats to an acceptable level but they may help, and include corporate governance requirements for those charged with governance to approve the appointment of auditors and the provision of non-audit services by auditors.

## 2.2.4  CONFLICT RESOLUTION

Ethical conflicts are inevitable. Firms should have established internal procedures for dealing with them under ISQC 1 but if a significant conflict cannot be resolved, advice

---

[12] ISQC 1 on firm-level quality control and ISA 220 on engagement-level quality control.
[13] Ethical Standard 1 on integrity, objectivity and independence.

from professional bodies or lawyers may be necessary. Advice on ethical issues does not involve breaching the principle of confidentiality provided the matter is discussed on an anonymous basis or with a lawyer under the protection of legal privilege. It is not acceptable for ethical conflicts to remain unresolved and professional accountants may have no choice but to withdraw from engagements where such conflicts exist.

## 2.3   CHANGES IN A PROFESSIONAL APPOINTMENT

### 2.3.1   COMMUNICATING WITH THE PREVIOUS ACCOUNTANT

Changes in professional appointment whether for tax, audit or any other work, require the *incoming accountants to assess whether there are any reasons that they should not take on the work*. The apparent reasons for changes in appointment can be misleading and sometimes mask disagreements. Incoming accountants need to know about this. Where there has been a difference of opinion, incoming accountants need to be happy that the client's position is reasonable. Some jurisdictions such as the UK have protocols providing incoming auditors with access to the working papers of outgoing auditors.

Reasons for not accepting appointment include any threats to the fundamental principles that cannot be reduced to an acceptable level, such as fraud, accounting irregularities, tax evasion or a client demonstrably misleading the predecessor accountant. These might all involve the accountant being associated with misleading information. Matters *possibly* affecting the decision to act include a client being economical with the truth in the past or refusing the incoming or outgoing accountant permission to communicate with each other.[14] Fee disputes and the inability to pay fees are not professional reasons for declining work but they are likely to amount to commercial reasons. Client complaints about the previous accountant may also be relevant.

> Incoming accountants communicate with the previous accountant using a *letter of professional enquiry* to *establish the facts and circumstances* behind the proposed change and *whether there are any reasons for not accepting the engagement, professional or otherwise*.

In practice, the position is often unclear. While they may be insignificant and worrying doubts, about, for example, financial reporting practices, appropriate safeguards may reduce the threats to an acceptable level. This will always involve obtaining an understanding of the business and its managers and owners. It might also involve getting assurances from the client to improve accounting records, controls, reporting practices or corporate governance practices, for example.

---

[14] Clients are more likely to fail to give accountants permission to communicate with each other rather than refusing it outright. Accountants need to consider the reasons for both very carefully.

The position for continuing engagements should be reviewed periodically.

*Incoming accountants:*

- *seek the client's permission* to communicate with the previous accountant, preferably in writing, explaining why and asking the client to confirm the change and authorise the previous accountant to communicate;
- *write* to the previous accountant asking if there are any reasons not to accept the engagement;
- *write again* or phone if there is no reply, finally sending a letter by registered mail[15] stating that in the absence of a response within a given time, say 14 days, they will assume that there are no reasons why the engagement should not be accepted;
- *where no response is received, take reasonable steps to obtain information about possible threats* by other means, through inquiries of third parties or background investigations of senior management or those charged with governance, for example;
- *consider declining* the appointment if the client *does not permit the previous accountant to communicate.*

*Previous accountants:*

- *obtain the client's permission* to communicate with the incoming accountant, preferably in writing;
- *respond promptly, giving details* honestly and clearly rather than referring to unspecified matters, and stating that there are no such matters where that is the case;
- *inform the incoming accountant if permission is withheld.*

Money laundering legislation, which is dealt with in more detail in Section 7, prohibits 'tipping-off'. This effectively means that in many jurisdictions the incoming accountant should not ask questions about any aspect of money laundering and previous accountants should not answer any such questions, if asked.

It is common practice to combine the letter of professional inquiry with a request for information and documents.

For audit appointments, regardless of whether the previous auditor resigns, is removed or is not re-appointed, there are often additional requirements to report to shareholders, professional bodies and regulators on the reasons for the change. This is dealt with in more detail below.

---

[15] Registered mail (in the USA) or registered delivery (in the UK) requires the signature of the addressee on receipt.

## 2.4  OBTAINING PROFESSIONAL WORK

### 2.4.1  ADVERTISING, PUBLICITY AND TENDERING

In many jurisdictions, advertising and marketing were once thought inappropriate activities for the professions. Marketing accountancy and audit services is still a relatively new area in some jurisdictions and practitioners often need help with it.

*Advertising and marketing pose a threat to compliance with the fundamental principle of professional behaviour.*

Professional accountants are required not to bring the profession into disrepute when marketing professional services which means being honest and truthful and not making:

- exaggerated claims regarding their services, qualifications or experience;

- disparaging references or unsubstantiated comparisons to the work of others.[16]

Professional bodies often permit firms to offer a free introductory consultation. Some bodies provide, for a fee, a service checking that advertisements are compliant with that body's requirements. Some professional bodies now permit unsolicited calls to potential clients (cold calling) provided it does not amount to harassment, but it is not a common method of obtaining professional work.

*Tendering*
Tendering for professional work is now not just good practice in many jurisdictions, but required in the public sector or under securities regulation, or effectively required under corporate governance codes with comply or explain approaches for listed company audits and other work.

When approached by an entity inviting the firm to tender for work a firm needs to consider:

- the potential client's timetable;
- whether the firm has the staff with the right skills and experience available when needed;
- whether additional training is required;
- the availability of any internal or external experts needed to perform the engagement.

The proposal document the firm prepares in response to the invitation to tender covers:

- the firm's skills and experience;
- the estimated fee and how it has been calculated and/or the basis on which the fees will be charged, including charge-out rates and the estimated time to perform the engagement;

---

[16] Justifiable factual statements are generally acceptable. National legal requirements regarding advertising also apply.

- the client's needs and how they will be met;
- assumptions made and proposed approach to the engagement;
- key staff to be involved in the engagement;
- the fact that the proposal is subject to a letter of professional inquiry.

### Professional bodies, branding and multi-disciplinary practices

Professional bodies manage their identities as brands. They have detailed rules about the content of advertisements, marketing, practice names and descriptions, letterheads, the use of the professional body's logo and restrictions on the use of terms such as 'Chartered Accountant'.

These matters are increasingly important as it becomes more common for:

- unqualified accountants to provide services traditionally provided by qualified accountants;
- non-accountants to invest, work in and control accountancy practices;
- accountants belonging to different professional bodies to work together;
- accountants to practise in partnership with non-accountants such as lawyers.

For example, Alternative Business Structures (ABSs) in the UK permit lawyers to practise with accountants and others in multi-disciplinary practices (MDPs).[17] Some accountants have advocated such 'one-stop shop' arrangements for professional services for many years because they enable firms to bring in new sources of funding, talent and clients. It remains to be seen if they are successful. The regulation of such practices may be complex and expensive, particularly where regulated activities such as audit are provided.

There is also a strong body of opinion in some parts of Europe and elsewhere that audit firms, particularly large firms with listed audit clients, should not provide non-audit services to their audit clients, despite the efficiencies.

Several large firms parted company with their consultancy practices in the early 2000s in some jurisdictions. In some cases the main reasons were commercial. Some consulting practices were very successful and no longer wished or needed to be associated with accountancy practice. In most cases there was also an element of regulatory pressure, but many firms have successfully developed new lines of non-audit work.

### Setting up in practice

Setting up in practice requires consideration of many matters including:

- sources of funding;
- whether to use a company, partnership, limited liability partnership or to operate as a sole practitioner;

---

[17] ABSs were permitted as of 2011.

- practice infrastructure including the technology to deal with administration, billing, methodologies and systems for compliance with professional standards;

- all of the normal business issues including recruitment, payroll, health and safety, and accounting systems for the practice itself;

- the security of systems, data protection and money laundering legislation;

- marketing, practice development and client management which are often overlooked.

*Companies* protect the assets of their directors and members but they must generally prepare and file accounts, and some clients prefer dealing with partnerships with unlimited liability. Obtaining loans and raising finance are sometimes easier for companies than for partnerships.

*Partnerships* generally have unlimited liability but unless they are very large, they are not required to prepare financial statements except for tax purposes.

*Limited liability partnerships*[18] are generally taxed as partnerships but their members have limited liability and they are required to prepare and file accounts.

*Sole practitioners*, particularly sole practitioners who operate without staff, must weigh the freedom of being able to work alone against the burden of having no-one to consult with and the very broad range of expertise that general practitioners are now expected to have. Arrangements with training consortia and local associations are likely to be essential for keeping up to date.

It is critical to consider realistically the attributes of the potential co-directors or partners. In partnerships, absolute clarity about the terms of the partnership agreement is essential.

*Audit firm use of electronic technologies*
Audit firm use of electronic technologies has improved significantly in recent years.

Intranets, the Internet, billing and customer relationship management systems and social media have all changed the way audit firms communicate internally and externally. The main areas in which technology is used include:

*Audit administration and planning*
Information about entities of all sizes, such as financial statements and press and other industry information, is now available on the Internet, some of it free, some of it paid for. Large firms of auditors may make it available on office intranets and relevant information can be stored electronically on permanent files. Constitutional documents and

---

[18] Limited liability partnerships are incorporated in the UK under the Limited Liability Partnerships Act 2000.

documents from other company advisers such as lawyers, banks and custodians can be scanned, even if the originals are not electronic.

Audit planning may involve the production of audit plans drawn from central databases, tailored to meet the needs of the individual client.

Audit administration covers budgeting and staffing using standard spreadsheet packages or specialised software, which can be used on notebooks and laptops as well as PCs. Such systems can be integrated with the firm's billing and payroll systems and held on office intranets.

Communication between the office, the audit team and the client can be by email, fax, secure web-sites, and instant messaging.

### Risk assessment, analytical procedures, materiality and sampling

Many computerised audit systems enable auditors to draw on a risk assessment database that provides examples of risk factors generally, and for particular industries, and will calculate the level of risk for a particular area.

Analytical procedures can be automated and updated annually so that comparative information can be prepared quickly and accurately. If a client's system can produce information in an acceptable format, information from management or financial accounts can be drawn directly from the client's system.

Materiality and performance materiality for the financial statements as a whole and for individual account areas can also be calculated automatically taking account of the results of analytical procedures, using a firm's own internal models. Tolerable error and deviation rates for sampling can be calculated automatically, as can samples and sample sizes.

### Working papers

Working papers can be prepared, updated, reviewed and stored electronically using word processing and other software. Systems can prompt staff to complete unfinished audit programmes and working papers. Working papers can be reviewed on-line or offline at a time to suit managers and partners.

Electronic cross-referencing of working papers is possible using web-links.

### Advantages and disadvantages

The main advantages of using electronic technologies include:

- consistent use of the firm's procedures;
- reductions in travel requirements, the movement of paper and clerical errors in the calculation of sample sizes;
- reductions in omissions and duplications;
- increased reliance on less experienced (and less expensive) staff to perform work because of the availability of central databases.

Audit plans are particularly useful for specialised industries where staff unfamiliar with a client or business are involved, because they help ensure that matters are not overlooked.

The main disadvantages include:

- reliance on technology which can fail and needs maintenance;
- infrastructure development, testing, and implementation costs, the costs of hardware, software and staff training;
- standardisation encouraging a lazy, mechanical approach to audits, discouraging the use of judgement;
- control and security issues, including the potential loss, corruption and unauthorised interception of confidential data, the need for policy and procedures on password changes, the security and integrity of portable hardware (such as not leaving laptops or notebooks in cars or using unauthorised data sticks), and the need for encryption, firewalls and back-up procedures for data, databases and systems.

***Cross-selling non-audit services to audit clients***    It was once commonplace for audit partners and senior engagements team members to be remunerated and promoted for selling non-audit services to audit clients, despite the self-interest threat and the need for the firm to be independent.

> *In the UK, ES 4[19] requires that no member of the engagement team may be remunerated or evaluated or have among their objectives the selling of non-audit services to the audited entity.*

In other jurisdictions, where audit team members are still compensated or evaluated on this basis, safeguards include:

- removing the individual from the audit team;
- reviewing the audit team member's work.

> *Key audit partners may not be evaluated or compensated based on their success in selling non-assurance services to the partner's audit client.*

### 2.4.2 SECOND OPINIONS AND ADDITIONAL WORK

The main problem for firms asked to provide second opinions, usually on financial reporting matters, is that they do not have all of the information available to the existing accountant.

Second opinions are usually sought where there are differences of opinion and differences commonly relate to what is relevant. If the existing firm takes account of an issue

---

[19]   Ethical Standard 4 on fees, remuneration, litigation, gifts and hospitality.

that the client considers irrelevant, the client is unlikely to provide the firm asked to provide a second opinion with that information.

For example, a difference of opinion might relate to a provision for slow-moving inventory. The existing firm may consider that an invoice for the sale of some of that inventory below cost is indicative of its value. The client may take the view that the invoice is irrelevant to the valuation of the remaining inventory because it was intentionally sold as a loss leader to a new customer as an inducement to enter into a much bigger contract. The entity seeking the second opinion might not mention this to the second firm. The risk is then that the client then puts pressure on the existing firm to agree to the valuation apparently agreed by the second firm, with an implied threat of removal, or at least tougher fee negotiations. Such situations are much less likely to arise if the *two firms communicate with each other*.

Safeguards applied by the firm from which the second opinion is sought include:

- seeking permission to contact the existing firm;
- describing the limitations surrounding any opinion in communications with the client;
- providing the existing accountant with a copy of the opinion.

If permission to communicate is refused, the firm needs to consider very carefully whether it is appropriate to provide a second opinion.

Similar risks arise where a second firm is asked to perform work in addition to work performed by the existing firm. In such cases it is appropriate to notify the existing firm of the proposed work, providing them with the opportunity to provide any relevant information.

## 2.5   PROFESSIONAL ETHICS: FEES

### 2.5.1   HIGH FEES

The most common complaints to professional bodies include complaints about poor service for high fees. However, *most professional bodies will not intervene in fee disputes, nor do they pass judgement on how fees are calculated or what rates their members charge.*[20] These are contractual issues.

*Professional bodies only act in response to allegations of wrongdoing* such as incompetence, negligence or fraud.

The mechanisms designed to establish, maintain and improve firm performance include quality control requirements and monitoring by professional bodies and independent

---

[20]   A few professional bodies and some other professions and governing bodies do have recommended minimum fees for certain types of activity.

regulators, as well as entry requirements for the profession and requirements for training, examinations and CPD. The market for professional accountancy services and a firm's reputation should also have a bearing on its performance.

***Professional accountants may quote whatever fee they deem appropriate.*** This is of little comfort to clients who consider themselves overcharged for a poor service but firms cannot charge whatever they please. They must not mislead clients regarding the fees to be charged or the services to be provided. The most common method of charging is still on an hourly basis, although an increasing number of firms charge fixed fees for certain services or charge on a value basis.

### 2.5.2   LOW FEES

Firms are from time to time accused of 'lowballing', i.e. charging excessively low fees in order to remove the existing firm in the hope of recovering the loss in subsequent years or by selling more profitable services to clients. What constitutes an excessively low fee is a matter of judgement of course and simply quoting a fee that is lower than that of another firm is not in itself unethical. Professional bodies and independent regulators do not intervene in commercial arrangements between firms and clients but they do *pay attention* to such arrangements though because they can be indicative of the quality of work, which is what they regulate. Uneconomic fees may make it difficult to perform the engagement in accordance with applicable technical and professional standards.

Pressure on fees during economic downturns can sometimes be dealt with by flexing the level and types of services provided.

Threats to the fundamental principles of integrity and competence arise when quoting low fees, and the commercial risks associated with client dissatisfaction when charging high fees, can be mitigated by safeguards such as:

• agreeing engagement terms in writing, clarifying charges and the services covered;

• having appropriate time budgets;

• assigning appropriate partners and staff.

### 2.5.3   CONTINGENT FEES

Contingent fees are common in certain non-assurance engagements and include fees charged on:

• a no-win-no-fee basis, often in disputes;

• the basis that the better the outcome of the service, the higher the fee, such as where the firm:

– advises the client when selling part of its business;
– provides tax planning arrangements.

There are potential advocacy threats in such cases because the firm promotes the client. A self-interest threat arises if the firm acts to maximise its own income rather than in the best interests of the client. Winning in disputes and getting the highest possible price is not always in the client's best interests, particularly where the client has or is likely to have an ongoing relationship with the other party, who may be a customer or supplier, for example.

Some jurisdictions, such as the UK, now prohibit some speculative tax planning arrangements sold wholly or partly on a contingency fee basis to audit clients, particularly where they take advantage of areas that are new or uncertain.

Where contingent fees are charged, safeguards include:

• agreeing engagement terms in writing;

• quality control policies and procedures;

• review of the work performed by an independent third party.

### 2.5.4  REFERRAL FEES AND COMMISSIONS

Many firms do not provide a full range of services. Where that is the case, they often have arrangements with other firms to refer potential clients to each other and it is common for a referral fee to be paid. Firms also take commissions from software suppliers and other third parties in connection with sales to clients.

Referral fees and commissions create a self-interest threat to objectivity and competence. Necessary safeguards are likely to include obtaining the client's agreement to such arrangements in advance. It is unlikely that the threat can be reduced to an acceptable level without disclosure of the arrangements, even if the amounts involved are relatively small.

### 2.5.5  AUDIT FEES

*Total fee income and audit clients*
When the total fees from an audit client represent a large proportion of the firm's total fee income, dependence on the client and worries about losing the client create self-interest and intimidation threats. Less well-established firms are likely to be more vulnerable. The more important the client to the firm, the greater the threat. This does not mean that firms outside the Big 4 should not audit large companies but where they do, this particular type of risk may require more management than it might for a larger firm. General safeguards include the use of internal engagement quality control reviews, external independent quality control reviews performed by another firm, a training consortium or a professional body for example, and/or consulting such bodies on key audit judgements.

Similar considerations apply where audit fees are significant to an individual partner or office. Profit-sharing arrangements have an effect on the significance of such threats.

> *In the UK, ES 4[21] requires that the engagement partner ensure that the provision of non-audit services does not influence or determine audit fees.*

### Fees from public interest audit clients

Where *for two consecutive years, the total fees[22] from a public interest audit client* and its related entities represent *more than 15% of the firm's total fees*, the firm must disclose that fact to those charged with governance and discuss the safeguards to be applied to reduce the threat to an acceptable level. Safeguards include:

- a pre-issuance review: i.e. an external independent engagement quality control review performed by another firm or a professional body prior to the issue of the audit opinion for the second year; or

- a post-issuance review: before the issue of the audit opinion on the third year's financial statements, a review of the second year's audit by another firm or a professional body. When the total fees significantly exceed 15%, a pre-issuance review may be preferable.

This situation can continue but continued disclosure to those charged with governance and safeguards is required.

> *In the UK, ES 4:*
>
> - *prohibits a firm acting as auditor if total fees receivable from a listed audit client and its subsidiaries audited by the firm will regularly exceed 10% (15% for non-listed entities) of the firm's total fees.*[23] Disclosure to the ethics partner and those charged with governance of the audited entity is required where the figure is regularly over 5% of total fees, together with consideration of whether safeguards are needed. Where the figure is over 10%, an external independent quality control review is also required before the audit report is finalised;
>
> - requires the *engagement partner to inform the ethics partner where the annual non-audit fees for listed companies are expected to be greater than the audit fees;*
>
> - requires new audit firms that are not yet established[24] to refrain from auditing listed companies where fees would represent 10% or more of the firm's total fees, and for two years have an external, independent quality control review for unlisted audits that represent over 15% of total fees.

---

[21] Ethical Standard 4 on fees, remuneration, litigation, gifts and hospitality.

[22] Total fees are the annual, combined audit and non-audit fees.

[23] The figure is also applied to parts (such as offices) used to calculate the engagement partner's profit share.

[24] New firms may find the requirements difficult to comply with in the short term. The first client of a new firm (and the last client of a firm winding down) always represents 100% of fees.

*Overdue fees and audit clients*

Overdue fees, particularly fees for substantial amounts not paid before the issue of the audit report for the following year, are akin to loans from the firm to a client. Firms are expected to require payment of the prior year's fee before the following year's audit report is issued. If fees remain unpaid, the self-interest threat needs consideration. Safeguards might include having another professional accountant who did not take part in the audit advise or review the work performed, but it is generally better for fees to be paid. The firm needs to consider whether it should continue to act in such circumstances.

---

*In the UK, ES 4 requires the previous period's audit fees and arrangements for payment to be agreed before auditors formally accept appointment for the following period.*

---

*Contingent fees and audit clients*

**Firms should not charge contingent fees for audit engagements.** Contingent fees in respect of non-assurance services sold to audit clients are prohibited if the fee is material to the firm. If the fee is not material, safeguards include reviews of the audit work and employing different teams to provide the audit and non-audit services.[25]

## 2.6   PROFESSIONAL ETHICS: CONFLICTS OF INTEREST AND HOSPITALITY

### 2.6.1   CONFLICTS OF INTEREST

Conflicts of interest and threats to objectivity and confidentiality may arise where:

- a firm performs services for two or more clients whose interests are in conflict, because they are direct competitors, for example, or in dispute;

- the firm's own interests conflict with those of the client, where fees or commissions are earned from sales to the client for example, or where a firm competes with a client or has a business arrangement with a major competitor of a client.

---

*Clients must always be notified about conflicts or potential conflicts and their consent obtained for the firm to continue to act.* If consent is not forthcoming, the firm cannot act.

---

Safeguards include:

- the use of separate engagement teams to work for competing clients;

- physical and other procedures to prevent information about one client being passed to another, such as secure data filing and the use of 'Chinese walls' whereby partners

---

[25]   In the UK, this extends to the part of the firm with reference to which the audit engagement partner's profit share is calculated.

and staff on the two engagement teams are not permitted to discuss their respective clients with each other;

- confidentiality agreements signed by the firm's partners and staff.

Some genuinely difficult issues arise. If client A has going concern problems and owes to client B a large sum of money that is unlikely to be paid, and is likely to be material to client B, confidentiality dictates that the firm may not inform client B about client A's predicament. The firm has a problem because it knows about a material error in client B's financial statements in the form of a receivable not provided for. The firm can:

- attempt to show that the debt should be provided for using information already in client B's records, such as a deteriorating pattern of payments, although it should not arouse suspicion by drawing unwarranted attention to the issue;
- delay, in the hope that client A's predicament will become public knowledge;
- ask client A for permission to disclose the problem to client B. This is very unlikely to be forthcoming as client B is likely to use this information to take action to recover the debt immediately, which will precipitate the collapse of client A.

These outcomes are not ideal.

## 2.6.2   GIFTS AND HOSPITALITY

Clients may offer gifts and hospitality to practitioners or their immediate or close family members. If gifts are accepted, intimidation, self-interest and familiarity threats may arise if the gifts are intended to influence behaviour, decisions or to obtain information. Gifts and hospitality may be publicised which may be embarrassing to the firm.

The value, nature and intent of offers matter.

The offer is in the normal course of business without the intent to influence decisions or to obtain information *if a reasonable and informed third party, taking account of the circumstances, would consider the offer trivial and inconsequential. In such cases, the threat to compliance is acceptable and no safeguards are needed.*

*For audit clients, unless the value is trivial and inconsequential, the firm and members of the audit team should not accept gifts and hospitality* because no safeguards can reduce the threats to an acceptable level.

> *In the UK ES 4* requires that *for audit clients, firms should have policies on gifts and hospitality.*
>
> It also requires that *gifts should not be accepted by the firm, those in a position to influence the outcome of the audit or their immediate families unless the value is clearly insignificant.*

> For hospitality, the prohibition applies to those in a position to influence the outcome of the audit and their immediate families who should not accept hospitality unless it is reasonable in terms of its frequency, nature and cost.

What is 'trivial and inconsequential', or 'clearly insignificant' is clearly culture-specific and the situation is complex in jurisdictions in which 'facilitation payments' are routinely expected. Laws and regulations intended to combat bribery are relevant here.[26]

## 2.7 PROFESSIONAL ETHICS: INDEPENDENCE AND OBJECTIVITY

Independence is the auditors' unique selling point. The fundamental principles are easy enough to understand but applying them is hard, particularly maintaining independence in appearance, i.e. being *seen* to be independent. Auditors are paid by the people they report on and standards of independence therefore need to be high.

We note above that objectivity is a state of mind and that it is possible to be objective without being independent. Independence is required for assurance engagements and, like objectivity, is a state of mind but independence in appearance is also required, i.e. the avoidance of situations likely to compromise integrity, objectivity, or scepticism in the eyes of third parties.

Auditors who own the businesses they audit, or who take 70% of their fee income from one client, are not likely to be objective or independent.

*Objectivity is required for all engagements.* Threats to objectivity arise from interests in, or relationships with, a client or its directors, officers or employees. Close family, personal or business relationships create a familiarity threat.

> *A professional accountant in public practice who provides an assurance service shall be independent of the assurance client.*
>
> IESBA *Code of Ethics for Professional Accountants* Section 280.2

*In many cases, safeguards simply involve not having those providing non-audit services to audit clients working on the audit team, or, if they do, having their work reviewed.*

### 2.7.1 DEFINITIONS

*Immediate family*: a spouse or equivalent, or dependant, which might include children under the age of 18 and elderly parents.

---

[26] The UK Bribery Act 2010 came into force in 2011 and criminalises bribery by UK companies and companies that do business in the UK, as well as UK citizens and residents, wherever in the world it takes place.

*Close family*: a parent, child or sibling who is not an immediate family member, which might include adult children, parents and siblings, none of whom are dependant.

The requirements below assume that those working in audit firms have knowledge of the financial affairs of their families and others. This may not be the case. Firms often require partners and staff to complete an ***annual independence declaration*** as part of the ongoing notification of personal financial interests in order to comply with ethical and quality control requirements. If partners and staff do not know whether their spouse or parent has shares in an audit client, for example, they simply state that fact.

*Key audit partner:* the engagement partner, the engagement quality control reviewer and other audit partners who make key decisions or judgements on significant matters on the relevant audit.

Depending upon the circumstances and the role of the individuals on the audit, 'other audit partners' may include audit partners responsible for significant subsidiaries or divisions.

*Network firm:* whether a firm is a part of a network is important because network firms must be independent of other network firms' audit clients.

Firms often form larger structures with other firms, variously described as associations, alliances, or networks, often using some sort of common branding. Whether these structures create a network depends not on whether the structure is described as a network, or on the legal separation of its members, but on the structure's particular circumstances.

---

*Networks are larger structures aimed at co-operation, with one or more of the following*:

- a *common system of quality control*;
- *significant professional resources in common* such as client data, billing and time records, technical departments, methodologies and training;
- a *common business strategy, branding, profit or cost sharing, or ownership or management arrangements*.

---

A structure that only refers work among members is not a network.

*Management responsibilities* include:

- setting policies and strategic direction;
- directing and taking responsibility for the actions of the entity's employees;
- authorising transactions and deciding which recommendations to implement;
- taking responsibility for financial statements and internal control.

## 2.7.2  FINANCIAL INTERESTS

Having a financial interest in an audit client, such as having shares in the client, may create a self-interest threat. Clearly the extent of the threat depends on the extent of the interest and the seniority and role of the person with the interest.

Financial interests are held directly or through intermediaries such as collective investment vehicles or trusts. Control over the investment or the ability to influence investment decisions determines whether the interest is direct.

*If any of the following have any direct financial interest or a material indirect financial interest in the audit client, no safeguards can reduce the self-interest threat to an acceptable level*:

- *the firm;*
- *members of the audit team* or their immediate families;
- *partners in the office in which the engagements partner works*, or their immediate families;
- *other partners or managerial staff who provide non-audit services to the audit client*, or their immediate families, unless the involvement is minimal.

> This means that *members of the audit team and some others within the firm and their immediate families should not have any direct financial interest, such as shares in an audit client, or a material indirect interest, such as shares in an audit client held in a trust.*

A member of the audit team may have a *close* family member with a direct or material indirect financial interest. Provided it is not a controlling interest, safeguards reducing the threat to an acceptable level include having the close family member dispose of the interest as soon as practicable, reviewing the team member's work, or removing the individual from the audit team.[27]

A firm's retirement benefit plans[28] may have a direct or material indirect financial interest in an audit client which may create a threat which needs to be managed.

Where financial interests arise through inheritance, gift or as a result of a merger, they should be disposed of or reduced to an immaterial level in the case of indirect interests, either immediately in the case of a firm, a member of the audit team or their immediate family members or as soon as possible in other cases.

---

[27] Threats may also be created if the firm or a member of the audit team, or their immediate family has a financial interest in an entity in which an audit client or its directors or owners also has in interest, but only if the 'joint' interests are material and the audit client can have significant influence over the entity. Removing the member of the audit team from the audit or disposing of the interest may be necessary depending on circumstances. Threats to independence also arise where financial interests are held through trusts.

[28] Retirement benefit plans include pension plans.

In the UK, ES 2[29] is more specific about arrangements for persons joining the firm with financial interests, for example.

### 2.7.3   LOANS AND GUARANTEES

> *Loans and guarantees of loans from banking or similar audit clients may only be taken by the firm, a member of the audit team or a member of their immediate family on normal commercial terms.*

If the loan is material to the audit client or firm receiving the loan, safeguards include having the work reviewed by a professional accountant from a network firm not involved with the audit or loan.

Loans include home mortgages, bank overdrafts, car loans and credit card balances.

Loans and guarantees from audit clients that are *not* banks or similar institutions may only be taken if the loan or guarantee is immaterial to lender/guarantor and borrower, and vice versa. This means that firms and members of the audit team or their immediate families should only make or guarantee loans to audit clients if it is immaterial to both parties.

These requirements do not prohibit bank deposits or similar on normal commercial terms.

### 2.7.4   BUSINESS RELATIONSHIPS

Close business relationships between a firm, a member of the audit team or their immediate family include:

• having a financial interest in a joint venture with the client or its senior management;

• arrangements to market combined auditor and client services or products;

• auditors distributing or marketing the client's products or services or vice versa.

Such arrangements are increasingly common, but not for audit clients. They should not be made with audit clients unless the financial interest is immaterial and the business relationship is insignificant. Audit team members involved should be removed from the audit team. Safeguards are needed where the relationship is between an immediate family member of an audit team member and the audit client or its management.

A significant level of goods and services purchased from an audit client by the firm might create a threat.

---

[29] Ethical Standard 2 on financial, business, employment and personal relationships.

## 2.7.5   FAMILY AND PERSONAL RELATIONSHIPS

Family and personal relationships between a member of the audit team and a director or officer or certain employees of the audit client may create self-interest, familiarity or intimidation threats. The more senior the people involved and the closer they are on the client's side to the financial reporting function, the greater the threat.

> *When an immediate family member of an audit team member is a director or officer or an employee in a position to exert significant influence over the accounting records or financial statements, the individual concerned should be removed from the audit team.*

In the case of:

- *close* family members of audit team members being in the position above;
- partners who are not members of the audit team having personal or family relationships with client staff in the position described above;
- employees who have a significant operational role;[30]
- members of the audit team having a close personal relationship with a member of client staff, as described above;

safeguards include:

- removing the individual from the audit team;
- structuring responsibilities so that the individual does not deal with matters that are the responsibility of the close or immediate family member or person with whom the audit team member has a close relationship;
- ensuring that the partner who is not a member of the audit team does not influence the audit.

## 2.7.6   EMPLOYMENT WITH AN AUDIT CLIENT

It is common for audit partners and staff to go and work for audit clients in senior positions after they leave the firm. This creates potential familiarity and intimidation threats and the more senior the staff, the greater the threat.

*If a director or officer of the audit client, or a senior employee* in a position to exert significant influence over the preparation of the client's accounting records or the financial statements *has been a member of the audit team or partner of the firm, no significant connection must remain between the firm and the individual.* This means:

- the individual must not be entitled to any benefits from the firm, such as profit shares, unless made in accordance with fixed pre-determined arrangements, such as a pension;

---

[30] Employees with an operational role may exert significant influence over the client's financial position, performance or cash flows.

- any amount owed to the individual must not be material to the firm;

- the individual must not continue to participate or appear to participate in the firm's activities by maintaining an office or appearing on the firm's letterhead, for example.

If any of these conditions apply, the firm may not continue as auditor. Even where these conditions are satisfied, safeguards may be needed such as modifying the audit plan, assigning more experienced staff to the engagement or performing additional reviews.

Similar threats are created when an entity for whom a former partner works becomes an audit client and when audit team members participate in the engagement knowing that they will, or may, join the client. Firm policies and procedures may require members of an audit team to notify the firm when entering employment negotiations with the client although this may be hard to enforce. Safeguards clearly include removing the individual from the audit team and reviewing any significant judgements they made while on the team.

### Public interest audit clients and employment with an audit client

The appearance of independence is compromised if key audit partners, or a firm's senior or managing partner or chief executive, join a public interest audit client in a key management position such as a director, officer or senior employee very shortly after leaving the firm.

> *There should be a gap of at least 12 months between the issue of the last set of audited financial statements and the employment of certain partners by audit clients, during which the firm should not act as auditor. In practice, this means that senior firm staff must agree to this as part of their contractual arrangements.[31] In the UK, under ES 2,[32] the gap required is 2 years.*

### 2.7.7  LOANS OF STAFF TO CLIENTS

> *Firms may lend staff to an audit client for a short period* provided such staff do not assume management responsibilities and the arrangement is not used to circumvent prohibitions on the provision of non-assurance services.

The client is responsible for directing and supervising the loaned staff and safeguards include ensuring that such staff are not subsequently involved in the audit of areas they worked on.

---

[31] There are exceptions to this requirement where the position arises from a merger of firms not contemplated at the time of departure.

[32] Ethical Standard 2 on financial, business, employment and personal relationships.

### 2.7.8   RECENT SERVICE WITH AN AUDIT CLIENT

Occasionally, client staff go to work for the audit firm. Threats to independence arise if an audit team member has to evaluate elements of the financial statements that they worked on while with the client. Such individuals should not be assigned to the audit team where they served as directors, officers or had responsibility for the accounting records or financial statements during the period audited. If they were in this position before the period audited, a review of their work as a member of the audit team may be needed.

### 2.7.9   SERVING AS A DIRECTOR OR OFFICER OF AN AUDIT CLIENT

A firm's partners and employees should not serve as directors or officers of an audit client.[33] Some jurisdictions such as the UK also specifically prohibit partners and employees from acting as company secretary and safeguards are needed where this is not prohibited.

Performing routine administrative services such as supporting a company secretary or providing advice do not generally create threats to independence provided management takes responsibility for decisions.

### 2.7.10   PARTNER ROTATION

Firms, their partners and staff who have been associated with a particular audit client for a long time may become over-familiar. Stories of companies not changing their auditors for decades generally over-simplify the issue but they do little to add to the appearance of independence.

Familiarity and self-interest threats are created by using the same senior partners and staff on an audit engagement over a long period. Safeguards include rotating them off the audit team, having a professional accountant who was not a member of the audit team review their work and independent internal or external quality reviews.

*Public interest audit clients and partner rotation*

> *Key audit partners should not work on public interest audit clients for more than seven years. After that they should not be a member of the engagement team or act as engagement quality control reviewer, provide consultation or otherwise influence the audit for two years.*

Key audit partners whose continuity is especially important to audit quality may in rare cases be permitted an additional year on the audit team due to unforeseen circumstances outside the firm's control such as the serious illness of the intended engagement partner. For other partners, rotating the partner off the audit team or regular independent internal or external quality reviews reduce threats to independence.

---

[33] UK law also makes directors or officers of a company ineligible for appointment as auditor to that company.

When an audit client becomes a public interest entity, if the key audit partner has served the client for five years or less they may continue to serve for seven years, less the number of years already served. If the individual has served for six or more years when the client becomes a public interest entity, the partner may continue to serve in that capacity for a maximum of two additional years.

Some firms have very few people with the necessary knowledge and experience to serve as a key audit partner on public interest audits and rotation may not be possible. Some independent regulators provide an exemption from rotation in such circumstances.

---

*In the UK, ES 3*[34] requires the firm to establish policies and procedures to monitor the length of time senior staff serve on each audit and assess threats and safeguards on that basis.

*Once an engagement partner on any audit has held the role for ten years, perceptions of objectivity may be impaired.*

*For listed entities:*

- *engagement partners may serve for 5 years, with 5 years off;*

- *engagement quality control reviewers may serve for 7 years, with 5 years off;*

- *other key audit partners may serve for 7 years with 2 years off.*

Safeguards are needed for senior staff and other partners in place for more than 7 years.

---

### 2.7.11   ACTUAL OR THREATENED LITIGATION

When a firm and client take adversarial positions through actual or threatened litigation that may be material to either of them, both will find it difficult to make full disclosure, which is necessary in an audit. Self-interest and intimidation threats are created. Litigation need not relate to an audit for these risks to arise.

Safeguards include removing any individual involved or implicated in the litigation from the audit team and having another professional review the work performed.

### 2.7.12   NON-ASSURANCE SERVICES

Firms in many jurisdictions have always provided their audit clients with a range of non-assurance services. Developments in business and particularly changes in IT mean that these services change. Before the firm accepts an engagement to provide any non-assurance service to an audit client, the firm determines whether providing such a service would create a threat to independence. If a threat cannot be reduced to an acceptable level with safeguards, the non-assurance service should not be provided.

---

[34] Ethical Standard 3 on long association with the audit.

*Threats clearly exist where non-assurance services materially affect the audited financial statements and are greater for public interest audit clients.*

> In the UK, ES 5[35] requires that *for any non-assurance engagement, the engagement partner consider whether a reasonable and informed third party would consider the objective of the engagement inconsistent with the objectives of the audit.*

### Internal audit and IT systems

The provision of internal audit services and IT systems to audit clients is dealt with in Section 4.5. The risk that auditors effectively take on management's role cannot be reduced to an acceptable level and as such *any internal audit services provided by external auditors must be of a technical rather than an executive nature.* Similar problems arise where auditors, or firms associated with auditors, provide IT services to audit clients. In some jurisdictions, such as the USA, both are effectively prohibited.

> *For public interest clients, external auditors may not design or implement IT systems that form a significant part of the internal control over financial reporting or generate information significant to the financial statements.*
>
> *For audit purposes no significant reliance can be placed on the internal audit or IT systems work performed for public interest audit clients.*
>
> *In the UK, ES 5[36] extends this requirement to all audit clients.*

There is a self-review threat where external auditors provide similar services to non-public interest clients. In such cases, necessary safeguards involve the client acknowledging full responsibility for internal control and decisions regarding the system, evaluating its adequacy and operating it afterwards. Again, using staff who are not members of the audit team is another obvious safeguard.

### Accounting services

Management is responsible for the preparation of the financial statements and for the underlying evaluations and estimates, systems, controls and accounting records. Providing an audit client with accounting services, including preparing financial statements, creates a self-review threat.

Normal discussions between auditor and client about the application of accounting standards, disclosures, internal controls and adjustments, and technical assistance with reconciliation problems or gathering information for regulatory reporting do not generally create threats to independence, provided the firm does not assume management's responsibilities.

*Where accounting services are of a routine or mechanical nature they may be provided to non-public interest audit clients* only where any self-review threat created is reduced to an acceptable level. These include payroll services and posting transactions

---

[35] Ethical Standard 5 on non-audit services.
[36] Ibid.

coded by clients to the general ledger, trial balance and financial statements. Safeguards clearly include having individuals who are not audit team members perform such services or, if they are performed by audit team members, having a suitably experienced member of staff not in the audit team review their work.

> *Except in emergency situations, accounting services should not be provided to public interest audit clients.*

Firms may provide some such services for subsidiaries and associates of holding companies if the relevant partners and staff are not members of the audit team and the entities are immaterial to the financial statements.

Accounting services may be provided in an emergency when it is impractical for the audit client to make other arrangements where, for example:

- only the firm has the necessary knowledge of systems to assist on a timely basis;

- to do otherwise would result in significant difficulties for the client, such as those resulting from a failure to make regulatory returns on time.

Again, those who provide the services should not be members of the audit team, the services should be provided for a short period, should not be expected to recur and the situation should be discussed with those charged with governance.

### Litigation support and valuation services
Many firms provide litigation support services: these include providing expert witnesses and calculating estimated damages or other receivables or payables arising from legal disputes. These amounts may have a material effect on the financial statements and create self-review or advocacy threats.

Performing valuation services for an audit client may also create a self-review threat if:

- the valuation is material and is a 'soft' number, i.e. inherently subjective and sensitive to changes in assumptions;

- there has been limited client involvement in determining the valuation methodology, the assumptions behind it or other significant judgements;

- the underlying data are not well controlled.

> Valuation services should not be provided to
>
> - *public interest audit clients if the valuations are material* to the financial statements;
>
> - *non-public interest audit clients if the valuation is material and subjective.*
>
> In other cases, and in the case of litigation support services, safeguards include a review of the estimation of damages or the valuation by a staff member not involved, and ensuring that staff providing such services do not take part in the audit in any capacity.

Not all valuations are subjective, particularly where assumptions and valuation or esti-mation techniques are established by law or regulation or are widely accepted, such as the valuation of pension funds or widely traded financial instruments. The key feature of such valuations is that the results are unlikely to be materially different if two or more parties perform the calculation.

### Corporate finance services

Providing corporate finance services to audit clients may create advocacy and self-review threats. Services include helping develop corporate strategies, identifying pos-sible acquisitions and disposals, assisting in raising finance and providing restructuring advice. The financial statements may reflect all of these.

Safeguards include using staff who are not members of the audit team to provide the ser-vices and having someone not involved advise the audit team on the accounting treatment.

Where the effectiveness of corporate finance advice depends on a particular account-ing treatment in the financial statements and the audit team has doubts about it, if the matter is material, the advice should not be given.

Firms do not promote, deal in or underwrite an audit client's shares because it creates advocacy and self-review threats that safeguards cannot reduce to an acceptable level.

### Tax Services

Issues arising where auditors provide tax services are similar to those arising where corporate finance advice is given. They can be complex, the client inexperienced and the matter material to the financial statements.

> Tax services include the preparation of *tax returns. This does not generally create threats* provided management takes responsibility for the return.
>
> *Tax calculations for the financial statements, including deferred tax, should not be provided for public interest entities except in an emergency.*[37]
>
> *Tax calculations create a self-review threat for non-public interest entities,* particularly if the issue is complex, a high level of judgement is needed, the amounts are material or the client is inexperienced. Safeguards include performance of the calculation by staff not involved in the audit or, if an audit team member does perform the calculation, having the calculation reviewed by someone else from within or outside the firm.

Providing tax planning services and assisting in resolving tax disputes may also create self-review threats where the outcome is reflected in the financial statements, as well as advocacy threats. Additional considerations include whether the tax authority has cleared the treatment, which is required in many jurisdictions, the degree of uncertainty in the area and the aggressiveness of the proposed treatment. As with the provision of corporate finance services, the less certainty and the more subjectivity there are in the area, and the greater the impact on the financial statements, the greater the threat.

---

[37] What constitutes an emergency for these purposes is similar to what constitutes an emer-gency for the purposes of providing accounting services to public interest audit clients.

Safeguards are as for the preparation of tax returns and calculations and include obtaining pre-clearance or advice from tax authorities where it has not already been obtained.

As with corporate finance services, where the effectiveness of the tax advice depends on a particular accounting treatment, the audit team has doubts about it and the amounts are material, the advice should not be provided.

Some jurisdictions have more stringent requirements in this area.

### Legal services

Legal services include litigation and contract support and advice on restructuring, mergers and acquisitions. Services that support an audit client in executing a transaction such as contract support, legal due diligence and advice on restructuring may create self-review threats. As always, the significance of threats depends on whether the service is provided by a member of the audit team and the materiality of the matter to the financial statements.

Safeguards include using staff who are not members of the audit team to perform the service and someone not involved reviewing the work.

Firms should not act in an advocacy role for an audit client in resolving a dispute or litigation when the amounts involved are material to the financial statements. Safeguards similar to those noted above are appropriate where the amounts involved are not material.

Firms should not provide staff to act as general counsel for legal affairs at an audit client.

### Recruitment services

Providing recruitment services to an audit client creates self-interest, familiarity and intimidation threats. If things go wrong, the client may blame the firm, the firm may find it difficult to criticise the work of the person recruited and the client may put pressure on the firm to accept the judgements of the person the firm recruited. The more senior the role recruited for, and the closer it is to the financial reporting function, the greater the threat. In practice, recruitment agencies affiliated to the audit firm sometimes perform such functions. In all cases, the firm should not assume management responsibilities and should not negotiate on the client's behalf. The hiring decision is left to the client but firms may filter applications, interview candidates and prepare a shortlist for the client to consider.

For a public interest audit client, firms should not search for or check the references of directors, officers or senior management in a position to exert significant influence over the accounting records or financial statements.

### 2.7.13  SMALLER ENTITIES

*In the UK, ES PASE*[38] *permits certain exemptions to auditors of smaller entities* that, for example, are not required to:

---

[38] Ethical Standard – Provisions Available for Smaller Entities.

- perform an external independent quality control review where total fees will regularly be from 10–15% of the annual fee income;

- apply safeguards to address the self-review threat where non-audit services are provided to audit clients provided that such entities have *informed management* and the firm extends quality control inspections of completed engagements;

- adhere to the prohibition on taking a management role in relation to non-audit services to audit clients provided this is discussed with those charged with governance and disclosed;

- have a 2-year gap between a former partner of the firm joining an audit client in a key management position.

## 2.8    APPOINTING AND REMOVING AUDITORS

Auditing is a regulated activity in most jurisdictions. The provisions below are requirements of UK companies legislation, much of which derives from European legislation and is therefore similar elsewhere in Europe.

### 2.8.1    WHICH ENTITIES ARE REQUIRED TO APPOINT AUDITORS?

Companies may be subject to audit requirements:

- under companies or other legislation, as in the EU;

- by securities regulators, as in the USA;

- by their constitutions;

- by banks, lenders or other creditors as a contractual condition of lending or credit.

Audit exemption levels have risen significantly in recent years in many jurisdictions but many entities still have audits voluntarily.

Shareholders are normally required to appoint auditors by ordinary resolution, i.e. a simple majority of votes, annually at the annual general meeting (AGM). In practice, the directors of larger companies recommend auditors and shareholders approve their choice. While they rarely disagree, some institutional investors now actively oppose the appointment of auditors in some cases.[39]

### 2.8.2    WHO MAY BE APPOINTED AS AUDITOR?

*To be eligible for appointment as company auditors, individuals and firms must be members of a Recognised Supervisory Body (RSB) and eligible for appointment under its rules.*

---

[39] Smaller private companies may elect not to have an AGM or the annual re-appointment of auditors, in which case auditors are appointed until they are removed or resign. Appointment can be made by written resolution. Such appointments are subject to objections by a 10% minority of shareholders.

*Individuals must hold appropriate qualifications and firms[40] must be controlled by qualified persons.*

*Direct authorisation by the Secretary of State is also possible.*

Company auditors may not be:

- officers or employees of the audited entity;
- partners or employees of officers or employees, or a partnership in which such persons are partners.

Qualification for membership of RSBs is via Recognised Qualifying Bodies (RQBs). ACCA and ICAEW are both RSBs and RQBs.[41]

Maintaining RSB and RQB status depends on continued compliance with the requirements for those bodies. The rules governing RSBs and RQBs are set (in part) at European level for the UK. The rules of RSBs must ensure that:

- those eligible for appointment are fit and proper, technically competent persons holding appropriate qualifications;
- audit work is conducted properly and with integrity;
- persons within firms who are not qualified persons are not able to exert an influence over an audit affecting independence and integrity.

RSBs need to deal with:

- admissions and expulsions;
- the investigation of complaints;
- compulsory PII;
- the requirements to provide publicly available registers of auditors.

---

[40] Firms may be sole practitioners, partners in partnerships, partnerships, LLPs and their members and auditing companies.

[41] There are five RSBs in the UK:

- the Association of Chartered Certified Accountants (ACCA);
- the Chartered Accountants Ireland (CAI);
- the Institute of Chartered Accountants in England and Wales (ICAEW);
- the Institute of Chartered Accountants of Scotland (ICAS);
- the Association of Authorised Public Accountants (AAPA).

All of these are also RQBs with the exception of the AAPA and there are two further RQBs:

- the Association of International Accountants (AIA);
- the Chartered Institute of Public Finance and Accountancy (CIPFA), currently in abeyance.

The entry-level educational requirements and the education and training requirements of RQBs are also set at European level and they attempt to ensure that those entering auditor training have degree level qualifications.

### 2.8.3 WHO APPOINTS AUDITORS?

In some jurisdictions directors routinely appoint auditors. In some cases it is their legal responsibility, in other cases it is a matter of custom.

In the UK, appointment of auditors is generally the legal responsibility of shareholders but directors, including directors on audit committees, may appoint auditors:

- before the end of the company's first period for appointing auditors, i.e. in its first year;
- after the end of audit exemption, before the company's next period for appointing auditors;
- to fill a casual vacancy in the office of auditor, when the auditor resigns mid-term, for example.

If directors and shareholders fail to appoint auditors, the Secretary of State may do so. This sometimes happens when companies with substantial assets are abandoned by their directors.

### 2.8.4 AUDITOR'S RIGHTS

Auditors have rights:

- of access at all times to the company's *books and records*;
- to require the provision of such *information or explanations* as they think necessary for the audit from officers, employees and staff of the company and its UK subsidiaries;[42]
- to receive all *notices* and other communications relating to general meetings;
- to *attend and be heard* at general meetings on matters concerning auditors.

It is now a criminal offence in the UK to knowingly or recklessly make false or misleading oral or written statements to auditors.

### 2.8.5 AUDITOR'S DUTIES

Auditors' legal duties require them to form an opinion on whether the financial statements:

- *give a true and fair view* of the entity's performance and position, etc.;

---

[42] The directors must obtain information from overseas subsidiaries for auditors.

- have been prepared in accordance with the *relevant financial reporting framework and companies legislation;*[43]

and to make statements by exception[44] if:

- *adequate accounting records* have not been kept or *adequate returns not received* from branches not visited;
- the *accounts do not agree* with the underlying records;
- all the *information and explanations necessary* for the audit have not been received;
- information issued with audited financial statements, such as the directors' report, is *inconsistent* with the financial statements;
- in the case of quoted companies, the auditable part of the company's directors' remuneration report does not agree with the underlying records.

Audit reports must state the name of the auditor and be signed and dated. Where the auditor is a firm, the report must be signed by the *senior statutory auditor* in his own name, for and on behalf of the firm.

Where the company is required to prepare a corporate governance statement and it is not included in the directors' report, auditors must make a statement in the audit report if the statement has not been prepared.

### 2.8.6   REMOVAL, RESIGNATION AND NON RE-APPOINTMENT

Most auditors do not resign, nor are they removed, they simply do not offer themselves for re-appointment when the audited entity has decided to appoint another firm. Whenever auditors resign, are removed or do not offer themselves for re-appointment, various statements must be made by the company and the auditors to the Registrar of Companies, shareholders, professional bodies and audit regulators.

Where they resign, auditors give notice of their resignation at the company's registered office. The company must send the notice on to the Registrar of Companies. Auditors may require the company to call a meeting to discuss the circumstances surrounding their resignation, although this rarely happens. Auditors who have been removed have a right to attend and be heard at the meeting at which their appointment would have ended.

Where auditors cease to hold office for any reason (resignation, removal or not seeking re-appointment) they must make a *statement of circumstances connected with their*

---

[43] The legal reporting requirements are similar to the reporting requirements under ISAs which require that auditors obtain reasonable assurance about whether the financial statements are free from material misstatement, whether due to fraud or error, and that they express an opinion on whether they are prepared in all material respects in accordance with the identified financial reporting framework.

[44] Statements by exception are made where there is a problem, so only if adequate accounting records have *not* been kept will a statement be made.

*ceasing to hold office that need to be brought to the attention of members or creditors, or make a statement that there are no such circumstances.*[45] The company must then either circulate it to members and others entitled to receive the accounts or object to the court.[46] Both auditors and the company must then send the statement to the relevant RSB, or if it is a 'major audit', to the Audit Quality Review team, formerly the Audit Inspection Unit (AIU).[47]

Statements of circumstances provide auditors with an opportunity to protest about inappropriate accounting treatments, and prevent auditors from resigning when things have gone wrong, without the effort and embarrassment of having to explain the matter to shareholders. There have been a few high profile cases in which auditors have made such statements and companies have objected to the courts about them, arguing that they should not be circulated because they present the auditors' biased or incorrect view of a disagreement.

## 2.9   AGREEING ENGAGEMENT TERMS

Agreement of engagement terms is an essential part of an audit despite the fact that audit is regulated. Engagement terms include commercial terms including fees and the basis on which they are payable.

Agreement is particularly important for the owners and managers of smaller entities who may not understand the statutory requirements. Agreement should establish a common understanding between auditors, those charged with governance and management. Agreement helps prevent misunderstandings, particularly misunderstandings about who is responsible for the preparation of the financial statements and the judgements therein.

### 2.9.1   PRECONDITIONS AND PREMISE FOR AN AUDIT

*Auditors should only accept or continue with an audit engagement if the preconditions for an audit are present.* If they are not, the engagement should not be accepted. The preconditions are:

- use by management of an *acceptable financial reporting framework* that is available to intended users;

- agreement to the *premise on which the audit is conducted*.

The *premise* is that management and, where appropriate, those charged with governance, acknowledge and understand their responsibility:[48]

- for the *preparation of financial statements* in accordance with the financial reporting framework and for the *internal controls* necessary to do so;

---

[45] The requirements are slightly different for quoted and unquoted companies.
[46] Objection is made to the court arguing that the company should not be required to circulate the statement on the grounds that it 'secures needless publicity for a defamatory matter'.
[47] The Audit Quality Review team is part of the UK's independent regulatory regime.
[48] ISA 200 on overall objectives paragraph 13 (j), and ISA 210 on engagement terms, paragraph 6 (b).

- to provide auditors with *access to all information* that management is aware of as necessary for financial statement preparation and with any *additional information that auditors request*;

- to provide *unrestricted access to people* within the entity as auditors consider necessary.

### 2.9.2   ACCEPTABLE FINANCIAL REPORTING FRAMEWORK

General purpose frameworks are presumed acceptable if they are established by *organisations authorised or recognised to promulgate standards that follow transparent and established processes involving consideration of the views of a wide range of stakeholders*.

IFRS and national standard-setters are examples of such bodies. If there is no such body, accepted accounting conventions or industry practice are relevant provided the conventions are more than a mere agglomeration of accounting conventions to suit a particular entity.[49]

In addition, acceptable financial reporting frameworks generally display criteria such as *relevance, completeness, reliability, neutrality and understandability*.[50]

Sometimes the financial reporting framework prescribed by law is unacceptable either for political or technical reasons. For example, governments in some jurisdictions make it a condition of investment that segment information is not disclosed in the investor's financial statements in order to hide, for example, poor performance or substantial profits where living standards are low. To the extent that this might be in direct conflict with the reporting requirements for the investing entity, such engagements should not be accepted unless:

- management agrees to additional disclosures so that the financial statements are not misleading;

- an emphasis of matter paragraph refers to the issue;

- the terms 'true and fair' or 'fairly presents' are not used;

- the audit report refers to the issue to prevent the financial statements being misleading.

Local law may override all of these conditions and some jurisdictions have the power to force auditors to accept certain appointments. Many governments hold this power in

---

[49] ISA 210 on engagement terms, Appendix 2 paragraph 5.

[50] These characteristics are similar to the qualitative characteristics of useful financial information in the IASB's *Conceptual Framework for Financial Reporting*. They are also the same as the characteristics of suitable criteria in the context of ISAE 3000 on assurance engagement other than reviews or audits of historical financial information, so they would be relevant to the suitability of a framework for reporting on greenhouse gas statements, for example.

reserve but rarely, if ever, use it. Others are more active in the appointment of auditors to large audits, particularly where the private sector is not well developed or has a history of government involvement.

### 2.9.3   WRITTEN AGREEMENT

Agreements need to be *in writing* and cover:

- the objective and scope of the audit;
- auditor and management responsibilities;
- the financial reporting framework;
- the expected form and content of the audit and other reports.

Where responsibilities are established in legislation, as they often are, a written agreement is not necessary except in respect of the premise on which the audit is conducted. The wording in the legislation is acceptable provided it is sufficiently close to the ISAs requirements.[51]

### 2.9.4   IMPOSED LIMITATIONS IN AUDIT SCOPE, RECURRING ENGAGEMENTS, CHANGES TO TERMS AND WRITTEN REPRESENTATIONS

Auditors are occasionally asked to accept appointments in which the client makes it clear that they have no intention of providing auditors with the necessary information, that they are not concerned about the performance of the audit and that they fully expect a disclaimer of opinion to be issued. *If auditors believe a disclaimer of opinion is likely to be necessary because of an imposed limitation in the scope of the audit, they should not accept an engagement unless required to do so by law or regulation.*[52] This does not apply to situations in which the limitation is imposed *after* the engagement has been accepted, although in such cases it may be necessary to consider withdrawing from the engagement. Equally, limitations in audit scope outside management's control, even if they may give rise to the need for a disclaimer, do not prevent auditors from taking on appointments. Such situations can arise where all or most of the accounting records are destroyed by fire, flood, electrical failure or other catastrophe, and the financial statements have to be reconstructed and are largely based on estimates.

For recurring audits, auditors consider whether it is necessary to revise the terms of engagement or remind the entity of existing terms. Significant change such as the acquisition of another company, a takeover, changes to the composition of senior management, those charged with governance or to reporting requirements might warrant a reminder or revisions to terms.

Changes to the nature of the engagement should not be accepted unless there is reasonable justification. Some clients may believe that a modified audit opinion might be

---

[51] ISA 210 on engagement terms, paragraph A22.
[52] ISA 210 on engagement terms, paragraph 7.

avoided if the engagement were changed to a review engagement. This is not the case because such a change would not be justified and, even if it were, auditors may not ignore the evidence already obtained. Reasonable justification might be a fundamental misunderstanding about the nature of the engagement, but the whole purpose of agreeing terms is to avoid this.

Some written representations are in areas of contention between auditors and clients and engagement terms should refer to the fact that they will be required towards the end of the audit. The premise of an audit includes acknowledgement that information will be provided to auditors, which includes written representations.

### 2.9.5  CONTENT OF ENGAGEMENT LETTERS

Engagement letters include:

- reference to legislation, ISAs, and ethical standards;
- *the expected form of the audit report and other communications,* such as those relating to weaknesses in internal control;
- reference to the *inherent limitations of an audit and the inherent limitations of internal control,* and the fact that there is an unavoidable risk that some material misstatements may not be detected, even though the audit is properly conducted;
- *arrangements for planning and performing the audit* including the composition of the audit team, the use of experts, other auditors and internal audit and communications with predecessor auditors in the first year;
- the *expectation of written representations;*
- management's agreement to *make draft financial statements and any other information available in sufficient time* to allow the auditor to complete the audit;
- management's agreement to apprise auditors of *facts that may affect the financial statements arising between the date of the audit report to the date the financial statements are issued;*
- the *basis on which fees are computed* and billing arrangements;
- any *agreed limitations of liability;*
- a request for management to *acknowledge receipt and agree the terms* of the letter

Section essentials: what you need to remember

- *The conceptual approach to ethics consisting of fundamental principles, threats and safeguards.*
- *The different aspects of auditor appointment: legal, professional, ethical and commercial.*

- *The need for firms to have systems to ensure compliance with ethical and other requirements.*

- *The difference between independence and objectivity, examples of the different types of conflict of interest.*

- *The need to agree engagement terms, including the preconditions of an audit, as well as the contents of an engagement letter.*

# SECTION 2, QUESTION

*Long association, PIEs and conflicts of interest*

Ethical requirements require that auditors do not become excessively familiar with their audit clients. Special considerations apply when auditors take on the audit of public interest entities (PIEs).

**Required:**

(a) Explain how the long association of senior audit staff with an audit client creates threats to independence and explain the ethical requirements in this area. (8 marks)

(b) Give six examples of the prohibitions in ethical requirements applicable to the provision of non-assurance services to PIE audit clients. (6 marks)

You are the auditor of Barco and Malco. Both are long-standing clients of your firm. On Monday, Barco asks you for help in preparing an offer to purchase a third entity, Otico. On Tuesday, Malco also asks for your help with its own bid for Otico. Both entities are aware that there are other entities bidding for Otico, but neither is aware of the identity of the other bidders.

(c) Explain the ethical issues as they apply to your firm and its relationships with Barco and Malco. (6 marks)

Total (20 marks)

# 3 HOUSEKEEPING: PLANNING, MATERIALITY AND DOCUMENTATION

**Covering:** ISA 300 *Planning an Audit of Financial Statements*, ISA 320 *Materiality in Planning and Performing an Audit*, ISA 230 *Audit Documentation*.

**Why do I need to read this section?**

*Planning, materiality and documentation are easy areas for examiners to set questions in, and they often do. It is rare for a paper not to cover at least one of the three areas. Understanding these areas will also help make sense of the remainder of the audit process.*

**What is important in this section?**

- *Understanding that planning and risk assessment are iterative processes, i.e. they need to be updated throughout the audit.*

- *Understanding the difference between the overall audit strategy and the audit plan and the content of these planning documents.*

- *The definitions of materiality, performance materiality, the concept of 'clearly trivial', and how they affect the audit work performed.*

- *The content of audit documentation, why it is needed, examples of audit documentation, what it is used for, and what is considered adequate.*

**What sort of questions come up in this area?**

- *Examiners often ask for the information about the audited entity auditors need to gather when planning and performing risk assessments.*

- *Questions in higher level papers may cover the administrative tasks that need to be performed, including timetabling and co-ordinating the many people involved in large or complex group audits.*

- *You are more likely be asked to suggest or calculate materiality levels in bigger case study-type questions in higher level papers but shorter questions in lower level papers also appear from time to time.*

- *Many questions in this area ask you to explain what materiality means, how it might be calculated and what effect it has on the rest of the audit.*

- *Examiners often ask how you would audit a specific area and what you would document. Documentation is covered in the final part of many questions.*

**How do I stand out from the crowd?**

- *Emphasise your understanding of the difference between materiality and perfor-mance materiality as applied to the financial statements as a whole and to individual account areas, transactions and disclosures.*

- *Emphasise the importance of judgement in determining materiality.*

- *Demonstrate your understanding of the purposes of audit documentation.*

# 3.1    PLANNING

Any complex logistical exercise that is to stand a chance of avoiding going over-budget requires planning. Some things will go wrong however good the planning, but a great deal more will go wrong without it. Much of what used to be included as audit plan-ning is now included in the risk assessment but pure planning remains an important part of the audit.

The elements of audit planning and its purposes are mainly common sense, as with many aspects of audit, but they can be hard to articulate properly. When exam ques-tions focus on these areas, students do not always do as well as they could.

## 3.1.1    PLANNING DOCUMENTATION

Planning involves developing:

- an overall audit strategy; and

- an audit plan.[1]

Both of these obviously need to be documented, as do any subsequent changes to either document. The overall audit strategy is often documented in an overall audit strategy memorandum. Planning necessarily involves liaison with the entity's management, although audit effectiveness may be compromised if management knows too much about how the audit will be conducted because audit procedures become too predictable.

Engagement team members are specifically required to discuss the susceptibility of the financial statements to misstatements arising from fraud, and this is likely to take place during planning or the initial risk assessment.[2] These discussions need to involve the engagement partner and key team members, not necessarily all of the team, but the engagement partner does need to determine how to communicate the team discussion to other team members.

The main *objective of audit planning* is to ensure that an *effective audit* is conducted.[3] This means:

---

[1]  ISA 300 on audit planning, paragraph 2.
[2]  ISA 240 on fraud, paragraph 15.
[3]  ISA 300 on audit planning, paragraph 4.

- ensuring that appropriate attention is devoted to important areas;

- identifying and dealing with potential problem areas early;

- selecting the right people for the audit team in terms of the skills and experience mix;

- ensuring that work gets reviewed properly;

- involving third parties such as component auditors, internal auditors and experts.

Auditors also need to determine what sort of analytical procedures to use in the risk assessment and what the materiality levels are likely to be.

---

Planning is an *iterative* process rather than a discrete phase of the audit. It overlaps with risk assessment because similar information is gathered for planning and risk assessment purposes. Planning and risk assessment need to be revisited and *revised as the audit develops.*

---

### 3.1.2   PRELIMINARY ENGAGEMENT ACTIVITIES

Preliminary engagement activities are compliance activities, making sure that *engagement terms* have been agreed, that *quality control* and *acceptance and continuation* requirements have been met, and that *ethical requirements* have been complied with.

### 3.1.3   PLANNING ACTIVITIES: OVERALL AUDIT STRATEGY AND AUDIT PLAN

*Planning activities* mean developing an *overall audit strategy* and, from that, an *audit plan.*

#### Overall audit strategy

The overall audit strategy covers the *scope*, *timing* and *direction* of the audit, i.e. *what* is to be audited, *when* and *how*. Determining what to audit involves thinking about the reporting requirements.

*Scope* issues, i.e. the nature and extent of the audit, are determined by the information management prepares and what auditors are required to report.

Reporting is determined by statutory, regulatory and contractual arrangements[4] and there may be audit requirements under companies, securities or tax legislation, for example. Regulatory audits are required for many entities in the financial services sector and for other regulated entities such as airlines and travel agents. Government and regional grants are often made on condition that financial or other audits are conducted. Simply identifying all of the subsidiaries that require consolidation in

---

[4]   Entities may agree with auditors that additional audit procedures or voluntary audits will be conducted, for example.

group audits can be a problem, compounded by some group companies having non-coterminous period-ends, and by the acquisition and disposal of subsidiaries and other components during the period.

The results of preliminary engagement activities and knowledge gained on previous engagements affect scope considerations.

*Direction* involves considering how the audit is conducted, supervised and reviewed, the resources required, who is involved and the reporting lines. This is a substantial exercise for some audits. A large part of directing the audit involves co-ordinating the availability of experts and staff with the right specialist skills, the logistics of reviewing their work, interaction with internal audit, and the timing of interim and final audits.

*Timing* issues include the timetable for inventory counts and the production of financial statements, reporting deadlines, particularly for large listed groups of companies, and deadlines for reporting to management on significant control deficiencies and other matters.

*Example: audit strategy document*

---

### Strategic Planning Memorandum

#### *AUDIT SCOPE*

*Administrative details*

Client, period-end:
Prepared by:
Approved by:

*Characteristics of the engagement*

Including, for example:

- Small/large, listed/unlisted, family owned.

- Major shareholders, transactions with related parties.

- Accounting framework such as IFRS or IFRS for SMEs.

- Other services provided the client's accounting function.

- The group structure, how business segments are managed, use of service organisations and internal audit.

- Extent to which work in prior periods, including work on internal controls, is to be used in the current period.

NB: *Documentation of continuing importance to the audit* such as information on the nature of the business, the economic and regulatory environment in which it operates, and its controls can be kept in a *permanent file*.

## AUDIT DIRECTION

### Materiality

- *For the financial statements as a whole*: based on a percentage of estimated profit before tax and/or a percentage of assets, adjusted for exceptional or unusual items, consistent with the basis of the calculation used in previous audits, or any change explained.

- *For specific areas:* depending on the needs of users of accounts in areas such as related party transactions.

- *Performance materiality*: in assessing risk and performing specific procedures, materiality is set at $x on the basis that there is a low/medium/high probability that the aggregate of uncorrected and undetected misstatements will exceed overall materiality.

- *Clearly trivial*: matters considered clearly trivial for the purposes of aggregating misstatements are set at the lower of 1% of performance materiality and $y.

### Internal control

- Documentation of the internal control system in the permanent file.

- Assessment of overall control environment.

- Plans to rely on any internal controls in specific account areas.

### Results of previous audit

Any matters identified during the previous audit which may be relevant to the current audit.

### Developments in the business

Details of planning meetings between management and senior members of audit team to discuss changes in the business, economic climate, the entity's performance, changes in values of assets, any developments which might affect the going concern status of the entity, and the planned nature, timing and extent of audit work.

### Risk assessment

- Commentary on the results of *preliminary analytical procedures* performed on management or interim accounts, budgets, forecasts and on the investigation of any unusual items.

- Identified *significant risk areas* such as the overstatement of inventory or other assets as a result of inappropriate write-downs, property valuations in volatile markets, the completeness of cash transactions, the understatement or overstatement of revenues where there are complex accounting policies, the potential for management bias and management override of relevant controls, and *how they will be addressed.*

### Resources required and allocated

- The engagement partner and senior manager(s) are [. . .], for [. . .] man-hours, representing a change/no change from previous members' periods.

- Audit team members consist of the following [. . .] audit seniors, [. . .] audit juniors and audit staff from other offices for [. . .] man-hours.

- Others involved in the engagement include: other offices of our firm, other firms, property valuation experts, lawyers, internal auditors, third party inventory holders, bankers.

- Other organisations that require co-ordination include service organisations [. . .] and [. . .].

- Total budgeted hours and costs.

## AUDIT TIMING

### Overview reporting timetable

- Client period-end, group reporting deadlines, deadlines for subsidiaries, associates and joint ventures.

- Interim and final audit dates.

- Deadline for auditor sign-off, approval of financial statements and management letter.

### Detailed reporting timetable

- *Planning and initial risk assessment*: planning meeting to discuss audit approach and audit strategy, discuss potential significant risks and the risks of material misstatement due to fraud, update permanent file, prepare audit programmes. Staff hours: [. . .] partner, [. . .] senior manager, [. . .] audit staff. To be completed by January 31, 20XX.

- *Interim audit work*: updating risk assessment and testing the design and implementation of internal controls and testing their operational effectiveness in areas such as sales, purchase and payroll. Limited substantive procedures in the same areas. To be completed by March 16, 20XX.

- *Final audit visit:* planning meeting to review results of interim visit. Amend audit strategy as necessary. Update of controls testing to period-end. Extensive substantive testing as appropriate. To be completed by April 26, 20XX.

- Inventory count: audit juniors to attend on December 31, 20XX.

- Manager and partner reviews to be completed by May 17, 20XX.

- Final client meeting for approval and sign-off of financial statements.

- Provisional audit report date June 26, 20XX.

### 3.1.4 AUDIT PLAN

The work involved in developing an overall audit strategy and audit plan involves gathering information that is also helpful to the subsequent risk assessment. Matters covered in developing the audit plan and in risk assessment might include:

- knowledge gained from previous audits;
- a preliminary assessment of materiality levels and high risk areas;
- forming a preliminary view on the overall effectiveness of controls in order to determine the broad audit approach;
- assessing significant business and industry developments and changes to reporting requirements.

The *audit plan* covers:

- the nature, timing and extent of planned *risk assessment procedures*;
- the planned *further audit procedures in response to risks* at the assertion level;
- *any other procedures* necessary to achieve the objectives of the audit, bearing in mind the requirement to consider the need for any additional procedures beyond those required by ISAs.

Standard *audit programmes* and checklists can be used covering each area to be audited, the associated risk assessments and schedules of tests of controls and substantive procedures. These need to be reviewed and approved before work starts. The audit plan also incorporates schedules dealing with the direction, supervision and review of work performed.

## 3.2   MATERIALITY

The objective of an audit is for auditors to obtain reasonable assurance about whether the financial statements are free from *material* misstatement, and to form an opinion as to whether they are prepared in all *material* respects in accordance with the applicable financial reporting framework.

Materiality and performance materiality are among the most significant audit judgements made. They are much more important than most students think. Small adjustments to these figures can make a substantial difference to the nature and extent of work performed and whether auditors need to re-engineer their audit approach, which involves time and money, or whether they can carry on as planned. Materiality drives the audit. The assessment of risk is the assessment of the risk of *material* misstatement. Materiality also affects the nature and extent of audit testing, sample sizes, deciding whether adjustments are required to the financial statements and audit reporting. The audit report states that the financial statements give a true and fair view of, or present fairly in all *material* respects, the entity's position and performance, etc., in accordance with the applicable financial reporting framework.

If systematic errors are found in sampling that may indicate a material misstatement by extrapolation, for example, the implications are serious. If in fact there is a material misstatement, an adjustment to the financial statements will be required in order to avoid a modified audit opinion. Auditors are also required to re-consider their original risk assessment and audit approach in such circumstances, as they are when anything unexpected arises.

If it transpires that risk should have been assessed as, say, moderate instead of low in a particular area, it will be necessary to re-visit the nature, extent and balance of testing of controls and substantive procedures to establish whether they were adequate. If not, more work will be required. It is therefore critically important at the outset to be clear about what an error actually is, and to ensure that, when errors are identified, they are in fact errors.

### 3.2.1  WHAT IS MATERIAL?

Most financial reporting frameworks define materiality in terms of misstatements, which individually or in aggregate *could reasonably be expected to influence the economic decisions of users based on financial statements*.[5] Users in this context can be expected to have a reasonable knowledge of business and be willing to study the financial statements, to understand the concept of materiality and to recognise the inherent uncertainties in the measurement of estimates.

Students sometimes make understandable but inappropriate associations between materiality and risk and assume that higher audit risk must result in lower materiality level. In practice, there may be a strong correlation between materiality levels and risk assessment and while materiality and risk both affect the nature and extent of work, to some extent, they do so *independently* of each other.

Materiality is based on what could influence users and it affects sample sizes and the assessment of misstatements independently of the risk assessment. So a high level of risk in an area that users are not concerned about because it is petty cash and small, say, may result in more audit work than would otherwise have been necessary, but that is because of the risk assessment and not because of the materiality level. Conversely, an area that users are concerned about, such as directors' remuneration, may be assessed as low risk but, because of user concerns, auditors may determine a lower level of materiality resulting in a greater level of testing.[6]

In practice, concerns over the sensitivity of areas such as the disclosure of directors' remuneration mean that some firms treat them as having a materiality level of zero, i.e. they will not tolerate any error in such areas.[7]

---

[5]  ISA 320 on materiality, paragraph 2.
[6]  While a high level of audit risk does not necessarily result in lower materiality, a low level of materiality *implies* a higher level of risk.
[7]  Legal requirements in some jurisdictions such as the UK to disclose certain transactions with directors and other related parties in the audit report if they do not appear in the financial statements add to this sensitivity.

## 3.2.2 PERFORMANCE MATERIALITY

*Performance materiality*

There is always a risk that errors in financial statements will remain undetected; in fact it would be fairer to say that in most cases this is a virtual certainty. Furthermore, some detected errors are not corrected because they are clearly trivial or inconsequential, which usually means very small and not simply immaterial.[8] Taken together, there is a risk that undetected and uncorrected errors will exceed materiality. This problem is addressed by working to a level of materiality that is lower than overall materiality and is designed to reduce that risk to an acceptable level. This is known as performance materiality.

... *performance materiality means the amount or amounts set by the auditor at less than materiality for the financial statements as a whole, to reduce to an appropriately low level the probability that the aggregate of uncorrected and undetected misstatements exceeds materiality for the financial statements as a whole.*

ISA 320 *Materiality in Planning and Performing an Audit* paragraph 9

## 3.2.3 DIFFERENT LEVELS OF MATERIALITY AND BENCHMARKS

Materiality and performance materiality can both be applied:

- at the overall financial statement level;
- at the level of transactions, balances or disclosures (account area).

Materiality applied at the level of transactions and balances might reflect higher risk or sensitivities associated with areas where there are detailed disclosure requirements, such as transactions with related parties, directors' remuneration, or key disclosures in a particular industry. It is not necessary to calculate a different level of materiality for each account area, though.

Factors affecting the calculation of materiality at the *financial statement* level include:

- whether users focus on areas in the financial statements such as key operating ratios;
- where the entity is in its life cycle;
- the industry and economic environment in which the entity operates;
- the way the entity is financed.

Where an entity has a high level of debt, for example, more attention may be paid to its assets than its earnings because users will be interested in the extent to which they will have recourse to its assets if the debts are not repaid.

---

[8]  ISA 450 on the evaluation of misstatements, paragraph 5.

There are no generally accepted methods of calculating materiality that will cover all situations.

Factors affecting the decision whether to calculate materiality for a particular *account area* depend on whether user decisions are likely to be affected and include whether:

- law, regulation or the financial reporting framework affect users' expectations in a certain area, such as capital maintenance ratios in the financial services industry and key industry disclosures such as research and development costs in the pharmaceutical industry;

- management draws attention to a disclosure, such as a newly acquired business.

### Qualitative aspects of materiality

Materiality is essentially about the size of an item because it is not practical to design audit procedures to detect misstatements based on their nature. Nevertheless, auditors may deem some items material, even if they fall below the materiality level.[9] These might include:

- adjustments that turn a profit into a loss or net assets into net liabilities;

- transactions with related parties that are significant to the related party;

- amounts that have the effect of showing an entity as having breached banking covenants, such as the maintenance of minimum asset to liability ratios;

- amounts that affect compliance with regulatory requirements, such as the maintenance of certain capital ratios in the banking and financial services sectors.

Auditors tend to focus on matters that are material because of their nature when evaluating misstatements, rather than at the planning stage.

### Percentages and benchmarks

Percentages are often applied to benchmarks such as profits or assets in calculating materiality. An overall materiality figure is sometimes calculated by taking an average of percentages of turnover, gross profit or profit before tax for continuing operations, and net assets. Benchmarks and percentages are adjusted if a business is a start-up, growing rapidly, going through significant change, experiencing volatility, or if there are changes in the composition of a group.

Calculations may be performed on the prior period financial statements, period-to-date results, or budgets and forecasts as adjusted for changes in the business, industry or economic environment in which the entity operates. Benchmarks such as profits may need to be normalised (adjusted) for non-recurring or unusual items. Amounts commonly added back to profits, for example, include director's remuneration for smaller entities.

Materiality is a matter of judgement and fixed formulae cannot and should not be applied. However, ISA 320 notes that where 5% of profit before tax might be appropriate as a starting point for calculating materiality for a manufacturing entity, 1% of

---

[9]   ISA 320 on materiality, paragraph 6.

total revenue or expenses might be appropriate for a not-for-profit entity. Benchmarks used vary and include:

- 0.5–1% of total revenue and gross profit;
- 5–10% of profit before or after tax;
- 0.5–2% of total assets;
- 2–5% of net assets.

In practice, *performance materiality* can be set, for example, somewhere between 50% of materiality in relatively high risk situations, such as capitalised research and development expenditure that users might be concerned about, and 90% in lower risk situations such as cash. A fixed percentage is not appropriate because, by definition, it needs to reflect the risks relating to aggregated uncorrected and undetected misstatements in the circumstances of the entity.

Materiality and performance materiality might be calculated as follows:

| *Materiality* | $ |
|---|---|
| 5% of profit before tax of $100,000 (average over 3 periods, say) | 5,000 |
| 0.5% total revenue of $900,000 | 4,500 |
| 0.5% of total assets of $1,500,000 | 7,500 |
| Average = | 5,666 |
| **Performance materiality** | |
| Research and development expenditure, say 60% of materiality | 3,400 |
| Cash, say 90% of materiality | 5,100 |

### 3.2.4 REVISIONS TO MATERIALITY

Materiality and performance materiality, like audit risk, need to be re-visited and may need revision as the audit progresses in the light of evidence obtained. Reasons for revising materiality include changes that occurred during the audit, such as decisions to dispose of or acquire a major business and new information about the entity. A change in the auditors' understanding of an entity may also result in a revision if actual results now seem likely to be substantially different from the budgeted results that were originally used to determine materiality.[10]

## 3.3 AUDIT DOCUMENTATION

Documentation is all auditors have to prove that they performed an audit that complies with auditing standards. Even if surgeons write no notes at all about the procedures

---

[10] ISA 320 on materiality, paragraph A13.

they perform, evidence as to the quality of their work is evident in the patient. Without audit documentation an audit is opaque. It is impossible to see what has been done or how well it has been done. Indeed, without audit documentation an audit has not been done at all because an audit requires documentation by definition.

Audit quality is not just about documentation, though. Audit quality also depends on the quality of the people entering the profession and performing audits, the training they get, the standards they apply and the regulatory infrastructure within which they operate. But without audit documentation, it is quite impossible to evaluate whether auditing standards have been applied or whether the objective of the audit, in terms of obtaining sufficient appropriate audit evidence to support the audit opinion, has been achieved.

### 3.3.1   PURPOSES OF AUDIT DOCUMENTATION

The *purposes of audit documentation* are to provide:

- an adequate record of *the basis for the audit report*;
- evidence that the audit was *conducted in accordance with ISAs.*[11]

Documentation, like planning, is also required as it is for any other complex logistical exercise to facilitate:

- planning, supervision, direction and review of the work;
- internal quality control reviews under ISQC 1 and external regulatory inspections;
- the accountability of the audit team.

### 3.3.2   PERMANENT FILE INFORMATION

Documentation also constitutes *a record of information that is of continuing significance to the audit*, often recorded in *permanent or systems files*. Documentation typically appearing in such files includes:

- systems manuals, flowcharts and narrative notes recording the entity's accounting and internal control systems: these are dealt with in more detail in Section 4;
- internal control questionnaire and internal controls evaluation questionnaires and results of walk-through tests;
- the entity's constitutional documents;
- details of other professional advisers such as bankers and lawyers;
- directors' service agreements;

---

[11] ISA 230 on audit documentation, paragraph 5.

- legal documents such as long-term leases, prospectuses and sales agreements;

- a history of the business;

- final financial statements;

- a long-term record of key performance indicators for the purposes of analytical procedures.

All of this needs to be updated annually.

### 3.3.3   ADEQUATE DOCUMENTATION

Documentation should be produced on a timely basis for the obvious reason that the later it is left, the more unreliable it is likely to be. But how much documentation is required, and of what?

---

Documentation must be:

*. . . . sufficient to enable an experienced auditor, having no previous connection with the audit, to understand:*

- *the nature, timing and extent of the audit procedures performed. . . .*

- *the results of the audit procedures performed, and the audit evidence obtained; and*

- *significant matters arising during the audit, the conclusions reached thereon, and significant professional judgements made. . .*

ISA 230 *Audit Documentation* paragraph 8

---

An experienced auditor is someone with practical audit experience and a reasonable understanding of ISAs, the regulatory framework and business environment in which the entity operates, and relevant auditing and reporting requirements.[12]

### 3.3.4   TYPES OF DOCUMENTATION AND WHAT TO LEAVE OUT

Documentation can be paper or electronic *information appearing on audit files* and includes:

- audit strategy documents;

- detailed risk analyses;

- audit programmes;

- working papers;

- issues memoranda and summaries of significant matters;

- correspondence on significant matters, including email;

---

[12] ISA 230 on audit documentation, paragraph 6(c).

- summaries of adjustments made and uncorrected (unadjusted) errors;
- confirmation and representation letters;
- checklists such as those covering going concern and the subsequent events review;
- copies or summaries of the entity's records, such as contracts;
- financial statements and disclosure checklists;
- draft reports to those charged with governance (the management letter).

*Audit programmes* include:

- audit objectives and the related risk assessment;
- substantive tests and tests of controls;
- sample selection methods, referring to standardised sample selection working papers;
- who prepared the programme, who reviewed it and when.

*Working papers* include:

- who prepared the working paper, performed the work, reviewed it, when and to what extent;
- the work performed and the detailed findings;
- the conclusions drawn.

What *not* to include is sometimes the bigger problem in practice and auditors are not required to keep *superseded drafts* of working papers or financial statements or *notes that reflect incomplete or preliminary thinking*.

It is also unnecessary and impracticable for auditors to document every matter considered and professional judgement made, or for auditors to document separately in a checklist compliance with matters where compliance is demonstrated by documents already on the file.[13] This means that if it is obvious that something has been done, there is no need to state that it has been done. So the existence of an adequate audit plan demonstrates that auditors have planned the audit, and there is no need to state that this is the case. The existence of a signed engagement letter demonstrates that engagement terms have been agreed.

Problems of interpretation arise in three areas: *significant issues*, the *detail of procedures performed*, and *oral explanations*.

*Significant issues* include:

- significant risks;
- matters that cause auditors difficulty;

---

[13] ISA 500 on audit documentation, paragraph A7.

- indicators that the financial statements could be materially misstated;
- indicators that that a revision to the risk assessment may be needed;
- findings that might require anything other than a 'clean' audit opinion.[14]

All of these issues involve the exercise of judgement and need to be properly documented. They are also areas that auditors are often reluctant to document.

Similarly troublesome areas include:

- the rationale for conclusions where auditors are required to 'consider' an issue;
- the need for auditors to demonstrate professional scepticism;
- bases for conclusions in subjective areas such as significant accounting estimates;
- the basis for conclusions where the authenticity of a document is called into question (which is rare).[15]

An area of contention between regulators and auditors is whether cleared review points should be kept on the audit file. There is no specific requirement to keep these on file even though they may be caught under the requirement to document significant issues. In practice some firms routinely keep them, and other firms routinely destroy them on the basis that they constitute notes that reflect incomplete or preliminary thinking and because, with the benefit of hindsight, it is perhaps too easy for regulators to challenge audit judgements. Documentation is required about discussions of significant issues with management and those charged with governance.

### 3.3.5  WHAT DOCUMENTATION SHOULD SHOW ORAL EXPLANATIONS

Regulators often complain that auditors over-audit and over-document in some areas, and under-audit and under-document in others. In terms of the detail of procedures performed, the documentation should show:

- *who performed* and who *reviewed* the work, *when,* and to what extent; and
- the identifying characteristics of *the specific items* or matters *tested.*[16]

The latter causes problems. Auditors might record that they have tested, say, 20 purchase orders selected using random number tables. What they should record is the *specific* identifying characteristics of the items tested, such as the purchase order numbers.

---

[14] ISA 230 on audit documentation, paragraph A8.
[15] ISA 230 on audit documentation, paragraph A10.
[16] ISA 230 on audit documentation, paragraph 9.

*Example working paper: sampling*

| | | |
|---|---|---|
| Client: | Chan & Co Furniture Manufacturers Group | Reference: B.3.4 |
| Period-end: | December 31, 20XX | Prepared by: M Bird |
| Subject: | Purchases Cycle | Date: January 4, 20XX |
| Reviewed by: | G Miller | Signature: |
| Date: | February 16, 20XX | |

Signature:

1.  **Objective** Ref Audit Strategy Document A.3.1

Substantive evidence supporting

*   the completeness, accuracy and classification of purchases in the income statement;

*   the completeness, accuracy and valuation of liabilities and disclosures in the balance sheet.

2.  **Work performed** Ref Audit Programme A.3.2.

Period-end substantive procedures on purchases and update of interim controls testing.

The initial risk assessment was LOW for the understatement of purchases and trade payables.

*   A statistical sample of orders selected at random from the period were traced to goods received notes, the relevant invoice, and to the purchase ledger and purchases account Ref S.5.6.

*   Inventory records were also examined as part of substantive inventory testing Ref C.2.1.

*   All orders were checked to the list of approved suppliers and all invoices were checked to ensure that they were signed as approved by the purchase ledger controller as part of controls testing Ref I.6.7.

The results of interim controls testing, Ref I.3.4, show that controls were operating effectively, as in previous periods.

3.  **Results**

One immaterial transposition error found in posting to purchases and the purchase ledger highlighted by an internal audit review and subsequently corrected.

| Order and Date | Auth? | GRN and Date | Invoice, Date & Value | Details | Auth? | Purchases account, purchase ledger? | Inventory Records |
|---|---|---|---|---|---|---|---|
| X23764/5 2 March | √ | Y347984 April | HLB/234 4 April $4367.87 | 25 – 35mm screws | √ | √ | √ |
| X43686/7 3 Feb | √ | Y2156 5 May | DAB/234 5 May $4064.87 | 2 – 2.5m piping | √ | √ | √ |
| Etc..... | √ | Etc... | Etc... | | √ | √ | √ |

4.  **Conclusions**

Our statistical sampling methods indicate that, based on the sample, purchases and purchase liabilities are not materially misstated.


*Example working paper: analytical procedures*

| | | | |
|---|---|---|---|
| **Client:** | Chan & Co Supermarkets Group | **Reference:** B.3.4 | |
| **Period-end:** | December 31, 20XX | **Prepared by:** M Bird | |
| **Subject:** | Bank and cash | **Date:** January 4, 20XX | |
| **Reviewed by:** | G Miller | **Signature:** | |
| **Date:** | April 4, 20XX | | |

**Signature:**

1.  **Objective**

Evidence supporting the completeness, existence, accuracy and classification of cash and bank balance disclosures.

2.  **Work performed**

Final analytical procedures on the bank and cash levels held at the period-end, by group and store, compared with prior periods and interim cash counts. Ref Audit Programme A.3.2

The results of interim internal control testing, Ref A3.4, show that controls are operating effectively, as in previous periods. Tests have not yet been updated to the period-end.

### 3. Summary of Results

Per draft financial statements

|  | Group cash in hand $m Ref B.3.4.1 | Group bank balances $m Ref B.3.4.2 | Average cash per shop $m* Ref B.3.4.3 |
|---|---|---|---|
| December 31, 20XX | 6.345 | 315.350 | 0.234 |
| June 30, 20XX | 7.002 | 200.345 | 0.345 |
| December 31, 20XY | 8.246 | 221.345 | 0.346 |

* Excluding A and B hypermarkets sold in Q3.

See working papers B.3.4.4–5 for details of cash, bank and average balances by region.

The overall decrease in group cash in hand is partially explained by better working capital management. Changes to inventory and cash management, including the introduction of a cash-back scheme have been introduced, Ref B.4.3.6. These figures are further improved when hypermarkets A and B are excluded, Ref B.4.3.1. However, the decrease may not be wholly attributable to these changes which were introduced in Q4 and while controls over cash counts at the shops appeared to be functioning effectively, investigations are taking place at two shops concerning allegations of the theft of substantial amounts of cash by employees, Ref B.4.3.7.

The increase in the group bank balance at the period-end reflects the sale of the loss-making hypermarkets A and B. The decrease in June reflects bulk cash purchases of garden furniture, Ref C.3.2.5. No other larger or unusual items.

### 4. Conclusions

Subject to confirmation of bank balances with banks, finalisation of analytical procedures on inventory and the outcome of investigations into theft of cash by employees, bank balances and cash do not appear to be materially misstated.

---

Of themselves, *oral explanations* by auditors do not constitute adequate audit evidence but they may be used to explain or clarify information contained in the audit documentation.[17] It can be difficult for auditors and regulators to agree on whether this apparently straightforward guidance has been applied.

Two other exceptional areas requiring documentation are *departures from relevant requirements,* and *procedures performed after the date of the audit report,* to accommodate changes made to documentation arising from audit inspection visits by regulators, for example.

---

[17] ISA 230 on audit documentation, paragraph A5.

### 3.3.6   ASSEMBLING AUDIT FILES

The final audit file should be assembled on a timely basis which is ordinarily *not more than 60 days from the date of the audit report.* Completion procedures should be purely administrative and include discarding superseded documentation and cross-referencing working papers.  The file should ordinarily be kept for not less than five years from the date of the audit report. Local regulation and tax legislation in particular may demand that files are kept for longer.

### 3.3.7   SMALLER FIRMS AND AUDIT DOCUMENTATION

The representatives of smaller practitioners often complain that the documentation requirements of ISAs are primarily designed for the audit of larger entities and that the most onerous aspects of ISAs are the documentation requirements. Completely irrelevant requirements, such as those relating to internal audit where there is no such department, or on the need to supervise staff where there are no staff and all the work is performed by the engagement partner, need not be complied with or documented. Even so, it is proving necessary for standard-setters, professional bodies and others to provide examples of documentation for smaller audits. In the UK, the Financial Reporting Council's Practice Note 26 provides examples of smaller entity audit documentation.

**Section essentials: what you need to remember**

• *The purposes of audit planning and audit documentation.*

• *The contents of the overall audit strategy, audit plans, examples of audit documentation and the standard of audit documentation.*

• *The definitions of materiality and performance materiality, what they mean, why they are important and how they are calculated.*

# SECTION 3, QUESTION

Calculating materiality involves the exercise of professional judgement. Working to an appropriate level of materiality is critical to prevent over-auditing, and to ensure that misstatements likely to affect user decision making are not overlooked. Performance materiality deals with risks relating to undetected and uncorrected misstatements.

**Required:**

(a) Explain the key elements of materiality and performance materiality. (5 marks)

(b) Give three examples of common benchmarks for the calculation of materiality and explain how the benchmarks might be used. (6 marks)

The following figures have been extracted from the draft financial statements of Rodco, which manufactures domestic electrical appliances.

Total revenue: 20XX = $950m (prior year $1,010m)
Profit before tax: 20XX = $150m (prior year $160m)
Net assets: 20XX = $1,500m (prior year $1,250m)

Competition in the market has increased resulting in several product lines being discontinued during the period. They accounted for $15m of revenue in the current and prior periods. A related provision for the write-down of inventory of $8m has been made in the current period.

**Required:**

(c) Explain the factors you will take into account when considering whether separate reference should be made to the discontinued product lines in the current period's financial statements. (5 marks)

(d) Explain the purposes of audit documentation and describe the test applied to determine whether it is adequate. (4 marks)

Total (20 marks)

# 4 THE CORE OF THE AUDIT

## 4.1 RISK ASSESSMENTS

**Covering:** ISA 200 *Overall Objectives of the Independent Auditor and the Conduct of an Audit in Accordance with International Standards on Auditing*, ISA 315 *Identifying and Assessing the Risks of Material Misstatement through Understanding the Entity and Its Environment.*

### Why do I need to read this section?

*Understanding the audit risk model, that all audits involve a risk assessment and that assessments depend on auditor judgement, is critical to understanding auditing. An audit involves more assessments and judgements than is generally appreciated. An audit opinion is just that, an opinion not a certification, and opinions sometimes differ. Students who realise that there is no one correct answer to a question on risk assessment or audit testing make better progress than those always looking for the 'right' answer which they think must exist and which the examiner is looking for. There are very few auditing and assurance papers that do not cover risk assessment in some form.*

### What is important in this section?

- *Understanding the risk model and how risk, controls, testing control effectiveness and substantive procedures fit together.*

- *Being able to give good examples of different types of risk, appreciating what auditors need to understand about a business, and how they will gain that understanding.*

- *Internal controls: what they are, the need to assess their design and implementation, how to test them and deal with deviations.*

- *The distinction between the various different types of internal control and the importance of higher-level controls.*

- *The difference between evaluating the design and implementation of controls and testing their operational effectiveness (control effectiveness).*

### What sort of questions come up in this area?

- *Questions that provide a scenario and ask you to explain the risk model and state what the main risks to the business as a whole are, and what controls should be in place to deal with risks in particular areas.*

- *Detailed questions on the controls you would expect to find in a given area and how you would go about testing their effectiveness.*

How do I stand out from the crowd?

- *Demonstrate an appreciation of the significance of higher-level controls such as the control environment and reviews of performance, and of management override of controls.*

- *Show that you understand how the constituent elements of the risk model fit together.*

- *Give good examples of risks and controls and make good quality links between them.*

### 4.1.1   RISK

Risk is a much used, abused and misunderstood concept in many spheres. Auditing is no exception and it is helpful to get to grips with the terminology used in ISAs up front.

### Categories of Risk

*Business risks*[1] are risks that could adversely affect the entity's ability to achieve its objectives such as making a profit, supporting a family, becoming a market leader, simply continuing as a going concern, or the risk of loss from litigation or adverse publicity, for example.

*Audit risk*[2] is the risk that auditors could express an inappropriate audit opinion when the financial statements are materially misstated, i.e. that auditors fail to spot a material misstatement and give an unmodified audit opinion where a modified one is appropriate. Audit risk is the product of the *risk of material misstatement* and *detection risk*.

*Risk of material misstatement/financial statement risk/entity risk* is the risk that the financial statements do not give a true and fair view of, or present fairly the entity's financial position and performance. It is the product of *inherent risk* and *control risk*.

*Inherent risk*[3] is the susceptibility of the financial statements as a whole, and of transactions, balances and disclosures, to material misstatement, regardless of controls or the audit. Inventory is inherently more risky than cash, and the financial statements of large established manufacturing businesses are generally less risky than small Internet start-ups.

*Control risk*[4] is the risk that material misstatement in transactions, account balances or disclosures will not be prevented, detected or corrected on a timely basis by the entity's internal control. Payables are generally subject to greater control risk than receivables. Control risk can never be eliminated because of the ***inherent limitations*** of internal control. These include human error, management override of controls, and the

---

[1]   ISA 315 on risk assessment, paragraph 4 (b).
[2]   ISA 200 on overall objectives, paragraph 13 (c).
[3]   ISA 200 on overall objectives, paragraph 13 (n).
[4]   ISA 200 on overall objectives, paragraph 13 (n).

avoidance of controls by collusion. For example, segregation of duties involves having different people deal with assets such as cash, and the related records, so that the asset cannot be misappropriated and the theft covered up in the records by the same person. This control can be evaded if the two people involved collude to misappropriate the cash and cover it up in the records. As with all elements of the risk model, some control risk will always exist.

*Detection risk*[5] is the risk that the audit procedures performed to reduce audit risk to an acceptably low level will fail to detect a material misstatement. Detection risk includes sampling risk and non-sampling risk. Sampling risk is the risk that samples will not be representative of the populations from which they are drawn. Non-sampling risk includes errors of judgement in selecting the sample or in interpreting the results, and errors in areas not involving sampling. Detection risk is a function of the effectiveness of audit procedures, i.e. how good audit tools or methodologies are, and of their application by auditors, i.e. how well auditors use them.

The assessment of inherent risk and control risk are audit judgements and they are fixed. The only variable is detection risk. The higher the assessed risks of material misstatement, the lower detection risk must be to keep audit risk at an acceptably low level. If audit risk is to be reduced, say, from 5% to 2%, only detection risk will need to be reduced as inherent and control risk cannot be reduced, at least not by auditors. Auditors will need to increase sample sizes, extend testing generally and obtain more persuasive audit evidence. Adequate planning, staffing, supervision and review enhance the effectiveness of audit procedures and reduce the possibility that auditors might select inappropriate procedures, misapply them, or misinterpret the results.

### Reducing, not eliminating risk

The inherent limitations of an audit and the limitations of financial reporting mean that audit risk and detection risk cannot be eliminated. The limitations of an audit include the fact that most audit evidence is persuasive rather than conclusive, that there are time and cost limitations to an audit, and that there is always the possibility of human error in the application of audit procedures. Limitations in financial reporting include the risk of fraudulent collusion and management override of controls in the preparation of financial statements, which cannot be eliminated either.

---

**Audit Risk = Inherent Risk × Control Risk × Detection Risk**

**Risk of Material Misstatement**

---

**Figure 4.1**   Audit risk model

---

[5]   ISA 200 on overall objectives, paragraph 13 (e).

There is in practice a significant overlap between business risks and the risk of material misstatement in the financial statements. Significant litigation and going concern risks, for example, almost always represent risks to the business and risks of material misstatement because they have a financial effect. But not all business risks have an immediate financial effect. Reputational risk, or the risk of an aircraft crashing, for example, are usually business risks. They do not become risks of material misstatement in financial statements unless and until reputation is actually lost, or an aircraft actually crashes, whereupon the financial effects crystallise and need to be reflected in the financial statements.

## 4.1.2   UNDERSTANDING THE BUSINESS

ISA 315 on risk assessment is one of the longest ISAs. It is the cornerstone on which all subsequent ISAs have been developed and it was one of the first revised ISAs published after the corporate collapses of the early 2000s, although its revision started well before the collapses happened. It was also one of the first ISAs to be revised as part of the IAASB's clarity project. Much of its excessive complexity has been removed as a result of clarification but much of its content is about understanding the business rather than risk assessment *per se*. Auditors perform risk assessments using their understanding of the business.

The requirement to obtain an understanding of industry, regulatory and other external factors and of the operations, ownership and governance structures are not what intuitively come to mind when thinking of risk assessment, but the full title of the document is clear: ISA 315 *Identifying and Assessing the Risk of Material Misstatement Through Understanding the Entity and its Environment*. The latter part of the title is often forgotten but risk assessment can only take place on the basis of a proper understanding of the entity.

**Understanding the Entity, its Environment and its Internal Control**

*Understanding the entity and its environment*
If asked, 'What do we need to find out about this business before we start the audit', students might suggest information about its operations, structure, objectives, strategies to deal with business risks, financing, ownership, governance, investments, accounting policies, and how it measures its financial performance. This is what the ISA requires.[6]

If asked to 'Find out something about the environment in which the business operates', students might suggest things very similar to the guidance in the ISA including information about the market in which the entity operates, business cycles, environmental and tax regulations, government policies affecting the industry, and any industry-specific regulation such as financial services legislation. Collectively, these are described as 'industry, regulatory and other external factors'.[7]

---

6   ISA315 on risk assessment, paragraph 11(b)-(e).
7   ISA315 on risk assessment, paragraph 11(a).

Understanding a business is not rocket science and it is not necessary for auditors to classify their understanding using the headings below, provided all areas are covered. Understanding the business involves gathering information about:

- the *entity*;
- its selection and application of *accounting policies*;
- its *objectives, strategies* and related business *risks*;
- how it measures and reviews its *financial performance*.

*Information about the entity*
Information about the entity might include:

- the complexity of its *structure*, particularly group structures containing potentially higher risk elements such as special purpose entities;
- the *ownership* of the entity;
- existence of and transactions with *related parties*;
- whether *operations* involve joint ventures, alliances or outsourcing;
- where the entity's *revenue streams* come from;
- the *location* of its facilities;
- whether *investments* involve non-consolidated entities such as partnerships and joint ventures;
- whether *financing activities* involve off-balance sheet financing, leasing arrangements or derivatives;
- whether *financial reporting* involves fair value accounting, and how revenue, foreign currency and unusual or complex transactions are accounted for.

SPEs are often related parties and have assets transferred to them by the reporting entity. The issue is often whether or not the risk relating to the relevant assets has genuinely been transferred to the SPE and whether, as a result, the assets and the SPE can be removed from an entity's balance sheet. The accounting can be complex and SPEs are often associated with higher audit risk.

The use of special purpose entities (SPEs) for fraudulent purposes is well documented but they have legitimate uses. They are generally established for a narrow, well-defined purpose such as the securitisation of financial assets such as mortgages or to carry out research and development activities.

*Selection and application of accounting policies*
The selection and application of accounting policies is a critical area in many audits but students sitting lower-level papers often forget it and focus on other aspects of understanding the business. Policies selected for significant and unusual transactions, policies that have changed and policies in emerging or new areas are all associated with higher audit risk and frauds such as earnings management.

*Objectives, strategies and related business risks*

Objectives are the overall plans for the business, such as sustainable growth and long-term profitability. Strategies are the means of achieving the objectives, through planned capital investment and sustained investment in training, for example. Related business risks are the threats to the achievement of the objectives, such as competition from those with a lower cost base, a lack of available credit or regulatory change.

Business risks arise from change, including changes in the business environment, from a failure to adapt to change, and because of inappropriate changes made by the business itself. New products and services may fail, or result in damage to the entity's reputation, and new markets may be inadequate to support new products.

Business risks overlap with audit risk but they are not the same thing. Business risks, especially unidentified risks, are associated with the risk of material misstatement. A poor quality customer base is a business risk. It might also give rise to a risk of material misstatement in the valuation of receivables, for example. In the longer term, it might also have an effect on the going concern status of the entity and would then be both a business risk and a reporting risk.

Indicators of material misstatement arising from business risks might include the following, many of which are also fraud risks:

- *regulatory investigations* which may give rise to penalties not accounted for, or affect the going concern status of an entity;
- a high level of *non-routine transactions or journal entries* at the period-end which are easy to manipulate when auditors are under pressure to complete the audit;
- *new accounting requirements, forward-looking transactions and uncertainties* such as pending litigation, contingent liabilities for environmental remediation or warranty claims and other areas involving a high level of professional judgement;
- *complex group structures* and/or frequent changes thereto which can be used to cover up fraud or simply lead to errors;
- significant *changes to IT systems, technology or key staff*;
- economic or market *volatility*.

*Measurement and review of financial performance*

Auditors need to take account of the fact that management measures things it thinks are important, and that performance measures not only create pressures to perform but sometimes provide a motive to misstate the financial statements.

Understanding the Business Checklist

*External factors: industry, regulation and economy*

- Market conditions and competition.

- Cyclical or seasonal factors.

- Accounting requirements, industry practices, environmental requirements, industry-specific legislation, taxation.

- General levels of economic activity, the effect of interest rates on borrowing and inflation.

*The entity*

- **Business**: sources of revenue, products and services, alliances and joint ventures, outsourcing, locations, key customers and suppliers, R&D, related parties.

- **Investments**: investment strategy; acquisitions and disposals of property, plant and equipment, acquisition of short- and long-term securities.

- **Financing**: bank loans and other debt financing such as loans from group companies and other related parties including directors, shareholdings, overdraft facilities, leases and derivative financial instruments.

- **Financial reporting**: accounting framework such as IFRS, industry specific accounting requirements, accounting for revenue recognition, fair values, foreign currency transactions, and financial statement presentation and disclosures.

**Entity objectives, strategies, related business risks**

| Objectives | Strategies | Business risks |
|---|---|---|
| Financial: profit, growth, asset-related | Investment, cost control, marketing, revenue growth | Availability of finance for investment; competition; cost of raw materials, effectiveness of marketing |
| Technical: new/leading products and services | Investment in innovation, HR and remuneration policies, IT | Competitor technologies, technical failure after product launch and associated reputational risk |
| Market share | Product/service bundling and pricing, investment in marketing, technology, IT | Effectiveness of competitor strategies |

*Performance measurement and review*

- Key ratios, operating statistics, performance indicators year to year
- Actual/budget variance analysis, analysts' reports, credit ratings

Figure 4.2   Understanding the business checklist

### Understanding internal control

The purpose of internal control is to address business risks that threaten the entity's objectives, i.e:

- the reliability of its financial reporting;
- the effectiveness and efficiency of its operations;
- its compliance with laws and regulations.[8]

The requirement here is for auditors to **understand controls relevant to the audit.** Virtually all of these are going to be financial controls rather than operational controls but not all financial controls are going to be relevant. Sophisticated operational controls for an airline might include controls over the maintenance of aircraft and controls over flight schedules, for example, which would not normally be directly relevant to the audit. Controls over the acquisition or disposal of a large fleet of aircraft on the other hand might primarily be for operational purposes, but are also likely to be relevant to the audit. A print media group might control the collection of statistics about circulation for compliance and advertising purposes and while in itself this is probably not relevant to the audit, if the statistics are used as a means of checking revenue, the controls might become relevant in conjunction with other controls over revenue.

**Smaller entities** have a different mix of controls to those of larger entities. They often rely on the day-to-day involvement of management to ensure the efficient running of the business and compliance with regulations, rather than on formal internal controls such as the segregation of duties. Segregation of duties often involves ensuring that those with custody of assets, such as cash, do not also have access to the related records, the cash book. In smaller entities, there are simply not enough people among whom to segregate the duties and control is exercised by the owner-manager 'keeping an eye on things', by performing ad hoc cash counts, for example, and the involvement of professional accountants which serves as a control over the financial statements. On the other hand, the owner-manager's control over assets, records and ability to override controls can mean a higher than usual risk of fraud, although this is equally true of larger entities even where exemplary systems of control and governance are in place.

> *The involvement of the owner-manager in the day-to-day running of the business can reduce control risk, or it can increase it, or both in different areas, depending on the integrity of the owner-manager and the way they exercise control. It is for auditors to make this judgement.*

### Evaluating design and implementation

Obtaining an understanding of controls involves **evaluating their design** and **determining whether they have been implemented**. The distinction between evaluating design and implementation and **testing control effectiveness** is simple and important

---

[8]  ISA 315 on risk assessment, paragraph A44.

but students (and practitioners!) sometimes fail to understand them. This means that any student who can demonstrate a clear understanding of these distinctions is going to impress examiners!

> Understanding the *design* and *implementation* of controls is required regardless of whether auditors intend to place any reliance on controls by testing their *effectiveness*.[9]

Testing control effectiveness is a third step. Evaluating design and determining implementation for risk assessment purposes must involve more than simply asking about them (inquiry). It needs to include observation, inspection or walk-through tests. The difficult distinction is between evaluating implementation, i.e. determining whether controls are in place (as designed), and testing effectiveness. How do you establish that a control, such as one that produces exception reports showing overdue receivables, has been 'implemented' without testing it? In many cases it will be efficient to look at implementation and effectiveness testing together. The fact that testing control effectiveness shows the control is working often means that it must have been implemented properly. In sophisticated systems there will be other ways of looking at implementation independently of effectiveness testing, sometimes using computer assisted audit techniques (CAATs), by entering dummy data into the receivables system and seeing if an overdue receivable shows up in an exception report in due course, for example.

A great number of controls are now both automated and very efficient. It used to be commonplace for audit firms to employ comptometer operators to add up computer printouts to ensure that the total was correct, because computer systems or the people who operated them were unreliable. Many of the most important entries in the records though are the non-routine, non-automated, journal entries put through close to the period-end when the final financial statements are being prepared, when things can easily go wrong in the pressure to meet reporting deadlines. Controls over the posting of final journal entries are often weak, but the entries can be significant either in size or impact and they are often made in haste, hence the risk of error or intentional misstatement.

Automated controls generally cover transaction processing (initiating, recording and reporting) whereas manual controls involve approval and reviews. Effective systems need both types but the risks associated with them are different. With manual controls, risks are often higher because they can be more easily by-passed, ignored or overridden than automated controls, and they are more prone to error. The risks associated with automated controls on the other hand are not only those of unauthorised access, and changes to and the loss or corruption of programmes and data. Risks also include inappropriate reliance on information produced by systems that have not been interfered with, but have not processed transactions properly simply because they were not designed well enough to do the job they were supposed to do, or were not implemented effectively.

---

[9]  Control effectiveness means operational effectiveness.

### Internal control components

The division of control into *five components* as suggested by ISA 315[10] is based on the well-established US COSO Framework.[11] Auditors can use other categorisations provided they cover all five areas. The five areas comprise:

- the control environment;

- the entity's risk assessment process;

- information systems;

- control activities;

- monitoring of controls.

### Control environment

The control environment is about the ***attitude, awareness and actions of those charged with governance and management.*** It sets the *tone* of an organisation and influences the *control consciousness* of its people. Elements include:

- *management's philosophy and operating style,* as evidenced by their selection of conservative or aggressive accounting policies, for example;

- the entity's *commitment to competence* as evidenced by the quality and extent of training, for example;

- *human resources policies and practices;*

- the extent and quality of *participation by those charged with governance.*

It is clearly not as easy to 'test' the control environment in the same way as other control elements can be tested. Nevertheless, auditors evaluate whether management has maintained a culture of honesty and ethical behaviour and whether any deficiencies in the environment undermine the other control components. The quality of the control environment has a direct bearing on the effectiveness of other control components. Evidence in this area might involve talking to employees about how management communicates its views on ethical behaviour, inspecting any code of conduct and considering whether management acts in a manner that supports this.

It may be difficult to document significant mismatches between what management and those charged with governance say they do, what they actually do and what they encourage employees to do.

The control environment is particularly important for smaller entities in the absence of other control components. Documentary evidence supporting the assessment of the control environment for such entities may include the fact that, for example, the owner-manager sets the right tone at the top by behaving with integrity, and that there is effective communication of the importance of ethical behaviour to staff.

---

[10] ISA 315 on risk assessment, paragraphs 14–24.

[11] COSO – The Committee of Sponsoring Organizations of the Treadway Commission, a joint initiative of, among others, the American Institute of Certified Public Accountants (AICPA), Financial Executives International (FEI) and the Institute of Internal Auditors (IIA).

A good control environment in larger entities counterbalances pressures on management arising from market demands or performance-related remuneration packages. It reduces the risk of error but is not an absolute deterrent to fraud.

*The entity's risk assessment process*
**An entity needs to assess the risks that threaten the achievement of its objectives so that it can manage them.** It can manage risks by *accepting* them if they are insignificant or unlikely, for example, by *mitigating* them or *transferring them* by means of insurance, for example.

A sports club might *mitigate* the risk of a cricket ball causing damage outside the club by putting a fence around the cricket ground. If no-one lives nearby and there is no property nearby, it might simply *accept* the risk, or it might decide to *transfer* the risk by taking out insurance against claims for any damage caused.

A common weakness in risk management systems is failing to update risk assessments when there are changes. Changes may involve new staff, new systems, changes in the operating environment in the form of new regulation, new technology, new competitors in the market, changes in social attitudes and the economy, and changes in business models and associated cost structures such as outsourcing.

Auditors are required to understand **whether the entity properly manages risks relevant to financial reporting,** i.e. whether the entity has a risk assessment process that identifies relevant business risks, estimates their significance, assesses the likelihood of their occurrence and decides what to do about them. If an entity does this, but auditors then identify financial reporting risks that the entity's system failed to pick up, auditors have to ask why, whether the risk assessment process has been designed and implemented properly, and whether there are other risks it might have missed.

If a business in the financial services sector fails to notice or respond to a downturn in the economy or the increasing popularity of ethical investments, for example, it is not managing its risks effectively and may not be profitable for very long. Such businesses need to have systems in place to respond to these matters by having a regular SWOT analysis on the board's agenda for example, and by reviewing business trends, revenue and profitability by comparison with competitors. These risks affect financial reporting when they start to represent risks to the entity's going concern status, perhaps where borrowing limits or banking covenants are approached or breached. They also give rise to an enhanced risk of fraud and error if managers are paid bonuses. Other examples of threats that have a similar effect on the risks relevant to financial reporting might include a failure to respond:

- to new providers of on-line financial services who keep costs down by outsourcing back office operations to cheaper jurisdictions;

- when outsourced operations are brought back in-house by competitors;

- when customers become increasingly willing to pay for good quality personal service rather than automated services on-line;

- when customers become increasingly sceptical about or unwilling to pay for ethical investments.

While the inertia of existing customers and repeat business may maintain volumes and profitability in the short term, it will not be sustainable in the long term unless the necessary investments are made.

*Smaller entities* generally do not perform formal risk assessment processes. This is unlikely to constitute a significant deficiency in internal control that needs reporting to management in many cases. *Owner-managers will usually go through a mental process that approximates to risk assessment, and act accordingly.*

The owner of a pizza delivery business might, for example, assess the main risks to the business as being a competitor arriving, an injury to a delivery person, food poisoning among customers or non-compliance with health and safety regulations. An event can be categorised as highly likely, moderately likely, or of low likelihood, perhaps. The potential *impact* of an event can also be categorised as high, moderate or low, but they are not the same thing. The risk of a competitor arriving might be low or moderate, for example, but the impact potentially high. The risk of a delivery person being injured might be high and its impact potentially high if a claim is made against the business. The risks associated with food poisoning might be low, and of non-compliance with health and safety regulations might be moderate, but the potential impact of both is high because inspectors could close the business down. If the principal means of managing risks are mitigating them, transferring them and accepting them, it might be appropriate for the business to do nothing in the case of a competitor arriving, unless and until one does arrive. The business might mitigate other risks by checking that those making deliveries have appropriate tax and insurance for themselves and their vehicles, by maintaining high food hygiene standards in kitchens, and transferring some elements of risk by maintaining general liability and workers' compensation insurance. The owner may not document all of this but if it is clear that the issues have been considered and addressed, auditors can document the thought processes in support of their control risk assessment.

### Information systems including relevant business processes

**Information systems consist of infrastructure, including hardware, and software, people, procedures and data.** Auditors need to understand how information systems work in their entirety. They need to establish which elements of information produced by systems are relevant to the audit, and evaluate the related manual and automated controls.

Controls should cover the initiation of transactions, through supporting documentation, ledger and journal entries to the financial statements. The information system is broadly the accounting system, including internal controls, and standard and non-standard journal entries. Related business processes are processes such as the production, sales and purchases systems that give rise to the accounting information relevant to the audit. Information systems are likely to include off-the-shelf packages for smaller entities.

For exam purposes, controls over computerised systems are often categorised as *general controls* and *application controls*. General controls are not specific to any applications and include controls over data centres and networks, and systems and software acquisition, development and maintenance. *General controls* include:

- controls over systems acquisition and development including:

  - standards for the acquisition, customisation and in-house development of systems and software including authorisation and approval controls and full documentation requirements;
  - segregation of duties between systems designers and operators;
  - testing procedures, which might include dry runs of new systems, parallel running of systems and data installation controls to ensure that data is not corrupted during transfer;
  - staff training.

- controls to prevent and detect unauthorised changes to systems including:

  - password controls over changes to programmes;
  - full records of programme changes;
  - restricted physical access to data centres using swipe-cards and locks, for example;
  - virus checks on software used and prohibiting the use of unauthorised software and hardware, such as unauthorised memory sticks;
  - policies on the use of the Internet and social media by staff;
  - the maintenance of programme logs showing who accessed the system and when;
  - read-only controls for programme files;
  - keeping back-up and control copies.

- controls to ensure that the right programmes are used and to prevent unauthorised amendments to data including:

  - the maintenance of programme libraries;
  - keeping control copies of programmes and comparing them with programmes in use;
  - proper job scheduling;
  - password controls.

- controls over operations and continuity including:

  - back-up and properly tested disaster recovery controls;
  - physical protection controls such as uninterrupted power supplies and fire and flood prevention, because many systems are still in basements;
  - proper maintenance and upgrading of systems.

Back-up and continuity procedures might include keeping back-ups of files at remote locations and having access to hardware that will run those files should there be a complete systems failure. Supermarkets and banks maintain such systems despite the high cost, sometimes in partnership with third parties who specialise in business recovery, because of the risks associated with systems failure.

Application controls are controls within individual applications such as inventory, receivables and payables and are dealt with below.

*Control activities*
Control activities relevant to the audit are what most people think of when they think about controls. They include ***authorisation controls, performance reviews, information***

*processing, physical controls and segregation of duties. They are relevant to the audit
if the related risk may give rise to a material misstatement.*

Many control activities serve more than one purpose. It is also common to find several
layers of controls in place to achieve a control objective, but it is not necessary for
auditors to consider all of them. For example, there may be a risk that inventories are
materially misstated. One objective of controls over inventories may be to ensure that
inventories are not materially overstated. Controls such as reviews of exception reports
highlighting inventories over a certain age, monthly, quarterly and period-end inventory counting procedures, and segregation of duties between those with responsibility
for inventories and those with responsibility for the records may all contribute to the
objective. It will not be efficient, or necessary to test all three sets of controls for these
purposes alone, particularly if the *principal* control for financial reporting purposes is
the period-end inventory count.

Examples of *authorisation controls* include automated controls over parameters,
such as sales systems that produce exception reports showing sales over a certain amount, and require special authorisation procedures for customers going
over a credit limit or for new sales where payment is overdue. Manual controls might
include a requirement for all credit notes over a certain amount to be authorised by a
credit controller and for large cheque payments or bank transfers to be signed by two
people. Once again, with smaller entities, the involvement of the owner-manager in
the day-to-day running of the business can remove the need for more detailed control
activities. Owner-managers are often the sole authority for granting credit to customers
and approving significant purchases, for example.

*Performance reviews* include comparisons of actual performance against budget, forecasts, prior periods and the performance of competitors. Financial data can be compared with operating data, such as an airline comparing the overall maintenance costs
of different types of aircraft with the number of miles flown. In many ways performance reviews are similar to the analytical procedures that auditors perform. Auditors
can use any information produced by an entity of this nature for their own analytical
procedures, provided they are satisfied that the source of the data used is accurate,
which usually requires some testing of the controls over the data.

*Physical controls* are designed to prevent the misappropriation of assets. The more susceptible assets are to theft, the better controls need to be. An entity that manufactures
gold jewellery will need a sophisticated physical control system. Such a system is likely
to incorporate security guards, manual and electronic locks, the use of swipe cards,
key-codes or biometric data to permit access and rigorous sanctions for any attempted
circumvention of such controls. Regular and ad hoc searches may also be needed to
prevent the theft of gold. Strong access and authorisation controls over access to parts
of information systems covering inventory and inventory counting might include the
prevention of physical access by unauthorised staff to those parts of a building where
records are maintained. Segregation of duties between those responsible for the gold
and those responsible for the related records helps prevent fraudulent collusion, i.e. the
theft of gold covered up by changes to the records.

*Segregation of duties* prevents the concentration of too much control in the hands of
one person. Segregation needs to be between those with access to assets and those with

access to records. For example, people receiving and checking inventory should not be the same people who update the inventory records from invoices or goods received notes. If they are, it is too easy to misappropriate the inventory and falsify the records to show that goods were never received. If there are sufficient people, the next level of segregation should be between those authorising transactions, and those with access to the relevant assets, and the relevant records. Staff, often within human resources (HR) departments, may be the only people authorised to make changes to master-files containing lists of authorised employees and pay rates. Their duties are segregated from those people processing the payroll to prevent fictitious (dummy) employees being set up on the payroll and their pay being misappropriated by the staff involved. Staff authorising purchase orders may be different from those approving purchase invoices. Those approving invoices and/or updating the records should check that what is being paid for is not only authorised but in line with company policy. This helps prevent unauthorised purchases. Similarly, if a manager who authorises the acquisition and disposal of cars also takes delivery of cars when they arrive, approves invoices for the purchase or sale of cars, and updates the records, the manager may authorise the acquisition of cars that company policy does not permit, or sell them to family members or friends at an inappropriate price. The manager may also be able to change some of the details of the car appearing in the records to cover this up.

Segregation of duties cannot prevent *collusion* between staff to circumvent controls. The same inappropriate purchases and sales can take place even if separate managers deal with the authorisation of the acquisition of cars, approval of purchase or sales invoices, taking delivery of cars and maintaining the records, if all of the relevant people collude. If staff in HR collude with staff in payroll, fictitious employees can still be created.

A common fraud is for staff in entity A to raise fictitious sales invoices for relatively small amounts to entity B, where they are approved by staff colluding with the staff in entity A. In practice, collusion is not always required because some entities with poor approval procedures will sometimes pay invoices for relatively small amounts for certain routine goods and services without checking that what should have been received has been received, such as invoices for entries in phone books or trade publications.

We refer to 'misappropriation' of assets rather than 'theft' or 'fraud' because the latter terms are legal terms and theft and fraud can only be established formally by the legal system. Misappropriation simply means taking without authority.

*Information processing controls* can be manual or automated. There are two types of control over computerised systems: general controls that cover all applications, and application-specific controls. General controls are dealt with above.

*Application controls* include:

- manual and computerised controls over the completeness and arithmetical accuracy of records including controls over input to systems, processing and output;
- maintaining and reviewing control accounts, such as receivables and payables control accounts and trial balances;
- application-specific reconciliations such as bank reconciliations.

Commonly used checks over the completeness, existence, accuracy and appropriate authorisation of inputs to systems, processing and output include:

- use of passwords limiting access to the system to those authorised, with requirements for them to be changed regularly, and prohibitions on sharing of passwords;
- batch totals, sequence checks and document counts for completeness;
- one-for-one checking of inputs to outputs;
- authorisation and existence controls that match master-files to transactions. Master-files contain standing data that does not change regularly, such as details of authorised employees, customers, suppliers and inventory. This ensures that only genuine employees are paid, credit is only granted to customers on the system, purchases are only made from authorised suppliers, and inventory sold exists and is in stock;
- arithmetic checks for accuracy and completeness, on whether an invoice adds up, for example;
- parameter (or range) checks and exception reporting for accuracy;
- check digit and alpha-numeric validity checks on customer or inventory codes, for example, for authorisation and accuracy;
- authorisation and reviews of input and output data including exception reports, and investigation of large or unusual items by credit controllers, purchase ledger controllers or financial controllers as appropriate.

Check digits are single figures appearing in codes such as bar codes. They are arrived at by applying algorithms to the rest of the code. If code is input incorrectly, the algorithm will calculate a different figure to the check digit and an exception report is produced. The algorithms are designed to deal with common input errors such as transposition errors.

### Monitoring of controls

*Entities monitor the effectiveness of controls to ensure that they continue to function properly.* Controls need maintenance. Auditors need to understand how entities do this and how they address deficiencies as they arise. In larger entities, this will involve internal audit and in all cases it will involve a review of reports. Management need to have a basis for their belief in the integrity of such reports.

If a control over cash involves the preparation of bank reconciliations, for example, monitoring that control might involve management reviewing whether they have been prepared for each month. If no-one ever checks that something is being done, those doing start to question whether it is necessary and eventually stop doing it. A legal department might periodically monitor an entity's contracts with customers to ensure that they are in line with company policy, an internal audit department might check that salesmen are only giving permitted discounts, and all entities should check that expense claims are being made in accordance with guidelines. A substantial part of an internal audit department's role might fulfil the monitoring of controls function, reporting regularly to management on strengths and weaknesses with recommendations for improvement.

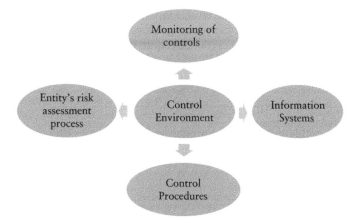

**Figure 4.3** Internal control components

Third parties such as customers, suppliers and regulators also perform a monitoring function. They are likely to complain if billing or payment are inaccurate, and regulators, such as those in the financial services sector, will report if inspections show that client money is not being handled properly, for example.

*Categorisation of controls*

For exam purposes there is often a focus on controls that can be tested directly. Most, but not all of these fall under the heading of control activities and a useful categorisation for exam purposes might be as follows:

- *Segregations of duties*: segregating those with access to records and those with access to assets to prevent fraudulent collusion;

- *Physical controls*: limiting access to assets and records to prevent misappropriation;

- *Arithmetical and accounting controls*: including computerised and manual controls over the completeness and accuracy of records (input to systems, processing and output) and maintaining reconciliations, control accounts and trial balances;

- *Authorisation and approval*: of documents, credit limits and changes to software, for example;

- *Monitoring controls*: use of budgets, forecasts and variance analysis and the use of internal audit to establish whether controls are being applied, are effective and to make recommendations for improvement.

Other control components are not so easily tested and have to be evaluated in other ways, but they do have a direct bearing on the nature and extent of detailed testing. They include the control environment, including the tone at the top, the attitude, awareness and actions of management, and the entity's risk assessment process. So, broadly speaking, the better the tone at the top and the better the entity's risk assessment process can be shown to be, the more auditors can reduce the extent and modify the nature of the substantive audit evidence required.

### Documenting auditor understanding of the entity's system

Deciding on how much documentation of systems is necessary can be difficult for auditors and having a structure helps. Structured documentation aids include:

- *narrative notes*: while these are comprehensive they can be difficult to read;

- *flowcharts and organisation charts*: these are concise but do not capture the importance of informal relationships and can be difficult to interpret;

- *Internal Control Questionnaires (ICQs):* the entity is asked whether it has in place a list of controls such as 'are purchase invoices authorised?' and 'are bank reconciliations performed on a monthly basis?'

- *Internal Control Evaluation Questionnaires (ICEQs):* these analyse the information in ICQs. They are a list of control objectives, such as the completeness of expenditure, together with the auditors' assessment of whether and how the client meets them.

### Examples of internal control objectives and supporting controls of relevance to the audit

Controls relevant to the audit are those that support the *financial statements assertions,* covered in more detail in section 4.2. They are, broadly, what management is assumed to be saying in the financial statements and what auditors are trying to prove, such as whether:

- an account area such as payables, is *complete;*

- assets such as inventory *exist* and belongs to the entity;

- the recording of transactions such as revenue are *accurate;*

- transactions such as purchases have been accounted for in the right period, i.e. *proper cut-off has been achieved;*

- the right *disclosures* have been made.

Table 4.1    Payroll system in a factory (excluding payment)

| Internal control objective How does the entity ensure: | Financial statement assertions | Example controls |
| --- | --- | --- |
| Employees are paid for the hours that they work | Completeness and existence | • Use of clock card systems by employees, i.e. a card is stamped by a machine showing the time and date of arrival and departure and use of sanctions where staff fraudulently clock in for each other |
| | | • Use of swipe cards, key-codes and biometric data such as fingerprints or retina scans on arrival and departure, recording the date and time |

| | | |
|---|---|---|
| Employees are paid at the right rates and are only paid for the hours they work | Accuracy and Existence | • Use of a master-file with authorised pay rates in preparing the payroll<br><br>• Periodic checking of rates of pay to the payroll |
| Correct tax and social insurance rates are deduced and paid to the tax authorities | Completeness, accuracy and existence | • Use of authorised tax and social insurance tables<br><br>• Authorisation of the payroll by the financial controller<br><br>• Maintenance and periodic checking of tax and social insurance control accounts |

*Table 4.2   Non-current assets*

| Internal control objective<br>How does the entity ensure: | Financial statement assertions | Example controls |
|---|---|---|
| All assets owned by the entity are included in the non-current asset register | Completeness and accuracy | • Use of bar codes or microchips to identify assets<br>• Authorisation of assets acquired<br>• Input controls over completeness and accuracy of invoices for assets acquired (batch totals, sequence checks, use of check digits for coding)<br>• Periodic checking by internal audit of invoices for new assets to the asset register<br>• Regular asset counts and reconciliation to the register<br>• Maintenance of non-current asset control account<br>• Segregation of duties between those authorising acquisition of assets, those with access to assets and those responsible for the related records |
| Only assets that exist are included in the non-current asset register | Existence and accuracy | • Authorisation of disposal of assets<br><br>• Regular asset counts and reconciliation to the register<br><br>• Input controls over invoices for the sale of assets or costs of disposal as above<br><br>• Segregation of duties, and periodic checking of disposal invoices by internal audit, as above |
| Assets are depreciated at the correct amount and assets written down to zero are not further depreciated[12] | Accuracy and existence | • Using a master-file of authorised depreciation rates to calculate depreciation<br><br>• Use of parameter checks to ensure that no asset can be depreciated for more than X years or by more than its original cost<br><br>• Periodic testing of master-file data and the asset register by internal audit to ensure that rates are up to date and that fully depreciated assets are not further depreciated<br><br>• Restricted access to the master-file using passwords limited to authorised persons<br><br>• Regular asset counts including a review of the condition of assets to ensure that additional depreciation provided where assets are damaged/have a shorter than expected useful life |

[12] An asset written down to zero might be further depreciated if its useful economic life were revised.

*The approach to the audit of internal control in the USA*
It can be helpful in answering questions about the importance of internal control in higher-level papers to be aware of the US approach to the audit of listed companies. This involves two parallel audits conducted at the same time, the audit of the financial statements and an audit of internal control over financial reporting, known as ***integrated audits***. Reporting on internal control has been on the agenda in Europe and elsewhere for a long time. While replication of the US reporting model is unlikely outside the US there will, in time, be parallels.

Reports to management, regulators and others on specific aspects of internal control, such as controls over client assets, have long been required in the financial services sector. Auditors also gain a great deal of insight into internal control over financial reporting more generally during their audit. Insights are often discussed with and reported privately to client management and those charged with governance but some investors, who pay for the audit, consider that they too can benefit from these insights.

The ***Sarbanes-Oxley Act 2002*** fundamentally altered auditors' approach to internal control over financial reporting in the US. The corporate collapses of the early 2000s influenced the implementation of the Act. Its objective is 'to protect investors by improving the accuracy and reliability of corporate disclosures...'

The Act established the ***Public Company Accounting Oversight Board (PCAOB)***[13] to provide *independent oversight* of auditors through the *registration of auditors*, *audit inspections*, auditing *standard-setting* and by *imposing sanctions* on non-compliant auditors.

The Act also contains ***auditor independence*** requirements that restrict the provision of non-audit services to audit clients. Other areas covered by the Act include audit committees, reporting requirements for off-balance-sheet transactions, the stock (share) transactions of corporate officers, and conflicts of interest with analysts, brokers and credit rating agencies.

The Act's most important changes:

- ***make senior executives responsible*** for corporate financial reports. The Act prescribes criminal and civil penalties for non-compliance. For example, Section 302 requires the company's principal officers, usually the CEO and CFO to certify the company financial reports;[14]

- require companies to have ***internal control over financial reporting***;

- require ***audits and reports by management on internal controls*** (section 404).

---

[13] www.pcaobus.org
[14] Section 1001 also requires the CEO to sign the corporate tax return.

Management are required to produce a *report affirming the responsibility of management* for establishing and maintaining *an adequate internal control structure* and an assessment of its *effectiveness*. The well-established *COSO Framework* is widely used in the US. Its 5-component model is recognisable in the description of internal control in ISA 315 on risk assessment.[15]

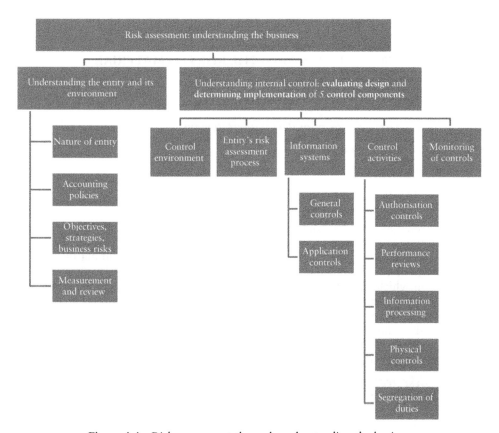

**Figure 4.4** Risk assessment through understanding the business

---

[15] Covering the control environment, risk assessment, control activities, the information system and monitoring of controls

The PCAOB's *Auditing Standard No. 5* provides guidance to auditors reporting on management's report. Auditors give their opinion on whether management maintained effective internal control over financial reporting in all material respects. The work required to support this opinion and the main audit of the financial statements are integrated, i.e. performed at the same time.

The Act applies to certain types of 'issuers', entities whose securities (broadly shares and loan stock) can be traded on US exchanges and who are therefore subject to regulation by the Securities and Exchange Commission (SEC). It does not apply to private companies.

### 4.1.3   IDENTIFYING AND ASSESSING THE RISKS OF MATERIAL MISSTATEMENT

Auditors are required to:

- *identify and assess the risks of material misstatement:*
  - *at financial statement level;*
  - *at assertion level;* and
- *relate identified risks to what can go wrong at the assertion level,* taking account of the effect of controls.[16]

A few risks, such as those relating to going concern, management integrity and the overall condition of accounting records apply at the financial statement level as well as affecting some assertions. Specific assertion-level risks though can cumulatively affect the view given by the financial statements as a whole. Auditors of larger entities in jurisdictions in which there has been no audit requirement in the past sometimes find themselves considering multiple modifications to several financial statement assertions. Collectively, these may have a pervasive effect on the financial statements and therefore give rise to a disclaimer of opinion.

### Risks Requiring Special Audit Consideration

*Significant risks require special audit consideration.* Controls are *not* taken into account in this assessment. *Auditors are required to understand and test relevant controls for significant risks, for period audited.*[17] The absence of any such controls may indicate a significant deficiency in internal control that should be reported to management and those charged with governance.[18]

Significant risks often arise in non-routine transactions that are unusual, involve judgement or require manual intervention, such as journal entries. Factors to take into account when considering the significance of risks include whether they involve:

---

[16] ISA 315 on risk assessment, paragraphs 25 and 26.
[17] ISA 315 on risk assessment, paragraphs 27 and 29. Some controls only need testing every three years. This is not the case for significant risks.
[18] ISA 265 on communicating deficiencies in internal control, paragraph A7.

- fraud or transactions with related parties;

- complexity or high levels of judgement or measurement uncertainty;

- recent significant accounting or other developments;

- unusual transactions including those outside the normal course of business for the entity.

There is a rebuttable presumption of a risk of fraud in revenue recognition.[19] This means that auditors assume that the risk of over- or understated income exists unless they can prove otherwise. For example, there is often a risk of overstatement of revenues where there are pressures on management to perform. Management might:

- recognise sales invoices too soon, before goods are shipped or services are delivered, for example, or over-estimate the stage of completion of long-term contracts;

- raise fictitious invoices shortly before the period-end using late journal entries that are reversed shortly after the period-end in the hope that auditors will not scrutinise them as carefully as they should do because of time pressures.

There is a risk of understatement in some smaller entities and entities such as car dealerships, casinos, and possibly restaurants and taxi firms where there is a high volume of cash transactions. Where this risk is a risk of *material* misstatement, it becomes a significant risk. The risk could be rebutted if, for example, there were a single and simple source of revenue, such as income from a property.

ISAs classify some types of the following risks as significant, but the list is not exhaustive:

- the risk of management override of controls;[20]

- the risk of material misstatement due to fraud;[21]

- risk involving high estimation uncertainty;[22]

- risk associated with related party relationships and transactions.

Several ISAs suggest specific procedures to address significant risks, including the need for:

- written and oral reports from experts;[23]

- engagement quality control review procedures to cover the identification of significant risks and how the engagement team dealt with them;[24]

---

[19] ISA 240 on fraud, paragraph 26.
[20] ISA 240 on fraud, paragraph 31.
[21] ISA 240 on fraud, paragraph 27.
[22] ISA 540 on accounting estimates, paragraph 11.
[23] ISA 620 on experts, paragraph A30.
[24] ISQC 1 on firm-level quality control, paragraph A54.

- the engagement partner review of the files to focus on significant risks;[25]
- auditors to consult the entity's external legal advisers for significant litigation risks.[26]

*Auditors need to communicate significant risks to those charged with governance together with information on how they propose to address them and their potential effects on financial statements.*[27]

### Risks for which Substantive Procedures Alone are Inadequate

Some testing of controls is likely to be necessary in addition to substantive testing where there is a large volume of routine transactions subject to automated processing. This is particularly relevant where there is little or no source documentation, where transactions are generated by the system itself, such as in on-line ordering from the Internet and airline ticketing, and even more so where the information is held in electronic form only. This is the principal type of risk for which substantive procedures alone are inadequate. Again, the requirement is for auditors to understand the relevant controls.

### 4.1.4  DOCUMENTATION

Documentation is required for:

- the engagement *team discussion* of the *financial reporting framework* and the *susceptibility* of the financial statements to material misstatement due to fraud or error;
- *key elements of auditor understanding* of the *entity* and its *environment*, its *internal control* overall and for *each component*;
- *risks of material misstatement* at the *financial statement* and *assertion* levels;
- *risks* that require *special audit consideration*, risks for which *substantive procedures are inadequate*, and related controls.

Section essentials: what you need to remember

- *The components of the audit risk model and how they affect each other.*
- *That understanding the business covers accounting policies, the business's objectives, strategies, risks and controls, and its measurement and review of its own financial performance.*
- *The difference between business risk and audit risk and significant risks.*

---

[25] ISA 220 on quality control engagement-level, paragraph A18.
[26] ISA 501 on audit evidence for selected items, paragraph A24.
[27] ISA 260 on communications with those charged with governance, paragraph A13.

- *The five types of internal control component and the impact of controls such as the control environment and monitoring of controls on the effectiveness of other controls.*

- *The difference between the understanding, the design and implementation of controls, and testing their effectiveness.*

- *How computer assisted audit techniques (CAATs) can be used in testing control effectiveness and substantive procedures.*

# SECTION 4.1, QUESTION

Required:

(a) Explain the significance of and relationships between audit risk,
    financial statement risk and detection risk.                    (10 marks)

Your firm is the auditor of Dazco, an importer and wholesaler of inexpensive,
non-branded clothes. It has a high turnover of staff, its accounting systems
are old and out-of-date and its controls, including credit control, are poor.
Accounting errors are frequent. Despite this, sales have increased. An economic downturn has resulted in a number of smaller customers being unable
to pay their debts but this has been more than compensated for by an overall
increase in sales of less expensive clothes. Dazco's customers comprise market
traders, independent shops and Internet retailers.

Required:

(b) Describe the risks likely to be associated with the audit of
    Dazco's receivables and an audit approach that is likely to reduce
    those risks to an acceptable level.                             (10 marks)

Total:                                                              (20 marks)

## 4.2   AUDIT EVIDENCE

**Covering:** ISA 500 *Audit Evidence.*

**Why do I need to read this section?**

*All auditing and assurance papers contain some basic audit evidence questions, often on revenue and receivables, purchases and payables, payroll or property, plant and equipment. Many papers have several such questions. A proper understanding of the financial statement assertions and the basic tests that provide evidence to support them goes a long way.*

**What is important in this section?**

*Understanding:*

- *that one audit procedure can perform several different functions. By checking various aspects of bank reconciliations, for example, auditors can understand the business by evaluating the design and implementation of a control, test its operating effectiveness, and perform a substantive procedure all at the same time;*

- *the fundamental difference between testing the effectiveness of a control and a substantive procedure;*

- *the significance of the direction of a test.*

**What sort of questions come up in this area?**

- *Questions on what is meant by 'sufficient, appropriate audit evidence'.*

- *Questions on risk assessment and further audit procedures, types of test and procedure and sources of evidence.*

- *Questions on the tests you might perform to provide evidence on a particular financial statement assertion.*

**How do I stand out from the crowd?**

- *Include a reference to the results of testing control effectiveness in answers to questions on substantive procedures. Testing control effectiveness, will, if successful, affect the nature and extent of substantive procedures.*

### 4.2.1   EVIDENCE

**Definitions**

> *The auditors' objective* is to design and perform audit procedures on the financial statement assertions and the financial statements as a whole to provide
>
> *...sufficient appropriate audit evidence to be able to draw reasonable conclusions on which to base the auditor's opinion.*
>
> ISA 500 *Audit Evidence* paragraph 4

Audit evidence is information used by auditors in arriving at the conclusions on which to base their opinion. This includes information in the accounting records and from elsewhere, such as industry information and information from banks, lawyers and third party inventory-holders.

Terminology is, unfortunately, important, although in exams showing that you understanding something is generally (but not always) more important than being able to reproduce or recognise a definition accurately. Practitioners, tutors and students all use terms inappropriately sometimes, often by using terms interchangeably or in the sense they were used a long time ago. Just because someone who should know what they are talking about uses a term in a particular way does not necessarily mean they are using it in exactly the right way for exam purposes!

The terminology of audit evidence is not particularly difficult provided students pay attention, but because the area *seems* straightforward, it is easy to get the concepts confused. Examiners are sometimes tempted to focus on this area, simply because students get it wrong so often!

There is only one pair of terms deemed equivalent under ISAs, and they are terms used in the auditors' opinion, i.e. that the financial statements give a *true and fair view of,* or are *fairly presented in all material respects,* in accordance with the identified financial reporting framework such as IFRS.[28] Examiners, fortunately, are not particularly concerned about the academic debate about what these terms mean. They have not changed much over the years and in any case, they make intuitive sense to most people. Instead, examiners focus on the requirements of ISAs. ISAs require auditors to gather evidence to support the audit opinion on the financial statements but this does not make auditors responsible for the financial statements. If management wants to prepare financial statements that are 'wrong', there is nothing auditors can do about it other than to give an opinion to that effect. Management is responsible for preparing financial statements that give a true and fair view or fairly present the position at the:

• financial statement level, overall;

• assertion level.

---

[28] ISA 700 on audit reports, paragraph 35.

*Financial statement assertions* include the *completeness, accuracy and existence of transactions,* such as revenue in the income statement, *balances* (such as receivables) *and disclosures* (such as depreciation rates). These are dealt with in more detail below.

Audit evidence comprises both information that supports and corroborates management's assertions, and any information that contradicts such assertions.[29]

## Risk Assessment Procedures and Further Audit Procedures

> *Audit evidence is obtained through the following audit procedures:*
>
> • *risk assessment procedures;*
>
> • *further audit procedures, i.e. tests of control effectivenes substantive procedures.*[30]

### Risk assessment procedures
Risk assessment procedures consist of

• inquiries;

• analytical procedures;

• observation;

• inspection.[31]

These procedures also serve as further audit procedures and are described in more detail below.

### Further audit procedures: testing control effectiveness and substantive procedures
Further audit procedures consist of testing control effectiveness and substantive procedures.[32]

### Testing control effectiveness
*Testing control effectiveness* enables auditors to *evaluate their effectiveness* in preventing, detecting and correcting material misstatements at the *assertion level*:

• testing control effectiveness involves deciding what evidence shows that the control is *effective;*

• *auditors only test the effectiveness of properly designed and implemented controls.* This is a key difference between understanding the design and implementation of controls, and testing their effectiveness. Auditors do not test controls that are not properly designed and implemented because they cannot be effective;

---

[29] ISA 500 on audit evidence, paragraph A1.
[30] ISA 500 on audit evidence, paragraph A10.
[31] ISA 315 on risk assessment, paragraph 6.
[32] ISA 330 on responses to risk, paragraph 4.

- the signature of the financial controller on a bank reconciliation together with a date might show that it has been reviewed, for example. However, a signature is not a guarantee that a review has actually taken place and, even if it has taken place, it may not be effective because of the qualities of the person performing it;

- a *poorly designed control* might be one where the person performing the bank reconciliation review is not competent to perform it. It cannot be effective and there is no point in testing it. If a control is *not implemented properly*, because the person performing the review lacks integrity and simply signs the reconciliation despite not having looked at it, or having only looked at it very briefly, again, it is ineffective and is not worth testing;

- understanding the design and implementation of controls often involves walk-through tests, by tracing transactions from source documentation, such as goods received notes, through invoices and ledgers to the financial statements and vice versa, to establish what controls are in place on the way. Testing control effectiveness requires more rigour using sampling methods that require auditors to investigate the nature and significance of deviations. It is possible to obtain the understanding and test controls at the same time, though;

- testing control effectiveness also involves deciding what constitutes evidence of *deviations*, i.e. departures from or non-application of the control procedure;

- the absence of a signature and/or date on a bank reconciliation, or evidence that despite the signature and date, a review has not been performed because there are obvious errors, might constitute deviations;[33]

- some deviations are likely to occur because of human error, and for other reasons. Audit *sampling* takes account of an *expected rate of deviation* but auditors may not assume that deviations in samples are isolated or rely on client assertions to that effect. Auditors have to show that deviations are isolated by further testing and they need good quality evidence for this because it is assumed that because of automation in transaction processing, *isolated deviations are rare;*

- deviations represent one of two things: either they are isolated and controls are in fact effective and working properly most of the time, or they suggest that the control is not working. The implications of the latter are serious because if the breakdown in the control is systematic, unless there are compensating controls, a re-assessment of the risk assessment and audit approach will be necessary, which may well result in substantial additional work.

When asked why a control has not been applied, clients may not understand, or wish to admit to auditors that there is a problem. Reasons put forward for the non-application of control procedures include the person performing the procedure being off sick, or having an 'off-day', or the issue being a 'glitch in the software that IT have sorted out now'. Properly designed and implemented control systems should be able to deal with this sort of thing and should not rely on one person alone. Systems generally provide for another individual to perform the control. If it is genuinely a short-term problem, when the person returns, they should apply the control procedure. Adequate systems

---

[33] ISA 500 on audit evidence, paragraph A29.

should not simply correct glitches in software. They should also correct any errors in the records that the software has created by applying the relevant control. Furthermore, regardless of whether the deviation is a manual or automated error, other higher-level controls or internal audit, if working properly, should detect them. In practice there may be many more instances of non-application of control procedures than client staff think.

*Substantive procedures*
**Substantive procedures are** designed to **detect material misstatements** at the **assertion level** and comprise:

- **tests of details** which are tests of individual **transactions**, such as sales, **balances**, such as receivables, and **disclosures**, such as a property, plant and equipment note.

  The issues noted above regarding the implications of **deviations in tests of control** also apply to **errors in substantive procedures**. Isolated errors in sampling are deemed rare. If 5% of a sample of invoices are understated, auditors need to provide a high level of evidence to show that 5% of all sales invoices, the population as a whole, are not understated.

- **substantive analytical procedures.**[34]

  Substantive analytical procedures are an **evaluation of an analysis of relationships among financial and non-financial data**. Auditors might predict that there will be a direct relationship between cost of sales, profitability and changes in the price of wheat for a bread manufacturer, for example. They might then schedule out the cost of sales, profitability and price changes on a monthly basis, compare it with prior periods, assess whether the relationship holds, and investigate and substantiate any significant variations from their expectations.

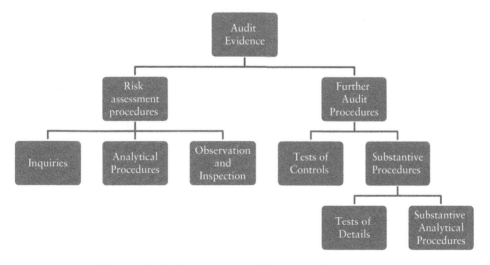

**Figure 4.5**   Risk assessment and further audit procedures

---

[34] ISA 330 on responses to risk, paragraph 4.

Section 4.3 deals with testing control effectiveness and substantive procedures in more detail.

**Sufficient, Appropriate Audit Evidence**

• *Sufficient* audit evidence is 'enough' audit evidence. It is a measure of quantity but not a precise one. It is a matter of judgement, affected by the auditors' assessment of risk and by the quality of evidence. Some types of evidence are more reliable than others.

• *Appropriate* audit evidence is of an appropriate quality, it is *reliable* and *relevant*.

*Reliable audit evidence*
*Reliable* audit evidence will stand up in court. It is a relative term. Some types of evidence are more reliable than others. It seems obvious that more 'assurance', (a technical term), or 'audit comfort', (a well-understood, non-technical term) come from *consistent evidence from different sources*. If there are inconsistencies, auditors cannot ignore them and need to resolve them. They also need to think about the implications.[35] Contradictory evidence from different sources might indicate a lack of control or management integrity, for example, or fraud. It also seems obvious that *independent evidence from outside* the entity, such as supplier statements, analysts' reports, or industry benchmarking data used in analytical procedures, is generally more reliable than internal evidence produced by the entity, such as accounting records or minutes of meetings. There are some grey areas, though, including a lack of consensus among firms about the strength and importance and usefulness of management representations, for example. This matters because of the time and effort involved in obtaining different types of audit evidence. Audits need to be efficient to maintain audit firm profitability.

*Factors affecting the reliability of audit evidence* include:[36]

• *its source* because, for example, third parties such as inventory holders may be well-informed about the entity, or they may not, and seniority is not necessarily a guide;

• *controls over its preparation and maintenance* because some records, such as records of cash, are often better controlled than others, such as records of payables;

• *its nature* because electronic records may be corrupted or deleted, for example;

• *the circumstances under which it is obtained,* because supplier statements obtained in a hurry, for example, might be prepared less accurately than they would be otherwise.

For exam purposes, the following generalisations about the reliability of evidence can be made, but be prepared to explain that there are exceptions.[37]

---

[35] ISA 500 on audit evidence paragraph 11.
[36] ISA 500 on audit evidence, paragraph A31.
[37] Ibid.

- evidence obtained from *outside* the entity is *more reliable than internally generated* evidence;

- internal evidence is *more reliable* when *effective and well-designed controls* are applied;

- evidence obtained *directly by auditors*, such as observation of the application of a control, is more reliable than *indirect audit evidence*, such as inquiry about the application of a control;

- *documentary evidence* including electronic evidence is *more reliable than oral evidence*, so a contemporaneous written record of a meeting is more reliable than a subsequent oral representation;

- *original documents are more reliable than copies* including photocopies, faxes, scanned or otherwise digitised documents.

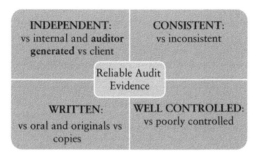

**Figure 4.6** Reliable audit evidence

### Relevant audit evidence

*Relevant* audit evidence is evidence relevant to financial statement assertions. *Financial statement assertions* are what management is 'saying' in the financial statements and they broadly relate to the income statement, balance sheet and disclosures. They comprise assertions about:[38]

- *classes of transactions* such as sales and purchases;

- *balances* such as receivables and payables at the period-end;

- *presentation and disclosure*.

*Assertions about classes of transactions*
Assertions about classes of transactions comprise:

- *occurrence:* recorded transactions and events have actually happened and pertain (relate) to the entity, roughly equivalent to the *existence* assertion for balances;

---

[38] ISA 315 on audit risk, paragraph A111.

- *completeness:* all transactions and events that should have been recorded have been recorded;
- *accuracy:* the details of recorded transactions and events (amounts and other data) have been recorded appropriately;
- *cut-off:* transactions and events have been recorded in the correct accounting period;
- *classification:* transactions and events have been recorded in the proper accounts.

A great deal of work takes place on completeness and accuracy but it is important not to underestimate the significance of the other elements. Outright frauds may show up in tests for occurrence, i.e. tests designed to show whether transactions actually happened, but *cut-off errors* give rise to many misstatements, i.e. moving transactions into or out of the accounting period around the period-end. Cut-off issues can arise for a whole host of reasons. Cut-off is not always a well-controlled part of the financial reporting process and may involve period-end journal entries. Errors often arise unintentionally. However, cut-off is often a higher-risk area not simply because of poor control, but because *intentionally* shifting transactions across the reporting date can be useful to:

- meet profit targets or manipulate bonus or tax payments;
- prevent the breach of banking covenants, i.e. promises to the bank not to exceed certain asset to liability ratios, for example;
- maintain or improve key performance indicators such as earnings per share, or simply keep them on the right side of industry averages.

*Classification* is often important for tax or regulatory purposes as well as for disclosures in the notes to the accounts. If expenditure is posted incorrectly to a capitalised research and development account, assets and profits are overstated and tax may be understated, among other things.

*Assertions about balances*
Assertions about balances comprise:

- *existence:* assets, liabilities, and equity interests actually exist;
- *rights and obligations:* the entity holds or controls the rights to assets, and liabilities are obligations of the entity;
- *completeness:* all assets, liabilities and equity interests that should have been recorded have been recorded;
- *valuation and allocation:* assets, liabilities, equity interests and any valuation or allocation adjustments are included in the financial statements at appropriate amounts.

Completeness and valuation are clearly important but auditors can be made to look very silly if they do not check on existence. There have been a number of celebrated cases in which auditors have not checked on the physical existence of assets by going and seeing them, or have done so in a very predictable manner. Inevitably, there have been cases where significant assets in the balance sheet turned out to be elaborate documentary fabrications. Auditors can never entirely rely on records, however good they appear to be and checking on existence at random or in an unpredictable manner improves the chances of fraud detection.

*Assertions about presentation and disclosure*    Assertions about presentation and disclosure comprise:

- *occurrence, rights and obligations:* disclosed events and transactions have actually occurred and pertain to the entity;

- *completeness:* all disclosures that should have been included, have been included;

- *classification and understandability:* financial information is appropriately presented and described and disclosures are clear;

- *accuracy and valuation:* financial and other information is disclosed fairly at appropriate amounts.

Presentation and disclosure are sometimes more important than the numbers. Two sets of financial statements may give identical figures but the overall view given by the set that discloses that all of an entity's assets are mortgaged to a bank is quite different to the view given by the set that does not.

Presentation and disclosure are increasingly important for two reasons. Firstly, there is far more scope for variations in presentation than there used to be because financial reporting has become more complex. Secondly, many more assets and liabilities are now carried at fair value. Disclosures were once about providing a more detailed breakdown of the figures in the financial statements for the benefit of those who were interested. Now they are also about valuation methods and the critical assumptions underlying them, without which it may be impossible to understand the financial statements properly. The current volume of mandatory disclosures is giving rise to serious concerns. Even financially literate readers can now find it difficult to navigate financial statements and there are worries about key disclosures being lost in a sea of unimportant ones.

Financial statement assertions can be combined and described differently provided they are all covered.[39] 'Accuracy' covers a lot but common themes for the income statement, balance sheet and notes are:

---

Financial statement assertions

- *Completeness*: is it all there?

- *Existence and ownership:* is what is there 'real', and do we own it?

- *Accuracy:* is it mathematically correct, properly valued, and in the right place?

- *Cut-off:* is it in the right period?

- *Disclosure:* is the entity telling us everything that it should be telling us?

A mnemonic for this is **DECCA**

---

[39] ISA 315 on audit risk, paragraph A112.

**Figure 4.7**   Financial statement assertions

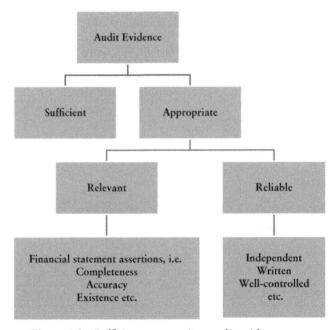

**Figure 4.8**   Sufficient, appropriate audit evidence

*Directional testing*

To return to the *relevance* of audit evidence, the relevance of a particular audit procedure is affected by the direction of testing.

*Directional testing* involves:

- tracing *from source documentation to the financial statements* which helps prove the *completeness* of the amount in the financial statements, as well as accuracy and cut-off, looking for *understatement*;
- tracing from the *financial statements to the source documentation*, which helps prove the *existence* of reported items, as well as their accuracy and cut-off, looking for *overstatement*.

For example: if the purpose of a procedure is to test for *overstatement* of accounts receivable, auditors trace from the financial statements through to the general ledger and the receivables ledger, back to the invoice, despatch note and order, i.e. the source documentation. If there is no source documentation, it may suggest a balance that has already been written off, or even a fraud in that a balance does not exist. If the source documentation is very old, it might suggest that that balance should be provided for or written off.

If the purpose is to test for the *understatement* of accounts payable, i.e. creditors that should be there but are not, or creditors that are understated, auditors trace in the opposite direction, from source documents such as orders and goods received notes through to invoices, the payables ledger, the general ledger and the financial statements. Other source documentation useful for testing the completeness of payables includes supplier statements and cash payments after the period-end, i.e. the most complete list of potential payables it is possible to find.

Broadly speaking, assets and expenses (debits) are tested for overstatement, and liabilities and income (credits) are tested for understatement. That is not to say that assets are never understated or that liabilities are never overstated, and it might seem odd at first glance that we should test for the overstatement of expenses (surely they will generally be understated?) and the understatement of income (will that not be overstated?).

It is important to remember that in testing assets for overstatement, we are also testing the related income for overstatement. Similarly, in testing liabilities for understatement we are also testing the related expenditure for understatement. So if in the examples above we trace the sales invoice to the sales account, as well as to the despatch note and order, we are testing both the receivable and the related income for overstatement. If we trace the purchase invoice to an expense account as well as to the general ledger and financial statements, we are testing both the payable and the related expenditure for understatement.

*It is recognised that if a mistake is made testing in one direction, the mistake will be replicated in the other direction.*

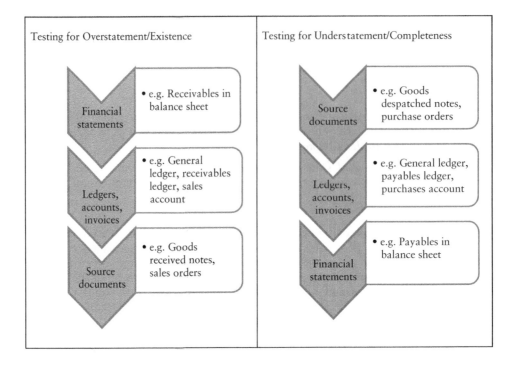

**Figure 4.9**    Directional testing

### Types of Audit Procedure

Different ways of performing risk assessments and further audit procedures are also described as 'procedures'. They might better be described as 'techniques', not least because they overlap with the definitions above. They comprise:[40]

- *inspection:* of the entity's and other *records* such as invoices or supplier statements, and documents of title to assets such as real estate and plant and equipment, and physical inspection of *assets*. Inspection of documents tends to provide better evidence regarding valuation, rights and obligations whereas inspection of assets tends to provide better evidence of existence, although these are not absolutes. Inspection of a building that appears poorly maintained, or inventory that appears to be damaged, for example, will provide some evidence as to valuation as well as existence;

- *observation:* of control *activities* such as inventory or cash counting while they are being performed. The evidence thereby obtained only relates to the point at which the observation takes place. People who know they are being observed tend to behave differently and observation is therefore of limited value;

- *external confirmation:* of bank balances, receivables and payables balances, inventory held with third parties and other *balances* and *contractual terms*, including terms that might not have been recorded;

---

[40] ISA 500 on audit evidence, paragraphs A12–25.

- *recalculation:* which amounts to checking the maths, either manually or electronically;

- *re-performance:* by auditors of *procedures applied by the entity*, such as the re-performance of a bank reconciliation by doing it again, or re-performing parts of an inventory count;

- *analytical procedures:* which are performed throughout the audit as part of *planning* and risk assessment, as *substantive procedures* and as part of the *overall review* of financial statements. At the planning and risk assessment stage, analytical procedures are used to identify risks or issues that auditors were previously unaware of as well as to confirm their understanding of the business. Many relationships between financial and non-financial data such as sales per square metre of retail space, for example, are very predictable and unusual or unexpected relationships can indicate error in the accounting records or fraud. High-level analytical procedures performed on monthly or interim financial information can be used as a basis for drilling down to the more detailed account areas. Smaller entities may not have monthly information and it may be necessary to wait for the draft financial statements to be produced before analytical procedures can be performed.

- *inquiry:* which involves seeking information from *knowledgeable persons* both within and outside the entity. It includes *formal and written* inquiries of banks and lawyers, for example, *informal and oral* inquiries made during the course of the audit and, importantly, evaluating the responses.

Inquiries may reveal new information that, if it is right, may require a revision to risk assessments and changes to the audit approach. New or unexpected information should always be corroborated, i.e. verified as far as possible. If inquiries of management indicate, for example, possible litigation against the entity of which auditors were previously unaware, they will need to corroborate that information by reference to formal inquiries of and correspondence with lawyers.

Corroborating management intentions is harder. If management indicate that it intends to take legal action against a third party, for example, but have not yet consulted or instructed lawyers, and the matter may be material and require disclosure, auditors are really relying on a statement of management's intention as audit evidence. The same is true where management intends to make a major capital investment in the near future, the only evidence of which is its own outline plans. The best auditors can do in such circumstances is obtain formal management representations, but it is important to remember that intentions that are likely to have a material effect on the financial statements are only intentions. Intentions may not satisfy the recognition criteria of accounting standards. If intentions have developed into plans, there should be some corroborating evidence. Inquiries and responses should be documented.

### Walk-through tests
A walk-through test is one that involves tracing a few transactions through the financial reporting system.[41] This means tracing a transaction from source documentation, such as a goods despatched note, through systems via, for example, the invoice, the sales account, the receivables ledger to the general ledger and vice versa. It may also

---

[41] Glossary of Terms.

include tracing such an item through the inventory records and the related payment through the cash book and the receivables ledger. Walk-through tests are used:

- because auditors are required to *document systems* under ISA 315[42] and a walk-through test establishes whether the auditors' or clients' record of the system is accurate;

- because of local requirements for auditors to report on whether *adequate accounting records* have been kept. This is partly determined by whether auditors think accounting system are adequate;[43]

- to determine whether *information obtained in prior periods remains relevant*, such as information on internal controls, which includes the accounting system. If auditors intend to use prior period information for the purposes of the current audit, which they usually do, walk-through tests help establish whether it is still current.[44] This is the only specific reference to walk-through tests in ISAs.

### Sources of audit evidence

Where does audit evidence come from? Sources of audit evidence are obvious but examiners sometimes require students to make it clear that all audit evidence ultimately arises from audit procedures. Procedures are performed on:

- accounting *records*;

- financial reporting *processes*;

- entity *assets*;

- *third parties* such as customers, suppliers, banks, lawyers and analysts;

- *publicly available information* about the entity such as public registries in jurisdictions where constitutional documents and accounts must be filed, for example, and industry information, and information generated by the media.[45]

### Section essentials: what you need to remember

- *The difference between tests of control effectiveness and substantive procedures.*

- *The financial statement assertions.*

- *The reliability of different types of audit evidence.*

- *Sources of audit evidence.*

- *The different types of audit procedure, walk-through tests and the significance of directional testing.*

---

[42] ISA 315 on risk assessment, paragraphs 32 (b) and 18, which require auditors to document key elements of their understanding of the entity's internal control, which includes its accounting system.

[43] ISA 700 on audit reporting, paragraphs 21 and 22, which refer to the auditors' 'opinion on other matters'.

[44] ISA 315 on risk assessment, paragraph A13.

[45] ISA 500 on audit evidence, paragraphs A7–A9.

# SECTION 4.2, QUESTION

Required:

(a) Explain the relationships between:

    (i)      substantive procedures and tests of control effectiveness    (5 marks)

    (ii)     the design, implementation and operational effectiveness of internal controls, giving examples.    (6 marks)

(b) Explain how auditors should deal with deviations from the application of control procedures arising in tests of control effectiveness.    (4 marks)

(c) Give five examples of financial statement assertions and explain their relevance to the audit.    (5 marks)

Total    (20 marks)

# 4.3   RESPONDING TO RISK

Covering: ISA 330 *The Auditor's Responses to Assessed Risks*; ISA 520 *Analytical Procedures, Controls, Tests of Control Effectiveness and Substantive Procedures.*

**Why do I need to read this section?**

*Virtually all audit and assurance papers cover responses to risk assessment in detail. A paper that does not is rare. Analytical procedures are almost always useful as examples in questions on evidence, and they are easy to understand and examine in their own right. The examples given at the end of this section emphasise controls over the revenue and expenditure in the income statement, but testing revenue necessarily means testing receivables, and testing expenditure necessarily involves testing payables. Detailed guidance on the audit of areas such as cash, inventory and other balance sheet items is covered in the next section.*

**What is important in this section?**

*Really understanding tests of control effectiveness and substantive procedures, what they are for, how they interact, the difference between them and, most of all, being able to give good examples of them.*

**What sort of questions come up in this area?**

- *Questions that ask you to provide examples of tests of control effectiveness and substantive procedures for the main balance sheet and income statement areas, i.e. revenues and receivables, purchases and payables, payroll, cash, inventory, and non-current assets such as investments and property, plant and equipment.*

- *Questions that ask you to describe the analytical procedures that could be performed on a given set of information, and questions that ask you to perform analytical procedures, particularly in higher-level papers in case-study style questions.*

**How do I stand out from the crowd?**

- *Demonstrate clearly your understanding of the difference between evaluating the design and implementation of controls and testing their effectiveness of controls, as well as the difference between tests of control effectiveness and substantive procedures, and how they all interact.*

- *Make imaginative and practical suggestions for comparing financial and non-financial data for the purposes of analytical procedures.*

- *Refer to the need to test the source of the data used for analytical procedures, to make predictions before the procedures are performed, and to corroborate explanations for unexpected variations.*

### 4.3.1  OVERALL RESPONSES

The risk assessment is a means to an end. Having performed audit procedures to assess risk, auditors perform further audit procedures to respond to the risks assessed. In practice, it is surprising how often in practice this does not happen. It is common for regulators to complain that auditors simply perform the procedures they performed the previous period without any clear rationale based on the risk assessment.

The higher the assessment of risk, the more persuasive the audit evidence must be in order to reduce overall audit risk to an acceptable level.

There is a common perception that, where there has been a corporate collapse shortly after the issue of an unmodified audit report, the auditors must have failed to identify significant risks. In practice, as subsequent investigations often show, it is more common for auditors to highlight problems and record them in the audit file, but to fail to appreciate their significance or follow them up. This failure to make appropriate connections happens in firms of all sizes. An appropriate response to an assessed risk is as important as the assessment itself.

The basic requirement is for auditors to design and implement responses at the overall financial statement level to address the assessed risk, and to perform procedures that appropriately respond to assessed risk at the assertion level.[46]

### 4.3.2  RESPONSES AT THE FINANCIAL STATEMENT LEVEL

A common example of what gives rise to a heightened risk assessment at the overall financial statement level is trading difficulties, or entities operating in a difficult economic environment. In practice this means that businesses are likely to be assessed as subject to higher audit risk in an economic downturn. This in turn increases the amount of resources that need to be allocated to audits at the same time as clients are most likely to put pressure on auditors not to increase audit fees. This tension is not an easy one to manage. Maintaining professional scepticism is important and heightened audit risk at the financial statement level means that auditors need to be more sensitive than usual to the possibility of fraud and error. Maintaining professional scepticism might be demonstrated by requiring better quality corroborations of management explanations, for example.

The overall response to heightened risk at the financial statement level generally involves more and sometimes different audit work, assigned to more senior audit staff, with a greater level of supervision than would be the case otherwise. More substantive procedures might be performed at the period-end instead of at the interim date, for example, more third party confirmations might be sought and sample sizes may be larger. Audit methodologies permit auditors to vary these elements in order to reduce overall audit risk to an acceptable level.

---

[46] ISA 330 on responses to assessed risks, paragraphs 5 and 6.

Other examples of heightened risk at the financial statement level might include situations in which the control environment is deficient, where management's operating style is aggressive and where there are poor general controls over IT. Poor general controls over IT are likely to give rise to less testing of control effectiveness and more substantive procedures overall. An aggressive management operating style might result in greater attention being paid to cut-off and accruals at the period-end, and an increase in the number of locations visited during the audit, because of the heightened risk of fraud and error.

At the overall financial statement level, *appropriate responses to heightened risk* in general might involve reducing detection risk by:

- more supervision of audit staff;
- emphasising the need for professional scepticism;
- using better qualified or more staff;
- obtaining more audit evidence or enhancing its quality by incorporating more unpredictability in testing;
- performing more substantive procedures rather than tests of control effectiveness and doing more towards the period-end rather than at the interim stage if the control environment is poor.

### 4.3.3   RESPONSES AT THE ASSERTION LEVEL

At the assertion level, a balance must be struck between tests of control effectiveness and substantive procedures, and between testing at the interim and final stages. A combination of tests of control effectiveness and substantive procedures is often appropriate. Testing control effectiveness is often efficient but if controls are poor, or if testing them would be inefficient for any other reason, substantive procedures alone may be appropriate, which may be the case for some smaller audits. Auditors should not assume that controls are too poor to test in smaller audits. Nevertheless, there are some rare cases, not necessarily in smaller audits, in which controls are so poor that it is not just impossible to test controls, but substantive procedures cannot be performed either and auditors cannot form an opinion. This might be the case where records simply have not been kept and cannot be reconstructed.

On smaller audits there is unlikely to be an interim audit and all audit work takes place at the period-end. If there is an interim audit, the bulk of control effectiveness testing and some substantive procedures are generally performed then. At the final audit, control effectiveness testing are updated to cover the intervening period and the bulk of substantive procedures are performed. The nature and extent of work performed at the final audit on the intervening period depend on:

- the results of testing at the interim period, which might suggest that controls are not in fact working properly;
- any changes to systems or assessed risks;
- the volume or nature of transactions processed.

Any significant changes in assessed risks might involve a change in audit approach and a change to the balance of control effectiveness testing and substantive procedures. If, for example, tests of controls over receivables at the interim stage indicate that they may not be operating effectively, and limited substantive procedures in the same area also highlight problems, it may be productive to abandon control effectiveness testing in that area altogether and adopt a wholly substantive approach at the period-end. If the situation is less clear-cut, as is often the case, perhaps because of a change in systems, it might be prudent to increase the substantive procedures at the period-end anyway but to continue to test controls during the intervening period.

---

It is helpful to remember that:

* *the purpose of testing control effectiveness is to allow auditors to reduce the level of substantive testing;*
* *some substantive procedures are always required* in all material areas, regardless of the risk assessment and regardless of whether internal controls are tested.[47]

---

### Tests of Control Effectiveness

Testing the operating effectiveness of controls is an efficient way of gaining audit evidence. Risk assessments are often based on the assumption that controls are working. If the assumption is made, it must be tested.

We have already seen that performing risk assessments involves evaluating the *design* of controls, i.e. whether they are set up so that they can do what they are supposed to do, and determining whether controls have been *implemented*, i.e. whether they have actually been put into place as designed. This is regardless of whether auditors intend to test their *operating effectiveness*, i.e. whether they are actually working for the full period under review.

For example, a computerised control might highlight postings made to the wrong account by showing all receivables balances over a certain age. The controls will be *designed* so that all receivables balances, whether debit or credit, are covered. If only debit balances are shown, the control is probably not fully effective and auditors must ask why it has been designed that way, given that receivables ledgers are likely to have credit as well as debit balances. Another method of evaluating the design of the same control might be for auditors to review the programming documentation, if they have the relevant programming skills.

The control will need to be *implemented* with appropriate parameters. If the intention is that balances over 90 days old are shown, but in fact only balances over 150 days old

---

[47] ISA 330 on responses to assessed risks, paragraph 18.

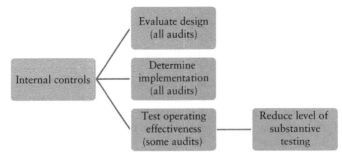

Figure 4.10    What to do with internal controls

are shown, the control will not have been implemented properly. Again, to determine whether proper implementation has been achieved auditors might:

- examine the software programme if they have the relevant skills;
- review lists of balances to see if balances over 90 days old appear to be shown;
- insert dummy data into the system to see if overdue balances are highlighted at the appropriate stage;
- walk existing transactions through the system from invoice to receivable to see if, when they become overdue, they are highlighted.

If auditors intend to test operating effectiveness, *it can be efficient to perform tests of the relevant controls at the same time as evaluating design and determining implementation.* In practice, it may also be possible to perform substantive procedures at the same time.

For example, the following procedures may serve as a combination of risk assessment procedures on the design and implementation of controls, tests of their operating effectiveness and substantive procedures:

- inquiry about the use of budgets (design);
- observing management's comparison of budgets to actual by attending a meeting (design and implementation);
- inspecting variance reports and analyses (design, implementation and testing if reports and analyses are produced every quarter, say);
- examining the underlying data and reconciling it or re-performing management's reconciliation to the variance reports (implementation, testing and substantive procedures);
- walking totals from that data through to the variance report (design, implementation, testing and substantive procedures);
- re-performing management's analyses of variance reports (implementation, testing, substantive procedures).

Performing substantive procedures concurrently with tests of control effectiveness is common: a dual purpose test such as establishing whether an invoice has been approved (controls test) and has been posted to the correct accounts at the correct amounts (substantive procedure) is one example.

*Risks for which substantive procedures alone are inadequate*
Many risks can be addressed using substantive procedures alone, although in the presence of controls a substantive approach will often be an inefficient and expensive way of going about it. Some risks though, can only be properly addressed by testing control effectiveness. For example, where there is a large volume of automated, routine transactions processing and there is little or no source documentation, substantive procedures are likely to be inadequate. Good examples are systems in which transactions are generated by the system itself, such as in airline ticketing, Internet and supermarket sales, and even more so where all the information is held in electronic form only.

*Evidence provided by controls tests performed in prior periods*
The nature, extent and timing of tests of control effectiveness is a matter of judgement. Auditors can use evidence from control effectiveness testing conducted in prior period audits. When they are considering when and to what extent they can reasonably do this, they need to consider the:

• significance of the control risk addressed;

• length of time since the control was last tested;

• overall effectiveness of the control environment, general IT controls and any changes.

If there have been no significant changes, auditors are required to test:

• *controls at least once in every third audit;*

• *some controls in each audit* to avoid testing all controls in one period and none in another;

• *controls relating to significant risks in every period.*[48]

Auditors are more likely to be able to leave a longer gap between testing automated controls than for manual controls, simply because automated controls are less likely to change and are generally lower risk.

Sometimes it is necessary to test 'indirect' controls which support 'direct' controls. A review of an exception report showing sales in excess of credit limits is a control directly relevant to the audit. Its effectiveness though is dependent on general IT controls over the accuracy of the information in the report, which are indirectly relevant to the audit. Testing the general IT controls may therefore be necessary.

---

[48] ISA 330 on responses to assessed risks, paragraphs 13–15.

*Deviations from the application of control procedures*

Deviations from the application of control procedures can be thought of as the non-application of controls. Deviations will always occur because of human error, among other things. Auditors must evaluate the deviations they encounter in control effectiveness testing and decide whether the deviations are isolated, or whether individually or collectively, the deviations mean that the application of the control procedure has broken down and that the control is not operating effectively. This evaluation is a matter of judgement.

Evidence of substantive misstatements in say, the payroll account, constitutes strong evidence that payroll controls are not working properly, but the converse is not so true.[49] The fact that substantive procedures provide no evidence of misstatements in payables provides only indirect and limited assurance that controls are operating effectively over payables.

A deviation from the application of a control procedure does not automatically mean that a control is not working, although deviations are problematic. While ISAs allow auditors to develop an *expected rate of deviation* arising from, for example, changes in staff, high volumes of transactions and human error, auditors have to decide whether deviations are isolated errors, or represent a systematic breakdown in the application of the control. If the *detected rate of deviation* is in excess of the expected rate, it indicates that the control is not reliable.[50] This has serious implications for the audit approach, and audit costs. Firstly, it suggests that the initial risk assessment, which assumed that controls were properly designed and implemented, might have been wrong. Secondly, it means that the cost of testing and its value to the audit may be lost. Thirdly, auditors now have to determine whether there are any compensating controls that can be tested, and if not, to abandon the approach and start again by testing the area substantively. All of this is time-consuming and expensive.

Reliable automated transaction processing means that anomalous deviations are extremely rare. A high degree of certainty that deviations are not representative of the population, by (extensive) additional testing is needed. The same applies to misstatements in samples used in substantive testing.[51] Despite this, strenuous efforts are sometimes made to prove that deviations in excess of the expected rate are isolated.

Controls sometimes have to be abandoned as ineffective. However, it is rare for an entity to rely solely on a single control, particularly in significant areas. There are usually several layers of controls such that if one does not work, there are often others auditors can test. For example, if controls over the input of the sequence of goods received notes into a system are not properly controlled, there may be gaps in the sequence that are not followed up, leading to the potential understatement of liabilities. However, if tests show that compensating controls are working, such as the matching of invoices to GRNs, together with good controls over inventory, the risk of unrecorded liabilities can be reduced to an acceptable level even though one control is not working.

---

[49] ISA 330 on responses to assessed risks, paragraph 16.
[50] ISA 330 on responses to assessed risks, paragraph A 41.
[51] ISA 530 on sampling, paragraph 15.

Where deviations occur, there is one of three outcomes[52] either:

- auditors need to show that errors are isolated, i.e. are *anomalies*, and that the control is in fact working by extending the sample or other procedures; or
- the *control is not working but there are compensating controls* which can be successfully tested; or
- the *control is not working and there are no compensating controls* in which case a wholly substantive approach may be needed in the relevant area.

### Substantive Procedures

We have seen that the purpose of testing control effectiveness is to allow auditors to reduce the level of substantive testing. We have also seen that some substantive procedures are always required in material areas, regardless of the risk assessment and regardless of whether internal controls are tested. However, the same is *not* true of tests of control effectiveness; tests of control effectiveness are not always performed.[53]

Substantive procedures consist of *substantive analytical procedures* and *tests of details*.

Substantive analytical procedures look at the bigger picture, at the financial statements as a whole at the risk assessment and final review stages, and at summaries of transactions as responses to risk assessment. Tests of details, as the name suggests, involve examining detailed transactions, balances and disclosures.

### *Tests of details*

Tests of details are tests of individual transactions, balances and disclosures. We have seen that relevant audit evidence relates to financial statement assertions such as completeness, existence, accuracy, cut-off and disclosure. Tests of details directly relate to these assertions. We have also seen that directional testing takes source documents such as purchase orders, and traces them through the invoice and payables ledger via journals if necessary to the financial statements when testing for understatement (liabilities and income), and in the opposite direction when testing for overstatement (assets and expenses).

Presentation and disclosure need to be complete and accurate. Disclosures about non-current assets, for example, need to show all third-party claims over the entity's assets, such as the claims of banks and other lenders over properties held as security for non-current asset investments held for sale should be classified and valued differently to other non-current investments.

Controls over financial statement finalisation are often weak and substantive procedures therefore need to be strong. As part of the financial statement closing process, auditors are required to:

---

[52] ISA 330 on responses to assessed risks, paragraph 17.
[53] Except where substantive procedures alone are inadequate and for significant risks.

- reconcile the financial statements with the underlying accounting records; and

- examine material journal entries and other adjustments made during the course of preparing the financial statements.[54]

Why journal entries? From a controls viewpoint they are often on the peripheries of the system. They are rarely as well-controlled as other areas despite their use in making material adjustments to the financial statements at the period-end, when everyone, including auditors, are at their most pressed. They are therefore easy for management to abuse and are often subject to a heightened risk of fraud and error.

*Errors in substantive testing*
Errors, or misstatements, become apparent in substantive procedures and particularly in tests of details. Often these are a result of deviations from the application of control procedures (i.e. control failures) and auditors need to consider not only the implications of the deviation for control effectiveness testing and risk assessment, but also the substantive error itself. Substantive errors often arise from control failures and control failures often result in misstatements.

There are almost always multiple layers of control to consider. Depreciation rates applied might be wrong because a change has not been properly authorised *and* has not been put through. Payroll deductions may be too high or too low because programmed parameter checks are not working *and* because no payroll reconciliation or review is performed by the payroll supervisor. Sales invoices may be wrong because incorrect product codes or quantities have been applied or both. Understated inventories might arise because a whole area was missed at an inventory count *and* because internal audit did not perform spot checks at the count.

When sampling, as with deviations in control effectiveness testing, **substantive anomalies are deemed rare** because of automated processing and strong evidence is required to support a conclusion that substantive errors are isolated.

Samples are taken as representative of the populations from which they are drawn. For example, if a sample shows that 3% of sales invoices are understated, auditors *project* (or extrapolate) the error to the population of invoices as a whole, to determine whether the error is potentially material. However, the relationship between errors in samples and errors in the populations from which they are drawn is not straightforward. This is partly because of sampling risk. If sampling risk is set at 5%, say, and sample sizes are calculated accordingly, 5 in every 100 samples will *not* be representative of the population, i.e. the sample will show no errors where in fact there are errors in the population, or the sample will show more or fewer errors than there actually are in the whole population.

## Substantive analytical procedures

*Definitions*

Analytical procedures are used at every stage of the audit. At the risk assessment stage, analytical procedures are performed at a high level on the financial statements

---

[54] ISA 330 on responses to assessed risks, paragraph 20.

as a whole, or on whatever information is available, such as management or interim accounts. Comparisons are made between preliminary results and prior periods in key areas. Having identified potential problem areas, auditors then drill down to the more detailed areas at the assertion level, which is where analytical procedures come into play as substantive procedures. Used properly, they are powerful audit tools that complement tests of details and tests of control effectiveness. Analytical procedures are also used during the overall review of financial statements.

Analytical procedures are:

> ....*evaluations of financial information through analysis of plausible relationships among both financial and non-financial data.*
>
> **ISA 520** *Analytical Procedures* paragraph 4

The key words to remember here are *analysis* and *evaluation*.

*Elements of analytical procedures*

Analytical procedures involve *comparisons* of actual information with prior periods, budgets, forecasts, industry benchmarks and expectations. They rely on predictable relationships between:

- *items of financial information* such as the costs of maintaining a fleet of salesmens' vehicles and sales, and sales and cost of sales; and

- *financial and non-financial information* such as sales and web-site traffic, and payroll costs and the number of employees.

Analytical procedures can be particularly important in the risk assessment performed on components in group audits.

The *analytical* element of analytical procedures involves the *comparison and analysis* of the data.

Auditors need to make *predictions* in performing analytical procedures. This is more difficult at the risk assessment stage than at any other stage because auditors have less information to go on.

For example, for an entity that sells insurance direct to the public through a sales team, and over the Internet, there is likely to be a direct and consistent relationship between the web-site traffic and sales, and between the costs of maintaining a fleet of salesmen's vehicles and sales. Scheduling out the web-site traffic, fleet costs and sales on a monthly basis enables auditors to see if those relationships are consistent and to focus audit attention and investigations on those periods where that does not appear to be the case. Similarly, for many entities there should be a direct relationship between the number of employees and the overall payroll cost, individual elements thereof such as tax and social insurance, sales or production levels, and various costs such as uniforms, motor vehicles and canteen costs, depending on what the entity does.

An important element of analysis is being satisfied about the quality of the information on which the analytical procedures are performed. If the information is not well-controlled or properly integrated with the financial reporting system, auditors may find that they have audited one set of information but reported on another. This can be a particular problem if draft financial statements are not available and auditors perform analytical procedures on management accounts, for example.

Having made predictions, auditors perform the analysis by scheduling out, for example, the gross margins for the period by comparison with prior periods.

The *evaluation* element of analytical procedures involves taking the analysis and dealing with unexpected variations, such as sudden spikes in a generally consistent relationship. This involves obtaining and corroborating explanations from management. Management will understandably try to find plausible explanations for unexpected variations where in fact there may simply be errors in the accounts, hence the importance of corroboration. An increase in gross profits for an umbrella manufacturer, for example, might be explained by a period of wet weather. It might also be explained by errors, attempts to meet sales targets by moving sales from one period into another, or both.

In performing analytical procedures, as in tests of control effectiveness, it is important to exercise professional scepticism and to ask 'why?' Why has the marketing expenditure increased, why did the monthly review of the marketing account not pick this up, why has a large adjustment to marketing expenses been made at the period-end? It is essential not only to document both question and answer, but to *corroborate* the explanation given. If the explanation of a large period-end adjustment is that there were substantial marketing costs posted to a suspense account in error, it will be necessary to check the suspense account and the substance of the entries transferred, to ensure that the explanation reflects what actually has happened. If the explanation for an unexpected increase in sales of soft drinks in a particular region is that there were unexpectedly high temperatures, it might be appropriate to check that that was in fact the case. The fact that an explanation sounds plausible does not mean that it is right.

Analytical procedures used as part of the risk assessment process should be clearly *linked* to the audit approach. Analytical procedures performed as part of the overall review of financial statements should be linked to the audit opinion. For example, if analytical procedures performed at the risk assessment stage indicate an unexpected fall in depreciation, it may be appropriate to assess risk as higher in that area and to respond by conducting more testing, either on controls, including automated controls over depreciation, more substantive procedures on the depreciation charge itself, or both. Three possibilities exist: either the recorded depreciation is wrong, or there is a reason for the increase that auditors are not yet aware of, such as disposals, or both. If it is wrong, it is either because errors have been made, or because someone has deliberately altered the figures. While auditors are required to exercise professional scepticism throughout the audit, this is not the same as assuming that everything that could be a fraud is one. If something is wrong, it is usually because of errors. Auditors generally encounter a few frauds in their professional careers but not many.

*Errors* may be the result of controls that do not exist or have not been implemented properly (i.e. do not work). If controls do exist, it is possible that management has overridden them and posted an inappropriate depreciation charge to smooth profits for tax purposes for example, or to ensure that targets are met so that bonuses are paid to management. This is one example of why it is always necessary to perform substantive procedures as well as tests of control effectiveness. Even if the controls appear to be working on a sample basis, substantive tests of the detailed depreciation charge and a review of the journal entries at the period-end might show that something has gone wrong.

*Analytical procedures at the detailed testing stage*
Analytical procedures are used at the planning and risk assessment stage to identify areas that require further investigation. At the detailed testing stage, the effective use of substantive analytical procedures requires auditors to:

- consider whether analytical procedures are *appropriate* as substantive procedures. If relationships cannot be predicted, they may not be;

- *link* them to the risks assessed;

- develop an expectation of relationships between items of data, consider whether the relationship is sufficiently *precise* to identify misstatements and determine the *level of difference* from expected values at which further investigation is required, depending on materiality and the risk assessment;

- evaluate the *reliability* of the data taking account of the controls over its preparation;

- *investigating* differences between expected values and recorded values.

Substantive analytical procedures are more likely to be *appropriate* where there are large volumes of well-controlled information where relationships can be predicted, such as in retail sales or a large payroll.

Some substantive analytical procedures are very detailed. For a steelworks, for example, it might be appropriate to schedule out the energy expense account for each week, month, quarter, half-year and year, for each plant, operating entity and on a regional basis, and to compare it to production levels. Much of the information might already be available from management or internal audit, but perhaps in a different format to that required by auditors.[55] At the other extreme, procedures may involve very few figures, such as:

- debtor days (or 'days sales in debtors') which shows the length of time debtors take to pay on average, calculated as trade receivables/sales × 365, an increase in which shows debtors taking longer to pay;

- creditor days which shows the length of time the entity takes to pay its creditors on average, calculated as trade payables/purchases × 365, an increase in which shows the entity taking longer to pay;

- 'proofs in total', which involve proving a single figure by reference to information supporting it.

---

[55] There can be high volumes of information available to auditors that are not relevant to the audit, unfortunately.

A proof in total for the payroll might involve multiplying the average number of employees on the payroll by an average of fixed rates of pay, to prove the total payroll cost. Similarly, total income for a hotel can be predicted by multiplying average room rates by the average occupancy rate. Such proofs can be used to justify reducing the level of detailed substantive testing in an area. However, it is important to note that a plausible relationship only provides indirect evidence about the items of data between which the relationship exists. A constant gross profit margin only provides indirect evidence about the sales or cost of sales figures, for example.

It is worth noting that frauds are more easily detected when they start or finish, i.e. when the change is noticeable. If fictitious sales go through every month, and they are not detected when the fraud commences, the fictitious sales become part of what auditors come to expect.

Where entities are growing or business is volatile, where information is not well-controlled, and where relationships are not predictable, analytical procedures are less effective and may not be appropriate.

Where expectations are insufficiently *precise* to identify a potential misstatement, it may be possible to drill down to the next level. For example, it might be more helpful to examine detailed inventory levels at the substantive procedures stage, rather than when examining the cost of sales figure. The level of *difference from expected values* that triggers investigation is based on materiality.

The *reliability* of data depends on controls, which auditors may test, but also on its source and nature. Information outside the entity such as industry average benchmarks – sales per square metre of retail space, for example – may be particularly useful. Achievable budgets and forecasts are more useful than aspirational ones.

*Investigating* significant differences involves inquiry of management and corroborating explanations provided.

### Substantive procedures responding to significant risks
*Auditors must perform substantive procedures that are specifically responsive to significant risks. If auditors have not tested controls over the significant risk, substantive procedures must involve tests of details and not just analytical procedures.*[56]

For example, if there is a significant risk that sales may be overstated to meet targets, auditors may consider obtaining confirmation not just of accounts receivable, but of the terms of trade covering delivery dates, rights of return and the dates of sales agreement. Inquiries of sales staff regarding changes in contract terms might also help. The types of significant risk for which auditors do not test controls include those that are outside the control of the entity, such as significant litigation against the entity. Analytical procedures would be unlikely to work in such cases anyway because the outcome is insufficiently predictable.

---

[56] ISA 330 on responses to assessed risks, paragraph 21.

It is nevertheless possible to rely on analytical procedures alone in certain circumstances, such as where the assessed risk is low, where there is a large volume of transactions that tend to be predictable over time, where controls are strong, or where the item is not material, such as for petty cash.

### Documentation

Documentation requirements for responses to assessed risks are straightforward and cover the:

- overall response to assessed risk at the financial statement level;
- further audit procedures performed;
- linkage of overall responses to assessed risks at the assertion level;
- conclusions about the operating effectiveness of controls obtained in previous audits where they are relied on in the current audit;
- reconciliation of the financial statements to the underlying records.

It is surprising how often the financial statements do not agree to the underlying records, usually because of late journal entries for significant amounts. In practice this can be a big headache for incoming auditors whose first job is to 'finish the job of the previous auditors', by reconciling the opening balances to the previous set of financial statements.

### 4.3.4  EXAMPLES: INTERNAL CONTROLS, TESTS OF CONTROL EFFECTIVENESS AND SUBSTANTIVE PROCEDURES

Questions on control effectiveness are worded in many different ways.

Questions cover:

- controls only:
  - what controls should there be? What are their objectives?
  - are the controls described designed and implemented adequately?
  - what are the weaknesses in the systems described and how might they be improved?
- tests of control effectiveness: what tests of control effectiveness should be applied to the controls described?
- any combination of the above, together with questions about substantive procedures on related items.

Some questions are best approached following transactions through from their source, such as a purchase order, through the system via invoicing and posting to ledgers, to the final payment, describing the controls that should be in place and the tests that can be performed on them along the way. For other questions, it may be more appropriate to divide controls into their different components.

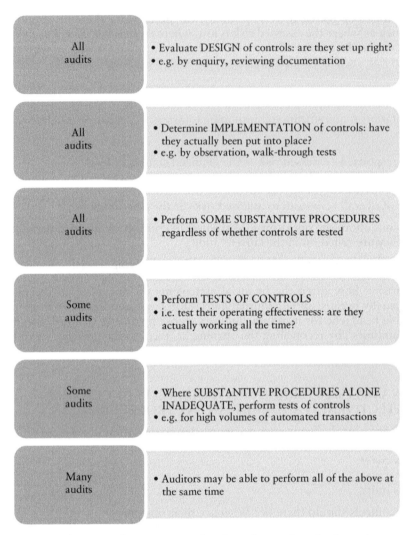

**Figure 4.11**   The design, implementation and testing of controls and substantive procedures

The following examples show some of the different ways of presenting material on controls. Some examples, like many exam questions, also refer to related substantive procedures. The next section focuses more specifically on substantive procedures for selected balance sheet items.

In questions that focus on controls, it is almost always helpful to mention the evaluation of control components other than control procedures, such as the control environment and the entity's risk assessment process, even though these are not generally tested directly. The auditors' evaluation of these components has an effect on the nature and extent of testing generally, as does the auditors' evaluation of general and application controls over the relevant computer systems which are also often worth mentioning. These are dealt with in more detail in the next section.

### Controls Only: Revenue Cycle in a Wholesale Mail-order Clothing Company

Customers submit their orders by email, using a simple secure web-site, or by telephone. Staff input details of orders, including those received via the web-site, to the company's computer system, which is integrated with the company's inventory control system. Standard credit terms are payment within 30 days of despatch. Most customers pay by bank transfer. Monthly statements are issued. The computer system applies credit limits authorised by the credit controller. New customers are not given credit. They are required to pay for goods prior to despatch for three months before this happens.

---

### Revenue Cycle in a Wholesale Mail-order Clothing Company

The overall control environment, which is evaluated as part of the risk assessment, and tests of general and application controls over the computer system, both have an effect on the nature and extent of testing.

**Internal controls over order processing and despatch, credit and payment might include:**

#### Order processing and despatch

- The system should produce a pre-numbered multi-part document with copies for the customer, despatch department and sales department.

- The system should automatically highlight orders for which goods are not available. Such orders should be referred to the customer for a decision whether to process the rest of the order, or wait.

- The despatch department should produce a despatch note (GDN) that should be cross-referenced to the order and the system should match despatch notes to orders, and any gaps representing unfulfilled orders should be investigated.

- The system should automatically produce an invoice for each GDN with prices drawn from a master-file. Invoices should be posted to the sales daybook, the sales ledger and the sales ledger control account.

- Periodic computerised sequence checks on the completeness of pre-numbered orders, GDNs and invoices in the system should be performed. Missing documents should be investigated.

- The sales ledger and the sales ledger control account should be reconciled each month and any differences investigated.

- Controls should ensure that goods returned and any discrepancies concerning prices, the nature or condition of the goods delivered should result in credit notes. These should be subject to the same controls as invoices and GDNs.

---

*Credit*

- When an order is taken, the system should reject or highlight orders from new customers and orders that exceed credit limits.

- The credit controller should authorise any override of credit limits.

- The despatch system should ensure that payment has been received from new customers prior to despatch by preventing a GDN from being raised until a reference to the related payment is found.

- There should be periodic reviews of credit limits and prices by the financial controller to ensure they are appropriately calculated and properly applied to individual transactions.

*Payment*

- The bank should provide a list of payments received by bank transfer. It should be matched with individual invoices and posted to the cash account, sales ledger, and sales ledger control account.

- Unallocated amounts received should be highlighted and investigated promptly to ensure that receivables are accurate and up to date.

- A list of overdue receivables should be produced at the end of each period and investigated, chased or a 'stop' put on accounts where amounts are significant or long overdue.

- A monthly bank reconciliation helps ensure that cash records are complete, accurate and up to date.

- Periodic calculations of the amount and age of the average outstanding receivable should be performed to highlight any weaknesses in credit control.

---

## Controls Only: Non-current Assets

Internal controls over non-current assets such as plant, machinery and office equipment should be designed, implemented and operated to achieve the objective of internal control. The objective of internal control is to address business risks that threaten:

- the reliability of an entity's financial reporting;

- the effectiveness and efficiency of its operations;

- its compliance with laws and regulations.

## Controls Over Non-current Assets

*Controls contributing to financial reporting reliability and compliance with laws and regulations.*

- Segregation of duties between those with *direct responsibility* for the non-current assets, those with responsibility for the *related records*, and responsibility for the *authorisation* of capital expenditure, disposals and depreciation rates.

- Preparation and monitoring of *capital expenditure budgets* by senior management.

- The periodic *review of asset lives and depreciation methods* by senior management to ensure that assets are being depreciated correctly, over an appropriate period of time.

- *Maintaining and reconciling a non-current asset register* to the general ledger and, periodically, to the assets themselves, i.e. performing asset audits, possibly by internal audit if there is such a department.

- The *periodic review of fully depreciated assets* to ensure that systems are not depreciating them after they have been written down to zero.

- *Periodic checks on disposals by internal audit or senior management to ensure that only assets authorised for disposal are being disposed of, that they are not being disposed of to related parties or staff without specific authorisation, and that disposals proceeds are appropriate and correctly accounted for.*

*Controls contributing to the effectiveness and efficiency of operations and compliance with laws and regulations.*

- Physical controls over access to assets such as locked doors and security systems, and electronic controls over access to assets such as computers, such as passwords and tokens.

- Maintaining firewalls and virus-checking software.

- Maintaining an appropriate fire and flood resistant environment and insurance against such disasters.

- Developing, testing and monitoring contingency plans.

- Indelible identification of all non-current assets which should be recorded in the asset register.

- Requiring staff who use entity assets off-site, such as laptops and motor vehicles, to take steps to ensure that they are secure, i.e. locked and out of sight when not in use.

- Prohibiting and preventing staff from using their own software on company equipment.

### Controls, Tests and Substantive Procedures: Payroll for a Software Development Company

Salaried staff are paid by bank transfer and a small number of hourly-paid staff are paid in cash. The principal audit risks in this area are likely to include the understatement of payroll liabilities and the associated expense. This might include any penalties for incorrect deductions of tax and social insurance and/or late payment of deductions to the tax authorities.

Management is also likely to be concerned with the overpayment of staff, payment for work not performed, dummy employees, similar frauds and the misappropriation of cash.

See Table 4.3.

### Controls, Tests and Substantive Procedures: Revenue, Receivables and Inventory for a Chain of Business Hotels

For a chain of hotels, the principal audit risks are likely to include the overstatement of revenue, receivables and inventory.

Associated business risks of concern to management are also likely to include:

- misappropriation or loss of revenue as a result of non-payment by customers, under-charging of customers whether intentionally or not;
- pilferage by customers and staff of inventory such as food, drink, linen and other consumables such as cleaning materials, and easily portable plant and equipment and fixtures and fittings such as cleaning equipment.

See Table 4.4.

### Section essentials: what you need to remember

- *Auditors always evaluate the design of controls and determine whether they have been implemented, regardless of whether they intend to test them.*
- *Tests of control effectiveness are needed if auditors want to rely on them and thereby reduce the level of substantive testing.*
- *The difference between substantive procedures and tests of control effectiveness.*
- *Examiners are looking for good quality examples of tests of control effectiveness and substantive procedures.*

Table 4.3 Controls, tests and substantive procedures: payroll for a software development company

| Principal Control(s) | Example Tests of Control | Substantive Procedures and Related Financial Statement Assertions |
|---|---|---|
| **Segregation of duties:** between those:<br><br>• who control cash, bank and payroll records;<br>• who authorise cash payments and bank transfers;<br>• with access to the assets, i.e. those who deal with bank transfers and cash payments;<br>• who control HR records and standing master file data such as employee numbers and salary details.<br><br>This helps prevent fraudulent collusion and the creation of fictitious employees or inflated payments. Having more than one person share a responsibility further reinforces segregation of duties and reduces the risk of fraudulent collusion.<br><br>**Physical:**<br><br>• Over access to buildings, departments (including payroll) and computers by means of door codes, touch-pads, key-cards or similar technology.<br>• The presence of two people when cash is paid to hourly-paid staff.<br><br>**Arithmetical and accounting:**<br><br>• Automated input controls (sequence, edit and batch controls) over the input to data files showing hours or days worked from login details and sickness records, for example.<br>• The production of exception reports showing gaps in sequences, gross pay or deductions over a pre-determined amount or percentage, negative pay and other potential indicators of fraud or error. | 1. Observe or test whether those with sole authority for authorising cash and bank transactions, such as financial controllers, also have access to the related cash and banks records, or standing master-file data or payroll records, or are able to make bank transfers and cash payments.<br>2. Observe cash payments to hourly-paid staff to ensure that two people are present and other physical controls (such as locked doors) are being applied.<br><br><br>1. Observe whether it appears to be possible to access buildings or computers without proper authorisation.<br>2. Check a sample of starters and leavers to ensure that the first and last payments to them are properly authorised with initials or signature.<br><br><br>1. Attempt to input fictitious staff numbers in the correct format to the system to establish whether they will be rejected as having no corresponding standing master-file or HR record (test data).<br>2. Input an incomplete sequence of payroll numbers, or existing payroll numbers in the wrong format to establish whether they show in exception reports or are rejected (test data). | **Analytical procedures**<br><br>Perform analytical procedures<br>• on total payroll costs using a proof in total (average salary multiplied by number of employees);<br>• on total and detailed payroll costs split into gross pay, tax, social insurance, sickness and other deductions and net pay, monthly and quarterly, with reference to changes in tax and social insurance rates, sales and other indicators of activity, and in total for the period as a whole, and by comparison with prior periods (completeness, accuracy and cut-off of payroll cost and completeness and valuation of liabilities).<br><br>**Tests of details**<br><br>• Check the details of a sample of payroll records to ensure that the calculations of salary or hours worked agree with contracts and tax and social insurance tables (completeness and accuracy of payroll costs and completeness and valuation of liabilities).<br>• Check a sample of starters and leavers to ensure that the first and last payments are correctly calculated (completeness, accuracy and cut-off for payroll costs, allocation of liabilities).<br>• Trace payroll entries from source documentation to the financial statements by checking hours worked for a sample of employees from authorisation (hourly paid) or salary details through to login details, payroll and cash records and the general ledger, ensuring the calculations are made correctly (completeness and accuracy of payroll costs).<br>• Trace payroll entries from the financial statements to source documentation by checking from payroll records in the general ledger back through the system to salary, login and authorisation details and to records of cash paid and bank transfers ensuring the calculations are accurate (existence and accuracy of recorded payroll costs). |

- Controls over the merging into the payroll of (a) data files as described above and (b) of standing master-file data covering salaries, payroll numbers, hours contracted, current tax and social insurance tables and starter and leavers details.
- Reconciliations of authorisations of work by hourly paid staff to records of hours actually worked, produced from login or other details.
- Production and review by the payroll controller of total and detailed payroll costs and deductions, and of exception reports showing relationships between, for example, gross pay and tax deducted that fall outside certain pre-determined parameters, and investigation of apparent errors.

**Authorisation and approval:**

- Approval of bank transfers and cash payments by the financial controller and checking after the event that the amounts authorised were the amounts transferred.
- Review of payroll by the financial controller.
- Password controls over access to the payroll system and bank and cash records, including regular changes.
- Approval of changes to standing master-file data and HR records such as:
  – inclusion and exclusion of starters and leavers and their first and last payments;
  – changes to tax and social insurance rates;
  – changes to salaries, payroll numbers, hours contracted.
- Maintenance of a secure HR department that keeps contracts signed by employees and other mandatory and non-mandatory employee data.
- **Monitoring:** management and internal audit review of monthly, quarterly and annual payroll charges, use of internal audit to test and monitor the application and effectiveness of other controls.

3. Review exception reports for evidence of checking of gaps in the sequence of payroll or other numbers and for errors in gross pay or deductions.

- Review the detail of exception reports and check that errors have been followed up (all objectives).
- Examine contracts signed by employees and trace details such as salaries through to HR records or standing master-file data and vice versa (completeness, existence and accuracy of recorded payroll costs and completeness, existence and valuation of liabilities).

1. Check that bank transfers have been authorised by appropriate staff by reviewing signatures.
2. Check authorisation of bank transfers to standing bank mandates, showing who the bank permits to authorise transfers.
3. Check for evidence of the follow-up of payroll and exception reports reviews, by initialling or signature and journal entries correcting errors, for example.
4. Check the existence of a secure HR department and controls over employee data that may be subject to data protection legislation.

Seek evidence by attending meetings or reviewing signatures that show that management reports have been produced and reviewed and that internal audit reports have been reviewed and actioned.

**Table 4.4** Controls, tests and substantive procedures: revenue, receivables and inventory for a chain of business hotels

| Principal Control(s) | Example Tests of Control | Substantive Procedures and Related Financial Statement Assertion |
|---|---|---|
| **Segregation of duties:** between those with access to cash and other assets and those with access to the related records. | 1. Observing whether those with access to cash appear to have access to the related records. | **Analytical procedures:** in all cases investigate and corroborate unexpected variations. |
| **Physical:** over assets such as food, drink, linen, other consumables and access to the hotel and rooms including electronic and manual locks. | 2. Observe staff using locks to access assets and hotel rooms.<br>3. Test controls over the issue and receipt of electronic key cards and similar devices giving access to assets. | • Analyse revenues on a monthly, quarterly and annual basis by hotel, region, and by business line (accommodation, restaurants etc.) and compare with budgets, forecasts, prior periods and expectations (completeness, accuracy and cut-off of revenues).<br>• Analyse predictable relationships between, for example, accommodation and restaurant volumes and the |
| **Arithmetical and accounting:**<br>• Automated controls over invoice numbering.<br>• Manual or automated batch controls over transaction input.<br>• Automated alpha-numeric format checks over input data such as customer numbers.<br>• Performance of bank reconciliations.<br>• Maintenance of sales ledger control accounts. | 1. Attempt to input dummy invoices into the system to establish whether those with incorrect alpha-numeric sequences are rejected (test data).<br>2. Attempt to access systems without valid passwords.<br>3. Check that bank reconciliations have been performed and reviewed for each period (by initialling or signature). | drinks/food ratio in restaurants and compare them with prior periods. Calculate and evaluate debtor days at the period end, for prior periods and on a monthly or quarterly basis if appropriate (indirectly, completeness, accuracy and cut-off of revenues, expenditure and the existence and valuation of inventory).<br><br>**Tests of details**<br><br>• Trace transactions from source documentation to the financial statements by checking written and elec- |
| **Authorisation and approval:**<br>• Password controls over access to different parts of the booking, checking in and out, billing and accounting systems.<br>• Approval of credit limits.<br>• Review of exception reports for overdue receivables.<br>• Manual and automated controls to prevent further bookings when receivables are overdue. | 1. Seek evidence of the review of exception reports from the revenue system, by initialling or signature.<br>2. Select a sample of large receivables balances and seek evidence that:<br>(a) credit limits have been authorised, by initialling or signature; and<br>(b) further bookings have not been taken without authorisation, by a review of the account. | tronic bookings for rooms through to check-in details, invoicing, payments received and the revenue and cash accounts in the general ledger, either using computer assisted audit techniques or manually, using print-outs from the system if available, or both (completeness of revenue, valuation of receivables).<br>• Trace transactions from the financial statements to source documentation by checking from cash received back through the system to bookings (existence of recorded revenue and receivables).<br>• Check transactions recorded around the period-end to ensure that they are accounted for in the correct period (cut-off of revenue, and valuation and allocation for receivables and inventory). |

**Monitoring:**

- Local management review of bookings, occupancy rates and other performance measures on a daily and weekly basis to identify trends, the effect of promotions and potential errors.
- Central management use of budgets and forecasts, comparison with actual results and analysis of variances.
- Internal audit testing and monitoring the application and effectiveness of controls.
- Regular and ad hoc asset counts by internal audit.
- Internal audit review the financial and operational performance of hotels.

1. Check that sales ledger control accounts have been prepared and reviewed for each period by initialling or signature.
2. Seek evidence that internal reports have been reviewed and actioned and review reports to form a view as to the effectiveness of the system.
3. Attend asset counts to establish whether procedures are being followed.
4. Perform independent ad hoc asset counts.

- Check entries in the bank reconciliations and sales ledger control accounts back through invoices and payments to source documentation such as written and electronic bookings, credit card receipts and bank statements (existence and valuation of cash and receivables).
- Consider performing an external confirmation of accounts receivable (existence and valuation of assets).
- Attend regular and ad hoc asset counts and:
  - perform test counts from assets to records and vice versa to establish whether the records are accurate;
  - establish whether count instructions are being followed (test of controls);
  - note the condition of inventory (existence and valuation of assets).

# SECTION 4.3, QUESTION

Required:

(a) Explain how analytical procedures are used in risk assessments and describe their limitations when they are performed before the period-end. (8 marks)

You have been asked unexpectedly to act as audit manager for the audit of Tonco. You are aware that Tonco specialises in the development of computer software and the sale of hardware for use in schools. Tonco is growing rapidly but is operating in an increasingly competitive market. The audit is due to commence tomorrow but the existing audit manager, who has worked on the audit for many years, has suddenly been taken ill and is due to go into hospital tomorrow. A planning meeting took place between Tonco and the existing audit manager a week ago but no notes have been written up.

You have been provided with a small amount of information relating to the year ended 31 December 200X. This has been produced quickly from management accounts.

|  | 200X | 201X |
|---|---|---|
|  | $'000 | $'000 |
| Revenue | 23,709 | 20,200 |
| Gross margin | 0.83 | 0.79 |
| Expenses as a percentage of revenue: |  |  |
| Distribution costs | 0.05 | 0.10 |
| Administrative expenses | 0.17 | 0.13 |
| Selling expenses | 0.18 | 0.25 |

You have scheduled a telephone call with the existing audit manager for this evening.

Required:

(b) Using the information above, in advance of this evening's phone call, prepare a list of questions you will ask and observations you will make about Tonco's performance. (8 marks)

(c) Describe what further information and explanations you will ask for from Tonco's management when the audit commences tomorrow, to support the figures above. (4 marks)

Total: (20 marks)

## 4.4   AUDIT TOOLS

**Covering:** ISA 505 *External Confirmations*, the audit of cash and bank, receivables and payables, ISA 501 *Audit Evidence – Specific Consideration for Selected Items, The Audit of Inventory*, ISA 540 *Auditing Accounting Estimates, Including Fair Value Estimates, and Related Disclosures, The Audit of Non-current Assets, Share Capital, Reserves and Long-term Liabilities*, ISA 530 *Audit Sampling* and Computer Assisted Audit Techniques (CAATs).

**Why do I need to read this section?**

*An auditing and assurance paper that does not include at least two of the areas presented in this section is rare. Accounting estimates cover a wide range of line items in financial statement including provisions for depreciation, old, slow-moving, damaged and obsolete inventory, doubtful receivables, warranty claims and many others. Estimates, along with external confirmations, are an important audit tool and, together with the audit of inventory, they are all easy and important areas to examine and, not surprisingly, often come up. Exactly which areas are going to come up is the issue and it is worth looking at recently set exam papers. If inventory has been examined heavily in the three previous papers, and payables were last examined over two years ago, payables are probably a better bet than inventory for the next paper.*

**What is important in this section?**

*Just about everything. There are so many different types of accounting estimate that are easily examined that it would be rare for a paper not to cover them in some way. Confirmations are important both in theory and in practice, as is the audit of inventory.*

**What sort of questions come up in this area?**

*The general principles applying to the audit of estimates can be used in answering the many different questions on receivables, inventory and non-current assets such as property, plant and equipment. Sampling, computer assisted audit techniques (CAATs) and confirmations often come up as questions in their own right but the techniques can be brought into answers to many other questions. Audit sampling and CAATs may appear to be relatively complex areas but they are not difficult. It is better to make the effort to understand them than simply to learn long lists of examples, because it is much more likely that you will be able to use them in answers to questions that way.*

**How do I stand out from the crowd?**

*Students who give examples of CAATs in answers to questions on audit evidence stand out because many candidates only mention them if they are answering a question specifically on CAATs. CAATs can be used in answers to questions involving sample selection for all but the smallest of audits, and in many financial statement areas.*

*Students who demonstrate a good understanding of perpetual inventory systems and how auditors go about auditing them often do well. So do those who clearly explain the purposes of attending inventory counts, i.e. why auditors are there, and not just what auditors do when they get there, and link that work to the work performed before and after the count.*

*Demonstrating an understanding of what can go wrong with confirmations and inventory counting, the frauds associated with them, and the limitations of audit techniques also stand out in answers.*

### 4.4.1   CONFIRMATIONS

The evidence provided by external (third party) confirmations is generally very strong because it comes from outside the audited entity. Confirmations can be of:

- bank balances and information about arrangements and transactions with the bank, entity assets held by banks and charges banks have over entity assets as security for loans;
- accounts receivable and payable and loan balances;
- inventories held by third parties;
- document of title (title deeds) to property and other documents held by lawyers;
- investments held by third parties such as stockbrokers;
- loans including their terms and any undisclosed 'side agreements' that might not appear in the entity's records.

If auditors can obtain third party confirmations of material balances, they will generally attempt to do so. Auditors have to gather a great deal of internally generated evidence to match the quality of evidence provided by confirmations that come from outside the entity.

**Confirmations and Financial Statement Assertions**

Confirmations do not cover all financial statement assertions though: confirmations of accounts receivable, for example, provide better evidence of existence than they do of recoverability. Only cash after date provides good evidence of recoverability.

Confirmation of quantities of inventory held by third parties again provides good evidence of its existence, but not of its value.

If a sample of trade payables for confirmation is taken from the payables ledger, no evidence at all is provided regarding completeness, which is a key area in the audit of payables. For this reason, samples of trade payables selected for confirmation need to be taken from a potentially more complete source of payables, such as a master-file, or the full set of purchase transactions during the period, or even from supplier statements held by the entity, rather than the period-end ledger. The objective is to highlight payables accounts that are missing from the period-end ledger as well as misstated amounts.

## Deciding Whether to Obtain Confirmations

Should auditors always try to obtain confirmations? The decision is not always straightforward. Confirmations can be time-consuming to process and do not always elicit a high level of response. Auditors need to take account of:

- the cost and time involved;
- the likely level of response;
- the likely quality of responses;
- the quality of controls over the population to be tested;
- the effect of the request on the relationship between the client and the third party.

Auditors need the permission of clients to approach third parties. The most common reason given for refusing permission is a potential adverse effect on the relationship between the client and third parties such as customers, suppliers, and less often banks, lawyers or third party inventory holders.

There is a presumption that revenue recognition constitutes a significant risk, which means that more and better quality evidence is required for revenue, and any associated receivables. Management and sales staff may be tempted to raise invoices before shipment, but not send them to customers, for example, which might show up in a response to an external confirmation request. Wherever there is pressure to meet targets, for whatever reason, auditors need to consider whether conducting external confirmations is likely to produce good quality evidence.

Responses may be less reliable if they come from related parties such as group entities.[57] Auditors are *required to consider whether to conduct external confirmation procedures*[58] and they may use them in response to an assessed risk of fraud.

## Positive and Negative Requests

### Positive requests
Positive confirmation requests *ask for a response in all cases,* regardless of whether the balance is agreed. Such requests can *either state the balance as per the client's records, or leave the respondent to supply it.*

If the balance is stated, the request asks the respondent to confirm it and provides for the insertion of a different balance if the one stated is not agreed, with a request for the respondent to provide details of differences.

---

[57] ISA 330 on responses to assessed risks, paragraph A 48 ff.
[58] ISA 330 on responses to assessed risks, paragraph 18 (b).

### Negative requests

Negative confirmation requests *ask for a response only where the balance stated is not agreed*. For this reason, *the balance must be stated* in negative requests.

Negative requests are, for obvious reasons, less reliable than positive requests. They rely on the assumption that the respondent will reply if there is a problem and do not take account of inertia. They are rarely used in practice except for the confirmation of well-controlled deposit accounts with some financial institutions. Historically they have been mandatory for larger entities in some jurisdictions such as the former Soviet Union.

Negative requests may not be used as the sole substantive procedure unless:

• the population has been assessed as being subject to a low level of audit risk;

• controls have been successfully tested;

• the population consist of a large number of homogeneous balances;

• there is no reason to suppose that the request will be ignored.

All of these conditions are present for many populations of deposit accounts. Requests to private individuals and smaller businesses are more likely to generate a response if something is wrong, particularly if the balance is too low, than requests to larger businesses.

### Stating the balance

The main issues with stating the balance, whether in a positive or negative request, are that respondents:

• are more likely to reply if the balance is stated and are able to provide details of differences; but

• might agree to any balance, in the knowledge that it is unlikely that there will be significant consequences even if it is wrong; and

• are particularly likely to agree to incorrect balances in their favour, such as understated receivables balances or overstated payable balances.

### The Confirmation Process

Auditors must control the confirmation process. The process consists of auditors:

• selecting the sample for confirmation;

• obtaining client permission to approach the third party;

• drafting requests on *client* notepaper asking for responses to be sent direct to the auditors;

• supervising the production and despatch of requests.

Pre-paid reply envelopes are often supplied to encourage responses.

**CONFIRMATION REQUESTS**

Auditors must CONSIDER requests as substantive procedures

They MAY be used to address fraud risk

| **POSITIVE REQUESTS** | **NEGATIVE REQUESTS** |
|---|---|
| Reply requested in ALL cases | Reply ONLY where balance NOT agreed |
| Balance MAY be stated | Balance ALWAYS stated |
| More persuasive than negative requests | Often used to confirm balances for well-controlled deposit accounts |
| In some cases, the only way to get adequate evidence | |

| **STATE THE BALANCE?** | **NEGATIVE REQUESTS** |
|---|---|
| Responses more likely BUT respondents more likely to agree regardless, especially where balance is in their favour | Not as sole substantive procedure unless: |
| | - risk assessed as low |
| Respondents more likely to provide details of reconciling items | - controls successfully tested |
| | - large number of small balances |
| | - no indication that request ignored |

Figure 4.12    Confirmations

### Client refusal to permit a confirmation request

If the client refuses auditors permission to request a particular confirmation, auditors must ask why, and evaluate the response. Is there a genuine commercial reason for refusing the request? It might interfere with negotiations for a large contract, for example. Alternatively, is the client trying to cover up a problem? In either case, auditors should not simply find another balance to confirm, but should instead seek to obtain evidence regarding the balance selected in some other way. In the case of receivables, this might involve examining cash received after the period-end, by conducting analytical procedures on the balance or by examining the invoices, credit notes and other elements making up the balance.

If, at the end of the day, the refusal is unreasonable or no other audit evidence is available, auditors should inform those charged with governance and there may be implications for the audit report. Whenever clients obstruct auditors, there is always the possibility of a qualified audit opinion resulting from an imposed limitation in audit scope, if the matter is material.[59] Questions about management integrity arise in such cases and have implications for the rest of the audit.

---

[59] It would be rare for a qualified audit opinion to arise solely relating to just one audit confirmation, although not impossible if the amount were the single most important feature in the balance sheet.

*Responses, non-responses and responses not agreed*

*Responses*
High-profile frauds involving audit confirmations entail interference with the request or the response by the client.[60] Firm methodologies and the ISA require that requests are controlled by the auditors and mailed from the auditors' office.

Auditors should examine responses to ensure that they appear to have come directly from the third party and that the client has not tampered with them. Clients have falsified responses to show balances as agreed, when they in fact are not, or have simply fabricated responses when the relevant third party does not exist. The client, for example, might offer to mail the letters for the auditors and interfere with them before they go out. If the ledgers contain fictitious balances, the client might fabricate details of respondent entities and send false replies. The use of post office box numbers or similar instead of regular addresses might be a warning sign of this.

There is increasing use of *electronic confirmations,* especially for bank confirmations. Auditors need to be satisfied about the origin and authority of the response and the identity of the respondent, all of which the client can falsify if auditors do not take appropriate precautions. Auditors generally use a secure environment to send requests and receive responses to mitigate these risks. That environment will validate the identity of the sender, encrypt the details of the request, and use digital signatures and procedures to verify web-site authenticity. Third parties sometimes provide electronic and other confirmation services commercially for a variety of audit firms. The quality of such services and the level of control and security provided affect audit risk.

Where there are doubts about the integrity of responses, if envelopes are open, for example, or if many responses arrive together, or an unusually high number are agreed, or appear to be in the same handwriting, auditors need to verify the source of the response, perhaps by telephoning the respondent. Auditors should in any case consider telephoning a sample of third parties, using publicly availably phone books or lists, to ensure that they exist.

Many responses, particularly from banks, contain restrictive language stating, for example, that the bank accepts no responsibility or liability for or in relation to the information provided. Of itself, this does not necessarily invalidate the response but it does potentially affect the reliability of the response. There is little auditors can do about these standard bank disclaimers.

*Non-responses*
In an ideal world, auditors receive all responses on time and all agree the balance stated. This never happens. If it were to happen, auditors would be rightly suspicious that some fraud might be involved.

---

[60] The Parmalat case involved a forged bank confirmation purportedly confirming balances of some $5.5bn with the Bank of America. It was alleged that the confirmation request was sent using Parmalat's internal mail and that the forged confirmation was put together by Parmalat employees using scissors and a scanner.

Second and third requests follow non-responses together with phone calls or emailed requests. However, telephone conversations and even emails constitute fairly poor quality evidence, even if scrupulous notes are taken about when the call took place, who was spoken to and what was said, and both should be followed up with a request for a proper written response.

Confirmation requests often result in a fairly high level of non-responses. Auditors are required to obtain evidence on the balances selected in some other way when second and third requests fail, as where the client refuses permission to seek a confirmation.

Alternative evidence for receivables and payables balances not circularised or confirmed includes:

• cash received or paid after the period-end;

• examination of shipping documentation, goods received notes and invoices;

• supplier statement reconciliations;

• analytical procedures on the balance at the end of each month.

If, however, assessed audit risk is other than low, and a confirmation is essential because there is no other way of obtaining adequate audit evidence, a non-response might, if it were material, result in a qualification of the audit report. Client records and controls would need to be particularly poor for this to be the case and there are usually ways around such problems involving the client putting pressure on the customer or supplier to help avoid such a qualification.

*Responses not agreed*
It is common for a large number of responses to positive requests to disagree with the balance stated with no details of differences provided. The vast majority of differences are timing differences such as cash and returned goods that have been recorded in the respondent's system that have not yet reached the client's ledger, and invoices and credit notes in the client's ledgers that have not yet appeared in the respondent's system.

*Bank confirmations*
Bank confirmation requests are often different to other types of requests and the protocols are determined by agreements between representatives of major banks and auditors in a particular jurisdiction. In the UK, a protocol exists between the British Bankers' Association and the Consultative Committee of Accountancy Bodies (CCAB) whereby members of those bodies, such as ACCA and ICAEW, send requests to banks for audit information in a standard format. This helps ensure completeness and comprehensibility of requests and that auditors and banks are able to process the many thousands of requests they send/receive. There are two forms of requests, simple requests for smaller or less complex entities and full requests where additional information is required.

In order for banks to reply to auditors, they need permission or authority from their customer, the audited entity. Two types of authority (or mandate) are possible: a

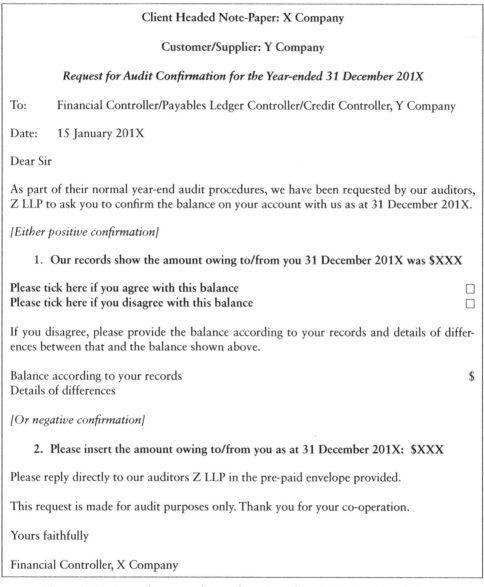

Client Headed Note-Paper: X Company

Customer/Supplier: Y Company

*Request for Audit Confirmation for the Year-ended 31 December 201X*

To:     Financial Controller/Payables Ledger Controller/Credit Controller, Y Company

Date:    15 January 201X

Dear Sir

As part of their normal year-end audit procedures, we have been requested by our auditors, Z LLP to ask you to confirm the balance on your account with us as at 31 December 201X.

*[Either positive confirmation]*

**1.  Our records show the amount owing to/from you 31 December 201X was $XXX**

**Please tick here if you agree with this balance**          ☐
**Please tick here if you disagree with this balance**       ☐

If you disagree, please provide the balance according to your records and details of differences between that and the balance shown above.

Balance according to your records                           $
Details of differences

*[Or negative confirmation]*

**2.  Please insert the amount owing to/from you as at 31 December 201X:  $XXX**

Please reply directly to our auditors Z LLP in the pre-paid envelope provided.

This request is made for audit purposes only. Thank you for your co-operation.

Yours faithfully

Financial Controller, X Company

**Figure 4.13**   Example request for confirmation of receivables/payables balance

standing authority that lasts for a fixed period or until revocation, or an authority sent with each confirmation request. Clearly the former should be administratively easier.

Standard requests cover matters such as:

• bank balances;

• the terms of trade;

- loans, and the conditions on which they are made;

- assets held by the bank as security and whether there are other charges on the asset.

Other details often requested include the repayment frequency and review date for loans and, where trade finance is provided by the bank, details of letters of credit, discounted bills, bonds, guarantees and indemnities and details of any derivatives and commodity trading.

## 4.4.2   THE AUDIT OF CASH AND BANK, RECEIVABLES AND PAYABLES

### The Audit of Cash and Bank

The audit of cash and bank, including bank overdrafts, comprises four main areas:

- testing control effectiveness over bank and cash accounts, including cash counts;

- the audit of bank reconciliations;

- obtaining bank confirmations and other substantive procedures.

Cash includes postal orders, travellers' cheques, regular cheques and other negotiable instruments such as bearer shares, as well as notes and coins.

*Control effectiveness*

- The effectiveness of controls over bank and cash has a direct effect on the nature and extent of substantive testing. As with all assets, there is a risk of overstatement. The auditors' evaluation of the control environment has an effect on the assessment of this risk.

- Controls over bank and cash accounts are generally good because of the obvious risk of theft. Whenever cash is handled, such as when cash is received in the post, at cash counts and when paying wages in cash, *ensuring that at least two people are present* where possible reduces the risk of fraud and error. It cannot eliminate the risk of fraudulent collusion, though. Auditors can observe the opening of post, the payment of wages and cash counts to test this control. As a substantive procedure they may also note payments or receipts made at the time, and check them to subsequent bank and cash records.

- *It is common to require two signatures* to authorise payments either by bank transfer or cheque for purchases, expenses or payroll. One person signing is usually independent. Auditors can check samples of cheques and authorisations for bank transfers to ensure that only those authorised to sign in accordance with the bank mandate have signed, and that the required number of signatures is present.

- In practice, it is not possible or necessary to have two signatures on every cheque or other document authorising the transfer of cash. Requiring only one signature for relatively small amounts is common. It is also a common source of low level fraud.

- *Automated controls over the processing of bank and cash transactions* from cash received through to the cash account, receivables or payables ledgers and control accounts, include using *check digits* to ensure that valid codes are used in posting cash to individual accounts, and *sequence checks* to ensure completeness of processing when batches of cash receipts or payments are posted. Auditors can test these using computer assisted audit techniques (CAATs) and/or by checking input to output. Substantive procedures can be performed at the same time ensuring that the correct amounts are posted to the correct accounts in the correct period.

- *Physical controls* over cash include the use of secure transportation of cash from retail outlets to cash centres, tills that only open when a sale is made, and minimising the cost and risks involved in moving cash by using cash-back schemes. They include keeping cash locked in safes or strong-rooms which can only be opened by two people with two keys. All of these controls can be observed and tested by auditors.

- *The performance of unannounced cash counts by internal auditors and senior management is a common control over cash and is part of a good overall control environment. External auditors may test such controls by observing them and may also perform such counts themselves as substantive procedures.*

*Bank reconciliations*

- *Performing and reviewing bank reconciliations* on a regular basis and investigating reconciling items is a control. Auditors test this by looking for evidence that the reconciliation has been performed, i.e. that it has been prepared each month, reviewed, i.e. that it has been signed, and reconciling items followed up, i.e. that it has no old outstanding items.

- *Substantive procedures performed on the bank reconciliation include tracing the unpresented cheques and other unpresented payments to the cash book and payables ledgers, the outstanding lodgements to the cash book and receivables ledgers, and both to the bank statement after the period-end. Contras and reconciling items need to be investigated paying particular attention to those that are large or old.*

*Bank confirmations and other substantive procedures*

Bank confirmations are *documentary third party audit evidence,* even though banks do not always provide the information requested. Obtaining a bank confirmation is often regarded as essential audit evidence, but some high-profile frauds have involved forged bank confirmations and it is essential that, as with all confirmation requests, auditors control their despatch and receipt. The bank must have authorisation from the business to provide auditors with information. This is either provided each time a request is made, or is a standing authorisation.

Information commonly requested, as noted above, includes:

- bank balances that can be checked to the bank statement;

- the terms of trade which may be relevant to the assessment of the entity's going concern status if cash flow is a problem;

- loans, and the conditions on which they are made;

- assets held by the bank as security and whether there are other charges on the asset which may require disclosure.

Substantive procedures other than those noted above include tracing receipts and payments through the cash books and ledgers and *analytical procedures* performed on total receipts, total payments and the balance at each period-end. Analytical procedures are particularly important in the audit of entities that deal with large volumes of cash, such as supermarkets, banks and casinos.

## The Audit of Receivables and Payables

As with the audit of bank and cash, the nature and extent of substantive testing is determined in part by the effectiveness of controls. Receivables are susceptible to overstatement, payables are susceptible to understatement.

The audit of receivables and payables comprises two common areas:

- testing control effectiveness and control accounts;

- obtaining confirmations and other substantive procedures including, in the case of receivables, procedures on allowances for doubtful receivables and receivables written off.

*Testing control effectiveness and control accounts*

- As with bank and cash, the auditors' evaluation of the quality of the overall control environment is relevant to the risk assessment. Auditors can also directly test general and application controls in the relevant computer systems.

- Automated controls over the processing of purchases and sales *orders* through to *invoices*, the *sales and purchases accounts*, receivables and payables *ledgers*, and receivables and payables *control accounts*, and *vice versa*, are similar to those required in other automated systems and include checking batch and hash totals to ensure the completeness of processing. Auditors can use computer assisted audit techniques (CAATs) in the form of test data to test controls over the completeness and accuracy of processing. They can also perform substantive procedures using audit software to analyse large samples of orders, invoices and receivables and payables balances.

- Checks on samples of invoices can be performed to ensure that they have been properly authorised and that the correct prices have been charged.

- The emphasis when testing *payables* will be to trace from source documentation, such as *goods received notes or a list of creditors*, through to *purchase invoices* and *ledgers*, to establish *unrecorded or understated payables*.

- When testing *receivables*, the emphasis is in the *opposite direction*, tracing from *receivables in the ledgers* through *invoices* to source documentation such as *orders and goods despatch notes*, to establish whether allowances for *doubtful receivables* need to be made or balances *written off*.

- *Control accounts* are maintained to act as a check on the accuracy of the other accounts such as the sales and purchase ledgers and sales and purchases accounts. They should be reconciled to them on a regular basis. Auditors can test this type of control by ensuring that reconciliations have been performed and reviewed on a regular basis, in the same way as they test bank reconciliations, noting large or old reconciling items. Auditors can also test the detail of the reconciliation for substantive accuracy at the same time, by tracing total cash received or paid to the cash book, and sales or purchases to the sales or purchases accounts.

*Obtaining confirmations and other substantive procedures*

- The processes for obtaining confirmations are described above. Consideration needs to be given to the source of information in the confirmation request, whether the request should be positive or negative and whether the balance should be stated.

- *Audit software* can be used to perform substantive procedures, including analytical procedures on purchases, revenue and the ageing of receivables and payables, and on allowances for doubtful receivables and receivables written off. Analytical procedures are a powerful audit tool provided the data the procedures are applied to is reliable. Reliability is in part determined by the results of controls testing.

- *Cash received after the period-end* is one of the most reliable sources of evidence for receivables in the absence of replies to requests for confirmations. The amounts paid after the period-end in respect of payables are relevant to the period-end figure.

- *Allowances for doubtful receivables* are accounting estimates. Auditors may review and test management's process for developing the estimate, including assessing the underlying assumptions and determining whether any changes are appropriate, or they can prepare their own estimate. Some formula or percentage is often applied to the total receivables figure to arrive at the allowance for doubtful receivables. Management's experience of calculating such allowances is relevant and receivables written off in the past can be compared to allowances made.

### 4.4.3  INVENTORY, LITIGATION AND CLAIMS AND SEGMENT INFORMATION

### Inventory

*Why is inventory important?*

The audit of inventory is important both in theory and in practice. Opening and closing inventories have a direct effect on profit. Provisions for old, slow-moving, damaged and obsolete inventory can be both complex and easily manipulated. The types of fraud commonly encountered involving inventory include:

- movement of inventory during a count so that it is double counted;
- false sales invoices being raised and inventory being moved off-site to disguise it;
- 'padding' inventory to give the appearance of greater quantities than are actually present;
- inappropriate estimation or valuation techniques;
- tampering with inventory count records and producing fictitious records.

### Planning attendance at counts

Planning inventory counts can be a major logistical exercise where inventory is material and held at many different locations. Auditors often need to:

- co-ordinate different offices of the firm;
- instruct other firms where the firm does not have a local office;
- liaise with internal auditors and in-house or independent valuers employed by management, such as quantity surveyors in the building industry;
- deal with component auditors in group audits and inventory held by third parties.

Chains of petrol stations, hotels and restaurants, and retailers may also use professional third party inventory counters.

In all cases it is essential to remember that auditors remain responsible for the audit opinion, regardless of who provides audit evidence whether they be internal auditors, auditors from other firms, third party inventory holders or their auditors, or professional inventory counters.

*Auditors may only use the work of others if satisfied with the independence and competence of those performing the work.* They must also determine whether the work performed is consistent with other audit work and whether the assumptions made are the same as the assumptions used by management in preparing the financial statements.

When dealing with expert valuations in the extractive industries, for example, auditors need to consider whether to employ their own expert. This has substantial cost implications. Clients may understandably be unwilling to pay for an auditors' independent expert as well as their own in-house or independent expert. Again, the key factor is whether management's expert is sufficiently independent and competent.

The audit approach to inventory depends on whether the entity maintains inventory records or not, and whether it engages in inventory counting during the period. If there are no records and no counting takes place during the period, it is very likely that a full count will be required at the period-end if the inventory figure is material.

### Perpetual inventory counting and inventory records

Management usually counts inventory at least once a year in order to prepare the financial statements, but not necessarily all in one go, and not necessarily at the period-end, particularly where perpetual inventory counting procedures are in place.

Perpetual inventory counting systems overcome many of the problems associated with full period-end inventory counts but not all of them. *Inventory records*, which are not part of the double-entry bookkeeping system, simply show how much and what sort of inventory is supposed to exist at any given point in time. Such records may or may not have values attached to them but they are often updated in parallel with the main accounting system from invoices or GRNs. However, if they are not regularly reconciled to actual inventory, they fall rapidly out of date. Many businesses maintain such records and count inventory quarterly, six-monthly or on an ad hoc basis. *Perpetual inventory counting*, however, as the term implies, involves *continuous counting* on a sample basis throughout the period. Such systems are essential for supermarkets and in high volume manufacturing businesses, for example, where inventory control is critical to profitability. Such businesses often operate 'just-in-time' inventory management systems in order to keep inventory at optimal levels, intended to achieve best balance between the cost of cash tied up in inventory, and the cost of stock-outs (lost sales). Perpetual inventory counting facilitates accurate inventory records that are essential to the development and maintenance of just-in-time systems.

Auditors can evaluate and *test controls over inventory counting and recording* as they can for other controls, enabling them to reduce the level of substantive procedures at the period-end. Where this is the intention, auditors need to:

• evaluate management instructions;

• observe counting during the year ensuring that management instructions are followed;

• perform test counts, much as they would at the period-end if no such system were in place.

If the intended approach is to rely on perpetual counting systems and perform relatively little work at the period-end, it is important that auditors are satisfied that:

• counting instructions are adequate and are being carried out;

• inventory records are adequate;

• differences between records and inventory are investigated and corrected on a timely basis.

If errors are extensive, controls may not be working, or were not designed or implemented properly and it may be appropriate to revisit the risk assessment.

### Risk assessment
Inventory does not form part of the double-entry bookkeeping system. While many systems incorporate inventory records, it is common for inventory records to be inaccurate in the absence of inventory counting because inventory gets lost, damaged, stolen, sent to the wrong place and misclassified.

Auditors need to evaluate the risks of material misstatement regarding inventory before making decisions about whether to assess and test counting systems. Risk is affected by:

• the nature, location and condition of inventory and its susceptibility to theft and damage;

- the reliability of accounting systems and controls over inventory, particularly physical controls;
- the timing and extent of inventory counts;
- the extent to which inventory levels fluctuate;
- the extent of work-in-progress and the difficulties associated with its audit.

As with all risk assessments, auditors will need to form an initial opinion as to the likely level of risk and then test any relevant controls, before reducing the level of substantive testing. Substantive testing usually forms a major part of the audit of inventory even where it is well controlled, particularly where inventory is material, because it is a 'soft' figure, i.e. easily manipulated.

Auditors do not necessarily need to visit every location at which inventory is held every year. They may attend inventory counts on a rotational basis. When considering which locations to cover, they need to assess the risks associated with inventory generally and the risks associated with particular locations. Deciding on which locations to visit depends on, for example:

- the client's views about problem locations;
- the results of analytical procedures on inventory levels, returns, provisions and gross margins;
- the quality of controls in different locations;
- the auditors' previous experience.

*Attending inventory counts*
*Auditors are required to:*

- *attend counts where inventory is material to the financial statements, unless impracticable;*
- *test the final inventory records to ensure that they reflect the count results.*[61]

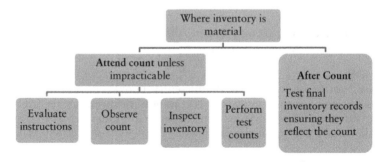

**Figure 4.14**    Auditor attendance at inventory counting

---

[61] ISA 501 on audit evidence for selected items, paragraph 4.

Impracticable means more than simply inconvenient, and refers to situations in which counting might be hazardous, for example. Difficulty, time and expense are not valid reasons for avoiding audit procedures for which there are no alternatives. At the count auditors:

- evaluate management's instructions;
- observe the performance of the count;
- inspect the inventory;
- perform test counts.

The purpose of attendance is to provide the best evidence available of the *existence and condition* of the inventory. The condition of inventory provides indirect evidence regarding its *valuation*. Attendance also provides evidence regarding *cut-off* and the *quality of controls* over inventory.

Attendance does not provide much evidence as to ownership. The fact that inventory is in the client's warehouse does not mean that it belongs to the client, or even that the client is free to dispose of it, particularly if there are charges over it or other restrictions on its movement or use. Such charges and restrictions often require disclosure.

Counting performed just before or just after the period-end is often for convenience, and avoids counting on New Year's Eve and similar dates.

*Evaluating instructions and observing performance*
Auditors are required to evaluate management instructions for counting. Theoretically this should be before the count so that auditors can make suggestions for improvement. In practice it can happen on the day of the count itself. If the instructions are not adequate and are not improved, auditors need to consider whether the count is adequate as a basis for the figure in the financial statements.

The sort of controls that auditors expect to see set out in management instructions cover:

- the *areas to be counted*, how they are to be identified and in what order;
- *The prevention of double-counting* by marking inventory as counted, for example;
- *spot-checking of counts* by management, internal auditors or other counters and procedures for re-counting where errors are found;
- the *segregation of duties* between counters and those with responsibility for the inventory, so that falsifications of records and/or theft of inventory cannot be covered up by those with day-to-day responsibility for inventory. This can be difficult as the only people available and capable of conducting the count may be those who deal with it on a day-to-day basis. It can be overcome by having staff count areas for which they have no responsibility, by having counters work in pairs (one knowledgeable, the other independent), or by having the count thoroughly reviewed;

- the identification of the *stage of completion of work in progress, slow-moving, obsolete or damaged* items and of inventory owned by third parties, i.e. inventory that should be excluded from the count;

- the *estimation of physical quantities* where precise measurement is not possible, such as coal heaps;

- *inventory movement* between areas counted, and the receipt and despatch of inventory before and after the *cut-off* date;

- *count documentation*: count documentation can range from part-completed forms in which the types of inventory are recorded but not the quantities, to completed forms which counters then check against the actual inventory. Controls need to prevent duplications and omissions usually by the use of pre-numbered forms to be completed. Documentation can be paper-based or electronic using scanners and bar codes, for example, or some combination of the two. Where inventory records are electronic, and there is no paper audit trail, auditors need to be satisfied that controls over the software are properly designed, implemented and are operationally effective by testing them. Automated and manual controls over such software should be designed to highlight, for example, negative quantities, and quantities outside certain pre-determined parameters.

Observing the performance of the count can be a test of controls by enabling auditors to form a view as to whether the instructions are adequately designed – whether there are enough staff, for example – and are being implemented and are operating effectively – whether counters are in fact working in pairs, as instructed, for example.

In practice, the organisation of inventory, whether specific items are easy to find, its general condition, whether it is grouped appropriately or scattered about, all give a good indication of whether inventory generally and the count in particular are well-controlled.

*Inspecting inventory and test counts*
Test counts may serve as either tests of control effectiveness or substantive procedures or both. Performing test counts provides substantive evidence but also tests control effectiveness by providing indirect evidence as to whether management's instructions are being carried out, such as whether controls over the movement of inventory during the count are being observed.

Observation of inventory generally, and specifically during test counts, provides substantive evidence as to the general quality and condition of the inventory.

Auditors normally obtain details of cut-off information, i.e. details of the last goods received notes and goods despatched notes, for example, for later follow up to the records used as a basis for the figure in the financial statements

**Test counts** trace from records to the inventory to confirm the **existence** of recorded inventory, and from the inventory to the records to confirm their **completeness and accuracy**.

Auditors sometimes conduct **test counts during the year** if there are inventory records, even if no perpetual inventory counting systems are in place. In addition to the test counts noted above, auditors may trace samples of goods received notes and goods despatched notes to the relevant invoices and to the inventory records, to ensure that quantities, descriptions and valuations are complete and accurate. The extent of such testing will depend on the auditors' assessment of the quality of controls over inventory and on the assessed level of audit risk. If controls or records are poor, auditors are unlikely to conduct such tests.

### After the count

Auditors usually perform analytical procedures on the final, adjusted records as well as the pre-count records. Procedures cover inventory levels, provisions for old, slow-moving, damaged and obsolete inventory, gross profit margins, and the levels of receivables and payables at the period-end, all of which should make sense when taken together.

Post-count adjustments are for a variety of reasons such as misclassifications, but it is easy to abuse such adjustments in order to manipulate the inventory figure. Post-count adjustments are not always well-controlled, for which reason auditors pay particular attention to them. They often involve journal entries.

### Testing the final records

Auditors trace their test counts to the final records to provide evidence regarding the **completeness** of inventory. This is not always straightforward as even where auditors have counted 20 red widgets, and there are 300 red widgets in the final records, it is not always clear whether those the auditors counted are included within the 300. Auditors can also check for appropriate provisions or write-downs for anything they noted as being in poor condition, to confirm the appropriate **valuation** of inventory.

Taking copies of sample count sheets and following them up later to the final inventory records helps ensure that the final records do not contain errors and have not been manipulated.

If, for whatever reason, auditors either cannot or simply do not obtain adequate audit evidence on inventory (regardless of whose 'fault' it might be), they need to consider whether a limitation in the scope of the audit exists and whether a qualified audit report is necessary.

### Cut-off testing

Analytical procedures provide some indirect evidence as to the accuracy of cut-off but are not a substitute for tests of details around the period-end.

Cut-off tests usually involve taking the last invoices, goods received notes and goods despatched notes issued immediately before the period-end, and the same information immediately after the period-end, and ensuring that:

- the correct quantities, descriptions and costs have been entered into the inventory records;
- the invoices have been included in the correct accounting period;
- any goods received and goods despatched not yet invoiced have been properly accounted for.

*Tests of control effectiveness and substantive procedures on inventory*
Students sometimes find it difficult to determine which tests of inventory are tests of control effectiveness and which are substantive procedures.

Tests of control effectiveness over inventory *counting* include:

- tests of controls over period-end counts and counts during the year, as described above, by observing whether management's instructions regarding counting in pairs and segregation of duties are being followed;
- test counts, which provide evidence as to whether controls to prevent double-counting are in place;
- tests of controls over post-count adjustments to inventory records, such as the authorisation of journal entries;
- cut-off tests as described above, to the extent that they constitute evidence that management's instructions are being carried out.

Tests of control effectiveness over inventory *records* include tests of:

- automated controls over inventory records similar to those over sales and purchases, which may involve using computer assisted audit techniques to test parameter checks for inventory quantities, exception reporting of negative inventory quantities, and the use of check digits within inventory codes, for example;
- password controls over changes to master-file data containing permitted inventory codes by attempting to access the system and make changes without an appropriate password, for example;
- physical access controls to inventory, such as the use of swipe-cards and keypads, by attempting to gain access using the invalid codes or cards;
- internal audit reviews of inventory levels and gross margins by ensuring that reviews have actually been performed.

*Substantive procedures* over inventory include:

- analytical procedures on inventory levels, returns, provisions for old, slow-moving, damaged and obsolete inventory, on gross profit margins, and the levels of receivables and payables at the period-end;
- tests of details including the test counts performed at inventory counts, and tracing these and a sample of completed count forms through to the final records;
- tests of details performed during the year on sales and purchase transactions where they are tied in with the inventory system;
- cut-off tests as described above to the extent that they involve checking that the individual transactions are in the correct accounting period.

*Auditor non-attendance*

Where auditors have not attended a count because of *unforeseen circumstances* (such as sudden illness, for example), they instead count or observe counting on another date, and audit the intervening transactions. If they have not attended because of *impracticability*, they need to obtain evidence as to the existence and condition of inventory by others means, possibly by counting on another date.

Where the counting takes place at a date other than at the period-end, auditors audit the intervening period, sometimes known as a 'roll-forward' or 'roll-back'. Clearly, the further the count from the date of the period-end, the more work is needed and the better controls need to be. The work performed on the intervening period is very similar to the work performed on cut-off. If the intervening period is significant, it may be necessary to test controls over inventory during that period, particularly if there have been changes of systems as this may affect audit risk.

### Inventory held by third parties

Where entity inventory is held by third parties, as might be the case where it is sold on a sale-or-return basis, or simply where there are very large volumes of inventory, evidence is obtained by: requesting confirmation from the third party as to the quantities and condition of inventory either by:

• visiting the third party, inspecting the inventory and performing other procedures such as test counts, much as they would if they were dealing with inventory held by the entity itself; or

• arranging for another auditor to do so; or

• obtaining another auditors' report on the inventory, where perhaps the third party only exists to hold the inventory of the audited entity, or where the audited entity is its main client, and it has its own audit; or

• obtaining the report of a service auditor specifically geared to the needs of third parties such as the audited entity.

### Auditing the lower of cost and net realisable value

Inventory is valued at the lower of cost and net realisable value (NRV) under many accounting frameworks, including IFRS and UK GAAP. US GAAP requires the lower of cost and market value. Inventory includes finished goods and work in progress.

*Cost*

Cost includes:

• costs of purchase, including transport and handling which can be traced to purchase invoices and invoices for, or allocations of, invoices for handling and transport;

• costs of conversion including fixed and variable manufacturing overheads;

• other costs incurred in bringing the inventories to their present location and condition.

The *routine audit of the purchases cycle* will provide some audit evidence in this area but auditors will also need to perform *analytical procedures* on the valuation of inventory and assess the quality of *management's past history* of inventory valuation.

| Before | During | After |
|---|---|---|
| • Consider the nature, location and risks associated with inventory through discussions with management, analytical procedures on inventory levels, gross margins, write-downs, receivables and payables and reviews of results of previous counts. | • Observe counting procedures. Are instructions being followed? Are inventory movements controlled? Is counted inventory marked as counted? Are counters working in pairs as instructed? | • Trace test counts and copies of count sheets taken at count to final count records. |
| • Are perpetual counting procedures in place and have procedures been tested? | • Inspect inventory for condition. Is it old, slow-moving or damaged? If so, record details for later follow-up. | • Trace cut-off details taken of last and first goods in and out to relevant invoices or accruals, ledgers and inventory records, ensuring they are accounted for in the correct period. |
| • Are inventory records adequate, i.e. up to date and differences investigated and adjusted for? | • Perform test counts from the records to inventory and vice versa. | • Ensure that appropriate adjustments have been made to inventory records and differences investigated. |
| • What is to be counted, where, when, and by whom (client staff, third party counters, internal audit)? | • Take copies of counted inventory sheets for later follow-up. | • Follow up details taken of inventory in poor condition to ensure appropriate valuation. |
| • Do third parties hold any inventory? Does client hold any for third parties? | • Take cut-off details of last goods in and out before the period-end, and first goods in and out after the period-end for later follow-up. | • Pay particular attention to post-count adjustments and consider the need to perform analytical or other procedures on inventory levels if adjustments are significant. |
| • Evaluate quality of management instructions, suggest improvements if appropriate. | • Consider the stage of completion of work-in progress; records might include photographs. | • Perform analytical procedures on the final records. |
| • Arrange for involvement of other offices, other audit firms, internal and group auditors. | • Form a view as to whether the count is adequate as a basis for the inventory figure in the financial statements. | • Consider the need for recommendations to management on how the count was conducted. |

**Figure 4.15**    Auditor procedures before, during and after inventory counts

Auditors need to pay particular attention to the ***allocation of overheads*** such as energy and administration costs. The risk is that costs will be inappropriately 'dumped' in inventory, reducing expenses, increasing assets and increasing profits. Posting overheads to the wrong account turns losses into assets. Where the amounts are material, auditors need to evaluate the system for cost allocation and be confident that it is properly designed and implemented, which should include regular reviews of the appropriateness of allocations. Systems need to ensure that only valid costs are allocated, excluding general overhead costs, abnormal waste, storage and selling costs, for example. Auditors need to test the controls in place to ensure that costs are in fact being allocated as they should be, and perform analytical procedures on allocations overall and tests of individual allocations.

Costs are net of trade discounts that may need tracing to period-end reconciliations where discounts are dependent on volumes purchased.

Some accounting frameworks such as IFRS permit or require borrowing costs to be included in the cost of inventory under very limited circumstances and, again, it is important to ensure that such costs are specifically attributable to the inventory.

The costing method, whether it be standard costing, the retail method, FIFO or weighted average may be used for the measurement of cost, provided it approximates actual cost.

*Net realisable value*
NRV is the estimated selling price in the ordinary course of business, less the estimated cost of completion and the estimated costs necessary to make the sale.

Analytical procedures are often used in auditing NRV and specific percentages of inventory over a certain age are sometimes provided for. Auditors need to be satisfied that such percentages are reasonable by reference to the actual amount of inventory that is eventually scrapped.

Selling price can be checked to invoices, contracts or cash received after the period-end. Costs of completion and costs necessary to make the sale might include re-packaging and marketing costs, which can be checked to the relevant invoices.

*Work-in-progress*
Work-in-progress (WIP), like finished goods, is valued at the lower of cost and net realisable value. Audit issues involve determining the stage of completion of part-completed manufactures. It is important to remember that the primary responsibility for valuation lies with the entity. Auditors firstly evaluate management's process for valuing WIP and consider testing control effectiveness over this. The valuation of WIP and write-downs to NRV are accounting estimates involving approximation. Auditors need to consider whether they are reasonable, largely in the light of subsequent events. It is possible that WIP as well as finished goods may need to be written down to NRV, where contracts for customised goods have been cancelled, for example, and where modifications are needed to make the goods saleable.

*Disclosures*
The audit of inventories always involves the audit of disclosures. These include accounting policies, the carrying amounts of various categories of inventory, write-downs and any reversals, and the cost of inventories recognised as expenses where permitted.

*Auditing work-in-progress*
Many accounting frameworks use the percentage of completion method to value partially completed construction contracts. It is permissible to recognise revenue and costs in proportion to the stage of completion (i.e. a proportion of profit), where the outcome of a construction contract in terms of total contract revenue, the stage of completion and the costs to complete the contract can be measured reliably. Where this is not the case, contract revenue should be recognised only to the extent that contract costs incurred are expected to be recoverable, i.e. revenues and costs are matched, but no profit is taken.

The stage of completion of a contract can be determined using surveys of work performed, the proportion of contract costs to date in relation to total estimated costs, or by reference to completion of a physical proportion of the work.

Auditors first of all need to agree with management's assessment as to whether the percentage of completion method should be used, which involves considering management's past record in this area, evaluating the systems used to determine whether the method is appropriate, and testing the controls applied. Where, as is often the case, the stage of completion is determined by surveyors, whether employed by the entity or not, auditors need to consider their independence and competence. They also need to review the work of such experts and consider the reasonableness of the assumptions and methods used and their compatibility with management assumptions.

Required disclosures often include the methods used to determine the stage of completion, the aggregate costs incurred, recognised profit, the amount of advances received and any retentions.

### Litigation and Claims

The main problem with the audit of litigation and claims is in the uncertainty involved. Will a case be won or lost and how much, if anything, will be paid or received?

The amounts involved can be significant and even when they are not, the reputational effects of litigation on an entity, and the powers of regulators to take action to shut down businesses, can have a knock-on effect on the going concern status of an entity.

Almost all accounting frameworks take a conservative view of litigation. Where potential liabilities are potentially material, they should be disclosed in the notes. If they meet certain recognition and measurement criteria, they should also be recognised in the income statement and balance sheet. The same is not true of potential assets, i.e. amounts awarded *to* an entity by the courts, which should only be recognised if there is more certainty, i.e. where it is virtually certain that they will be received.

Auditors are mainly concerned with completeness, ensuring that *all* litigation and claims that might give rise to a material misstatement are appropriately dealt with. Procedures include:

- inquiry of management and in-house lawyers;
- reviewing minutes of meetings with lawyers and with those charged with governance;
- reviewing legal expense accounts.

Where these procedures indicate that there is a risk of material misstatement, auditors are also required to communicate directly with the entity's external lawyers.

As with other external confirmations, a letter is prepared by management asking lawyers to communicate directly with the auditors.

In some jurisdictions, direct communication with auditors is prohibited either by custom, law or by the lawyers' professional body, in which case auditors need to perform alternative procedures. If such procedures are ineffective, i.e. auditors cannot obtain the evidence they need in relation to completeness, or if management or lawyers refuse to respond to requests, there may be a limitation in the scope of the audit.

Auditors are also required to request written management representations to the effect that all known actual or possible litigation whose effects should have been considered in preparing the financial statements has been disclosed to auditors, as well as properly accounted for.

Communications with lawyers are often problematic. Ideally, auditors should make general enquiries: are there any claims of which lawyers are aware, and what is their estimate of the financial implications? Even if direct communications with auditors are not prohibited, lawyers in many jurisdictions refuse to respond to such general requests. They will only respond to requests to confirm the reasonableness and completeness of *management's* list of litigation and claims and *management's* assessment of the financial implications.

Where matters are complex or auditors have assessed the matter as a significant risk, or where the client and lawyers disagree, it may be appropriate for auditors to request management to arrange a meeting at which matters are discussed, which auditors also attend.

### Segment Information
There are specific requirements for auditors to:

- understand the reporting requirements for segment information and management's processes for dealing with them;

- test management's processes if necessary;

- perform analytical procedures on segment information.

Segment information is important because it is politically sensitive and because entities sometimes manipulate the information to hide poor performance. Most accounting frameworks align disclosures with the way in which entities report and manage segment performance.

Entities can find themselves in a difficult position when operating in countries whose governments do not want public exposure of the extent of the entity's investment, revenues or profits, and make it a condition of investment that such information is not disclosed in the investor's financial statements. There can be tensions between such conditions and the disclosure requirements of the relevant accounting framework.

Relevant audit procedures might include comparing disclosed segment information with prior periods and budgets, and considering how revenue, costs, assets and liabilities are allocated and disclosed in the financial statements, how they are managed in budgets and management accounts, and where they are allocated in practice.

### 4.4.4  ESTIMATES

#### Types and Characteristics of Accounting Estimate

There are many types of accounting estimate. For exam purposes, they usually include:

- provisions for depreciation of tangible assets and sometimes amortisation of intangibles, including depreciation methods and asset lives;
- allowances for uncollectable and doubtful accounts receivable, also known as bad and doubtful debt provisions;
- provisions for ageing, slow-moving, damaged or obsolete inventory;
- warranty provisions;
- profits or losses on long-term contracts;
- costs arising from litigation.

Other useful examples less often examined are provisions for the write-down of investments and the valuation of complex financial instruments such as derivatives. The latter rarely appear in auditing and assurance papers partly because valuation models on which they are based are complex and are outside financial reporting syllabi. They are perfectly good as examples of estimates, though.

By definition, the measurement of estimates is imprecise. Differences between estimates and the actual outcome are expected, but very large differences may amount to misstatements. Estimates are often described as 'soft' numbers, which are more difficult to audit than 'hard' items such as cash, although some accounting estimates, such as complex financial instruments, are a great deal softer than others, such as inventory. Soft numbers are subject to higher levels of estimation uncertainty than hard numbers, because the nature and reliability of information available to management to support estimates vary widely. The higher the level of estimation uncertainty, and the greater the susceptibility to management bias, intentional or otherwise, the higher the risk of material misstatement of accounting estimates.

*Estimation uncertainty*
*Low estimation uncertainty* exists where, for example, estimates:

- are made routinely, lack complexity and require little judgement;
- are relatively insensitive to changes in assumptions;
- are made using recognised measurement methods and models;
- are produced from external data, or from data that can be corroborated externally.

Low estimation uncertainty is often associated with *depreciation* calculations, and certain generally accepted models used in fair value measurements, such as those used for interest rate swaps. The inputs to such models include asset prices, interest rates and mortality rates for pension fund valuations, and other readily available published 'observable' data, such as records of transactions in a particular security produced by independent third parties. Where there are active open markets for investments measured at fair value, there is very little estimation uncertainty, although adjustments are *sometimes* required for large holdings which if dumped might skew the market.

*High estimation uncertainty* exists where a wide range of outcomes is possible, such as for:

- the outcome of *litigation* involving a high level of judgement;

- *derivative financial instruments* valued using specialised models developed by the entity itself, or where inputs to the model are 'unobservable'. Unobservable inputs reflect the entity's own assumptions about how the market would price the asset or liability because there is little or no publicly available trading data either because there are few trades and/or trading does not take place on a public exchange.

Where the level of estimation uncertainty is so high that it does not meet the recognition criteria of the financial reporting framework, the asset or liability is often disclosed in the notes, but not recognised on the face of the financial statements.

Most financial reporting frameworks call for *neutrality* and estimates are notoriously subject to management bias. *Bias* can be intentional and can amount to fraud, but most instances of bias arise from management's unconscious desire to achieve a particular result.

Bias is difficult to detect because it often manifests itself in a general tendency to over-optimism. Taking a positive view in individual areas such as assets' lives, interest and exchange rates, sales growth or cost savings, for example, may be justified but auditors need to look at the overall tendency to bias in aggregated estimates, and the overall trends in and accuracy of estimates over a number of accounting periods.

Auditors are specifically required to review the judgements and decisions made by management in order to identify indicators of possible management bias. The *objective* of the audit of any estimates is to ensure that they are *reasonable* and that the related *disclosures are adequate,* whether estimates are recognised on the face of the financial statements or simply disclosed in the notes.

### Understanding Accounting Estimates
For all estimates auditors are required to obtain an understanding of:

- the *financial reporting requirements*, which are likely to cover recognition, measurement and disclosure. Where there is a range of alternatives for the estimate, *recognition criteria* may require management to make *point estimates* either by assessing the most likely outcome, or by using *probability-weighted expected values*. Either method could be applied to the outcome of litigation where, say, a high payout is most likely, but a lower payout or even no payout is also possible but less probable;

- *how management identifies the need for accounting estimates* to be recognised or disclosed in the financial statements. Management of very small entities might establish the need for estimates simply by knowing their own business. Very large entities may have a risk management function tasked with oversight of the area but all but the smallest of entities need some method, formal or informal, to prevent the omission of necessary estimates, which can be a significant risk. New estimates may be required because of changes in regulation, such as the need for new provisions for environmental clean-up costs, or changes in trading, such as new warranty provisions.

- *how management makes estimates*, and *what data* it uses to do so. This covers management's:

  - *method*, whether prescribed by the framework or developed by the entity, including any models;

  - *internal controls*: period-end estimates are often not part of the main internal control system, and are prone to error and bias. Controls over the development of accounting estimates as a minimum need to comprise some level of review and approval, and there needs to be some segregation of duties between those with responsibility for calculating the estimates, such as those calculating fair values of investments, and those with responsibility for the assets themselves, such as a treasury managers;

  - *expert valuers*, such as those valuing oil and gas reserves;

  - *assumptions* underlying the estimates. Some of these are within management's control, including asset maintenance programmes that affect the useful life of assets, others are outside management control, such as assumptions about interest rates and the likelihood and timing of future cash flows for a new production facility;

  - *assessment of estimation uncertainty*.

### Changes in estimate calculations

Should there have been a change from the prior period in the estimating method used? Auditors are required to review the outcome of prior period estimates, partly to form a view as to how good management is at making estimates, which might let them lower their assessment of audit risk in the area, and partly to provide evidence regarding the estimates in the current period.

While auditors are not required to question the judgements made in the prior periods based on information available at the time, ISA 240 on fraud requires a retrospective review of judgements and assumptions. Analytical procedures often suffice for routine estimates such as depreciation and accruals but particular attention should be paid to individual estimates subject to high estimation uncertainty, estimates that have changed significantly and to changes in methods, models or assumptions. Changes in methods, models and assumptions require close attention where they constitute deviations from industry practices, or where they appear arbitrary or biased and cannot be associated with a change in circumstances.

### Auditing Accounting Estimates: Responding to Assessed Risks

Some estimates have ceased to be estimates by the time the audit report is signed. The sale of all inventory that existed at the balance sheet date provides more or less conclusive evidence regarding its valuation, including any provisions. The same applies to receivables, including any allowances or provisions, which a review of subsequent cash receipts can help confirm, particularly when there is a long gap between the period-end and the date of the audit report, and where there is a high volume of low value receivables which normally turn over quickly, i.e. where customers pay promptly. If a review of such events occurring up to the date of the auditors' report provides sufficient evidence, no more is required. If not, auditors are required to perform one or more of the following:[62]

- *test how management made the estimate,* including their measurement methods, assumptions and the data on which it is based;

- *test controls over the estimate,* and perform appropriate substantive procedures;

- *develop a point estimate ($x), or range ($x–$y),* to evaluate management's point estimate. Where a range is developed, outliers are eliminated so that all outcomes in the range are considered reasonable.

*Testing how management made the estimate*
Testing how management made the estimate involves:

- re-calculation;

- testing management's review and approval process: if management do not review and approve the calculation of estimates, methods will be applied incorrectly and errors will slip through, regardless of the possibility of any management bias;

- considering the completeness, quality and reasonableness of the data and assumptions used to make the estimate: audit work on sales has a bearing on the work of warranty provisions because warranty provisions are normally based on sales data. Reasonable assumptions are internally consistent, consistent with the auditors' knowledge of the business and neutral.

Management's track record of bias and doing what they say they will do when assumptions are about management's future actions is relevant to the reasonableness of assumptions. If the valuation of long-term contracts, for example, depends on management obtaining new finance or re-allocating existing staff, auditors need to consider whether there are adequately documented, budgeted and approved plans for this. Auditors need to consider whether management has been successful in obtaining new finance in the past, whether it has taken the steps it said it would take, and whether it generally succeeds in managing staff change internally and appear to be succeeding in this case.

*Testing control effectiveness*
Testing the effectiveness of controls over the estimate is straightforward where the estimate is derived from the accounting system, where systems automatically produce expense accruals for power or insurance at the end of each period, for example. Where estimates are only made once a year or are being made for the first time, though, review and approval controls are more important.

If the review of a material estimate for profits on long-term contracts for a construction company is prepared by management and approval is performed by an audit committee,

---

[62] ISA 540 on accounting estimates, paragraph 13.

the overall strength of controls, and the extent to which substantive procedures can be reduced, is enhanced. *Smaller entities* sometimes rely on their auditors to help prepare the financial statements and controls may be non-existent in such circumstances. This does not relieve the entity of responsibility for the controls, all it does mean is that a fully substantive approach will need to be taken and that auditors will need to take care to obtain appropriate management representations.

*Developing a point estimate or range*
Developing a point estimate or range for comparison with management's estimate can be time consuming and expensive and auditors are unlikely to do this where the associated risk of material misstatement is relatively low. It is more appropriate where the estimate is significant and non-routine, for provisions relating to litigation, for example. Auditors also develop their own range or estimate where management's estimates in prior periods have proved reasonable but where controls are weak or non-existent, where there are alternative models or assumptions available, and where events after the period-end appear to contradict management's estimate.

It is common for auditors developing their own estimates to use different assumptions, models and methods to those used by management to assess the sensitivity of management's estimate. It is important though for auditors to understand management's approach properly and in sufficient detail to be comfortable that their own point estimate or range takes account of all relevant variables, to facilitate a proper evaluation of significant differences.

*Risk assessment and significant risks*
There is a high level of correlation between high estimation uncertainty and audit risk. Other factors that need to be taken account of in making the risk assessment include the absolute value of the estimate, the involvement of experts if any and whether management has a track record of making good quality estimates. An apparently immaterial estimate may have the potential to cause a material misstatement if there is a very high level of estimation uncertainty. Auditors are not only required to evaluate the degree of estimation uncertainty associated with estimates, they are also required to determine if any estimates that do have high estimation uncertainty constitute *significant risks*.

*Substantive procedures in response to significant risks*
For significant risks, auditors are required to perform substantive procedures that respond specifically to that risk and to evaluate:

* *how management has dealt with alternative assumptions* or outcomes, i.e. how it has addressed estimation uncertainty, through the use of alternative assumptions and models, for example. Where management has not done this for a significant risk, auditors consider whether it is necessary to develop their own range to evaluate the reasonableness of management's estimate. If management has failed to perform a sensitivity analysis of the effect of changes in interest rates on cash flows for a major project that is highly leveraged, for example, auditors need to consider why it has not done so and whether they, the auditors, need to perform their own sensitivity analysis. There may be good reasons for not doing so, where interest rates are

very stable, for example, or where financing is fixed, but in practice it is more likely that time pressure and a desire not to have to explain why a more pessimistic view should not be taken are the real reason.

- whether the *significant assumptions* used by management are reasonable, regarding interest or exchange rates when valuing simple derivatives, for example;

- *management's intent* to carry out specific courses of action and its ability to do so where relevant. Estimates of profits on long-term contracts are dependent on the entity having sufficient resources to complete the contract, for example.

Auditors are also required to obtain evidence regarding the **measurement basis** and management's **decision to recognise estimates**. Most financial reporting frameworks require that an item that can be adequately measured is recognised on the face of the income statement and balance sheet. Where a decision to do this has been made, auditors focus on whether the measurement is in fact reliable enough to warrant recognition. Where a decision *not* to recognise an item has been made, auditors focus on whether the recognition criteria have in fact been met.

The tendency is for management not to recognise liabilities or provisions for losses in the income statement or balance sheet where they should, such as those arising from litigation, because they can in fact be measured, albeit not precisely. The opposite applies to assets and income.

### Misstatements

Potentially material misstatements arise where there is a difference between the auditors' and management's respective point estimates. They also arise where auditors have developed a range of possible reasonable outcomes and management's point estimate falls outside this. The misstatement in that case is the difference between management's point estimate and the nearest (end) point in the auditors' range.

*Misstatements and point estimates*

**Figure 4.16**   Management and auditors both calculate a point estimate

### Disclosures and Written Representations

*Disclosures* are critical regardless of whether an estimate is recognised or merely disclosed. Most accounting frameworks require disclosure of key assumptions and other sources of estimation uncertainty, ranges of possible outcomes, assumptions used and qualitative disclosures about risk.

Management's point estimate ($z)

↕    Difference – misstatement

Upper limit of auditor range of reasonable outcomes ($a)

↕    Acceptable range

Lower limit of auditor range of reasonable outcomes ($b)

↕    Difference – misstatement

Management's point estimate ($c)

**Figure 4.17**    Management calculates a point estimate, auditors develop a range

For estimates that give rise to significant risks, particular attention needs to be paid to the adequacy of estimation uncertainty disclosures and consideration should be given to whether an emphasis of matter might be appropriate.

*Written representations* are required on whether management believe that the significant assumptions used in making accounting estimates are reasonable.

Documentation is required of the basis of conclusions about the reasonableness of estimates, the disclosures that give rise to significant risks, and indicators of possible management bias.

### 4.4.5    THE AUDIT OF NON-CURRENT ASSETS, SHARE CAPITAL, RESERVES AND LONG-TERM LIABILITIES

**The Audit of Non-Current Assets**

Non-current assets usually comprise intangible assets such as brands and goodwill, and tangible assets such as land and buildings, plant and equipment, motor vehicles, fixtures and fittings and office equipment.

The nature and extent of substantive testing are determined by the effectiveness of controls. All assets are susceptible to overstatement. The auditors' evaluation of the quality of the overall control environment is relevant to the risk assessment but there are less likely to be automated controls over non-current assets than there are over receivables, payables or cash, particularly in smaller entities.

The audit of non-current assets comprises two areas:

- testing control effectiveness over acquisitions and disposals and asset registers;

- substantively testing cost, valuation, depreciation or amortisation and disclosures.

*Control effectiveness over acquisitions and disposals and asset registers*

- Acquisitions and disposals should be planned for and authorised within a *capital expenditure budget* in larger entities. Auditors can test a sample of acquisitions and disposals to ensure that they have been authorised, and at the same time test the cost or disposal proceeds to cash accounts, invoices, orders and contracts. Acquisitions from and disposals made to *related parties* and staff may require *disclosure* in the financial statements.

- *Assets registers* should be reconciled on a regular basis to the asset accounts and to the assets themselves on a sample basis, possibly by internal auditors if such a department exists. Auditors can check whether such reconciliations have been performed and reviewed, as evidenced by a signature, for example, and at the same time perform substantive tests on the existence of assets by tracing from the register to the asset, and in the opposite direction to ensure completeness of the records.

*Cost, valuation, depreciation or amortisation and disclosures*

- Auditors consider whether management has made *appropriate valuations and depreciation or amortisation calculations in the past* by comparing recorded asset lives with actual asset lives, for example.

- *Inspections of assets during inventory counts* give some indication as to the condition of assets and may indicate the need for write-downs.

- *Assets carried at valuation* in accordance with the requirements of the *relevant financial reporting framework* are likely, in the case of *property or intangible assets,* to be valued by an *expert*.

- *Experts* should be objective, if not *independent, and competent*. Auditors are required to *obtain an understanding of the assumptions* and methodologies used and consider whether they are reasonable in the light of their understanding of the business.

- It is usually straightforward to trace the *cost* of an asset to the original invoice if the asset was acquired relatively recently. Records of cost are sometimes lost in which case it may be necessary to make assumptions about cost when assets are revalued, and to prevent their continued depreciation or amortisation after they have been fully written down.

- *New property* can be checked to title deeds and any public registers of property ownership. *New motor vehicles* can be checked to registration documents. Both can be checked to insurance documentation and *maintenance and repairs and renewals accounts*.

- Auditors should test controls ensuring that *assets fully written down are not written down further* and that assets such as land are not amortised.

- Where an entity has large amounts of similar non-current assets such as a fleet of motor vehicles, *analytical procedures* can be performed on cost and depreciation charges.

- *Depreciation and amortisation are estimates*: auditors either *review and test the process used by management* to develop the estimate or use an independent estimate for comparison with that prepared by management.

- *Reviewing and testing the process used by management* is most common and involves *evaluating the data and assumptions* on which the estimate is based, such as the asset life and the depreciation method, and considering the *reasonableness of any changes*. It also involves *checking a sample of calculations for accuracy* and considering the approval *process*.

- For each different category of non-current assets, disclosures are generally required for cost and depreciation or valuation *brought forward*, which can be checked to the prior-period financial statements, *changes* during the period, and figures *carried forward*.

- There are often requirements for the disclosure of the *qualifications of valuers, valuation and revaluation policies, and any charges over assets* held as security for loans.

## The Audit of Share Capital, Reserves and Long-term Liabilities

Controls in this area are unlikely to be automated except in the largest of companies with complex financing arrangements. Control is likely to reside in the expertise of the company's lawyers, the company secretary and professional advisers. Auditors can evaluate the effectiveness of the control environment in this area which will have a bearing on the nature and extent of substantive procedures.

Areas to be audited include:

- changes in share capital, if any, including any share premium;

- transfers to and from reserves, including the transfer of profit from the income statement and transfers to revaluation reserves;

- *changes in long-term liabilities.*

In all cases, changes and transfers should be properly *authorised*. Auditors can check authorisations to board minutes and minutes of shareholders' meetings where appropriate.

For *share capital,* shares can be agreed to the company's constitutional documents and/or the figures brought forward. Any share issue should be authorised and the amounts checked to the cash, share capital and share premium accounts, and to share certificates.

*Dividends paid* and payable should be checked to ensure that they are legal, and to cash accounts.

*Transfers from the income statement to reserves* should be checked to ensure that they are in accordance with the entity's constitution and are legal.

Transfers to *revaluation reserves* should be checked to ensure that they correspond to the revaluation. Audit work performed on the revaluation itself is relevant.

For share capital, share premium, all reserves and long-term liabilities, figures *brought forward from the prior period* can be checked to the *opening balances in the current period.*

The allocation of payments to reduce *long-term liabilities* to *capital and interest* should be checked and appropriate disclosures made.

Separate *disclosure* is likely to be required for *share issues, new long-term liabilities, dividends paid and movements on reserves.* It is also often required for the issue of shares to *related parties.*

## 4.4.6 SAMPLING

### Definition of Sampling

All auditors perform tests on samples in order to be able to draw conclusions about the population as a whole.

It is generally impossible and unnecessary to test all transactions anyway because in practice there are now so many of them that it would take too long and cost too much. Even if that were not the case, testing 100% of a population does not reduce the risk of missing an error to zero because of human error, regardless of whether testing is performed manually or using computer assisted audit techniques (CAATs). However, for the audit of significant risks, sampling, i.e. testing less than 100% of the population, is *not* generally appropriate.

*Sampling is the application of audit procedures to less than 100% of items...such that all sampling units have a chance of selection....to provide the auditor with a reasonable basis on which to draw conclusions about the entire population.*

ISA 530 *Audit Sampling* paragraph 5

### *Statistical and non-statistical (judgement) sampling*
Two basic types of sampling are generally recognised, statistical sampling and non-statistical sampling, sometimes known as judgement sampling. The former involves the use of statistical techniques to select the sample and interpret results and can only be applied where certain conditions are present. The latter can be applied in a wider range of situations. Broadly speaking, the remainder of this section applies to statistical sampling.

Statistical sampling involves random selection of the sample items and the use of probability theory to evaluate sample results. Judgement sampling relies on the auditors' judgement to do the same. *Both* methods involve the use of judgement. While it is arguable that the scope for errors of judgement is narrowed where statistical techniques are used, there is a certain 'spurious accuracy' to statistical techniques. The results can appear very precise but they are based on broad unquantifiable auditor assessments such as the level of risk associated with a population, and quantifiable but imprecise judgements such as the materiality level.

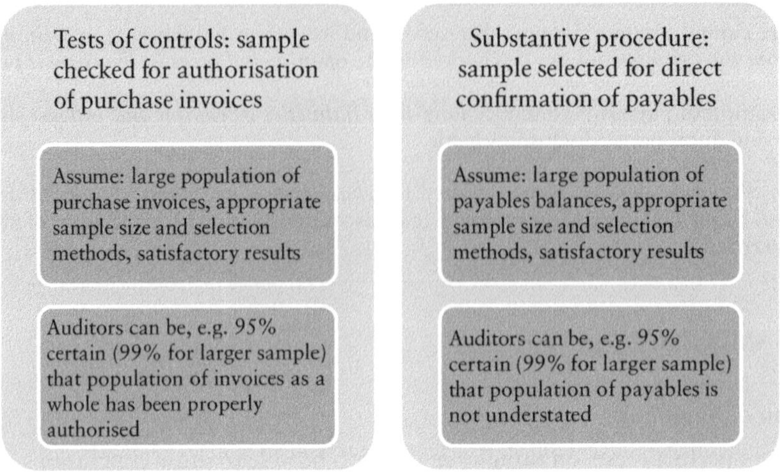

**Figure 4.18**   Sampling examples

> *95% (or 99%) certain: in every 100 samples taken from a population, 5 (or 1) samples will not be representative of the population, i.e. the sample will be unrepresentative and appear to show that invoices are not authorised when they are, or vice versa, or that payables are not materially understated, when in fact they are.*

The main advantages of statistical sampling are that:

- the process permits less experienced staff to use the techniques;
- there may be more rigour and more defendable, precise results;
- there may be less scope for errors or abuse of judgement.

The main disadvantages of statistical sampling are its cost, the risk that more junior staff will not apply the techniques properly or misinterpret the results, and that the results can appear to be more accurate than they are.

The main features of judgement sampling are that it is relatively cheap, more easily understandable to those without statistical training, but requires more experienced auditors overall to use their judgement in selecting samples and interpreting results. The technique can be applied to a wider range of populations than can statistical sampling.

### Sample Selection

Each firm will have its own methodology for sample selection. An understandable error often made by students is to assume that there is a direct relationship between the size of a population, the level of materiality, and sample sizes. While there is such a relationship and the larger the sample size, the less the risk that the sample is unrepresentative of the population from which it is drawn, the relationship is not linear. Doubling the sample size does not halve the risk and halving the sample size does not double the risk.

### Conditions for statistical sampling

There are a few basic conditions and rules for statistical sampling which apply to all methodologies. If these conditions are not met, judgement sampling must be used. Statistical sampling requires that:

- each item in the population must have *some quantifiable chance of being selected*, although not necessarily an equal chance, which means that block selection methods, such as selecting invoices from one month only, which exclude other parts of the population, cannot be used;

- the population needs to be *large*; sampling can work on small populations but adjustments need to be made;

- the population must be *homogeneous*, subject to the same controls and subject to the same level of audit risk. This condition is often absent. Heterogeneous populations of items containing distinct sub-categories subject to different control procedures and levels of audit risk include receivables and payables ledgers because they often comprise a few very large balances dealt with in one way and a large number of smaller balances dealt with in another. Such populations are often stratified, i.e. split into their constituent elements, and samples taken separately from each of them in order to reduce sampling risk.

### Sample selection methods

There are a number of sample selection methods including the following:

- truly *random* selection, which requires the use of random number generators or tables. For a population of plant and equipment with sequential asset numbers, a random number generator could be used to generate a sample of assets to examine physically using the complete range of asset numbers;

- *interval* selection, which is a form of random selection which takes every 'nth' item, the first item being selected at random. So for a population of invoices of 2,500 items, where a sample of 25 items were required, the first item would be selected from the first 100 items at random, say the 86th item, and then every 100th item beyond that, so items 186, 286 and 386, etc., would be selected;

- *block* selection in which one part of a population is selected for testing, such as all of the receivables balances over a certain amount, or all of the receivables balances dealt with by a particular credit controller, or all balances with account names beginning with the letter 'P'. This does not generally constitute an adequate basis for sample selection because some of the items within a population stand no chance of being selected, unless it is argued that the selection method, say on the basis of a letter, approximates to truly random selection;

- *haphazard* selection, which involves auditors simply picking items 'at random' and is also sometimes put forward as an approximation to random selection but this method is vulnerable to bias, conscious or otherwise, on the part of auditors who may, understandably, avoid items that look as if they might be a problem, and as such it is not generally acceptable as a selection method;

- *monetary unit* selection, which involves selecting items within a population *by reference to* the monetary unit they represent. In a population of receivables, if the total value of the ledger is $30,000, and a sample of 15 items is required, every 2,000th 'monetary unit' might be selected. By definition, a balance of say $5,000 (anything over $4,000) will be selected more than once because of the sampling interval of 2,000. This is not of itself a problem, but it is important to recognise that the sample of receivables balances tested will in fact comprise less than 15 balances, because at least one balance represents two of the monetary units selected.

### Deviations and Misstatements

One of the most difficult aspects of sampling is dealing with *deviations and misstatements*.

### *Deviations*

We have seen that deviations are deviations from the application of control procedures, i.e. where they have not been applied properly. Examples include credit notes that should have been authorised not being authorised because a member of staff was off sick, or where a bank reconciliation that should have been checked was not checked.

Some deviations can be expected because of human error and auditors assess an *expected rate of deviation* in a population. If this is very high, testing control effectiveness may not be appropriate.

The *tolerable rate of deviation* permits some level of deviation while still concluding that a control is effective. Auditors must decide whether deviations beyond the tolerable rate of deviation are isolated deviations, i.e. *anomalies*, or whether they are symptomatic of a breakdown in the application of a control.

Anomalies are deemed rare, partly because of the high level of automation in transaction processing and a high level of evidence is required to support a conclusion to the effect that deviations are isolated. Auditors are required to investigate similar items taking account of the likelihood of systematic deviations (and misstatements) and the extreme rarity of anomalies.[63]

Even if deviations do represent a breakdown in control, there are usually *compensating controls* on which auditors can rely. All good control systems have several layers of control, recognising that if one fails, others are needed. So should a bank reconciliation, which is a control procedure, be performed incorrectly, the review of reconciliation,

---

[63] ISA 530 on audit sampling, paragraphs 13 and A17.

another control procedure, might pick the error up. If so, fine, but the risk assessment still needs to be re-visited and the nature, extent and balance of testing considered. It is important to determine very clearly at the outset what constitutes a deviation, and to ensure that what appears to be a deviation actually is a deviation.

*Misstatements*
We have seen that errors arise in substantive tests, such as where a sales tax is calculated incorrectly in an invoice because an incorrect product code has been applied, or where incorrect inventories are recorded during an inventory count. As with deviations, anomalies are deemed rare and a high level of evidence is required to support a conclusion to the effect that misstatements are isolated.

If systematic errors in sampling indicate a material misstatement by extrapolation, the implications are serious. If in fact there is a material misstatement an adjustment to the financial statements will be required in order to avoid a modified audit opinion. Auditors are also required to re-consider their original risk assessment and audit approach in such circumstances. If it transpires that risk should have been assessed as, say, moderate, instead of low in a particular area, it will be necessary to re-visit the nature, extent and balance of testing of controls and substantive procedures to establish whether they were adequate. If they were not adequate, more work will be required. It is therefore critically important at the outset to be clear about what an error actually is, and to ensure that when errors are identified they are in fact errors.

It is also important to remember that tests of control and substantive procedures can be performed at the same time and are interrelated. Substantive misstatements can indicate control failures and control failures often result in misstatements. The failure to apply a control often results in a substantive error. The cause of the incorrect sales tax calculation may be the failure of a computer control, and perhaps the failure of a credit controller to review invoices, because there are always multiple layers of control to consider. This is also why it is important for auditors to re-evaluate audit risk and reconsider the audit approach and the need to test controls whenever deviations or misstatements occur.

## Deviations, Misstatements and Sampling Risk

We have seen that audit risk, i.e. the risk of an unqualified opinion where there should be a qualified one, is a function of inherent risk (the risk that material errors will occur), control risk (the risk that controls will not prevent or detect those errors) and detection risk (the risk that auditors will not pick up those errors). We have also seen that detection risk is a product of sampling risk and non-sampling risk. Non-sampling risk encompasses human error and poor judgement and includes using inappropriate audit procedures, misinterpreting audit evidence and failing to recognise misstatements or deviations.

*Sampling risk is the risk that the sample is unrepresentative of the population from which it is drawn.*[64]

---

[64] ISA 530 on audit sampling, paragraph 5.

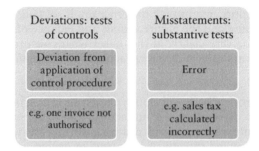

**Figure 4.19**   Deviations and misstatements

Sampling risk is the risk that the sample does not have the same characteristics as the population from which it is drawn. Generally, if a large population of invoices has a 3% error rate in it, there is a very high chance that a sample taken from it will also have a 3% error rate in it, provided the sample is properly selected. Proper selection means among other things that all items within the population have a chance of being selected, not necessarily an equal chance, but some chance.

Sampling risk is the unlikely risk that out of a population of 1,000 receivables in which 5% are actually uncollectible or doubtful, auditors happen to pick a sample in which over 15% appear to be uncollectible or doubtful: auditors just happened to pick all of the balances with problems. This happens less often than might be expected and is quantifiable. The larger the sample, the less likely it is that it will be unrepresentative of the population, but, as noted above, the relationship is not linear.

Sampling risk means that that controls may appear to be more effective than they actually are, or that a material misstatement may appear to exist when it does not, or does not appear to exist when it does. Both erroneous conclusions are problematic because errors in a sample that are not in fact representative of the population result in more audit work, and errors in a population not reflected in a sample ultimately mean that auditors may fail to detect a material misstatement in the financial statements and give an unmodified opinion where a modified one is warranted.

### Projecting Misstatements

For tests of details, auditors are required to project misstatements found in the sample to the population.[65]

Auditors seek to obtain assurance through substantive procedures that the actual misstatement in a population does not exceed an amount known as ***tolerable misstatement***. This is the absolute amount of misstatement that auditors can tolerate and still

---

[65] ISA 540 on audit sampling, paragraph 14.

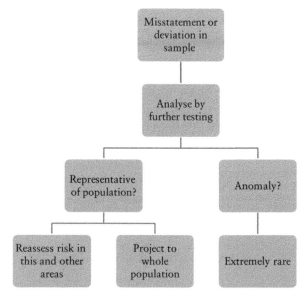

**Figure 4.20** Deviations and misstatements in sampling

be assured that the financial statements are not materially misstated. We have seen in the context of materiality that tolerable misstatement addresses the risk that the aggregate of individually immaterial, misstatements may cause the financial statements to be materially misstated, and provides a margin for possible undetected misstatements. It is the application of performance materiality to sampling. Tolerable misstatement can be the same as or lower than performance materiality.

### 4.4.5 COMPUTER ASSISTED AUDIT TECHNIQUES (CAATs)

Despite widespread automation of transaction processing in entities of all sizes, auditors still focus a great deal of audit effort on inputs, outputs and what goes on 'around the computer', rather than what goes on 'through the computer'. But the days of simply ignoring the computer are long gone, not least because transaction processing is a great deal more reliable than it was even a short time ago, and it therefore makes more sense now for auditors to test controls over processing than it used to.

CAATs are still thought of, though, as being relevant to larger audits with highly automated systems for which audit software and test data have to be customised by expert computer auditors. This remains true, but there is an increasing number of off-the-shelf CAAT packages designed to interface between widely used accounting packages and proprietary audit systems.

## Types of CAAT

There are broadly two types of CAAT, *audit software* and *test data*. A simple example of the use of audit software would be for auditors to download or import details from a client's receivables ledger into a spreadsheet, and to perform an ageing or other analytical procedures on that information. A simple example of test data would be for auditors to insert a dummy invoice into the client's system to see if it produced an overdue receivable in due course, or to see if the application controls in the system performed as expected by rejecting the invoice. Auditors might reasonably predict that a system would reject an invoice with a non-existent customer code or product reference, or a reference that was not in the correct alpha-numeric sequence or a code with an incorrect check digit, for example. If the invoice was not rejected, something would appear to be wrong with the controls that were supposed to be operating.

Test data is used to test application controls which we have already seen in section 4.1.

## Usage of CAATs

### *Audit software*
Audit software can be used for many types of analytical procedures such as:

- ageing receivables or payables ledgers, i.e. splitting them into those due within 30 days, 60 days, 90 days and so on, for the review of trends by comparison with prior periods and the client's ageing, for example;
- calculating debtor or creditor days and reviewing trends by comparison with prior periods;
- recalculating the depreciation in non-current asset schedules and comparing it to client calculations;
- re-performing calculations on large volumes of transactions such as calculations of taxes and totals within individual invoices and account totals in sales or purchases accounts;
- calculating allowances for uncollectible and doubtful receivables;
- extracting large items with particular characteristics for further testing, or items such as transactions with an individual or entity that has been identified as a related party.

### *Test data*
Test data might be used to test controls in a payroll system as follows:

- attempting to enter a fictitious employee into a payroll master or transaction file without a proper employee number, tax code or social insurance number, or attempting to duplicate an existing employee, all with the expectation that the system will:
    - reject the attempted input;
    - accept it but produce an exception report;
    - accept it but the item be highlighted during manual approval of system outputs.

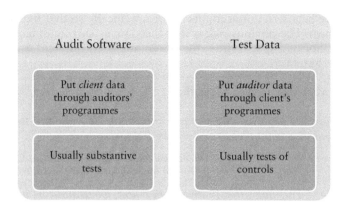

**Figure 4.21**   Audit software and test data

- attempting to process an unrealistically high number of hours worked or a large bonus, for a bona fide employee to see if parameter checks are working and reject the amounts involved;
- attempting to alter tax or social insurance rates, employee social insurance numbers or basic salary information in master-files without proper authorisation.

### Are CAATs Worth the Effort?

CAATs cost money and take time to set up. When deciding to develop or use them, auditors need to take account of whether:

- the entity is likely to change systems in the near future;
- auditors are likely to be able to use the CAATs developed in subsequent periods;
- it is essential to test controls over processing, or whether it is just as easy or easier to audit around the computer and test controls over inputs and outputs.

CAATs may not be appropriate where there is:

- a low volume of transactions;
- an expectation of poor processing controls;
- a poor relationship with the client.

If there are strong input and output controls, CAATs may not be necessary.

Getting test data (dummy data) into a system is one thing, getting it out again might be quite another and an ***integrated test facility,*** whereby auditors are allocated a ring-fenced section of each of the client's systems to be tested is one way of getting around this problem. It avoids potential corruption or contamination of client data.

There may therefore be a series of accounts set up specifically so that the auditors can post test data to them. The obvious risk is that the systems surrounding and controls over the auditors' allocated space within the system might be different to the controls over the rest of the system.

### Section essentials: what you need to remember

- *The difference between negative and positive confirmations, when to use them, and the advantages and disadvantages of stating the balance.*

- *The major stages in the audit of accounting estimates: they can be used in answers to questions on provisions for depreciation, inventory, receivables and many others.*

- *Procedures before, during and after an inventory count, when auditors have to attend them, why, and the issues involved in perpetual inventory counting systems.*

- *The difference between audit software and test data, what sort of tests they are used for and the conditions needed for them to be used.*

- *Sampling, CAATs and audit confirmations can be brought into answers for many questions, not just questions about those subjects.*

- *Examiners rarely ask students to calculate sample sizes.*

# SECTION 4.4, SHORT-FORM QUESTIONS

SFQ 1: Explain why the audit of inventory is important.                              (3 marks)

SFQ 2: Describe the audit tests you might perform during the audit of
finished goods in an entity that assembles electrical appliances.     (6 marks)

SFQ 3: Describe how auditors should deal with a provision for claims made
under a 1-year manufacturing warranty provided by an entity that
manufactures electrical appliances.                                  (4 marks)

SFQ 4: Describe judgement sampling and statistical sampling.          (3 marks)

SFQ 5: Describe how you would audit a 5-year bank loan.               (4 marks)

SFQ 6: List the substantive procedures you would perform on trade
payables, purchase accruals and expense accruals.                   (5 marks)

Total:                                                               (25 marks)

## 4.5    MORE AUDIT TOOLS: USING THE WORK OF OTHERS

*Covering: Internal Audit and ISA 610 Using the Work of Internal Auditors, ISA 620 Using the Work of an Auditor's Expert, ISA 600 Special Considerations–Audits of Group Financial Statements (Including the Work of Component Auditors), Outsourcing and ISA 402 Audit Considerations Relating to an Entity Using a Service Organization, ISAE 3402 Assurance Reports on Controls at a Service Organization.*

**Why do I need to read this section?**

*Using the work performed by others as audit evidence is an increasing and inescapable part of auditing. Technological developments resulting in ever-increasing specialisation mean that auditors are forced to work with those with expertise outside accounting and auditing. The rise of multinational groups and the use of service organisations mean that auditors have to work with other auditors, often outside their own jurisdiction. Commercial pressures mean that clients want external auditors to take more account of work performed by internal auditors.*

*Some of the issues involved in relying on others are complex, especially in group audits, but there are a few general principles that can be applied whenever auditors need to work with others, whether they be internal auditors, component auditors in group audits, experts or the auditors and management of service organisations. A grasp of these principles will help in answering any question that comes up in this area.*

**What is important in this section?**

*Questions on internal audit often combine elements of how internal audit departments work, and how external auditors can work with them and use the work they have performed. The area has been examined for many years. Auditor reliance on the work of experts has also been examined for many years, for valuations of specialist inventory, property portfolios and other assets and liabilities. Referring to possible reliance on the work of internal audit and/or experts will be relevant to answers to questions in many areas in all but the smallest of audits.*

*The use of third party service organisations for high volume back-office transactions processing is now well established and while it is a relatively new area for examiners it is likely that there will be an increasing number of questions set in this area, particularly in higher-level papers.*

*Group audits tend to be examined in higher-level papers and are often excluded from lower level papers.*

**What sort of questions come up in this area?**

*Questions on external auditor use of internal audit tend to focus on whether it is appropriate to use the work of internal audit and, if it is, to what extent, in what areas and what additional work external auditors need to do on the work of internal audit.*

*With experts, the position is more complicated and questions tend to focus on whether it is possible to use the work already performed by an expert employed by management, and/or whether it is necessary to incur the cost of involving an auditors' expert and, if so, how to go about it.*

*With service organisations, questions revolve around the extent to which the audited entity relies on the organisation in areas that may be material to the financial statements, whether a service auditor routinely provides a report on controls, what type of report is produced, whether it is useful and what additional work auditors need to do beyond obtaining a report.*

*The issues associated with group audits tend to appear within case-study style questions, as parts of larger questions and in multiple choice and short form questions; the same is also true to a lesser extent of service organisations.*

**How do I stand out from the crowd?**

*None of the areas covered in this section are areas that are covered in every auditing paper. Even so, external audit use of internal audit and experts' work is relatively straightforward, examined at all levels and worth the time and effort it takes to understand it. Knowledge of these areas is relevant to many different questions.*

*Where there is a choice of questions, students who choose unpopular questions stand out. While markers do their best to be impartial, there is considerable scope for judgement and for giving or withholding the benefit of the doubt. While markers will attempt to curb their instinct to reward courageous students who attempt unpopular questions disproportionately, there are fewer students to compare the student against which may work in students' favour. So there is an argument for spending some time on the less popular areas, but if a student really knows very little about an unpopular or obscure area, it generally shows and it is probably better to marginally pass a question on depreciation than to marginally fail a question on the use of service organisations.*

### 4.5.1 GENERAL PRINCIPLES APPLYING WHERE AUDITORS SEEK TO USE THE WORK OF OTHERS

1. ISAs require auditors to take responsibility for the whole audit, regardless of who has performed the work. They **do not permit auditors to divide responsibility** with others, even though some jurisdictions such as the USA permit divided responsibility in some circumstances.

2. Where auditors use the work performed by others, whether they be component auditors, service organisation auditors, experts or internal auditors, they

must obtain evidence to satisfy themselves that those whose work is used are *objective or independent* as appropriate, and *competent*. Auditors remain alert during the audit for indications that their initial assessment of objectivity or independence and competence might no longer be appropriate.

3. Where auditors use the work performed by others, they must *perform procedures to satisfy themselves that the work performed is adequate* for the purposes of the audit, they cannot simply accept a report or assertions that the work has been done. This often means that they need to test the work performed, evaluate the context in which it has been performed and understand the bases and assumptions underlying it, to ensure consistency with the auditors' knowledge of the business.

4. Auditors are *not permitted to refer to reliance on the work of others in the audit report*, except where necessary in order to explain a modified audit opinion, even though some jurisdictions permit this. Where references are necessary because of modifications, there should be no inference that responsibility is divided.

Objectivity means not allowing bias, conflict of interest or undue influence of others to override professional or business judgements. Independence is a state of mind unaffected by influences that compromise professional judgement, allowing an individual to exercise objectivity. Maintaining the appearance of independence means avoiding situations in which a reasonable third party would be likely to conclude that the individual lacks objectivity.

Objectivity is a necessary precondition for independence but it is possible to be objective without being independent. Internal auditors, for example, cannot be independent of the entities they audit because they are instructed and paid by those entities, but they can be objective provided that they do not report to the people they audit, i.e. they should report to those charged with governance in addition to or instead of management. Experts employed or engaged by the client may be objective but they are unlikely to be independent, because they are being paid by the entity they report on. If auditors engage the expert, it is more likely that the expert will be independent as well as objective. In group audits, it is essential that component auditors are independent of the entities they audit. Similarly, there is an expectation of independence in auditors of service organisations.

## 4.5.2   INTERNAL AUDIT

Working with internal audit is an important part of large external audits. The scope of internal audit work is now much wider and more sophisticated than it used to be. It is common for internal auditors to be involved in evaluating corporate governance and risk management and to have a rounded view of the business as a whole. External auditors also need a holistic understanding of the business and internal audit can help provide that. Internal audit's detailed work on risk assessments, systems and controls, and substantive testing in the area of financial reporting often overlap with external audit work. Management understandably wants internal and external auditors to work together as much as possible and to avoid unnecessary duplication, particularly when budgets are tight. The requirement for external auditors to be independent gets in the way of this.

Internal audit cannot by definition be independent of the entity. There are always concerns about the threats to independence, i.e. the self-review threat, where external auditors provide internal audit services and where internal audit staff work for external auditors.

Internal auditing is described as:

*. . . an independent, objective assurance and consulting activity designed to add value and improve an organization's operations. It helps an organization accomplish its objectives by bringing a systematic, disciplined approach to evaluate and improve the effectiveness of risk management, control, and governance processes.*[66]

## What do Internal Auditors Do?

Larger entities are more likely to need internal auditors than smaller entities. Internal audit functions are not generally compulsory but there is a strong expectation that listed entities will have them. The UK Corporate Governance Code 2010 for listed entities, for example, requires audit committees to consider whether there is a need for an internal audit function if one does not exist. It also notes the need for explanations in the annual report where there is no internal audit function. The relationship between internal audit and audit committees is dealt with in Section 5.

Internal audit is considered part of an entity's internal control system, often part of monitoring of controls. This is critically important in regimes in which management and external auditors are required to report on the effectiveness of internal financial controls, such as under S404 of the Sarbanes-Oxley Act 2002 in the USA.

Internal audit activities are still often described as including:

- *monitoring internal control:* reviewing controls, monitoring their operation and recommending improvements;

- *examining financial and operating information:* reviewing the process for producing financial and operating information, performing tests of control effectiveness and detailed testing of transactions, balances and procedures;

- *reviewing the economy, efficiency and effectiveness of* operating activities including non-financial activities, i.e. value for money audits;

- *reviewing compliance* with laws, regulations and management policies.

ISA 610 on internal audit expresses internal audit's role as follows:

> *Internal audit provides **assurance and consulting activities** to management and those charged with governance **designed to evaluate and improve the effectiveness of the entity's governance, risk management, internal control processes.***[67]

---

[66] *The Professional Practices Framework, The IIA Research Foundation, January 2004. In the UK, the Chartered Institute of Internal Auditors is a member of the IIA.*

[67] ISA 610 on internal audit, definitions.

Assessment of **governance processes** may involve establishing whether the entity has achieved its objectives on ethics, values, performance management and accountability.

Assessment of activities relating to **risk management** may involve identifying and evaluating significant risk exposures and improving risk management and internal control.

Assessment of **internal control** activities may involve testing and providing assurance on the design, implementation and operating effectiveness of internal control and examining financial and operating information. These are similar to external audit activities. Reviews of economy, efficiency and effectiveness and of compliance with laws and regulations are also included.

Some internal audit departments focus on value for money audits that provide assurance on the economy, efficiency and effectiveness of operations. This is not generally relevant to external audit.

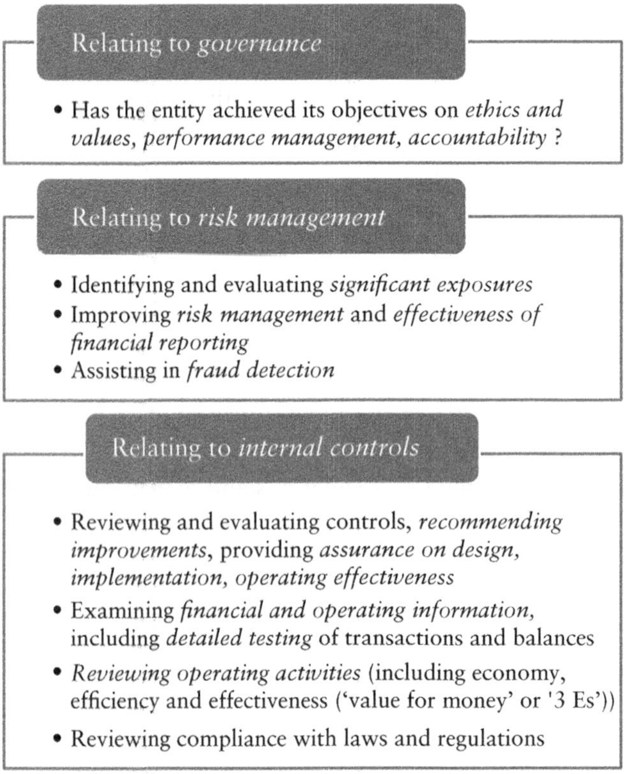

Relating to *governance*

- Has the entity achieved its objectives on *ethics and values, performance management, accountability* ?

Relating to *risk management*

- Identifying and evaluating *significant exposures*
- Improving *risk management* and *effectiveness of financial reporting*
- Assisting in *fraud detection*

Relating to *internal controls*

- Reviewing and evaluating controls, *recommending improvements*, providing *assurance on design, implementation, operating effectiveness*
- Examining *financial and operating information*, including *detailed testing* of transactions and balances
- *Reviewing operating activities* (including economy, efficiency and effectiveness ('value for money' or '3 Es'))
- Reviewing compliance with laws and regulations

**Figure 4.22**   Internal audit activities

In practice, the effectiveness of internal audit depends largely on whether it is adequately resourced and structured. It should have a direct reporting line to those charged with governance as well as to management. If internal audit is to be effective:

- it should not report on its own work, i.e. while it may make recommendations for improvements to internal control, it should not decide on what improvements to make, and it should not make the improvements;

- its work should be reviewed by, and it should ultimately report to, those independent of the functions being examined, such as an audit committee;

- the head of internal audit should have sufficiently senior status within the entity and be appointed on the recommendation of the audit committee;

- its staff should have a proper balance of skills, experience and qualifications and be rotated periodically.

### Ad hoc internal audit assignments

Ad hoc internal audit assignments include the following list, which is growing:

- *Value for money* audits evaluate the three 'E's, economy, efficiency and effectiveness of an entity, function or department. Economy involves balancing quality of resources with their cost, efficiency covers obtaining the best outputs using those resources, and effectiveness covers the extent to which objectives are achieved.

Table 4.5   Differences between internal and external auditors

|  | *External Audit* | *Internal Audit* |
|---|---|---|
| Purpose | To provide reasonable assurance on the financial statements | Part of the internal control system – monitoring of controls |
| Report to | Shareholders (sometimes directors) | The audit committee or other non-executive directors charged with governance, as well as or instead of management |
| Appointed by | Shareholders, on the recommendation of directors, as advised by any audit committee | Directors, as advised by any audit committee |
| Objective | To give an independent opinion on the true and fair/fair presentation of the financial statements | To evaluate and report on internal control, risk assessment and governance processes and make recommendations for improvement |
| Independence and objectivity | Must be independent and objective | Must be as objective as possible, not reporting on or determining the scope of their own work, or to those responsible for the work scrutinised |
| Scope of work | Determined by legislation, regulation and ISAs | Determined by the audit committee, others charged with governance and management |

Value for money exercises are often performed in the public sector on corporate services such as IT procurement, out-sourced services such as refuse collection and road maintenance, and social services. Benchmarks for economy might be the cost per hour of care workers or the rent per square metre of social housing. Efficiency might be measured by the number of people visited per care worker and effectiveness might be measured quantitatively by the reduction in the number of people requiring residential care, or qualitatively by measuring satisfaction levels within a community about refuse collection.

- *Best value* audits are broader than value for money audits and are also performed in the public sector. Best value performance indicators look at *strategic objectives*, such as efficient IT services, *service delivery outcomes*, such as response times at call centres, the *quality* of services delivered, such as error rates in invoicing and fair access to services, across different regions, for example.

- *IT audits* might involve assurance on whether IT services provide value for money, whether a procurement process is effective, and maintenance standards.

- *Procurement and supply chain audits* and internal and external assurance on them are increasingly important in the context of corporate social responsibility. They have always been essential in industries such as aircraft manufacture and defence.

- *Financial audits* might cover the effectiveness of processes for producing management information, budgets, interim information and prospective financial information. *Operational audits* cover a wide area of operations including treasury and credit management.

*Assignment processes*
All audit and assurance processes follow broadly the same approach. *Terms of reference* for the assignment help maintain focus and prevent misunderstandings. The *objectives* of the entity, department or function and of the audit need to be clear so that *risk assessments* can be performed, analysing the threats to the achievement of both.

In a supply chain audit, the objective might be for auditors to provide assurance that the entity's supply chain requirements, such as those relating to labour practices and waste disposal, are met by major suppliers. The risk assessment would evaluate the risk that the entity's requirements were not being met, which might be higher for suppliers a long way away from the entity, or in jurisdictions with no local legislation covering such matters or with a history of disregard for them. The controls exercised by the entity over the supplier, the quality and frequency of inspections of supplier facilities and the quality of documentation would affect the risk assessment. The assessment would also account for the risk that the internal auditor's procedures fail to detect non-compliance with the requirements.

*Evidence-gathering* might involve tests of relevant controls and substantive procedures, perhaps by means of re-performance of control visits, by reviews of inspectors' reports and by reviews of other required documentation.

*Internal audit reports*

Internal audit reports can be formal or informal and structured as presentations, memoranda, formal reports or all three. Formal reports are likely to contain:

- a cover sheet;

- an executive summary;

- recommendations and agreed actions;

- key findings;

- appendices, including objectives, terms of reference, methods used, detailed findings and a list of persons conducting the audit.

## Can External Auditors Use Internal Audit Work?

Formally, internal audit is an element of monitoring of controls. The risk ISAs require auditors to include in their risk assessment *inquiries of appropriate individuals within internal audit* and to obtain an understanding of internal audit's responsibilities, its organisational status and its work.[68] This is *regardless of whether auditors expect to be able to use internal audit's work*. It is important to recognise that auditors cannot simply decide to disregard the requirement to make inquiries on the basis that they think it unlikely that internal audit work will be relevant. Making the inquiry is required in order to understand the business. Auditors cannot assume that they understand the business without making the inquiry!

Inquiries of persons within the risk management function may be relevant. Reading internal audit's terms of reference, strategy and planning documents may help and establishing how management deal with internal audit recommendations often provide a good indication of the strength of the function. Establishing links with appropriate individuals within internal audit early in the engagement creates the right environment for internal audit to be able to help external auditors assess risk and respond to it.

External auditors look to establish whether the internal audit function:

- is structured organisationally to support *objectivity and competence* in its staff;

- applies a *systematic and disciplined* approach as evidenced by the use of proper audit plans and manuals, risk assessments, work programmes, documentation, reporting protocols, quality control procedures and the use of standards set by professional bodies such as the Institute of Internal Auditors (IIA).

These are the necessary preconditions to the use of internal audit by external auditors. If they are not present, the work cannot be used.

The main risk for internal audit functions is that they lack objectivity, because they report on and to the same people. If an internal auditor prepares a report on the

---

[68] ISA 315 on risk assessment, paragraphs 6 and 23.

receivables system which is the ultimate responsibility of the finance director, and internal auditors are hired, trained and promoted by staff who report to the finance director, it is likely that internal auditors will be less critical than they might be were they to report their findings elsewhere. It is therefore important that internal auditors have a reporting line to those who are not responsible for areas it reports on, usually those charged with governance, such as an audit committee.

It is likely that external auditors will seek to use its work if the internal audit function:

- reports to, or at least has unhindered access to, those charged with governance;
- is not constrained in the scope of its work;
- recruits and trains its staff properly with the oversight of those charged with governance;
- has proper operational processes, such as a plan of work and an up-to-date audit manual;
- employs members of professional bodies obliged to uphold standards of objectivity;
- maintains internal policies that uphold standards of objectivity.

*Usage of internal audit work does not reduce the external auditors' responsibility for the audit.*

*External auditors must make all significant judgements in the audit and less use will be made of internal audit work if:*

- there is a high the *risk of misstatement*, especially for *significant risks;*
- more *judgement* is required;
- the function's organisational status and policies and procedures do not support *objectivity*;
- the function is not *competent*.

Competence may be compromised where the internal audit function is not adequately resourced, where there are no established policies for recruitment and training, and where staff are not members of professional bodies that oblige them to comply with standards requiring them to keep up to date.

External auditors need to communicate the planned usage of internal audit work to those charged with governance.

### Evaluating Internal Audit's Work

Having decided to use internal audit's work, external auditors perform very similar procedures on that work to those they would in reviewing the work of their own staff.

Table 4.6   Internal audit work that may and may not be used by external auditors

| *Internal audit work that MAY be used by external auditors* | *Internal audit work that MAY NOT be used by external auditors* |
|---|---|
| Tests of control effectiveness | Assessing the risk of material misstatement |
| Substantive procedures involving limited judgement | Evaluating the sufficiency of audit work |
| Observing inventory counts | Evaluating the appropriateness of management's use of the going concern assumption |
| Audits and reviews of components that are not significant in a group audit | Evaluating significant accounting estimates |
| | Extensively, in relation to risks assessed as significant |

External auditors are required to:

- *read internal audit reports* in relevant areas;
- *perform sufficient audit procedures on the body of internal audit work* as a whole, sufficient to evaluate its adequacy in the areas used.[69]

This includes evaluating whether the work has been properly planned, performed, reviewed and documented, whether sufficient evidence has been obtained and whether conclusions are reasonable in the circumstances. What is 'sufficient' depends on the extent of intended use of internal audit work, the level of judgement involved and the degree of competence and objectivity of the function but it *must include re-performance of some of internal audit's work*.[70] Re-performance does not need to cover all areas but it does need to cover items actually examined by internal audit and, if this is not possible, a sufficient number of similar items.

If internal auditors have examined controls over transactions in a real-time ticketing system in which there is little or no source documentation by using CAATs, external auditors may need to use the same CAATs or similar CAATs to establish whether the system did actually perform as expected. Re-performance is likely to focus on areas that involve high levels of judgement or audit risk, such as inventory rather than cash.

### Direct Assistance

> Where internal auditors perform external audit procedures under the direct supervision of external auditors they are providing *direct assistance*.

It seems self-evident to some audit clients that from a commercial viewpoint, internal audit staff, particularly junior internal audit staff, can and should, 'go and work for the

---

[69] ISA 610 on internal audit, paragraphs 20 and 21.
[70] ISA 610 on internal audit, paragraph 22.

external auditors' while the external audit is being performed. The external auditor is short of time and using under-utilised internal audit staff should be cheaper than using the audit firm's staff. On the other hand, it is equally self-evident that there is a very real risk that such situations are very likely to end in entities effectively auditing themselves. In some jurisdictions, direct assistance is prohibited. There are significant restrictions on situations in which internal auditors are permitted to provide direct assistance to external auditors.

---

*It is important to distinguish as clearly as possible between:*

- direct assistance; and

- the more normal circumstances in which external auditors use work performed by internal auditors who are not answerable to, and do not report to external auditors and whose work plan is developed independently of external auditors.

---

### How much direct assistance can be provided, and in what areas?

As always, direct assistance does not reduce the external auditors' responsibility for the audit and external auditors cannot delegate the entire audit to internal audit whether by direct assistance or otherwise. The nature and extent of work performed by 'direct assistants' depend on judgement, risk and the significance of any threats to the assistants' objectivity. Circumstances that would prevent external auditors using the work of internal audit generally are similar to those that prevent internal auditors providing direct assistance to external auditors. Direct assistance is not provided where:

- there are *significant threats to the objectivity or competence* of internal auditors;

- the relevant audit area involves *significant judgement* or a *higher risk* of material misstatement, or involves a discussion of fraud risks;

- internal auditors have been *involved in the department audited* for which they are providing direct assistance;

- the issue is the *evaluation of the internal audit function* or *decisions to use the work of internal audit,* which would amount to the function evaluating its own independence and competence and making the decision to use itself!

Inquiries of internal auditors providing direct assistance about fraud risks might be acceptable, but discussions would not. Similarly, while internal auditors might help with assembling information about confirmation requests, external auditors need to control them. Checking the accuracy of the ageing of receivables would be acceptable if performed by those providing direct assistance, evaluating a provision would not.

This is all in contrast to the more normal situation in which internal auditors are not providing direct assistance, but external auditors are instead seeking to rely on their work, in which case discussions with and evaluations performed by internal auditors are relevant to the external audit. In practice, external auditors may seek to use the work of internal auditors for, say, the audit of receivables by, say, discussions with senior internal auditors about the associated risks and at the same time use more junior internal audit staff to provide direct assistance in the audit of payables.

In practice, the dividing line between the two types of co-operation with internal auditors is not as clear as it might be, particularly given the extent to which internal auditors sometimes modify their independent work plans to accommodate the desires of external auditors.

Those charged with governance need to be satisfied that the nature and extent of the *planned direct assistance are not excessive* in the circumstances.

Where direct assistance is planned, external auditors need to obtain *written agreement* that internal auditors will *follow external auditor instructions without interference*, and that they will *keep information confidential* and inform the external auditor about any threats to their objectivity.

Documentation is required for all key areas: internal audit's competence and objectivity, the basis for the decision to use of direct assistance, who reviewed the work, the written agreement authorising the use of internal auditors, and the working papers prepared by the internal auditor.

### Direction, supervision and review of internal auditors providing direct assistance

The nature and extent of direction, supervision and review depend on the levels of risk and judgement associated with the work performed. They depend in particular on the external auditors' evaluation of the internal auditors' objectivity.

Threats to objectivity might include internal auditors being accountable to the people they audit, i.e. management rather than those charged with governance, and any family or personal relationships, or any association with the entities, departments or functions they are likely to be working on.

The higher the risk, the more judgement involved and the greater the threats to objectivity, the more detailed are the direction, supervision and review. Procedures might include external auditors checking back to the underlying audit evidence for some of the work performed by internal auditors, i.e. re-performing some of their work.

As always, external auditors must remain alert for evidence that their initial evaluation of the competence and objectivity of internal auditors is not appropriate.

### May External Auditors Provide Internal Audit Services to Audit Clients?

The issue is not straightforward. The idea is attractive because the synergies can result in reduced overall audit fees, but the threat that auditors will take on management responsibilities and the self-review threat to independence are obvious. Internal audit is an internal control and it can easily appear as if auditors are auditing their own work, even if they are not in fact doing so, either because the service is provided in an operational area unrelated to the financial statement audit, or because those providing the service are entirely independent of those performing the audit.

**Similarities: less use of internal audit where**

- more judgement
- higher risk
- less competence
- less objectivity

**Similarities: level of use and reliance**

- where using internal audit work, external auditor must be sufficiently involved; for direct assistance, use must not be excessive
- use communicated to those charged with governance

**Similarities: external auditors remain alert for**

- evidence that their initial evaluation of the competence and objectivity of internal auditors is not appropriate

**Differences**

- *using* internal audit work: internal audit plans its own work and does not answer or report to external audit
- *direct assistance:* internal audit staff 'loaned to' or 'go to work for' external auditors

**Figure 4.23**    Similarities and differences: use of internal audit work and direct assistance

Similar problems arise where auditors, or firms associated with auditors, provide IT services to audit clients. In some jurisdictions, such as the USA, both are effectively prohibited.

IESBA's *Code* notes the self-review threat to the independence of external auditors who provide internal audit services to audit clients.[71] Safeguards can reduce this threat to an acceptable level. The risk that the auditors take on management responsibilities cannot be 'reduced to an acceptable level' and as such any internal audit services provided by external auditors must be of a technical rather than an executive nature.

External auditors *may not provide the following services* to audit clients:

- setting internal audit *strategy* or policies;
- taking *responsibility* for internal control or for the actions of internal audit employees;

---

[71] S290.195–200.

- deciding *which recommendations* made by internal audit *to implement*;

- *reporting the results* of internal audit activities to those charged with governance;

- *performing control procedures* such as approving changes to staff data access privileges;

- for *public interest clients*, services covering a significant part of *internal control over financial reporting*, systems that generate information that is *significant to the financial statements* or amounts or disclosures that are *material*.

External auditors *may provide internal audit services to audit clients where*:

- the client designates an appropriately *senior member of management* to be responsible for internal audit and acknowledges responsibility for internal control;

- management or those charged with governance *approve the scope* of internal audit services, evaluate its adequacy and determine which recommendations to implement;

- *management report* significant internal audit findings and recommendations to those charged with governance.

The significance of the self-review threat depends on factors such as materiality and the risk of misstatement in the relevant financial statement area. If the areas in which external auditors provide internal audit services are insignificant to the financial statements, or low risk, or if the external audit evidence does not involve using internal audit work, the threat is lower. Obvious safeguards include using staff who are not members of the audit team to perform the internal audit service.

IESBA's *Code* also deals with *IT Systems Services*.[72] These include the design or implementation of hardware or software and may or may not have an effect on financial reporting. As with internal audit services, providing systems services may create a self-review threat. Unlike internal audit, though, these provisions have implications for smaller firms helping their clients with accounting packages.

The following IT systems services *do not to create a threat to independence*:

- design or implementation of IT systems unrelated or insignificant to financial reporting;

- implementation of off-the-shelf accounting or software packages if customisation is not significant;

- making recommendations for systems developed or operated by the client or third parties.

---

[72] S290.201–206.

For *public interest clients*, as with internal audit services, external auditors may not design or implement IT systems that form a significant part of the internal control over financial reporting or generate information that is significant to the financial statements.

There is a self-review threat where external auditors provide similar services to non-public interest clients. In such cases, necessary safeguards involve the client acknowledging full responsibility for internal control and decisions regarding the system, evaluating its adequacy and operating it afterwards. Again, using staff who are not members of the audit team is another obvious safeguard.

### 4.5.3   EXPERTS

With internal audit, external auditors increasingly seek to use the work of internal audit in appropriate circumstances, because it is efficient. With experts, external auditors seek not to use them, unless necessary, because they are expensive if engaged or employed by the firm, and they may lack objectivity if engaged or employed by the client.

Experts are not used for accounting or auditing matters. They are only used in areas that are likely to be material and involve technically complex issues that are outside the expertise of most auditors, such as valuations of:

- oil, gas and mineral reserves, precious metals, antiques, or works of art;
- intangible assets such as brands;
- liabilities for environmental clean-up costs;
- actuarial liabilities associated with retirement benefit plans;
- the interpretation of contracts, laws and regulations.

It is no longer acceptable (if it ever was) for auditors to simply use the bottom line figure provided in the expert's report, without any critical assessment. Auditors are required to obtain some understanding of the relevant field of expertise and to evaluate the adequacy of the expert's work. As always:

> *The auditor has sole responsibility for the audit opinion expressed and that responsibility is not reduced by the auditor's use of the work of an auditor's expert.*
>
> ISA 620 *Using the Work of an Auditor's Expert* paragraph 3

The lines dividing accounting, auditing and other skills are not always clear. A taxation lawyer is likely to be an expert for audit purposes because taxation law is not a mainstream accounting or auditing skill, a deferred tax specialist is not, because deferred tax is an accounting skill, even if both are employed by the audit firm.

Problems are compounded in areas such as complex financial instruments where a very small group of people is skilled in the accounting requirements for and the valuation and use of financial instruments.

*Auditors need to determine whether an expert's work is needed and, if so, to determine whether the expert's work is adequate for the purposes of the audit.*[73]

Experts can be individuals or organisations. They may not be needed if auditors have experience in auditing the relevant area and/or can obtain sufficient understanding of it by discussions with other auditors who have performed similar audits. Experts can be used at all stages of the audit.

### Should Auditors Use an Expert?

Among other things, the decision to use an expert depends on:

* the *risk of misstatement* in the area of expertise;
* the auditors' *knowledge of the area;*
* the auditors' *previous experience* of the expert;
* whether the expert is an *internal expert*, i.e. employed by the firm and therefore bound by the firm's or network firm's quality control requirements, or an *external expert* and not so bound;[74]
* whether the expert has the necessary *competence*, i.e. technical expertise, and *capabilities*, i.e. resources and *objectivity*.

Cost is also a factor but it cannot be the deciding factor.

Auditors need to determine what work the expert is to perform and evaluate its adequacy when it is finished. *For auditors' experts, agreement of terms is needed* which should be in writing where appropriate and cover the nature, scope and objectives of the work, the roles and responsibilities of auditors and the expert, the need for confidentiality, and the form of report and any other communications between the expert and auditors. If there is no engagement letter or other written agreement, which is more likely when an internal expert is used, the planning documentation and audit firm policies need to cover the area.

### *Is the expert competent and objective?*
Auditors are required to make inquiries about interests and relationships that may threaten the expert's objectivity. They cannot simply rely on an expert's reputation, qualifications or marketing material. Auditors should inquire about any financial, business and personal relationships and the extent of any other services provided by the expert to the client.

Any experience of working with the expert is relevant, as are the expert's qualifications, specialisations, knowledge of relevant accounting requirements, membership of professional bodies and any publications.

---

[73] ISA 620 on experts, paragraph 5.
[74] Some jurisdictions treat all auditor experts as members of the engagement team and bound by quality control requirements.

### Understanding the expert's field of expertise

Auditors are required to understand the data, assumptions, methods and models used by the expert and the existence of any professional standards or legal requirements in the area. Assumptions about a pension fund, for example, might be actuarial assumptions about the length of life of employees, often determined by government, associations of actuaries or pension fund regulators. Sometimes assumptions are determined by common industry accounting practices, such as assumptions about the length of life of mineral reserves.

The auditors' own experience, training, and discussions with other auditors and the expert are all relevant.

### Is the Expert's Work Adequate?

Auditor evaluation is required of:

- the *reasonableness and relevance* of the expert's overall findings and significant assumptions and methods;
- the *consistency* of the expert's work with other audit evidence.

This can be difficult. Specific procedures may include discussions with the expert, a review of their working papers, observing their work, performing analytical procedures and re-performing calculations. Sometimes it will be important for auditors to develop their own point estimates. Assumptions made need to be generally accepted within the field, consistent with accounting requirements and with management assumptions in the same area, on the length of asset lives, for example. Auditors also verify the origin of the data used, and test controls over it.

If the expert's work is not adequate, auditors need to agree on additional work. That might involve the engagement of another expert, which would be expensive.

> ### Reporting
>
> *The auditor shall not refer to the work of an auditor's expert in an auditors' report containing an unmodified opinion unless required by law or regulation to do so.*
>
> ISA 620 *Using the Work of an Auditor's Expert* paragraph 14

The explanation of a modified opinion may of necessity require some reference to the expert where, for example, there is a modification, because the expert's work is inadequate. Reference to the use of the work of experts is required in some jurisdictions. When any such reference is made, auditors must indicate in the report that they have sole responsibility for the opinion, despite the reference to the expert.

### Management's Expert

Generally, where management employs or engages an expert to perform a valuation, auditors will seek to use the work already performed, despite the lack of independence and objectivity compared to an auditors' expert. Nevertheless, if there is a history of incompetence, if the relevant valuation is pervasive to the financial statements, or if the expert has a significant role in the preparation of the financial statements, for example, auditors may seek to use their own expert anyway.

Almost by definition, the use of an expert by management increases audit risk because of the technical complexity that gives rise to the need for an expert. In some cases, it may be necessary for auditors to employ their own expert to help them understand the field of expertise, or to assess the work performed by management's expert.

The resources made available to management's expert and any restriction on their work is relevant but, for most purposes, the criteria used by auditors in determining whether to use management's expert's work are very similar to those applied to an expert engaged by auditors.

---

### Checklist for Experts

- Are they *needed*? Can auditors obtain sufficient understanding of the area without help? Does management employ or engage an expert?

- Is the expert, management's or auditors', *competent, capable and objective*?

- Set out *scope* of their work in writing.

- Obtain an *understanding* of their field of expertise.

- *Evaluate* their work: is it consistent with other audit evidence? Are significant assumptions and methods relevant and reasonable? Is the source data used relevant, complete and accurate?

- If the work is inadequate, agree further work, perform other procedures or employ another expert.

- Reporting: *do not refer to the expert* unless the report is modified, and indicate that this does not diminish the auditors' responsibility for the report.

---

### 4.5.4   OUTSOURCING AND SERVICE ORGANISATIONS

#### Outsourcing

*Outsourcing* is contracting out business functions to third party service providers and has become increasingly common. Outsourcing may be to an overseas organisation, in which case it is also *off-shoring*.

*In-sourcing* is bringing business functions back in-house, which may involve *on-shoring* the function if previously outsourced off-shore, but outsourcing and in-sourcing need not involve any overseas organisations.

All of these terms should be distinguished from *shared service centres* in which different parts of an organisation, or members of a group, are provided with services such as

IT, marketing or event management, i.e. common services that were previously 'dupli-cated' within an organisation or across a group. The main advantage of shared service centres is economies of scale. The main disadvantages are the loss of control, detailed understanding of the business and quality of service, at least to begin with. Similar issues arise when outsourcing is considered.

### What can be outsourced?

Service organisations now provide a very wide variety of services to organisations of all sizes. They had their origins in computer bureaux that were used to process payroll transactions but the development of secure electronic communications, data processing and software expertise means that large parts of the finance function, among others, are now transferred to service centres within organisations, or outsourced. Third party service organisations now often provide:

- high-volume back-office transactions processing;

- transaction initiation and maintenance of accounting records;

- asset management in financial services or for fleet or property management;

- tax returns and financial statements for smaller entities.

### Benefits of outsourcing

Benefits of outsourcing include:

- cost savings, cash flow improvement, avoidance of waste;

- reduction in operational redundancy where business volumes are seasonal;

- the technical expertise of the service organisation;

- freeing up resources to concentrate on the core business;

- keeping the business agile and responsive to external developments;

- not having to keep up to date with developments in legislation and technology;

- reducing and transferring the risk of error and fraud to the service organisation.

### Drawbacks of outsourcing

Expecting to eliminate drawbacks simply by outsourcing them is often wrong and out-sourcing creates its own problems. Drawbacks of outsourcing include:

- unpopularity with customers;

- costs savings may not be achieved or cannot be measured;

- loss of quality of service leading to staff morale problems;

- potential conflict with the service provider taking up management time;

- the need for new systems or procedures to conform with service organisation requirements.

*Outsourcing internal audit*

All of the benefits and drawbacks of outsourcing noted above apply to outsourcing internal audit.

Cost control, keeping up with current developments in audit methodology and enhanced independence are all important factors in the decision to outsource internal audit. Outsourcing internal audit is increasingly common but there are important ethical and reputational issues to deal with when considering outsourcing internal audit services to external auditors. As with all outsourcing, it needs proper management if its benefits are to be realised.

Outsourcing does not of itself eliminate the problems that internal auditors have highlighted and entities should avoid outsourcing as a means of 'shooting the messenger', particularly when a high proportion of internal audit staff go to work for the outsourcing organisation, which sometimes happens. Where it does not, problems may arise from unfamiliarity with the business.

As with external audit, the fact that the organisation providing internal audit services can be replaced and is being paid means that there is a risk that it will produce reports that management or those charged with governance want to hear. Long-standing internal auditors employed by the entity and who are secure in their positions may be *more* independent in such circumstances.

## Service Organisations

The following broad categories of functions are commonly outsourced:

- data processing and IT;
- finance and asset management;
- internal audit;
- pensions and benefits.

The issue for auditors is the need to understand the significance of the service organisation to the audited entity, and to obtain evidence by testing controls and performing substantive procedures at an organisation with which auditors have no relationship.

*Communication between auditors and service organisations including their management and their auditors must be authorised by the client and management of the service organisation.*

A service organisation sometimes uses a sub-service organisation, which further complicates the issue for auditors.

## Understanding the Services Provided and Responding to Assessed Risks

*Obtaining an understanding*

Auditors are required to obtain a thorough understanding of the services provided by the service organisation and of how the entity manages the relationship.

As much evidence as possible is gathered from controls operated by the client over the movement of data and information to and from the service organisation, known as *complementary user entity controls*. This minimises the need for direct involvement with the third party service organisation and substantive procedures.

Obtaining an understanding involves considering, among other things:

• the nature of the *services provided* and the extent of user entity controls;

• the *materiality* of the transactions processed;

• the *significance* of the *financial reporting processes* affected;

• the *interaction* between the service organisation and the entity, and contract terms.

The greater the level of interaction between the service organisation and the client, the more likely it is that the client will be able to exercise control over the service organisation.

Many organisations still use service organisations to process payroll transactions. If such an entity compares the data sent to the information returned, performs sample re-calculations to ensure that individual deductions are correct, reviews the information overall and regularly calculates a proof in total or performs other analytical procedures, auditors will seek to test such controls and to avoid the need for testing controls at the service organisation.

Where there is relatively little interaction there will be fewer controls for auditors to test and auditors will need to deal with controls at the service organisation. If a service organisation initiates individual transactions, such as purchase invoices from despatch documentation without specific authorisation from the client beforehand, and subject only to a review afterwards, auditors are much more likely to need to understand and test controls at the service organisation, rather than at the client.

---

Auditors *obtain an understanding of an entity's use of a service organisation* including how the transactions processed are controlled by reviewing manuals, systems notes and contracts and by discussions with the client.

Only where the *evidence available from the user entity is insufficient as a basis for risk assessment* should auditors either:

• *obtain a type 1 or type 2 report* from a service auditor, either the service organisation's own auditor or another auditor; or

• *visit the service organisation* to obtain the information; or

• *use another auditor* to obtain the information.

Auditors need *permission* from the client and the service organisation for any communications to take place.

*Type 1 and type 2 service auditor reports*

*Type 1*
Type 1 reports are reports on the description by management of the service organisation of the design of controls. The description covers the system, control objectives and controls that have been designed and implemented at a specific date. The service auditor's opinion states that:

- management's description *fairly presents* the system as *designed and implemented* at a given date;

- *controls* as described were *suitably designed*.

Type 1 reports are only used *to obtain an understanding* of the service organisation.

*Type 2*
Type 2 reports are as for Type 1 reports but management's description may cover a period rather than being at a specific date and the operating effectiveness of controls for that period. The service auditor's report is as for type 1 reports and:

- *covers a period* rather than a specific date;

- covers the *operating effectiveness* of controls;

- includes a *description of the tests of controls* performed and *results*.

Type 2 reports are used to *obtain an understanding and respond to assessed risks*.

Where an entire finance function or a large part of it is outsourced, a service auditor's report may not be available and it may be necessary to visit the organisation.

*Responding to assessed risks*
Auditors firstly determine whether adequate audit evidence is likely to be available from the records held at the client. If not, they either perform tests at the service organisation, or have another auditor do so, which might include obtaining a type 2 report if the risk assessment includes an expectation that controls are operating effectively.

If auditors perform tests at the service organisation, the types of tests of controls and substantive procedures they perform are very similar to those that they would perform at the entity were the records kept and controls implemented there. Generally, there is a balance to strike between examining records held by the entity and records held by the service organisation.

**Using a Service Auditor's Report: Obtaining an Understanding and Responding to Assessed Risks**

As always when using the work of others, auditors cannot simply rely on the service auditor's report but must assess the quality of evidence it provides. This depends on:

- the *service auditors' independence and competence* and whether they belong to a professional organisation and have used recognised standards, such as ISAE 3402 *Assurance Reports on Controls at a Service Organisation*;

- the *standards used* in preparing the report;

- whether the service organisation's report refers in the description to *complementary user entity controls*, and if it does, whether they are actually implemented at the client;

- the *date of the report or the period covered:* the service auditor's report may be prepared for a number of different users and for a period that does not correspond to the client's accounting period. The larger the gap, the greater the additional audit evidence required to cover the intervening period. The factors to consider here are similar to the factors considered when there is a gap between the period-end and physical inventory counting, including the strength of the control environment. If the period is relatively short and there is nothing to suggest that there has been a significant change in systems, it may be possible to rely on analytical procedures, for example;

- in the case of *type 2 reports*, evaluating whether the tests of control effectiveness and results described in the service auditor's report are *relevant* to the client's audit;

- in the case of *type 2 reports*, evaluating the significance of 'exceptions' to the application of control procedures identified in the description of tests of controls and results thereof, or of a modified service auditors' opinion; neither *exceptions* nor a *modified opinion* mean that the report is not useful.

Where a service organisation uses a sub-service organisation, the service auditor's report may 'carve out' any responsibility in that area. In such cases auditors must consider whether the work of the sub-service organisation is of sufficient significance to the audit to warrant further work.

### Making Reference to the Service Auditor

> *The user auditor shall not refer to the work of a service auditor in the user auditor's report containing an unmodified opinion unless required by law or regulation to do so.*
>
> **ISA 402** *Audit Considerations Relating to an Entity Using a Service Organisation* **paragraph 21**

As always, there is no reference to the use of the service auditor's work in the auditors' report unless reference is necessary in explaining a modification. Modifications arise where auditors are unable to obtain sufficient appropriate audit evidence from the service organisation, for example. The report should indicate that the reference does not diminish the auditors' responsibility for the opinion.

### 4.5.5   GROUPS

#### Group, Parent Entity and Component Audits

A *group audit* is usually the audit of a set of consolidated *group financial statements.*

Group audits are performed in addition to the audit of any individual *parent* (holding) entity financial statements and individual *component* entity financial statements.

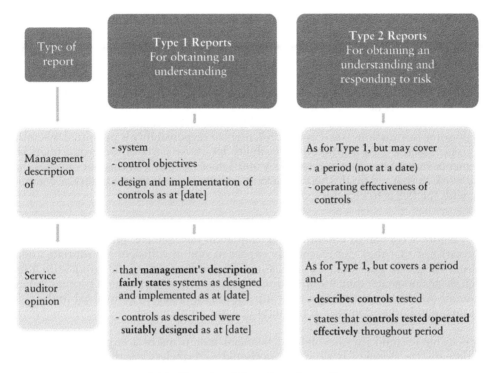

**Figure 4.24** Type 1 and Type 2 service auditor reports

Applicable accounting requirements determine what constitutes a group, a component and the requirement to prepare group accounts. Components usually include subsidiaries, associates and joint ventures.

The main audit issues with group audits are:

- the *responsibility* for the group audit and understanding the group;
- *risk assessment*;
- determining which components are *significant,* which are *non-significant*;
- determining the *work to be performed on components* for group audit purposes;
- *evaluating* and *working with component auditors*;
- the audit of the *consolidation process*.

### Responsibility

Where the group auditor is also auditor of all of the components, many of the difficulties associated with group audits are avoided. It is common, though, for components to be audited by many different firms for historical, legal, commercial and ethical reasons. These include requirements in some jurisdictions that local firms are appointed. In others, group auditors are not appointed to audit components because they already act for competitors. Often, other firms simply have more expertise locally than the group auditor.

In all cases, however, the ***group auditor takes responsibility for the group audit,*** regardless of who actually does the work. This means that no reference is made to the use of the work of component auditors in the audit report unless required by law or regulation. In some jurisdictions, such as the USA, divided responsibility is permitted whereby the group auditor does not take responsibility for those parts of the group financial statements audited by other auditors. ISA 600[75] does not prohibit this but requires the same work as that required where the group auditor has sole responsibility, if compliance with the ISA is to be achieved.

While ***there is no minimum proportion of the group that the group auditor must audit,*** before accepting or continuing a group audit engagement, group auditors need to be satisfied that they can reasonably expect to obtain sufficient appropriate audit evidence for group audit purposes. This includes ***understanding the group structure,*** which means understanding group-wide controls and the consolidation process. A key feature of ISA 600 is that it requires group auditors to be actively involved in the risk assessment and other elements of the audit of some components.

It is possible to audit the consolidated financial statements of a large group without auditing any components at all. Auditors should nevertheless ask themselves whether they want to do so, and if it is right to do so given their level of involvement. The answer may well be 'no' and regulators, and some investors, may take a dim view of some such arrangements.

### Significant and Non-significant Components

All components are either significant or non-significant. This is an audit judgement. Significant components may be significant because of their size, or because of the specific risks to which they are exposed.

---

Work on components is required as follows:

- *Individually financially significant components require an audit using component materiality;*
- components that are significant because of associated risks require an audit, review, or specific audit procedures to address risks;
- *non-significant components require analytical procedures;*
- *selected non-significant components also require audit, review or specific audit procedures where analytical procedures at group level, work on significant components and testing of group-wide controls do not provide sufficient evidence.*

---

[75] ISA 600 on group audits

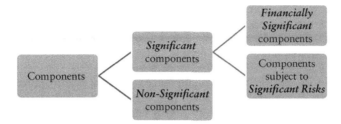

**Figure 4.25**   Components

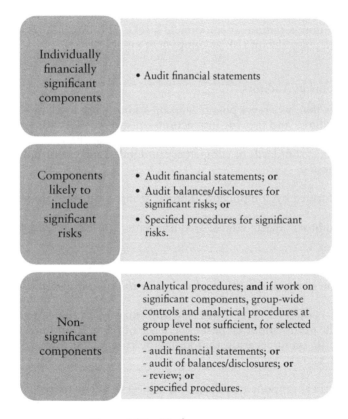

**Figure 4.26**   Work on components

*Materiality*

Calculations are required for ***group level materiality*** and materiality for specific trans-actions, balances and disclosures.

***Component materiality*** also needs to be calculated where components are subject to audit or review. For group purposes, component materiality is effectively performance materiality in as far as it deals with the possibility that undetected and uncorrected misstatements will, in aggregate, exceed group materiality. Performance materiality needs to be smaller than group materiality. This means that a large number of insignificant components is likely to result in a lower level of performance materiality than a small number of significant components.

Component auditors also need to calculate materiality and performance materiality for the purposes of local statutory audits. All other things being equal, these amounts are likely to be lower than materiality and performance materiality for group purposes, however, it is possible that there will be some areas which are particularly risky for group purposes that are not risky at component level. In such cases, adjustments to local materiality levels may be needed for group purposes, or additional work performed for group purposes. For example, if environmental liabilities represent a high risk area for the group as a whole because it is involved in oil and gas extraction, that area may require more attention at component level for group audit purposes even if it does not represent a significant risk at component audit level.

### Evaluating Component Auditors

Efficiency dictates that, wherever possible, group auditors use work already performed by component auditors and provide instructions on specific work for group audit purposes, rather than performing it themselves.[76] This may not be possible if component auditors do not meet standards of competence and independence or fail to provide the information requested.

To use work performed by component auditors, group auditors evaluate whether:

- component auditors meet ethical requirements, including *independence* and *competence*;

- component auditors are subject to proper audit *oversight*;

- the extent of the *group auditors' involvement in the component audit* is adequate.

The information needed to make this evaluation may be available from component firms and from the group auditors' past experience of them, from third parties such as network firms in the same location that know the component firm, or from national oversight or professional bodies.

Determining whether component auditors are subject to adequate regulatory oversight in distant locations may not be easy. Audit regulation is a fast-developing area and new regulatory bodies may have appropriate aspirations in line with international norms, but they may not have the resources of more established bodies. Imposing oversight and quality control standards on new professional bodies and firms that are not accustomed to them can be challenging for all concerned. Nevertheless, group auditors need

---

[76] This does not mean that group auditors can delegate their *own* responsibilities for involvement in the component audit to component auditors.

to make the evaluation and professional bodies and regulators usually have a web-site and produce annual reports that can be examined if the firm does not have knowledge of or connections in the relevant jurisdiction.

It may be necessary to visit component auditors or to ask them to complete a questionnaire about the professional standards they use (auditing, accounting and ethical), although these need careful drafting to ensure good quality responses.

There is no distinction between network and non-network firms for these purposes. The same audit evidence is required but clearly it will be easier to obtain where networks operate common methodologies and quality control procedures, as well as branding.

### Group Audit Process

The group audit process, like any other audit process, involves a group audit plan, risk assessment and response, and testing of group-wide controls and controls over the consolidation process either by the group or by component auditors, all in order to reduce substantive testing.

Group auditors communicate with group management and those charged with governance regarding the group audit plan, audit findings, any limitations in the scope of the audit, suspected fraud and internal control deficiencies in the same way as they would for any other audit.

*Group auditor involvement in component audit work*
*As a minimum, group auditor involvement in component audits should include:*

- discussing **significant business activities** with component auditors or management;

- discussing financial statement **susceptibility to material misstatement** with component auditors;

- reviewing component auditor **documentation of identified significant group risks and responses** thereto.

Additional work might include reviewing the component auditors' audit strategy and plan, participating in opening and closing meetings and meeting with component management or auditors.

*Communications with component auditors*
Even where component auditors are well-known auditors in advanced jurisdictions, there can be communication problems. In many jurisdictions such as the UK, there is a legal requirement for component auditors to provide group auditors with information for group audit purposes. In other cases, group auditors may have no right to ask for information either from the component or its auditor and they have no right to reply to any such request without the permission of component management. For this reason, it is essential that group auditors agree before the audit commences that the parent entity will do what is necessary to ensure that component entities and their auditors provide

the group auditor with the information needed for the group audit. In all cases, the following information is obtained, usually from component auditors:

- *financial information* for inclusion in the consolidated financial statements;
- information about the *conduct of the audit* and *the component auditors' conclusions*;
- *confirmation of completion of the work* required by the group auditor on group audit risk;
- information about the *independence, competence and oversight* of component auditors;
- information about the *auditing, ethical and accounting standards* used.

Group audit questionnaires covering all of the above can be lengthy and complex. This acts as a deterrent to their completion. *Group auditors need to let component auditors know when this information is needed to allow them time to complete the questionnaire.* Group auditors may find that component auditors are using a variation on ISAs and IESBA ethical requirements, which may be difficult to evaluate.

If the component auditors' work cannot be used for whatever reason, work for group audit purposes has to be performed by the group auditors. Component auditor work might not be acceptable because, for example, component auditors lack independence, or because group auditors cannot obtain information about independence. Even if component auditors are independent and competent, they may simply fail to respond to requests for information. This always has cost implications and group auditors need the permission of the parent and component entity if they wish to perform the work themselves. In the event that group auditors do not obtain sufficient appropriate evidence for whatever reason, a modified audit opinion will result.

### The consolidation process and accounting requirements
In an ideal world, all group entities should have the same period-end and use the same accounting policies. This is often not possible because of local regulatory requirements. Financial information about the component required for group purposes includes accounting policy adjustments and adjustments for significant events between group and component period-ends.

Specific risks arising from the consolidation process include attempts to consolidate information based on incompatible accounting policies, for example. Fraudulent misstatements as well as errors such as non-consolidation of an entity that should be consolidated may arise because of weak controls over the process. Responses to that risk might include more detailed substantive work on the consolidation.

Particular attention needs to be paid to:

- *non-routine* consolidation *adjustments*;
- *adjustments* or *disclosures* required for subsequent events where there are components with *non-coterminous period-ends*;

- *related party transactions*;
- *materiality*;
- *uncorrected misstatements*;
- non-compliance with *laws and regulations*;
- evidence of *management bias*;
- *significant deficiencies in internal control*.

### Reviewing component auditor work

In practice, group auditors will hope to use the response to the group audit question-naire without reviewing the component auditors' files. Group auditors are required to discuss significant matters arising with component auditors, component management or group management and determine whether they need to review component audit documentation.

It may be necessary to obtain translations of key audit schedules if component audit files are in another language, as is common.

## Joint Audits

In a joint audit, two or more firms of auditors take joint responsibility for the audit. This means that *both firms are fully responsible for the full audit*. In some jurisdic-tions, joint audits are compulsory for some entities, partly because of the public interest element in entities such as banks, and partly in some cases to encourage growth in the profession locally. The issues surrounding joint audits are as follows:

- *cost*: even if the two firms split the audit work between them, both firms will want to perform procedures in some key areas. Engagement partners will seek to review all of the work of the other firm, and engagement quality control reviewers are also likely to cover both sets of work. All of this can involve considerable duplication. However, some argue that the presence of another firm helps keep costs down;
- *liability*: each firm is responsible for the work of the other firm;
- *quality*: having two firms of auditors audit the financial statements should improve audit quality but there is a risk that some matters will 'fall between the cracks', pos-sibly because of incompatible audit methodologies.

### Section essentials: what you need to remember

- *The fundamental principles: auditors must be satisfied with the independence and competence of the persons whose work they use, auditors must perform proce-dures on that work to justify using it and, regardless of the extent to which exter-nal auditors use the work of others, the responsibility for the audit opinion is not divided.*

- *The nature and extent of work that external auditors need to perform on the work of internal auditors and experts depend on the assessed level of risk associated with relevant audit areas, and external auditors always involve considering whether the assumptions and bases used are consistent with their knowledge of the business.*

- *The requirement for auditors to assess the extent to which the work performed by service organisations is relevant to the financial statements.*

- *The type of work performed by service organisations and whether user entities control data sent to them and information received back.*

- *Whether entities outsource an entire function to service organisations and exercise only high-level management controls.*

- *Whether service organisations provide Type 1 reports describing the system and providing an opinion on whether system design and implementation are adequate, or Type 2 reports, which also provide an opinion on the operational effectiveness of controls, and a description of tests conducted.*

- *The need for external auditors to be actively involved in the risk assessment of some components for group audit purposes and to be satisfied regarding the competence, independence and oversight of component auditors.*

- *The difference between significant and non-significant components and the different types of work to be performed on them; the content of group audit questionnaires and the need to review component auditor files.*

# SECTION 4.5, QUESTION

One of your larger audit clients, Jillco, distributes parcels nationally and internationally in association with a number of overseas partners. Jillco is considering whether to outsource a large part of its accounting function, including a high volume of automated transactions, to an overseas entity. Some of Jillco's partners outsource their accounting functions.

Jillco is expanding rapidly and despite a highly automated accounting function, the accounting systems and internal controls have struggled to keep pace with the growth of the business.

Required:

- (a) Explain:

    - (i)   why Jillco might want to outsource its accounting function;

    - (ii)  the types of outsourcing arrangement that Jillco might consider;

    - (iii) the potential drawbacks of outsourcing for Jillco.          (6 marks)

- (b) Describe the problems outsourcing basic accounting functions can create for external auditors and the risks external auditors are required to assess arising from the use of service organisations.          (6 marks)

    Much of the work performed by internal auditors is relevant to the work of external auditors. Many entities wish that their internal and external auditors were able to work more closely together than they do.

Required:

- (c) Explain why it is not always possible for external auditors to use all of the work performed by internal auditors, even though it may be relevant to the external audit.          (3 marks)

- (d) Compare and contrast the contents of internal audit reports, and external audit reports prepared under International Standards on Auditing (ISAs).          (5 marks)

Total          (20 marks)

## 4.6   RELATED PARTIES, INITIAL ENGAGEMENTS, OPENING BALANCES AND COMPARATIVE INFORMATION

**Coverage:** Covering ISA 550 *Related Parties*, ISA 510 *Initial Audit Engagements – Opening Balances*, ISA 710 *Comparative Information – Corresponding Figures and Comparative Financial Statements.*

### Why do I need to read this section?

*It is helpful to have an overview, at least, of the areas covered in this section. While lengthy questions in these areas are uncommon, the requirements for the audit of related parties are more extensive than they once were, and are now more easily examinable as part of risk assessment as well as audit finalisation. There is scope for bringing the audit of opening balances and comparative information into answers to many questions but not many students do this.*

### What is important in this section?

*Related parties tend to be examined in higher-level papers and are often excluded from the syllabuses of lower-level papers. Different jurisdictions have different requirements for the presentation of comparative information and few students can clearly articulate the difference between comparative figures and comparative financial statements, which is a shame, because the area is not so very complex. In all cases, ISAs require auditors to obtain audit evidence on opening balances and comparative information because they affect the current period's financial statements. ISA also require auditors to assess the risks associated with transactions with related parties. This is regardless of jurisdiction-specific requirements for the audit of comparative information and disclosure requirements for transactions with related parties.*

### What sort of questions come up in this area?

*Questions that focus solely on the risks associated with transactions with related parties are possible but the area is still more likely to be examined as part of a larger question or in multiple choice or short-form questions.*

*In almost any question on a specific income statement or balance sheet area, whether it be expenses, receivables, long-term liabilities, property, plant and equipment or share capital, almost all financial reporting frameworks require comparative information from the prior period to be provided in some form. For this reason, some mention of the audit of comparative information can be made legitimately in answers to many different questions.*

How do I stand out from the crowd?

*Risk assessments must always cover the risks associated with transactions with related parties, and audit work on opening balances and comparative information. Few students mention these areas in answers to questions on planning or risk assessment and those who do stand out.*

## 4.6.1   AUDITING RELATED PARTY TRANSACTIONS AND DISCLOSURES

Virtually all major corporate collapses have involved transactions with related parties. Part of the audit of related parties relationships and transactions involves evaluating the related fraud risks.

Financial reporting frameworks often define related parties[77] and commonly include the directors of entities, their immediate families and other dependants, and group entities, where there is control or significant influence.

Where the financial reporting framework provides minimal or no requirements, ISA 550 on related parties provides definitions and argues that auditors need to understand related party transactions regardless of accounting requirements because they are *always relevant to the fair presentation of financial statements*. They are also *always relevant to compliance frameworks* because, for example, non-disclosure of the fact that a substantial proportion of an entity's transactions were with a related party might render a set of financial statements *misleading,* even if there were no requirement to disclose such transactions.

While many transactions with related parties such as group companies are in the normal course of business, others, such as the sale of assets to directors or their spouses, are not. Special attention is paid to the *risk of material misstatement* in this area because:

• IT *systems may fail to capture* related party transactions;

• related party transactions are a *feature of fraudulent transactions*;

• related party transactions are *not undertaken on normal commercial terms*.

Materiality and performance materiality in this area are often set at lower levels than in other less sensitive areas.

### Related Parties in Smaller and Larger Entities

In practice, smaller entities often rely on their accountants or auditors to tell them who related parties are and what needs disclosing. They have few if any controls in the area and, as with all aspects of smaller entity audits, the general attitude and integrity of the owner-manager can increase or decrease risk in this area.

---

[77] Such as IAS 24 *Related Party Disclosures.*

In an ongoing relationship, auditors may gather information about related parties in the first instance by inquiry, inspection of documents and observation of the quality of the owner-manager's oversight. Auditors can give this information to owner-managers in the first year so that in subsequent years the information can be given to auditors by the owner-manager, instead of the other way round.

### Dominant influence, fraud risk factors and significant risks

Related parties who exercise dominant influence over an entity, particularly if they tend to override normal controls, may constitute a fraud risk factor. A significant risk arises where this combines with other fraud risk factors such as a high turnover of senior staff, the use of intermediaries for no obvious reason or the preoccupation of the dominant individual with accounting estimates or similar matters.[78]

Additional procedures where there is a significant risk that management do not account for or disclose related party transactions include further investigation of transactions with intermediaries and other related parties. Additional procedures are also required where there is an identified significant risk of fraud due to the presence of a related party with dominant influence.[79]

Owner-managers of smaller businesses may exercise dominant influence but charismatic personalities also sometimes exercise inappropriate dominant influence over the boards of larger entities. Local legislation may require the approval of some transactions with related parties but entities of all sizes often prefer not to disclose transactions with related parties unless they have to. Even larger entities may have poor controls over such transactions, because the significance of such transactions is not understood, or they are considered unimportant, or because there may be no disclosure requirements.[80]

### Understanding Related Parties

Auditors are required to:

- discuss within the engagement team the susceptibility of the financial statements to material misstatement due to *fraud or error arising from transactions with related parties*;

- ask management about *who* related parties are, and about *transactions* with them;

- perform procedures to understand any *controls* over related parties (over identification disclosure and authorisation of transactions, for example);

- *remain alert* to the possibility of undisclosed transactions when performing the audit;

- *inspect documents* such as bank and legal confirmations, and any minutes of shareholder and other meetings for evidence of undisclosed transactions with related parties;

---

[78] ISA 550 on related parties, paragraphs 18 and A30.
[79] ISA 550 on related parties, paragraphs A32 and A33.
[80] ISA 550 on related parties, paragraph A18.

- ask whether any *significant transactions outside the normal course of business* are with related parties. If they are, they are treated as significant risks;

- obtain *written representations* about the completeness of disclosures.

### Unidentified and Undisclosed Related Parties

Problems arise when auditors uncover related party relationships and transactions that management did not tell them about. When this happens, auditors need to ask why controls failed to identify them, why management did not disclose them, and whether there are any more transactions with them or other undisclosed relationships. Auditors also need to consider whether their original risk assessment needs to be changed.

### Normal Course of Business and Arm's Length Transactions

#### *Transactions outside the normal course of business*
Transactions outside the normal course of business are transactions which the entity does not normally engage in, such as real estate property transactions for a manufacturing entity. They also include transactions with offshore entities with weak tax laws and circular arrangements such as sales with commitments to re-purchase.[81] The Valukas report into the failure of Lehman Brothers noted that 'repo 105' transactions, i.e. circular sale with commitment to repurchase arrangements, were used to move billions in debt off its books in the months before it collapsed.

Where transactions outside the normal course of business involve related parties, such as the sale of a company aircraft to the husband of a director of a property construction company, auditors are required to:

- obtain evidence that the transaction has been *approved,* because many jurisdictions require shareholder or director approval of such transactions;

- inspect the underlying documentation to establish the *business rationale* for the transaction, whether the transaction may have been for *fraudulent purposes* and whether its terms are consistent with management's explanations.

#### *Arm's length transactions*
Transactions on normal commercial terms are known as *arm's length* transactions.

Transactions above or below normal prices or on unusual terms, such as extended credit or with very low interest rates, are not at arm's length. Such transactions are of interest to shareholders and some financial reporting frameworks require disclosure of any such transactions with related parties. Transactions at under or overvalue between group companies are common for tax planning, cash flow and operational purposes and accounting frameworks may not require the disclosure of such routine transactions. However, transactions with individuals, particularly if they are at undervalue, are always of interest to shareholders if they are significant. For these reasons, where

---

[81] ISA 550 on related parties, paragraph A25.

entities assert that related party transactions are on normal commercial terms, they need to provide auditors with evidence to support that assertion.[82]

### Special Purpose Entities

Special purpose entities (SPEs), sometimes known as SPVs (special purpose vehicles), are usually established for legitimate reasons. They have, however, featured in numerous corporate collapses such as that of Enron, whose executives used SPEs to hide losses and take liabilities off the balance sheet by means of circular transactions in which Enron guaranteed loans for the purchase of its own stock by SPEs, and did not consolidate them in the group financial statements. Accounting for SPEs is often far from straightforward.

SPEs may be established for narrow and well-defined purposes such as research and development, to facilitate leases, and for the securitisation of financial assets such as mortgages, i.e. bundling and selling them on.

SPEs may take the form of companies, trusts, partnerships or unincorporated entities. Assets transferred to them often involve the de-recognition of assets and liabilities in the transferor, i.e. the entity that set up the SPE, even though certain rights and responsibilities and funding relating to the assets are not fully transferred.[83]

SPEs are not often designed to be consolidated in the group financial statements. However, the SPE may be a related party of the reporting entity if the reporting entity controls it, even though it does not own it.[84] The engagement team discussion of fraud may cover SPEs and how they might be used to facilitate earnings management.[85]

### 4.6.2   INITIAL ENGAGEMENTS: OPENING BALANCES

The title of ISA 510[86] is misleading in that it can be read as implying that it deals only with entities undergoing their first audit, which is not the case. ISA 510 also deals with the much more common situation in which there has been a change in auditors. The basic requirement is for auditors to obtain evidence about whether:

- *opening balances* contain *misstatements* that *materially affect the current period;*
- *accounting policies* have been *consistently applied*, or changes appropriately accounted for and disclosed.

Opening balances are defined as including opening disclosures, such as those for contingencies, based on the closing balances of the previous period. The closing and opening figures are not necessarily the same because of adjustments made in the preparation of financial statements. Such adjustments are obviously open to abuse though and they warrant attention, particularly if they are material.

---

[82] ISA 550 on related parties, paragraph 24.
[83] ISA 315 on risk assessment, paragraph 26.
[84] ISA 550 on related parties, paragraph A7.
[85] ISA 550 on related parties, paragraph A10.
[86] ISA 510 *Initial Audit Engagements – Opening Balances.*

Evidence on opening balances is obtained by:

- *reading* the prior period financial statements;
- determining whether the prior period closing balances have been *properly brought forward* or restated, and whether opening balances reflect *appropriate accounting policies*;
- performing one or more of the following:
  - *reviewing the predecessor auditors' working papers:* this is not often an option and the competence and independence of the auditors would be important;
  - using *current period procedures* to provide evidence on opening balances: this is the most efficient option because current year work on receivables provides evidence regarding the brought forward balances, for example;
  - performing *specific audit procedures* on opening balances: for the opening inventory figure, for example, observing an inventory count just after the beginning of the period might provide evidence, as might performing analytical procedures on inventory levels and gross profit margins, and work on valuation methods. For non-current assets, inspection of plant and equipment at the beginning of the period might provide evidence and for liabilities, external confirmations of balances brought forward might be possible as well as documentary evidence held by the client.

If there is any indication of misstatements in the opening balances that affect the current period, or if there is a modification in the prior period audit report, auditors establish whether there are any effects in the current period. This is very likely where modifications affect opening inventory, for example. If a lack of evidence led to a qualified opinion on the income statement and balance sheet for the prior period, and insufficient evidence is available from current period work on inventory, it is likely that a qualified opinion will be given on the current period's income statement because opening inventory affects profit in both periods. The current period balance sheet, however, will not be affected by the qualification but there are implications for comparative information, particularly where it is presented as corresponding figures which are integral to the current period financial statements.

A qualified opinion or disclaimer of opinion is necessary if there is insufficient information to form an opinion. If in fact there is an uncorrected material misstatement that affects the current period, a qualified or adverse opinion will be given.

### 4.6.3 COMPARATIVE INFORMATION: CORRESPONDING FIGURES AND COMPARATIVE FINANCIAL STATEMENTS

*Comparative information* is, in short, last year's figures, provided to help readers of financial statements make sense of current period information. Financial reporting frameworks require the provision of comparative information in one of two ways:

- *comparative financial statements*: separate, comparable sets of financial information are presented together, and the auditors' opinion is given on each period presented, as in the USA;

- *corresponding figures*: a selection of figures and disclosures is provided to correspond with what is presented for the current period. The figures are integral to the current period financial statements and auditors do not give a separate audit opinion, as in the UK.

The fact that no opinion is given on corresponding figures does not mean that no work is required. Where the figures are required, they need to be right in order for the current period financial statements to give a true and fair view, or to be fairly presented.

However presented:

- *comparative information should agree with what was presented in the prior period,* or be properly restated;
- prior period *accounting policies should be consistent* with the current period, or properly accounted for and disclosed if they have changed.

Complications arise where:

- there are *changes in auditors*: for both comparative financial statements and corresponding figures, where predecessor auditors reported on prior periods, an *other matter paragraph* is used in the audit report to state that fact and to provide details of the type and date of the report;
- *the prior period was unaudited*: in both cases, an *other matter paragraph* is used to state that fact, but auditors are still required to ensure that there are no misstatements in the opening balances affecting the current period financial statements;
- *a modified opinion was given in the prior period*: for corresponding figures, where the matter is unresolved, the *modification is made again* in the current period if the current period is affected, as might be the case where no depreciation was provided. Where the current period is not affected, where prior period expenses were misstated, for example, the current audit opinion is still modified because of the lack of comparability in the corresponding figures.

For comparative financial statements, if information comes to light that suggests that the *prior period figures audited by other auditors are unreliable,* i.e. an unmodified opinion was given where a modified one was appropriate, auditors communicate that fact to management and those charged with governance, requesting that the other auditors be informed. A new audit report is sometimes issued. For corresponding figures that have not been restated to deal with such an issue, a qualified or adverse opinion is given because of the error in the corresponding figures. If a restatement has been made, an emphasis of matter can be given.

Auditors seek written representations confirming that the written representations made in prior periods on the comparative financial statements still stand.

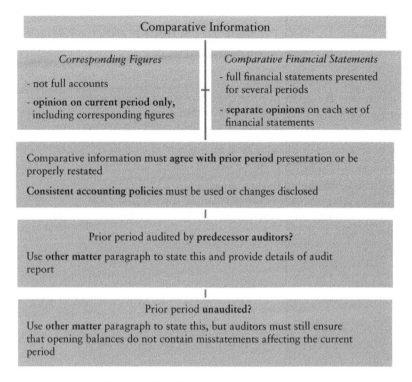

**Figure 4.27**  Comparative information

## Section essentials: what you need to remember

- *The risks associated with the audit of related party transactions are similar to those associated with fraud risks and should be treated in the same way.*

- *Many opening balances have a direct effect on the current period financial statements, such as opening inventory which has a direct effect on profits, and opening receivables and payables which have an effect on revenue and closing receivables and payables.*

- *Comparative information can be either corresponding figures in the current year's financial statements, or comparative financial information in which prior period financial statements are shown alongside current financial statements.*

# SECTION 4.6, QUESTION

Required:

(a) Explain why the audit of related parties is important and explain the auditors' main responsibilities in that area. (9 marks)

(b) Explain the two main ways in which comparative information can be displayed in financial statements and the auditors' main responsibilities in that area. (6 marks)

(c) Briefly describe the additional work required of auditors where an audit engagement is being performed for the first time because an entity has grown and is no longer exempt from audit requirements. (5 marks)

Total (20 marks)

# 5 CORPORATE GOVERNANCE, PROFESSIONAL LIABILITY, REGULATION AND OTHER CURRENT ISSUES

## 5.1 CORPORATE GOVERNANCE

**Covering:** *Differing systems of corporate governance, the OECD Principles of Corporate Governance, the UK Corporate Governance Code, Audit committees.*

**Why do I need to read this section?**

*Students often avoid optional questions in this area. This is a shame because difficult questions are rarely set. It is understandable, though, because the terminology can be confusing and the area is sometimes poorly presented in study material. Many requirements in auditing standards assume an understanding of how corporate governance works and why it is important, including numerous requirements to report significant or unusual matters to the audit committee, for example. Students often simply forget to mention this because they do not really understand why it is important. These ISA requirements should make more sense in the context of the background provided by this section and help you gain the easy marks that are often available.*

**What is important in this section?**

*Auditing and assurance papers differ in the extent to which they examine corporate governance. Lower-level papers often cover it in considerably more detail than higher-level papers. Lower-level papers focus on details and the basic requirements for entities to have audit committees, for independent directors, and for auditors to communicate certain matters to them. Higher-level papers sometimes focus on the bigger picture, on what corporate governance is and how auditors contribute to good corporate governance.*

**What sort of questions come up in this area?**

- *Straightforward knowledge-based questions on the nature of corporate governance, and on the purposes and benefits of audit committees and auditors' communications with them.*

- *Questions on how an entity should set up corporate governance structures in a given scenario.*

**How do I stand out from the crowd?**

- *Show an awareness of the basic types of corporate governance systems, particularly in questions on group audits.*

- *Remember in questions in other areas, that many ISAs require auditors to report significant or unusual matters to the audit committee.*

### 5.1.1   WHAT IS CORPORATE GOVERNANCE?

There is no generally accepted definition of corporate governance. It is about the way in which companies (corporate bodies) are governed. Descriptions of it include terms such as the following:

*. . . frameworks, systems, rules, processes and practices used by management and those charged with governance to ensure accountability and by which companies are directed and controlled . . .*

An adequate description for exam purposes is as follows: *corporate governance deals with the way companies are directed and controlled and the relationships between their directors, shareholders and other stakeholders.*

Some descriptions include the way companies are *operated* but corporate governance is often distinguished from the day-to-day operational management of the business.

Particularly important among other stakeholders are employees. Other stakeholders include creditors, tax authorities and governments but these tend to have a lesser role in day-to-day corporate governance.

In some jurisdictions, the board is legally required to act in the interests of the company, taking account of shareholders, employees and the public good. In others, it is best practice.

Corporate governance exists because of the separation of ownership (shareholders) and management (directors) in companies. Like audit, it is necessary to help manage the tensions between directors and shareholders by aligning their interests where possible. Corporate governance discourages the misuse of corporate assets by management for its own benefit or for the benefit of selected shareholders at the expense of minority shareholders, and management for short-term gain at the expense of longer-term sustainability.

**Corporate Governance in the USA, UK and Europe**

Corporate governance operates within jurisdiction-specific legal, regulatory and commercial frameworks, i.e. 'corporate governance' means different things in different places.

Corporate governance in the USA developed in an environment in which financial reporting and auditing operate in the context of federal securities laws, originally developed in the 1930s in reaction to abuse of the markets by dishonest market participants for personal gain at the expense of other participants. Federal securities laws seek to promote efficient capital markets through regulation that facilitates the management of companies without excessive regulatory or shareholder interference.

Company law and the rights of shareholders feature more prominently in the UK. UK corporate governance developed in the context of corporate law and regulation, originally developed in the late 19th century in reaction to the abuse of shareholder funds by dishonest company promoters. Corporate law and regulation focus on the obligations of management to the companies they run and to their shareholders.

Company law is about how companies are run. Securities law is about how markets are operated.

In continental Europe, many companies operate *two-tier board systems* with a *supervisory board*. Elected shareholder and employee representatives sit on a supervisory board that oversees and appoints members of the management board. Supervisory boards approve major business decisions.

The *unitary* systems of the UK and the USA prevail in many English-speaking jurisdictions.

In many jurisdictions, oversight and separation of potentially conflicting interests and duties are stipulated by many corporate governance codes requiring the establishment of *audit, risk and remuneration committees* and through the *separation of the role of chairman and chief executive*.

## Corporate Governance Codes

Many codes of corporate governance exist, sometimes described as rules rather than codes. Some are high-level and principles-based, others are sets of detailed rules and some operate in the public sector.[1]

There is no single, generally accepted model of good corporate governance and in many jurisdictions, including the USA and the UK, there are several codes covering different aspects of corporate governance from the viewpoint of different stakeholders. For example, the *UK Corporate Governance Code 2010*[2] has a 'comply or explain' approach and exists alongside the *UK Stewardship Code, Guidance on Audit Committees* and *Guidance on Board Effectiveness*. Corporate governance requirements in other jurisdictions are mandatory and are found in a single document.

It is, unfortunately, difficult to prove that compliance with codes of corporate governance actually improves either the overall quality of governance or corporate

---

[1] A global list of codes can be found on the European Corporate Governance Institute's web-site www.ecgi.org (independent research into corporate governance) and a discussion of current corporate governance issues can be found at the web-site of the International Corporate Governance Network www.icgn.org (institutional investors) and the Global Corporate Governance Forum www.gcgf.org (corporate governance in emerging markets and developing economies).

[2] Financial Reporting Council, June 2010 www.frc.org.uk/corporate/ukcgcode.cfm.

performance. The effects of compliance (or non-compliance) on performance are difficult to disentangle from the effect of business cycles and the quality of operational management, for example and some large entities with exemplary corporate governance structures and practices have nevertheless been the victims of major frauds perpetrated by their own directors. Good corporate governance cannot eliminate dishonesty, although it discourages it, and encourages integrity in corporate life and appropriate corporate behaviour.

The coverage of codes varies: the OECD *Principles of Corporate Governance*, for example, go into some detail on shareholder rights whereas the UK Code focuses on the board, mainly because shareholders' rights are well established in UK company law.

### Auditor reporting on corporate governance statements

Auditors are often required to review and report on corporate governance statements and on other mandatory corporate statements on going concern and directors' remuneration, for example.

In the UK, auditors are required to review the objectively verifiable provisions of the corporate governance statement made by directors including matters such as:

- responsibility for preparing financial statements;
- the report on internal control and risk management;
- membership of the audit committee and its terms of reference;
- the audit committee's responsibility for whistle-blowing, internal audit, the appointment of external auditors and the non-audit services which they provide.

UK auditors are also required to review the mandatory going concern statements made by directors. The work performed on such statements might include reviewing the documentation prepared by the entity to support its assertions, reviewing the statement for consistency with the auditors' knowledge of the business and the adequacy of the disclosures. The requirements of other ISAs dealing with audit reporting also cover these statements.[3]

Reporting on these matters can be complex because of the interaction between legislation, listing rules and regulation but reporting is generally either *explicit*, particularly in the case of reporting on risk assessment and internal control over financial reporting processes and about capital structures, or *by exception*, i.e. only where there is a problem.

### Corporate Governance Objectives and Outcomes

Good corporate governance should provide incentives to management to pursue objective that are in the interests of the company and its shareholders, rather than their own interests. It should also facilitate effective monitoring of management performance by requiring transparency (i.e. disclosure). Corporate governance should help generate confidence and lower the cost of capital.

---

[3]  ISA 720 on other information applies to information issued with audited financial statements in the annual report.

In practice, unfortunately, many corporate collapses in recent years have involved entities in which all of the prerequisites for good corporate governance were in place: audit committees, separate chairmen and chief executives, and well-resourced risk and remuneration committees. These structures can lend the appearance of legitimacy to activities that in substance serve to maximise remuneration, bonuses and other benefits to management without any significant corresponding enhancement of shareholder value.

Aggressive earnings management fuelled by the need or desire to meet or exceed market expectations, weakness in GAAP, complex group structures, transactions with related parties and aligning executive compensation with shareholders' interests are difficult to address through corporate governance, although attempts are made every time a series of corporate crises arises.

*Sarbanes-Oxley*
The accounting scandals of the early 2000s influenced the development of the Sarbanes-Oxley Act 2002 in the USA. It requires, among other things, that senior executives, such as the CEO and CFO take ***individual responsibility*** for corporate financial reports (section 302) and imposes criminal penalties for non-compliance. It also requires ***reports by management on internal controls over financial reporting and external audits of controls*** (section 404). Such requirements are costly; there is some consensus that companies benefit from these requirements although many consider them onerous for smaller entities.

No system is perfect. It is clear that in 'comply or explain' regimes, for example, there are some poor explanations of why elements of codes have not been followed. Despite this, 'comply or explain' regimes have taken root. For example, since corporate governance codes have been in place in the UK, the number of non-executive directors has increased substantially, as have the number of entities disclosing risks. Statements of full compliance with relevant codes have also increased substantially and an ever-smaller number of listed companies gives minimal explanations of why they do not comply, although these give cause for concern. Audit committees were unusual to begin with, they are now the norm and the vast majority of UK listed entities have them. The most commonly reported non-compliance relates to the level of independence of boards and committees; a small number still combine the role of chairman and chief executive.

## 5.1.2   THE OECD PRINCIPLES OF CORPORATE GOVERNANCE

The OECD[4] *Principles of Corporate Governance ('Principles')*, first published in 1999 were revised in 2004. They underpin many jurisdiction-specific codes. ***Auditing and***

---

[4]   The Organisation of Economic Co-operation and Development (OECD) is a 34-member developed-country forum of countries 'committed to democracy and the market economy'. It seeks a high level of sustainable growth, employment, rising living standards and financial stability, contributing to world trade and economic development. It covers economic, environmental and social issues and acts through peer pressure by implementing soft law, i.e. non-binding instruments. It cooperates with businesses, trade unions and other representatives of civil society. Collaboration regarding taxation, for example, has fostered the growth of a global web of bilateral tax treaties. www.oecd.org.

*assurance papers based on international standards usually examine those aspects of the* Principles *that deal with internal control and auditors.*

The *Principles* note that policy makers, companies and investors are now more aware of how good corporate governance contributes to financial stability, growth and investment. They note that investors, particularly pension funds, now realise that they have a role in good corporate governance. This is important in the light of increasing reliance on the private sector for retirement pensions.

The *Principles* apply to publicly traded (listed) companies. They are non-binding and focus on the governance problems that arise from the separation of ownership and management. They note the importance of the behaviour of controlling shareholders and the legal rights of minority shareholders, employees and creditors. The *Principles* deal with:

- effective corporate governance frameworks;
- the rights of shareholders;
- the equitable treatment of shareholders;
- the role of other stakeholders;
- disclosure and transparency;
- board responsibilities.

### OECD Principles Affecting Auditors

*Disclosure and transparency*
The *Principles* state that:

- corporate governance frameworks should require timely and accurate disclosure of all material matters including the financial position performance, ownership, and governance of the company, i.e. most of the matters already found in annual reports;[5]
- access to company information whether it be hard copy or website information, should be available to all entitled to it and it should be up-to-date. Simultaneous reporting of information to all shareholders is a fundamental equitable principle and avoids insider trading problems;

---

[5] Such information includes the identity of major shareholders, remuneration policy for board members and key executives including the link between remuneration and performance, information about board members including their qualifications and other company directorships, and related party transactions including those with major shareholders and their families.

- *an annual audit should be conducted by an independent, competent and qualified auditor to provide objective assurance to the board and shareholders that the financial statements fairly represent the financial position and performance of the company . . . ;*

- *external auditors should be accountable to shareholders and owe a duty to the company to exercise due professional care in the conduct of the audit.*

The independence of auditors and their accountability to shareholders have been reinforced in recent years by the trend towards the replacement of the *self-regulation of auditors*, in which professional bodies set standards for and disciplined their own members, with *independent auditor oversight*. Bodies that are not controlled by accountants and auditors now generally set accounting and auditing standards. This trend, which started in the mid-1990s, was advanced by the corporate scandals of the early 2000s.

The Professional Oversight Board (POB) in the UK was established in 2004,[6] the Public Company Accounting Oversight Board (PCAOB) was established in the USA under the 2002 Sarbanes-Oxley Act, and IFAC's Public Interest Oversight Board (PIOB) that oversees its standard-setting activities was established in 2005.

*Board responsibilities*
These include the *strategic guidance* of the company, effective *monitoring of management* and *accountability* to the company and shareholders.

Board responsibilities involve ensuring:

- *the integrity of accounting and financial reporting systems, including the audit;*

- *that appropriate systems of control are in place and, in particular, systems for risk management, financial and operational control;*

- *compliance with the law and relevant standards.*

This means:

- developing strategy, risk policy, budgets and business plans, setting performance objectives and monitoring performance and overseeing major capital expenditure and disposal;

- monitoring the effectiveness of governance;

- selecting and monitoring key executives and aligning executive and board remuneration with the longer-term interests of the entity;

- ensuring a formal transparent board nomination and election process and managing potential conflicts of interest including the misuse of assets.

---

[6]  The POB was preceded by the Professional Oversight Board for Accountancy (POBA).

Board members should act in the best interest of the company and the shareholders, treat all shareholders equally and take account of the interests of other stakeholders. Self-assessment by boards is now common practice as are performance reviews of individual board members. Remuneration committees, with a majority of non-executive directors, should deal with policy and contracts for board members and key executives. For unitary boards, separation of the role of the chair and chief executive is desirable and where there are supervisory boards, the head of the lower board should not automatically become chairman of the supervisory board.

In some jurisdictions, some board members are required to be independent of dominant shareholders and there are requirements for independent audit, nomination and remuneration committees.

Board members should be able to commit themselves effectively to their responsibilities and should have access to good quality information.

### OECD *Principles* in Other Areas

The following are examples of the application of the *Principles* in areas not affecting auditors:

*Corporate governance frameworks* should be in the public interest and consistent with the rule of law. This means that they should be transparent (everyone should have access to them) and enforceable (there must be some sanctions for non-compliance). They should clearly articulate the division of responsibilities among different supervisory, regulatory and enforcement authorities, all of which should be properly funded. Public consultation is an essential element of good practice.

*Shareholder rights* should be protected by corporate governance frameworks. Key shareholders' rights in all OECD jurisdictions include the right to:

- elect board members;
- amend the company's constitution such as changes in what the company does;
- approve extraordinary transactions such as the sale of all the company's assets;
- transfer shares;
- obtain information in sufficient time for shareholders to attend meetings and vote;
- question the board, place items on the agenda of general meetings;
- propose resolutions, subject to reasonable limitations;
- make their views known on remuneration policies, by means of an advisory vote;
- approve the equity component of compensation schemes (i.e. share options).

Institutional investors casting proxy votes on behalf of smaller shareholders should be transparent about their use of proxy votes and provide shareholders with the opportunity to disagree. Institutional investors should disclose their overall corporate governance and voting policies. Companies should disclose capital structures that enable some shareholders to obtain control disproportionate to their ownership, such as additional voting rights.

Capital markets rules should be clear to investors. Companies should not use anti-takeover devices to shield management and the board from accountability.

### Equitable treatment of shareholders
Provisions include the following:

- all shareholders of the same category should be treated equally;

- changes in voting rights should be subject to approval by those negatively affected;

- minority shareholders should be protected from abuse by controlling shareholders;

- it should not be unduly difficult or expensive to cast votes;

- insider trading should be prohibited;

- board members and key executives should disclose transactions with the entity.

There are well-established legal rights of shareholders to take action against management and board members in many jurisdictions provided certain conditions are met to prevent excessive litigation, but there should be a 'safe harbour' for management's business judgements.

### Employees and other stakeholders
Provisions include the following:

- Employee and other stakeholder rights should be respected;

- employee share-ownership schemes should be permitted;

- employees and others should not be punished for exercising their whistle-blowing rights.

## 5.1.3   THE *UK CORPORATE GOVERNANCE CODE 2010*

The first UK corporate governance code (the Cadbury Code) was published in 1992. Its most recent revision was in 2010. Key areas cover:

- *leadership:* the board, which should have a clear division of responsibilities between the running of the board (the chairman) and responsibility for running the business (chief executive). Non-executive directors should challenge and help develop proposals on strategy;

- *effectiveness:* the board should have an appropriate balance of skills, knowledge, experience and independence. There should be a rigorous and transparent procedure for the appointment of new directors. Directors should be able to allocate sufficient time to the company to discharge their responsibilities effectively, i.e. they should not have too many directorships. The board should evaluate its own performance and that of its committees and individual directors. Directors should be re-elected at regular intervals, subject to continued satisfactory performance;

- *accountability:* the board should present a balanced and understandable assessment of the company's position and prospects. The board determines the risks it is willing to take in achieving its objectives. It should maintain risk management and internal control systems. There should be arrangements for maintaining an appropriate relationship with auditors;

- *remuneration:* rewards should be linked to corporate and individual performance, and be sufficient to attract the right quality of directors, but no more. There should be transparent procedures for developing executive remuneration policy and for fixing remuneration packages. Directors should not be involved in deciding on their own remuneration;

- *shareholders:* the board has a collective responsibility for ensuring that there is a dialogue with shareholders and it should encourage their participation at the AGM.

### 5.1.4   AUDIT COMMITTEES AND INTERNAL AUDIT

Audit committees with independent non-executive directors are established good practice for listed entities in all developed jurisdictions.

In the USA, audit committees are a requirement. In the UK, listed entities are required either to comply with the *UK Corporate Governance Code 2010* that requires audit committees, or explain why they do not. In unitary board systems (as in the UK and the USA) audit committees are a sub-committee of the board. In two-tier board systems, audit committees are often sub-committees of the supervisory board that sits above or alongside the board. In both cases, they serve as an intermediary between external auditors, internal auditors, the board and management. Their independence should enable them to act in the interests of shareholders and other stakeholders.

Audit committees should be prepared to take a robust stand. Information should be freely available to audit committees from the board and auditors, who must listen to committee views and talk through the issues openly.

Among other things, audit committees oversee the monitoring work performed by internal audit.

Audit committee members, and particularly chairmen, need to have enough time to do the job and require, like members of the board, induction and possibly training.

The areas noted below are taken from the UK *Guidance on Audit Committees* and cover most of the areas dealt with by similar codes internationally.

## Membership, Procedures and Resources

Many requirements are designed to protect audit committees from pressure to 'rubber stamp' board decisions. In the early days, audit committees were often pressurised in this way.

Audit committees should have *at least three independent non-executive directors*. At least one member should have *recent relevant financial experience*, preferably a professional accountancy qualification.

The board should make appointments to the audit committee for *up to three years* on the recommendation of the nomination committee if there is one. There should be *at least three meetings each year*, the external auditor and the finance director should be invited regularly and no-one other than the chair and members is automatically entitled to attend. Chairmen of boards at one time thought they were entitled to attend such meetings, which inhibited frank discussion.

Audit committees should be *adequately resourced* and the board should make *funds available for independent legal advice* where the audit committee thinks it necessary. The board should review the audit committee's effectiveness annually. Disagreements between the board and the audit committee that cannot be resolved – a rare and embarrassing situation and one to be avoided – may be reported by the audit committee in its report to shareholders in the annual report. Audit committees should have written terms of reference. A *report on the membership of the audit committee and on its activity should appear in the annual report*.

## Financial Statements and Internal Control
Audit committees should:

- monitor the *integrity of the financial statements and review significant judgements*;
- *review internal financial controls* and other controls and risk management systems and the board's statements in the annual report on internal control and risk management, unless there is a risk committee to do this;
- *review the adequacy of whistle-blowing arrangements* whereby staff can raise concerns about corporate improprieties. Many jurisdictions have legislation in place requiring that companies and other entities set up such arrangements.

## Internal Audit
Audit committees should monitor and review the *effectiveness of internal audit*, and approve internal audit's remit and resourcing. Where there is no such function, audit

committees should assess the implications and make any necessary recommendations to the board. Audit committees should consider:

- whether the head of internal audit reports to the audit committee and has access to the chairman of the main board of directors;

- whether the internal audit work plan is adequate;

- internal audit reports and management's response thereto;

- meeting with the head of internal audit, without management, at least once a year.

## External Audit

### Appointment
Audit committees should:

- make ***recommendations*** to the board on external ***auditors' appointment***, remuneration and other terms of engagement. This should cover group situations and the decision to use firms from more than one network, or joint auditors. Shareholders are asked to approve the board's recommendation. The board should explain in the annual report why they have not taken the audit committee's advice where that is the case, although again this would be a rare and embarrassing situation;

- monitor and ***review*** the external auditors' ***independence*** and the ***effectiveness of the audit*** process each year and investigate the reasons when auditors resign;

- ***explain*** in the annual report ***how the auditors have been chosen***, the tendering frequency and any contractual obligations that restrict the choice of auditors in any way. This is partly because of fears, well-founded or otherwise, of 'Big 4 only' conditions in lending contracts;

- review and ***agree the engagement letter*** each year and be satisfied that an effective audit can be conducted for the ***fee payable***. This is to prevent audits being used as loss-leaders for the sale of non-audit services, and to prevent 'low-balling' whereby auditors quote a very low fee that will not cover costs in order to obtain the work, in the belief that once appointed they can recoup their losses in later years or obtain more profitable non-audit services.

### Ethical requirements
Audit committees should:

- develop and implement ***policy*** on external auditor engagement to supply ***non-audit services***, which should cover the firm's fees, skills base and safeguards. The annual report should explain how independence is safeguarded where non-audit services are provided. The policy should specify non-audit services:

– that are *pre-approved*, such as routine audit-related tax and filing services, where the fee is relatively small (limits may be specified),
– requiring *specific approval*, such as internal audit services, although these are prohibited in some jurisdictions,
– that are *prohibited*, such as human resources and financial systems design and implementations systems;

- consider *investor perceptions* where there are proposals for the *external auditors* to provide *internal audit services*, and consider how it is explained in the annual report;

- consider whether in the absence of an internal audit function, the audit committee is over-reliant on the external auditor;

- agree with the board a *policy for employing former employees of the external auditor*, which may be more rigorous than the ethical requirements. IESBA's *Code* notes self-interest, intimidation and familiarity threats when former members of the audit team go to work for the audit client, particularly audit partners and particularly if the move is to a senior position at the audited entity;

- monitor the *firm's compliance with the audit partner rotation requirements*.

*Annual audit*
Audit committees should review:

- the *appropriateness of the audit plan*, and whether *materiality levels* and resources to be devoted to the audit are adequate;

- the *external auditor's findings* including major issues arising, especially unresolved issues and errors identified, particularly unadjusted errors;

- the *representation letter* before it is signed by management, paying particular attention to non-standard issues;

- the *management letter and management's response* to it;

- the *effectiveness of the audit* when completed by obtaining feedback from senior staff involved such as the finance director and head of internal audit, and by assessing the quality of the management letter and considering whether it demonstrates a good understanding of the business, for example.

### Section essentials: what you need to remember

- *The nature and purpose of corporate governance.*

- *The broad areas covered by corporate governance codes including the rights of shareholders and other stakeholders, accountability, disclosure and transparency, board responsibilities, leadership, board effectiveness and remuneration.*

- *The role of audit committees, their membership, resources that should be made available to them, and the scope of their oversight, including internal control and risk management, internal and external audit.*

## 5.2  PROFESSIONAL LIABILITY, REGULATION AND OTHER CURRENT ISSUES

**Covering:** *Professional liability under statute, in contract and tort, managing professional liability, regulating the profession and other current issues.*

**Why do I need to read this section?**

*Professional liability is important when things go wrong because a firm does not necessarily just lose a client, it may be sued. If the firm is a partnership it may have unlimited liability. Even if the firm is incorporated, and the firm has done nothing wrong, the time, effort, cost and worry of fighting a negligence claim or any other claim can be very damaging. Liability needs active management.*

*Current issues are examined in some higher level papers. The high-level issues do not change much: regulation, auditor independence, the expectations gaps and auditor liability have been problems for the profession in different ways for many years. The detail clearly changes but many issues can be brought under these headings. The profession does move on, but slowly.*

**What is important in this section?**

- *The different ways in which a professional accountant can be liable when things go wrong;*
- *The duty of care owed by auditors;*
- *The ways in which professional liability can be managed;*
- *The nature of the expectations gap and what might be done to reduce it, how auditor independence can be improved, the issues surrounding professional regulation and auditor judgement.*

**What sort of questions come up in this area?**

- *Questions tend to focus on the solutions rather than the problems of liability and current issues but they often also ask for an explanation of the problems.*
- *Auditing and assurance papers rarely ask for the detail of case law but using it where appropriate to illustrate the principles will be credited.*

**How do I stand out from the crowd?**

- *By answering optional questions on professional liability;*
- *By demonstrating an awareness of the different sides of the arguments in questions on current issues, and expressing a conclusion or opinion where it is asked for.*

### 5.2.1  PROFESSIONAL LIABILITY

This section is based on UK case law but the principles are recognisable in many jurisdictions.

The vast majority of professional bodies require practitioners to carry professional indemnity insurance (PII). This is because professional accountants can be liable to third parties in several different ways when things go wrong. To whom, and for how much, varies according to jurisdiction. However, despite differences in legal systems, there are more similarities than might be expected across jurisdictions, not least because legislators and judges are influenced by precedents set abroad, even though they are not bound by them.

The categories of liability in common law jurisdictions include:

- criminal liability;
- civil liability;
- liability in contract;
- liability in tort;
- statutory liability.[7]

These categories overlap. Liability in the tort of negligence is liability for a civil wrong, for example, but some torts are created by statute, such as liability for defective products under consumer protection legislation. Similarly, liability in contract is also a civil wrong, but statutory liabilities such as fraudulent misrepresentation also apply to contracts.[8]

Practitioners are liable like other private individuals and businesses for crimes and wrongs they commit under general legislation applying to everyone, such as employers' liability, liability for insider trading, fraud and theft, in addition to crimes and wrongs that specifically relate to their work. Practitioners are also answerable to professional bodies they belong to as a condition of membership. Professional bodies have the power to investigate professional wrongdoing by their members and to impose financial and other sanctions, including expulsion. Conviction of crimes involving financial misconduct is usually sufficient to warrant expulsion but other serious crimes are also relevant.

Sole practitioners and partners in partnerships have unlimited personal liability for the debts of the business if it defaults. Practitioners operating through companies and limited liability partnerships are not liable in this way because the members of the company or the LLP have limited liability. Nevertheless, the courts and legislation sometimes find or hold the directors of companies and partners in LLPs liable for their debts in any case where, for example, a company has been engaged in fraudulent or wrongful

---

[7] Anything 'statutory' is created by legislation.

[8] There is also an overlap between civil and criminal wrongs. For example, in common law jurisdictions such as the UK, even if the crime of murder cannot be proved 'beyond all reasonable doubt', the civil wrong of 'causing wrongful death' which requires proof 'on a balance of probabilities' might be. Signs that say 'Trespassers will be prosecuted' demonstrate misunderstandings about criminal and civil law. Trespass is a civil tort in which the 'plaintiff' sues the 'defendant'. Only if it constitutes criminal trespass, which usually involves crown (military or royal) property, will there be a crime, in which there is a 'prosecution' of the 'accused'.

trading under insolvency legislation. The directors can be ordered to contribute to the company's assets in such circumstances.[9]

### Statutory Liability

Practitioners, particularly auditors, may be statutorily *liable to creditors* under insolvency legislation, or *liable to investors* under financial services, tax and securities legislation.

In an increasing number of jurisdictions, auditors are criminally liable in statute, as in the UK under the Companies Act 2006, for:

- *knowingly or recklessly causing an audit report to include anything materially false, misleading or deceptive;*

- *acting as auditors while ineligible.*

Penalties include fines or imprisonment.

### Liability in Contract

Auditors can be liable in contract for simply failing to provide an audit report. They can also be liable for breach of contract if they perform the obligations negligently. They are required to apply 'reasonable skill and care', which will generally be as set out in auditing and other professional standards. The contract is between the company and the auditors, which means that only the company can sue the auditors. In practice, auditors are sometimes sued both in contract and in tort.

### Liability in Tort

Auditors can be liable in the *tort of negligence* to third parties such as investors in the audited entity. This requires that:

- auditors *owe a duty of care* to the third party;

- auditors *have breached that duty;*

- the plaintiff *has suffered a loss as a direct result of the breach.*

Much of the case law relates not to the standard of care owed or whether the duty of care was breached, i.e. whether or not auditors were in fact negligent, but to whether:

- a duty of care is owed in the first place;

- the loss suffered is a *direct* result of the auditors' negligence, or a result of something else.

---

[9]  The courts 'pierce the veil of incorporation' when finding the directors liable for an entity's debts. Fraudulent and wrongful trading involve continuing to trade where the directors knew or ought to have concluded that there was no reasonable prospect of avoiding insolvent liquidation, and did not take every step to minimise losses to creditors. Fraudulent trading is a criminal offence and requires a higher burden of proof than wrongful trading, which is a civil offence.

*How is the duty of care breached?*
A duty of care may *be breached* if the auditors did not:

• apply appropriate and up-to-date auditing, accounting and ethical requirements, which includes employing competent well-trained and supervised staff;[10]

• comply with the agreed terms of engagement.

---

**Re Kingston Cotton Mills (1896)**

Lord Justice Lopes

*'It is the duty of an auditor to bring to bear on the work he has to perform that **skill, care, and caution which a reasonably competent, careful, and cautious auditor would use.** An auditor is not bound to be a detective, or, as was said, to approach his work with suspicion, or with a foregone conclusion that there is something wrong. **He is a watchdog, but not a bloodhound.** Auditors must not be made liable for not tracking out ingenious and carefully laid schemes of fraud, when there is nothing to arouse their suspicion . . . So to hold would make the position of an auditor intolerable.'*

---

*To whom is the duty of care owed?*
Whether a duty of care is *owed* has been established over the years in different cases but a duty of care may be owed where:

• the auditor *knew or should have known* that the party suffering loss would rely on the financial statements;

• the party suffering loss *did in fact rely* on the financial statements and would have behaved differently if the financial statements had shown the true picture;

• there was sufficient *proximity* (closeness) between the auditor and the party suffering loss.

Parties believing that auditors owe them a duty of care include existing and prospective shareholders, banks and other lenders. The courts have been reluctant to allow auditors to owe a duty of care to a wide group of people such as prospective investors, for fear of opening the 'floodgates of litigation'.

---

*Caparo Industries Plc vs Dickman and Others (1990)*

Caparo bought shares in Fidelity several times in 1984, before the date of the audit report, on the date of the audit report and, relying on the audited accounts, they bought more shares, bid for the remainder, and acquired control later that year. They claimed that the accounts were misleading and showed a pre-tax profit of £1.3m that should have been a loss of £400,000. They argued that the auditors, Touche Ross, owed them a duty of care as investors and potential investors.

It was held that the auditors of a public company owe no duty of care to members of the public who decide to buy its shares, and that existing shareholders contemplating additional

---

[10] The pace of change in accounting, auditing and ethical standards means that it is not a rare thing for audit inspectors to find a small minority of practitioners using out-of-date standards.

investment are in the same position. The purpose of the audit is to fulfil a statutory require-ment, *to provide shareholders as a body with information* relevant to their proprietary interests in the company. There is no suggestion that the audit is to protect the interests of investors in the market.

*Auditors owe a duty of care to the company and to the shareholders as a body, not to indi-vidual shareholders.*

This narrow interpretation created a problem for those seeking to rely on the audited financial statements. Attempts were made to create a contractual relationship between auditors and third parties. In *ADT Ltd v Binder Hamlyn (1995)*, ADT considered bid-ding for the Britannia Security Group. In a meeting during the run up to the acquisi-tion, before the audit was finished, an audit partner told ADT representatives that he 'stood by' the accounts when asked to confirm that the accounts gave a true and fair view and that he had heard nothing subsequently to cast doubt on them. The group was found to be worth less than ADT paid for it and the auditors were held to owe a duty of care in contract to ADT. In a subsequent case, *Peach Publishing Ltd v Slater & Co (1997)*, it was held that auditors do not automatically owe a duty of care to pur-chasers to whom they made oral assurances. The case involved management accounts that auditors said were 'right', but unaudited.

Banks seek to establish a relationship with auditors so that they will be owed a duty of care by requiring as a condition of loan agreements that they will have access to the audited financial statements.

**Royal Bank of Scotland v Bannerman, Johnstone, Maclay and Others (2002)**

The bank provided an overdraft to a company whose accounts were overstated due to a fraud which they claimed the auditors were negligent in not detecting. The auditors claimed that they did not owe a duty of care to the bank. It was held that because of the work performed by the auditors, they would have known that the bank required audited accounts as part of the overdraft arrangement and knowing this, could have disclaimed liability to the bank. They did not do so and were liable to the bank.

Some firms now routinely use 'Bannerman clauses' in audit reports stating that:

- the *report is made solely to the company's members* as a body in accordance with companies legislation;

- the purpose of the audit work is to report to members as required, and *for no other purpose*;

- to the fullest extent permitted by law, the firm *does not accept or assume responsibil-ity to anyone other than the company* and the company's members as a body, for its audit work, report or opinions.[11]

---

[11] This type of wording is suggested by ICAEW. ACCA suggests that using disclaimers as *stan-dard* in audit reports may devalue them.

## Managing Professional Liability

As noted above, practitioners operating as partnerships and sole traders have unlimited liability for their work unless they limit it. General methods of managing practitioner liability include:

- operating through a company or limited liability partnership;
- maintaining PII covering claims made by third parties arising from the practitioners' work, and fidelity guarantee insurance covering claims made in respect of the misuse of assets held in trust by the firm, such as client money;
- agreeing a limitation of liability with clients;
- ensuring that engagement terms are agreed, auditing and quality control standards followed and disclaimers issued where permitted.

Until recently, auditors in the UK were not permitted to limit their liability in respect of audit work, although they were in relation to other work. UK companies legislation[12] now permits auditors to limit their liability provided that:

- the terms of the agreement are disclosed to and authorised by the members of the company;
- the agreement is fair and reasonable.

Any type of limitation may be agreed, including a fixed cap or a multiple of fees.[13] Such methods are used in jurisdictions outside the UK. Germany, Austria, Greece and Slovenia have statutory caps, for example. Australia has a system of proportionate liability.

## Directors and Auditors: Who is Responsible?

It is helpful to remember that when auditors do not detect a material misstatement in the financial statements, it is the directors who are responsible for the misstatement.

Unlimited liability for auditors remains a problem because:

- auditors are required to carry PII, directors are not and plaintiffs will sue those who are most likely to be able to pay rather than those who are to blame;[14]
- the principle of joint and several liability is entrenched in UK law and means that even if auditors are only partly to blame where things go wrong, they may bear all of the costs;
- the commercial insurance markets will not provide large firms with sufficient PII, meaning that they are forced to insure themselves.

---

[12] Section 534 of the Companies Act 2006 permits limited liability agreements.

[13] The Association of British Insurers (ABI), National Association of Pension Funds (NAPF) and PIRC generally oppose auditor liability limitation agreements and as a result very few have been agreed to by UK listed companies.

[14] As at 2013, ICAEW requires practitioners to carry a minimum level of PII of £1.5m for any one claim or claims in total. Where the firm's gross fees income is under £600,000, this is reduced to the greater of 2.5 time gross fee income and £100,000.

Suggested methods for dealing with these problems include:

- compulsory insurance for directors;
- modification of the joint and several liability regime;
- clarifying directors' responsibilities.

### Clarifying directors' responsibilities: UK

Until fairly recently, the duties of directors have been ill-defined. In the UK directors' duties have now been consolidated in companies legislation and guidance for directors and audit committees.[15] In the USA the Sarbanes-Oxley Act 2002 has clarified directors' responsibilities.

UK companies legislation[16] requires directors to promote the success of the company for the benefit of members as a whole having regard for:

- the likely long-term consequences of decisions;
- the interests of the company's employees;
- the need to foster the company's business relationships with suppliers, customers and others;
- the impact of the company's operations on the community and the environment.

### Clarifying directors' responsibilities: USA

The objective of the Sarbanes-Oxley Act 2002 is 'to protect investors by improving the accuracy and reliability of corporate disclosures . . .'.[17]

The Act established the *Public Company Accounting Oversight Board (PCAOB)*[18] to provide *independent oversight* of auditors by means of *registration of auditors, inspections,* auditing standard-setting and sanctioning of non-compliant auditors.

The Act also contains *auditor independence* requirements, including restrictions preventing auditors from providing certain non-audit services to audit clients.

Other areas covered include audit committees, reporting requirements for off-balance-sheet transactions, the stock (share) transactions of corporate officers, and conflicts of interest with analysts, brokers and credit rating agencies.

---

[15] Much UK guidance for directors is issued by or under the auspices of the Financial Reporting Council (FRC) www.frc.org.uk.

[16] Section 172 of the Companies Act 2006.

[17] It is also intended to 'deter and punish corporate and accounting fraud and corruption, ensure justice for wrongdoers, and protect the interests of workers and shareholders'. President George W. Bush.

[18] www.pcaobus.org.

The Act's most important changes:

- *make senior executives take individual responsibility* for corporate financial reports. The Act describes criminal and civil penalties for non-compliance. For example, Section 302 requires the company's principal officers, usually the CEO and CFO, to certify the company's financial reports;[19]
- require companies to have *internal control over financial reporting* for assuring the accuracy of financial reports;
- mandate *audits and reports by management on internal controls* (Section 404). This is the most costly aspect of the legislation for companies to implement.

Management is required to produce a report *affirming the responsibility of management* for establishing and maintaining an *adequate internal control structure* and an assessment of the *effectiveness* of the internal control structure.

US managers generally use the well-established and detailed COSO framework for internal control. Its 5-component model is recognisable in the description of internal control in ISA 315 on risk assessment, i.e. the control environment, risk assessment, control activities, the information system and monitoring of controls.

The PCAOB's Auditing Standard No. 5 provides guidance for auditors reporting on management's report. Auditors give their opinion on whether effective internal control over financial reporting was maintained in all material respects by management, in addition to the financial statement opinion. These are described as *integrated audits*.

The Act applies to companies that issue securities, i.e. whose shares can be traded on US exchanges and who are therefore subject to regulation by the Securities and Exchange Commission (SEC). It does not apply to 'private' companies.


## 5.2.2 REGULATION AND OTHER CURRENT ISSUES

Accountancy, like every other profession, has its critics. As with all criticism, some of it is justified, some is not. Like other professionals, accountants have from time to time denied problems and defended the status quo where perhaps they should have been more willing to change. The slow movement away from self-regulation to independent external regulation is in part a result of this intransigence but it probably would have happened anyway, and it is not unique to the accountancy profession. Lawyers, doctors and architects are also subject to a great deal more external inspection than they once were and there are now very few professional bodies taking full responsibility for regulating the activities of their own members.

Professional activities are now a great deal more transparent than they once were. Developments in technology have facilitated the standardisation of processes and procedures in medicine and law as well as in accounting and auditing.

---

[19] Section 1001 also requires the CEO to sign the corporate tax return.

These trends have already made it clear that a professional is not simply someone in possession of esoteric knowledge. However adept we become at researching our ailments, property law or tax cases, and however sophisticated expert diagnostic systems become, most of us still find it necessary to consult doctors, lawyers and accountants from time to time. We do not understand what the basic information we have found means, or how to use it. Training, skill and a lot of experience are what we pay for in a professional. We seek their advice because we value their opinions and respect their judgements.

### Professional Judgement

The problem with professional judgement is that it is easily abused. Despite continuing exhortations by academics for policy and practice in many areas to be more evidence-based, they remain largely unsupported by any sort of evidence, sometimes because evidence is ignored but mostly because the evidence is not there.

High-quality evidence is invaluable, and while the tools for the collection and manipulation of data are better than they ever have been, evidence can rarely be provided as fast as policy-makers would like and it is often inconclusive. For these reasons, a certain amount of suspicion always surrounds professional judgements. Is the surgery advised because the patient will benefit, or because the surgeon will benefit? Is the accounting treatment accepted by the auditor appropriate, or has the auditor accepted it in order to keep the client? These questions can only be answered in the context of the wider regulatory regime.

Auditors receive a thorough technical training and training in ethics. They are required by legislation, professional standards and professional bodies to use their judgement independently and objectively. They are required to act with integrity. Bodies independent of the profession develop the standards they apply. If auditors do not behave appropriately, independent audit inspectors and professional bodies take action against them. But this has not always been the case.

### Self-regulation and Independent Regulation

The accountancy profession in the UK has long argued that principles are better than rules. Rules create a compliance mentality, a tick-box approach and stifle innovation, creativity and judgement. They discourage the brightest and best from entering the profession. But the rules keep on coming. Less than 30 years ago, there were three short auditing standards and five auditing guidelines in the UK. UK auditing standards and guidance now take up over 1,500 pages. The same trend is evident in accounting standards. Why?

*Quis custodiet ipsos custodes?* means 'who guards the guards?'. Regulation is about who audits the auditors. Self-regulation is no longer seen as acceptable in any of the professions, if it ever was. The first accounting and auditing standards in the UK were developed in the 1970s in response to concerns about inconsistencies in reporting.[20] Each wave of corporate collapses and frauds since then from BCCI and

---

[20] The Hansard Report into the fraud at the Peachey Property Corporation dated 1979 notes that '. . . the ways in which accounts are qualified has to be seriously looked at . . .', although the development of the first UK auditing standards were already under way by then.

Polly Peck in the 1980s and 1990s, through to Enron and WorldCom in the early 2000s, gave rise to, or was accompanied by, changes in company law and corporate governance requirements and accounting and auditing standards.

Over the same period, the Big 8 firms became the Big 5 and, with the demise of Arthur Andersen, the Big 4, partly reflecting the globalisation of clients. In the 1970s, professional bodies in the UK set auditing, accounting and ethical requirements. The UK's independent Financial Reporting Council (FRC) now sets them all. Similar moves towards independent regulation have been made all over the world.[21]

The combined effects of independent regulation and the adoption of international auditing and accounting standards in the mid-2000s have probably improved audit quality and consistency in financial reporting, but no-one seems much happier. Annual reports are cluttered, complex and lengthy. Investors do not seem satisfied with the information in them and they now question more than ever the value of audits, the appropriateness of IFRS and whether global convergence of standards is a good thing.

### Expectations Gap

The expectations gap is as old as the profession itself and shows no sign of going away. Outsiders have always expected auditors to act as financial policemen, to detect frauds, to publicise the financial wrongdoing of errant companies and to give warnings before companies collapse. This is not the same as what auditors are actually tasked with, which is forming an opinion on the historical financial statements. It is important in this context to understand that:

- many of the large figures in the financial statements are soft, subjective estimates rather than hard figures and are therefore legitimately a matter of opinion;

- auditors are no more able to foresee than anyone else a major loss of confidence by investors in the markets.

In practice, a great deal of negotiation takes place between auditors and clients, particularly over accounting treatments. Frauds and misstatements are detected by auditors and dealt with by clients. Much of this is never publicised though. Audit is sometimes described as a hygiene factor in that it is only noticed when it is not done properly.

Elements of the expectations gap include a:

- *standards gap*: the belief that auditing standards require auditors to do more than they do, or should require auditors to do more than they do;

- *performance gap:* where auditors do not apply standards properly as highlighted by reports on firm performance published by regulators such as the UK's Audit Quality Review team;

- *a liability gap:* the expectations gap proper, i.e. the difference between what auditors are in fact required to do, and what people believe they are required or should be required to do.

---

[21] UK professional bodies now train professional accountants, supervise the audits of smaller entities, and represent and discipline their members. These remain substantial undertakings.

The profession has long maintained that the best way to *bridge the expectations gap* is to *educate the public* about what auditors actually do. The public has doggedly resisted this type of education despite numerous changes to the audit report clarifying what auditors do and do not do, and continues to insist that auditors ought to do more.

Auditors have always been willing to admit that *improvements in performance* are possible and the requirements of auditing standards are now more demanding than they ever have been.

Auditors currently appear to be more receptive to suggestions that they *provide more information about key audit judgements*. Auditors have also maintained that auditor liability and the threat of a claim that could wipe out a firm have made them reluctant to provide more information.

### Improving Auditor Performance and Perceptions of Audit

#### EC draft legislation

Many current issues are covered in recent draft EC legislation on reform of the audit market. It comprises:

- a regulation on the quality of audits of public-interest entities;
- a directive to enhance the single market for statutory audits.[22]

The objective of the legislation is to improve the internal market for audit services and the quality of audits for public interest entities (PIEs). The draft legislation covers:

- *mandatory audit firm rotation:* public interest entities (PIEs) would not be permitted to engage the same firm for more than six years. The initial appointment would be for a minimum of two years, renewable once, with a four year cooling off period. The arguments for and against mandatory firm rotation are mixed. On the one hand, if a firm knows it is going to have to hand over to another firm in the near future it is likely to make sure that all is in order. On the other hand, unfamiliarity with the client means that things may slip through the net in the first years of audit. Changing auditors is time-consuming and expensive. The small amount of academic evidence about the effects of mandatory firm rotation in jurisdictions such as Italy, Brazil, India, Singapore and South Korea suggests that the overall effect on the cost of capital and shareholder value of mandatory rotation is neutral or negative. The profession and preparers of financial statements have opposed mandatory audit firm rotation;
- *mandatory tendering:* PIEs would be required to undertake a tendering process involving at least two audit firms, one of which must earn no more than 15% of its total audit fees from PIEs. This is intended to encourage the growth of

---

[22] Regulations apply directly. Directives must be implemented by Member States.

smaller firms to bridge the now substantial gap between the size of the Big 4 and their nearest rivals. It might also encourage the appointment of joint auditors. Where a PIE has voluntarily appointed joint auditors, the maximum duration of the engagement would be nine years under the provisions above. Joint audits are still required in some jurisdictions, partly to encourage the growth of smaller firms. They were once common in the UK for financial institutions. Their cost, and an increasing disinclination on the part of larger firms to risk working with other firm because each firm is liable for the work of the other firm and because of incompatible audit methodologies, mean that they are now unusual in the UK. The lack of choice of auditors among larger entities, who sometimes struggle to obtain professional services because of the combined effects of independence requirements and specialisation, is of concern to competition authorities.[23] The vast majority of entities on a number of stock exchanges are audited by the Big 4. Forcing the break-up of larger firms would be a last resort, and having audit-only firms might go some way to alleviate concerns;

- *audit-only firms:* firms taking more than a third of their audit revenues from large PIEs would be prohibited from providing other services to those entities except for related audit services[24] which would be capped at 10% of the total audit fee. Many argue that this would be inefficient and ineffective;

- *audit reports:* audit reports would be expanded considerably to cover details of audit methodology, key audit risk areas and materiality levels. The report would not be longer than four pages or 10,000 characters. It would identify each member of the audit engagement team. Reporting proposals have also been made recently by both the IAASB and the PCAOB;

- *audit committees:* PIEs, with some exceptions, would be required to have an audit committee. At least one member of the audit committee would have auditing competencies and at least two members would have accounting and/or auditing competencies. Auditors would provide extended reports to audit committees with detailed information on going concern issues and material audit findings;

- *non-audit services:* non-audit services auditors would be prohibited from providing to audit clients would include accountancy services, designing and implementing internal control or risk management systems, certain internal audit and IT services and expert services unrelated to the audit. Some services could be provided subject to the approval of the audit committee, such as some recruitment, IT and due diligence services.

Many of these requirements are already present in some form in ethical requirements.

---

[23] The UK's Competition Commission is investigating the market for audit services in the UK.
[24] Related audit services would include audits of interim financial information, assurance on corporate governance, corporate social responsibility statements and other statutory and regulatory returns.

### Audit report proposals

Audit reports used to be a lot shorter than they are now. Their length has increased partly because auditor reporting requirements have become more complex, but mostly because auditors have been encouraged to communicate the work they have performed and the value of the audit more clearly.

More effective auditor communication comes not only through the audit report but through enhanced communications with audit committees and those communications are more extensive than they used to be, but they are not made public. Some professional investors want this information, or similar information, to be made public. The main issue with audit reports that are in the public domain has always been that they consist largely of a pass/fail audit opinion, which is valuable to users, and a great deal of boilerplate, i.e. standardised wording.

The main obstacles to auditors providing more entity-specific information, such as information about significant audit issues, have been:

• the potential liability for auditors;

• the belief that the type of information that professional investors wish to read is information that should probably come from the entity itself, rather than auditors, whose job it is to express an independent opinion, rather than provide original information about the entity. If auditors provide information covering the same area as the entity, there is the potential for confusion, or worse.

Pressure on auditors to provide more information than they currently do, in the form of an auditor commentary[25] on the audited financial statements and/or the audit itself, has resulted in proposals from the PCAOB and IAASB in this area. Some jurisdictions already provide some such information. The additional information would highlight matters that, in the auditor's judgement, are likely to be most important to users' understanding of the audited financial statements or the audit. It would be required for public interest entities.

Proposals also focus on the possibility of referring to material going concern uncertainties in the audit report and on any material inconsistencies between the audited financial statements and other information.

### Audit firm governance and annual transparency reports

Some audit firms are big businesses, employing large numbers of people and operating in many ways on a multinational basis. Until very recently, because they operated as partnerships, they produced very little information about their affairs, unlike the businesses they audited.

Regulators were probably less concerned about the financial affairs of large firms than about the need for them to be seen to be operating proper quality control systems, and

---

[25] The auditor commentary might parallel the management discussion and analysis (MDA) provided by the directors of US companies, i.e. an auditor discussion and analysis.

having proper governance systems in place to ensure that commercial considerations did not override professional requirements.

The UK's *Audit Firm Governance Code* applies to eight audit firms that together audit about 95% of the companies listed on the Main Market of the London Stock Exchange. Other audit firms are encouraged to adopt it.

The Code takes a 'comply or explain' approach and is based on the UK's corporate governance requirements for listed entities. The Code recognises that the governance challenges faced by audit firms are different from those faced by listed companies. It establishes the principle that audit firms should appoint independent non-executives within their governance structure. It also codifies existing good practice.

The EU was the first jurisdiction to require audit firms to publish *annual transparency reports*. The USA now has similar requirements. Australia has followed suit.

The type of information required in annual transparency reports is intended to provide existing and potential clients and other stakeholders with factual information about the operation of the audit firm. Information included covers the firm's:

- legal, governance and ownership structure, including information about any network;

- risk management and internal quality control systems;

- independence practices, CPD and whistle-blowing policies;

- public interest entity clients;

- summary financial information;

- partner remuneration.

*Other current issues*
Current issues in standard-setting are dealt with in Section 8. More current issues can be found at the web-site accompanying this text www.wiley.com/go/bagshaw_essentials.

## Section essentials: what you need to remember

- *The main categories of professional liability.*

- *The principle ways in which liability can be managed.*

- *The constituent elements of the expectations gaps, the main issues with auditor independence and how it might be improved, the importance of independent regulation and professional judgement.*

# SECTION 5, QUESTION

Required:

(a) Explain how internal auditors contribute to good corporate
    governance and risk management.                    (6 marks)

A very high proportion of listed companies in many jurisdictions have audit
committees. Their functions include liaison between external auditors and the
main board of directors to help maintain, amongst other things, the external
auditors' independence and the integrity of published financial information.
Nevertheless, some large entities with seemingly good quality corporate governance structures, including well resourced audit committees, have collapsed
unexpectedly in recent years.

Required:

(b) Explain why audit committees have not always warned about or
    helped prevent corporate collapses in recent years.   (7 marks)

Discussions between audit committees and auditors may cover limitation of
liability agreements. Audit firms have many methods of avoiding litigation
and claims.

Required:

(c) Discuss the advantages and disadvantages of restricting auditors'
    liability and describe how firms may limit their exposure to
    litigation and claims generally.                    (7 marks)

Total                                                    (20 marks)

# 6 AUDIT REPORTING

## 6.1 AUDIT FINALISATION

Covering: ISA 520 *Analytical Procedures*, ISA 450 *Evaluation of Misstatements Identified during the Audit*, ISA 560 *Subsequent Events*, ISA 580 *Written Representations*.

**Why do I need to read this section?**

*The material in this section is straightforward and much of it is relevant to general questions on audit evidence as well as to questions on audit finalisation. When prompted, it is clear that students know that written representations, final analytical procedures and similar matters are relevant towards the end of an audit but they sometimes have difficulty in pulling the issues together. Students somehow run out of steam at this stage of the audit!*

**What is important in this section?**

*Evaluating misstatements properly can make the difference between issuing an appropriate audit report and an inappropriate one. Subsequent events are important in practice and in theory and the ability to distinguish between what needs an adjustment and what needs disclosing is important. Knowing how to deal with problems arising after the issue of the financial statements, and whether a new audit report can be issued is also critical because auditors cannot simply change their minds!*

*Written representations are probably the most contentious issue in practice. It is important to know that some representations are mandatory, i.e. those covering the responsibility of management for the financial statements, and that others depend on the client's circumstances.*

**What sort of questions come up in this area?**

*Knowledge-based questions on subsequent events and on mandatory written representations are common but the need for written representations is relevant to many questions on audit evidence. General questions on audit finalisation and how auditors arrive at the overall audit conclusion drawing together all of the issues covered in this section come up from time to time.*

**How do I stand out from the crowd?**

*Not many students distinguish clearly between analytical procedures as used at the risk assessment stage, as substantive procedures and as used at the final review stage. Students who do make this distinction stand out.*

*Markers are impressed by students who demonstrate an holistic knowledge of how and why the various strands of the audit need to be brought together in order to form an overall conclusion of the financial statements. This is a higher-level skill and students should try to show the thinking of the partner asked to sign the audit report, rather than the junior or manager presenting files for review.*

### 6.1.1   FINAL ANALYTICAL PROCEDURES AND THE FINANCIAL STATEMENT CLOSING PROCESS

**Final Analytical Procedures**

Analytical procedures performed near the end of the audit are designed to provide evidence that the financial statements are consistent with the auditors' understanding of the entity. Analytical procedures are performed on high-level aggregated data when forming an overall conclusion. At the detailed testing stage, procedures are performed on lower-level more disaggregated data. To an extent, procedures performed at audit finalisation resemble the analytical procedures performed at the risk assessment stage.

Analytical procedures at the audit finalisation stage should corroborate conclusions formed based on the substantive procedures and tests of control effectiveness performed on financial statement components at the detailed testing stage. Auditors are looking for evidence of management bias at this final stage and for the effect of any significant late journal entries that are often poorly controlled, and can be used to manipulate the view given by the financial statements as a whole.

**The Financial Statement Closing Process**

The financial statement closing process is often a higher risk area. Auditors and clients are under pressure to complete the audit and reporting process on time. For these reasons, auditors are required to *perform substantive procedures on the closing process* including:

- *reconciling the financial statements to the underlying records;*

- *examining material journal entries* and other adjustments made during the course of preparing the financial statements.[1]

### 6.1.2   EVALUATING MISSTATEMENTS

Reports of investigations into major corporate collapses sometimes observe, albeit with hindsight, that the evidence of the relevant fraud or accounting irregularity was not hidden from auditors. Reports note that such evidence was sometimes recorded in the audit file, but that auditors did not appreciate the significance of the issue, follow it up or make the right linkages. Reports by professional bodies and independent regulators on audit firms highlight the same problem. Audit failure is more likely to involve errors of judgement and a failure to evaluate audit findings properly than deficient audit methodologies, or sampling risk, for example.

---

[1]   ISA 330 on responses to assessed risks, paragraphs 20 and A52.

Evaluating misstatements is a critical part of audit finalisation. Some misstatements are routine and automated, such as a failure to apply the correct sales tax rate to an invoice. Evaluating something as simple as this, though, involves more than correcting the immediate misstatement. Evaluation involves consideration of whether, for example:

- there are further financial implications, such as a penalty sales tax;
- the error is isolated, or whether it represents a breakdown in controls, and the implications of that for the level of substantive procedures and assessed risks;
- controls have been overridden, and the implications of that for risk assessment and the assessment of management integrity.

Where misstatements are not automated, such as erroneous journal entries close to the period-end adjusting the inventory valuation, even more questions need to be asked.

*Misstatements are the difference between the way*:

- *items are reported in the financial statements;*
- *they should be reported,* in accordance with the applicable financial reporting framework.

Clearly, there can be differences of opinion between auditors and clients. Misstatements can be *factual* where there is no doubt, *judgemental* where auditors and clients differ on matters such as estimates and how accounting policies are to be applied, and *projected* misstatements, i.e. the auditors' best estimate of misstatements in populations based on projections from samples.

Matters affecting the evaluation of misstatements include:

- materiality levels;
- compliance with regulatory requirements, banking or debt covenants;
- whether the matter is subject to very specific disclosure requirements such as transactions with related parties and directors' remuneration.

### Communicating Identified Errors

Auditors are required to *accumulate misstatements identified during the audit* other than those that are clearly trivial.[2] In particular, they consider whether misstatements:

- could be material when taken together with undetected misstatements; or
- approach the level of materiality.

---

[2] ISA 450 on evaluating misstatements, paragraph 5. Clearly trivial means clearly inconsequential, either individually or in aggregate, and is of a wholly different order, i.e. smaller than anything material.

If misstatements could be material, as described above, revisions to the overall audit strategy and plan may be needed.

Misstatements arise from fraud or error. Any misstatement that is not a fraud is, by definition, an error. While entity controls should detect misstatements, the inherent limitations of internal control, including the risk of management override of controls and collusion, mean that some misstatements will not be detected by the entity. There is also the risk that auditors fail to detect misstatements either because of sampling risk – the sample may not show errors but the population as a whole might – or because of non-sampling risk, i.e. auditors may simply make a mistake. It is for this reason that auditors need to take account of the possibility of undetected misstatements.

In practice, auditors discover many misstatements. In an ideal world, the client would correct all of them but the work involved is often considered not worth the effort, particularly where the amounts involved are small.

Auditors are required to *communicate all misstatements to management on a timely basis*[3] and to ask for them to be corrected to prevent a build-up that might be material. If management refuses auditors need to understand why, and consider the implications, such as whether the refusal might indicate management bias.

Auditors report uncorrected misstatements to those charged with governance, in summary if there are many small items, together with a request for them to be corrected.

Auditors also *seek written representations asking management to confirm their belief that uncorrected misstatements are immaterial*.

Documentation should include:

- a schedule of accumulated errors;
- a schedule of uncorrected (unadjusted) errors;
- a note of the level below which errors are considered clearly trivial.

### Evaluating Uncorrected Misstatements

A corrected misstatement is no longer a misstatement. Uncorrected misstatements may be material either individually or in aggregate. Individual misstatements may be offset against each other but only if they are within the same account class. A material misstatement in revenue cannot be offset against a misstatement of a similar size within expenses on the basis that the effect on profit is immaterial. Individually material misstatements that are not offset are likely to be corrected by the entity to avoid a modified

---

[3] In many jurisdictions, anti-money laundering legislation prevents auditors from 'tipping-off' (warning) a client about a matter if it might prejudice investigations into illegal acts. For this reason, it may not be possible for auditors to communicate matters to management in some cases.

audit report, provided it is agreed that the misstatement is in fact a misstatement. Auditors are more usually in the more difficult position of considering the aggregate effect of misstatements. This includes the effect of uncorrected misstatements of prior periods that may have a cumulative effect, either in individual account areas or on the financial statements as a whole.

### 6.1.3 SUBSEQUENT EVENTS

Some large audits involve audit staff being at the client's premises almost all year round. Some events occurring after the financial statement date require adjustment or disclosure in the financial statements. Others event are accounted for in the following period. The decision depends on whether the event provides evidence of conditions existing at the financial statement date, or of conditions that arose afterwards. A major customer becoming insolvent in March for an entity with a financial statement date of 31 December may well constitute evidence of both, i.e. a bad debt in both periods.

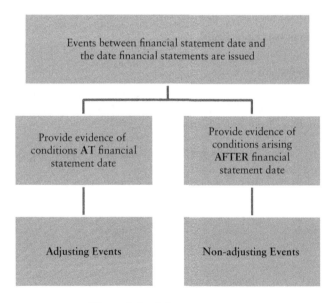

**Figure 6.1** Subsequent events

IAS 10[4] includes within adjusting events those that indicate that the going concern assumption is not appropriate.

---

[4] IAS 10 *Events after the Reporting Period.*

> *Adjusting events* require *adjustments* to the financial statements and often some disclosures.
>
> *Non-adjusting events* should be *disclosed* if non-disclosure would affect the ability of users to make proper evaluations and decisions. Disclosure is of the nature of the event and an estimate of its financial effect, or a statement that an estimate cannot be made.

Adjusting events might include, where significant:

- the unsuccessful outcome of litigation in progress at the financial statement date;
- receipts from the sale of inventory below the amount stated in the balance sheet.

Non-adjusting events might include, where significant:

- the successful outcome of litigation in progress at the financial statement date;
- restructuring (mergers, acquisitions, disposals, changes in debt or equity);
- acquisition or disposal of assets;
- expropriation of assets by government;
- destruction of assets by fire or flood.

### Auditors' Responsibilities

*Auditors are required to actively search for subsequent events between the financial statement date and the date of the auditors' report. After that, they are only required to deal with issues that come to their attention.*[5]

In practice, matters coming to light very late in the next period are dealt with in the subsequent period's financial statements.

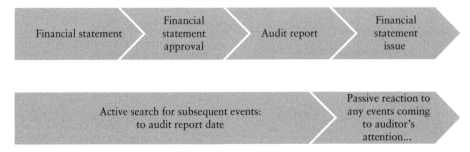

**Figure 6.2**   Subsequent events: key dates and auditors' actions

---

[5]   ISA 560 on subsequent events, paragraphs 6 and 10.

*Between the financial statement date and the audit report date*
The audit report cannot be issued until management or those charged with governance have taken responsibility for the financial statements, i.e. approved them, because the financial statements do not exist, technically, until that has happened.

Evidence that all subsequent events requiring adjustment or disclosure have been identified is obtained through *procedures between the financial statement date and the audit report date, including*:

- *understanding management procedures* for dealing with subsequent events;

- *inquiring* of management and any legal advisers *about subsequent events*;

- *reading minutes* of management and shareholder meetings;

- *reading financial information* such as interim or management accounts and budgets;

- considering whether *written representations* are needed.

*Between the audit report date and the financial statement issue date*
Auditors only need to consider taking action in this period where matters come to their attention. They are not required to search for events. They are required to *discuss with management any subsequent events that do come to their attention, including whether the financial statements need amendment.* That might be the case if the events that come to light might have caused auditors to issue a different audit report had the matter been known at the time the report was signed. An unexpected outcome to significant litigation might constitute such an event, for example.

*If management make a necessary amendment to the financial statements,* auditors audit the amendment, update the subsequent events work for the rest of the financial statements and issue a new audit report. In some jurisdictions such as the UK, there are legal provisions dealing with such revisions of financial statements. In other jurisdictions such as the USA, 'dual dating' is permitted, meaning that the amendment is audited, but the subsequent events work is not updated for the rest of the financial statements. The financial statements and audit report bear two dates, one the original date, the other date is restricted to the amendment made. The new or amended audit report contains an emphasis of matter referring to the restriction in such cases.

*If management do not make a necessary amendment to the financial statements,* provided that the audit report has not been supplied to the entity, a modified audit report can be issued. If the audit report has been supplied to the entity and the financial statements are issued without amendment, auditors are in a difficult position and need to take action to prevent reliance on the audit report. Such situations are rare and in practice it would mean taking legal advice.

In many jurisdictions including the UK, auditors have the right to speak on audit related matters at the AGM, and if they choose to resign, they are obliged to make a statement concerning the reasons for their resignation.

*After financial statements are issued*

If events requiring adjustment or disclosure come to the auditors' attention after the financial statements are issued and the financial statements are amended, a new audit report can be issued, but this is very rare. If they are not amended, legal advice, resignation or speaking at the AGM are possible with the objective of preventing reliance on the audit report.


## 6.1.4    WRITTEN REPRESENTATIONS

The significance of written representations as audit evidence is a matter of opinion. Some firms obtain them because ISAs require them to but attach little value to them, others take a more positive view. The requirements in this area have changed in recent years and firms are no longer permitted, if they ever were, to ask for blanket written representations confirming all areas involving the use of judgement. Nor are they permitted to use written representations as a basis for obtaining little or no additional audit evidence in the relevant area.

The mandatory representations concerning management's responsibility for the financial statements and the provision of information to auditors are now very detailed. This can be a problem in smaller audits because client management may not understand why it is asked in the representation letter to take responsibility for the financial statements that it has paid the firm to prepare. At best, such clients consider it unfair. Firms of all sizes continue to spend some time agreeing the representation letter with clients.

Written representations are a ***necessary but not sufficient*** source of audit evidence in some areas and the fact that management have provided representations does not reduce the extent or quality of other audit evidence required.


### Representations on Responsibility for the Financial Statements

Written representations are from management to auditors. If those charged with governance have greater overall responsibility for the financial statements, auditors seek written representations from them instead. Representations are required stating that in accordance with engagement terms management has:

- *fulfilled its responsibility for the preparation of financial statements* in accordance with the applicable financial reporting framework, and that they give a true and fair view of/fairly present in all material respects the position, performance and cash flows in accordance with the identified financial reporting framework, as appropriate;

- provided auditors with *all relevant information and access to information* and that *all transactions have been recorded* and reflected in the financial statements.


### Other Representations

Other representations are required by specific ISAs, or are needed to support other audit evidence on specific assertions in the financial statements.

Specific representations *required by ISAs* include representations that:

- all known *litigation and claims* have been disclosed to auditors;[6]
- the identity of *related parties* and all transactions with them have been disclosed to auditors and included in the financial statements;[7]
- all *subsequent events* have been adjusted for or disclosed as appropriate;[8]
- *significant assumptions* used in accounting estimates are reasonable;[9] and
- full disclosure has been made to auditors in relation to *fraud risks* and compliance with laws and regulations.

Representations to *support other audit evidence* might include:

- the appropriateness of *accounting policies* selected;
- *management plans or intentions* that affect the carrying value of assets;
- the completeness of actual and *contingent liabilities*;
- confirmation of *title to assets* and any assets pledged as collateral for loans;
- that management has communicated to auditors all known *deficiencies in internal control*.

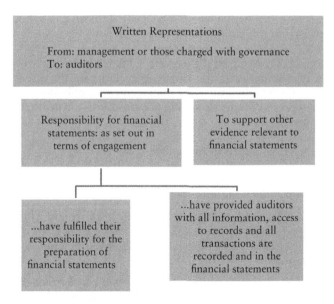

**Figure 6.3** Written representations

---

6 ISA 501 on audit evidence for selected items, paragraph 12.
7 ISA 550 on related parties, paragraph 26.
8 ISA 560 on subsequent events, paragraph 9.
9 ISA 540 on accounting estimates, paragraph 22.

### Format and Date

Written representations are dated as near as possible to the audit report date and take the form of a letter addressed to auditors. In practice, auditors usually draft the letter and negotiate its contents with the client.

Legislation often makes entities responsible for the financial statements, and requires them to make statements about those responsibilities either in the financial statements or elsewhere. Management may, understandably, point to such statements and ask why they do not suffice for audit purposes. Management does not want to repeat such statements in representation letters using the wording suggested by auditors that is likely to be slightly different to the wording used in legislation. Where management makes such statements of responsibilities publicly, they may suffice for audit purposes. However, the mere fact that such statements appear in legislation does not suffice, nor does a statement of compliance with legislation, without specifying what the legislation says.

### Representations not Provided or Doubts as to Reliability

If auditors have doubts about the competence, diligence or integrity of management, or if there are unresolved inconsistencies between representations and other evidence, auditors must consider whether written representations are reliable. If, after discussion, management refuses to make the representations auditors consider necessary, auditors need to reconsider management's integrity. In both cases, auditors also need to consider an impact on the audit report.

A disclaimer of opinion is required if there are sufficient doubts about the integrity of management that representations regarding responsibility for the provision of information to auditors cannot be relied on, or if management simply does not provide those representations or representations regarding responsibility for the financial statements. This does not happen often.

### Section essentials: what you need to remember

- *Mandatory written representations deal with responsibility for the financial statements and provision of information.*

- *Subsequent events require adjustment in the financial statements if they reflect conditions existing at the balance sheet date, and disclosure if they reflect conditions that did not exist at the balance sheet date but non-disclosure would affect the ability of users to make decisions.*

- *High-level final analytical procedures are performed on the financial statements as a whole and are designed to corroborate conclusions formed based on audit procedures performed on financial statements components.*

- *In evaluating misstatements, auditors accumulate misstatements identified during the audit, and consider whether they could be material when aggregated with undetected misstatements, or whether they approach the level of materiality.*

## 6.2 MODIFIED AND UNMODIFIED AUDIT OPINIONS

**Covering**: ISA 700 *Forming an Opinion and Reporting on Financial Statements*; ISA 705 *Modifications to the Opinion in the Independent Auditor's Report*.

**Why do I need to read this section?**

*The basic concepts underlying audit reports have not changed significantly for a long time. Reports have, however, become longer. The opinion given at the end of the audit report on truth and fairness or fair presentation has remained largely unchanged for decades. The material above it, explaining what has been done and who is responsible for it, has lengthened. Examining reporting is therefore well established but the style of questions has changed over the years and it is now unlikely that students would be asked to reproduce a full audit report in an exam.*

**What is important in this section?**

*A clear understanding of the terminology used in audit reports and their significance is important, mainly because students often understand the subject but fail to make that clear by using imprecise or incorrect terminology. This is one of the few areas where terminology is very important.*

**What sort of questions come up in this area?**

*Case-study style questions asking what sort of audit opinion would be appropriate, together with an outline of the content of the rest of the report are common, as are questions asking students to draft a modified opinion. Short questions on what type of audit report is appropriate in a given set of circumstances are easy to set.*

**How do I stand out from the crowd?**

*Students who clearly distinguish between the various types of modified opinion, reports on other legal and regulatory requirements, emphases of matter and other matter paragraphs, are rare, and stand out. Students also stand out if they demonstrate a good understanding of the content of audit reports outside the opinion paragraph, and of when and how it is acceptable to change the standard wording.*

### 6.2.1 AUDIT REPORTS

The principles underlying opinion paragraphs have not changed in recent years but this does not mean that they will not do so in future. Audit reporting appears to be in a state of transition and there is much discussion about whether auditors should report on more than the truth and fairness or fair presentation of financial statements. These discussions are not new though, and it remains to be seen whether auditors will in future report on matters such as areas of audit risk and materiality, as has been suggested. The current debate in this area among professional bodies, standard-setters and regulators seems more likely to result in real and far-reaching change this time than on previous occasions.

One significant issue is about who provides information. Currently, auditors report on information prepared by management but do not provide any other information about the entity that is not already provided by management. Some argue that in order for the audit to retain its value, it is essential that independent auditors continue to report on information prepared by management, rather than providing information themselves. However, some investors and others would like to see more 'original' reporting by auditors on, for example, matters discussed with those charged with governance which include audit risk, materiality, areas of significant audit judgement, significant difficulties encountered during the audit and what was discussed with management.

### General Purpose, Compliance and Fair Presentation Frameworks

A great deal of the value of an audit report lies in the opinion paragraph. The audit opinion depends on the financial reporting framework used. *General purpose* frameworks that meet the common information needs of a wide range of users are either *fair presentation* frameworks or *compliance* frameworks. Auditors are required to form an opinion on whether the financial statements are prepared in all material respects in accordance with the applicable financial reporting framework.

*Compliance frameworks* only require compliance with the requirements of the framework. The audit opinion states that the financial statements have been prepared in all material respects in accordance with the identified financial reporting framework. In extremely rare cases, it is possible that such financial statements are misleading, in which cases auditors need to consider whether the framework is actually acceptable.

*Fair presentation frameworks* require more than simple compliance with the framework's requirements. They acknowledge that it may be necessary to **provide disclosures beyond the framework** and, in extremely rare circumstances, to **depart** from framework requirements, to achieve fair presentation.[10] The latter requirement must be explicit. Such frameworks require departures from their own requirements in order to achieve compliance with their own requirements, which may seem odd. The audit opinion states that the financial statements *give a true and fair view of . . .* or *fairly present in all material respects the position, performance and cash flows . . . in accordance with the identified financial reporting framework.* The two sets of terminology are equivalent under ISAs. The need for departures from the framework in order to achieve fair presentation is known in many jurisdictions as the *true and fair override.*[11]

---

[10] ISA 200 on overall objectives, paragraph 13.

[11] If law or regulation prescribe the wording of the opinion in terms that are significantly different to these requirements, that wording can be used provided users are not misled, which may require some additional explanation. If even this is not enough, the engagement should not be accepted unless required by law or regulation, and the audit cannot be described as having been conducted in accordance with ISAs. These provisions are similar to those applying to agreement on the wording of the preconditions for an audit.

## Forming an Opinion

Matters to consider in forming an opinion include whether:

- sufficient appropriate evidence has been obtained;
- uncorrected misstatements are material;
- qualitative aspects of accounting practices include indicators of management bias;
- accounting policies are adequately disclosed and appropriate;
- accounting estimates are reasonable;
- information is relevant, reliable, comparable and understandable.

Issues that might result in a modified audit opinion arising from the considerations above include:

- the selective correction of misstatements and management bias when making estimates, which represent a cumulative lack of neutrality. When taken together with uncorrected misstatements these might cause a material misstatement;
- situations in which compliance with the applicable financial reporting framework is qualified, and the financial statements are described as being 'in substantial compliance with IFRS', for example.

## Content of Audit Reports
Audit reports include:

- *a title*: indicating the auditors' *independence;*
- *an addressee*: usually *shareholders* or those charged with governance;
- *an introductory paragraph*: identifying the *entity*, stating that financial statements have been *audited*, identifying the *title* of each statement audited, often using *page numbers, the date(s) or period(s)* covered and referring to the *accounting policies* used;
- *management responsibilities*: for the *preparation of financial statements* in accordance with the framework that are free from material misstatement whether due to fraud or error, for *internal controls* that enable it to do this, for the selection of *accounting policies;*
- *and auditors' responsibilities*: to express an *opinion* based on an *ISA* audit, requiring compliance with *ethical* requirements and to obtain *reasonable assurance;* referring to *procedures* performed on amounts and disclosures, to the *risk* of material misstatement due to fraud and error, to *judgement, internal controls*, evaluating the *appropriateness of accounting policies*, the *reasonableness of estimates*, the *overall presentation* of financial statements and whether sufficient appropriate *evidence* has been obtained;
- *an opinion*: on *compliance* with the framework or a *true and fair* or *fair presentation* opinion, on any *other legal* and *regulatory requirements* and on any specific procedures requested by the client;

- *a signature*: by the firm(s), the individual auditor(s), or both and usually the individuals' professional designation(s);

- *a date*: no earlier than the date on which auditors have obtained sufficient appropriate audit evidence which requires that the *financial statements are complete* and those with responsibility for their *preparation have asserted that they have taken responsibility* for them, usually in the management representation letter;

- *an address*: the location in which the auditors practise, usually a city.

A mnemonic for this is *Adam's toad.*

Where law or regulation require the use of different wording to that stipulated by ISA 700, particularly for the audit opinion, there is a risk that users might misunderstand the report, even with additional explanation. ISA 700 recognises local requirements as equivalent provided the ISA's basic requirements are met. If they are not, ISA 210 on engagement terms states that auditors should not accept the engagement unless law or regulation requires it. If law or regulation do require it, auditors cannot assert compliance with ISAs.

Audit reports can make reference to more than one financial reporting framework or more than one set of auditing standards, such as national auditing and accounting standards as well as IFRS and ISAs. It is important in such cases that full compliance is achieved if it is asserted, and that there is no conflict between the reporting requirements.

Any information beyond what is required by the financial reporting framework presented with the audited financial statements must be clearly differentiated from what has been audited, by being labelled 'unaudited', for example.

**An unmodified audit report might read as follows:**

---

INDEPENDENT AUDITORS' REPORT to the SHAREHOLDERS OF ABCCO

**Report on the Financial Statements**

We have audited the financial statements on pages x to y of ABCCO, which comprise the statement of financial position as at December 31, 20XX, and the statement of comprehensive income, statement of changes in equity and statement of cash flows for the period then ended, and a summary of significant accounting policies and other explanatory information.

*Management's Responsibility for the Financial Statements*

Management are responsible for the preparation and fair presentation of these financial statements in accordance with International Financial Reporting Standards, and for such internal control as management determine is necessary to enable the preparation of financial statements that are free from material misstatement, whether due to fraud or error.

---

*Auditors' Responsibility*

Our responsibility is to express an opinion on these financial statements based on our audit. We conducted our audit in accordance with International Standards on Auditing. Those standards require that we comply with ethical requirements and plan and perform the audit to obtain reasonable assurance about whether the financial statements are free from material misstatement.

An audit involves performing procedures to obtain audit evidence about the amounts and disclosures in the financial statements. The procedures selected depend on the auditors' judgement, including the assessment of the risks of material misstatement of the financial statements, whether due to fraud or error. In making those risk assessments, auditors consider internal control relevant to the entity's preparation and fair presentation of the financial statements in order to design audit procedures that are appropriate in the circumstances, but not for the purpose of expressing an opinion on the effectiveness of the entity's internal control. An audit also includes evaluating the appropriateness of accounting policies used and the reasonableness of accounting estimates made by management, as well as evaluating the overall presentation of the financial statements.

We believe that the audit evidence we have obtained is sufficient and appropriate to provide a basis for our audit opinion.

*Opinion*

In our opinion, the financial statements give a true and fair view of [or present fairly, in all material respects] the financial position of ABCCO as at 31 December 20XX, and (*of*) its financial performance and its cash flows for the year then ended in accordance with International Financial Reporting Standards.

**Report on Other Legal and Regulatory Requirements**

*[Form and content depend on local reporting responsibilities].*

Signature(s):

Date of audit report:

Address(es):

The paragraphs above that are most likely to change depending on circumstance are the opinion paragraph, for a modified opinion, and the report on other legal and regulatory requirements. The part of the management responsibility paragraph that refers to fair presentation would not do so for a compliance framework. The opinion paragraph for a compliance framework might appear as follows:

*Opinion*

In our opinion, the financial statements of ABCCO for the period ended 31 December 20XX are prepared, in all material respects, in accordance with XYZ Law of Jurisdiction X.

## 6.2.2 MODIFIED AUDIT OPINIONS AND OTHER PARAGRAPHS COMMONLY APPEARING IN AUDIT REPORTS

### Summary and Introduction

The wide range of audit reports issued often confuses students. Modified opinions, reports on other legal and regulatory matters, emphases of matter and other matter paragraphs can easily blur into one another. Part of the problem arises from the use of loose terminology. It is important to remember that in ISA terminology it is the audit *opinion* that is modified, not the audit *report*. Unfortunately, discussions often to refer to *modified reports* and students should avoid this because ISAs do not use this term. It is confusing because audit reports can be modified in many different ways, without the opinion being modified.

A few other rules aid comprehension in this area.

- There are three types of *modified* audit opinion:
  - *qualified* opinions: issued where there is a *material lack of evidence* or *misstatement* giving rise to an *except for* opinion in both cases;
  - *disclaimers* of opinion: a *pervasive lack of evidence* resulting in auditors being unable to form an opinion;
  - *adverse* opinions: a *pervasive material misstatement*.

  There are effectively four types of modified opinion because, as noted above, there are *two types of qualified opinion*, both of them *except for* opinions issued where there is *a material lack of evidence* or *a material misstatement* that is not pervasive.

  *Pervasive* means affecting the view given by the financial statements as a whole.

  *Unmodified audit opinions* are opinions that are not qualified, disclaimers of opinion, or adverse opinions. This means that a *report on other legal and regulatory requirements*, an *emphasis of matter* or an *other matter* paragraph in an audit report does not make the audit opinion a modified opinion.

- Any audit report may include an *Emphasis of Matter* paragraph that draws users' attention to matter(s) in the financial statements that are *fundamental to users' understanding of the financial statements*. The inclusion of such a paragraph does not make the audit opinion a modified opinion.

- Any audit report may include a paragraph entitled *Report on Other Legal and Regulatory Requirements*. This deals with *local reporting requirements* such as whether the entity has kept adequate books and records. The inclusion of such a paragraph does not make the audit opinion a modified opinion.

- Any audit report may include an *Other Matter* paragraph that draws users' attention to matters that are relevant to the *audit, the auditors' responsibilities or the audit report* that are *not* in the financial statements. The inclusion of such a paragraph does not make the audit opinion a modified opinion. Such paragraphs are rare.

- The order in which paragraphs generally appear is as follows:
  - *audit opinion* (which may be modified, i.e. except for, disclaimer or adverse);

– any *emphasis of matter*;

– any *report on other legal and regulatory requirements*.

Any *other matter* paragraph appears *either* below any emphasis of matter but above any report on other legal and regulatory requirements, *or* as a sub-paragraph within or below any Report on Other Legal and Regulatory Requirements depending on the subject matter.

The audit opinion is what matters in an audit report. Investors who read the report look at this first. A modified audit opinion, certainly for a large entity, means that there has been a problem with the audit or that there is a problem with the financial statements.[12] Emphases of matter, such as those drawing attention to a significant uncertainty about a going concern problem, often do give rise to concern even though technically they are not modifications to the audit opinion. However, *Reports on Legal and Other Regulatory Matters* rarely highlight anything that has not also resulted in a modified audit opinion because qualified opinions arising from insufficient audit evidence often go hand in hand with a lack of adequate books and records for example. *Other matter* paragraphs referring to matters not in the financial statements relating to the audit, the auditors' responsibilities or the audit opinion, such as inconsistencies between the audited financial statements and other information in the annual report, are rare.

### Modified Audit Opinions

Auditors *modify audit opinions because*:

- the *financial statements MAY be materially misstated*: auditors do not know because they *cannot obtain sufficient appropriate audit evidence*, sometimes known as *a limitation on the scope* of the audit; or

- in the auditors' opinion, *there IS a material misstatement* in the financial statements: auditors *disagree* with some aspect of the financial statements as presented by management and management refuses to change the financial statements. This does not necessarily mean that management believes it is right and the auditors are wrong, it may be that management is deliberately misstating the financial statements.

The latter category of modification is rare by comparison with the former. Auditors inform those charged with governance when they believe that they will need to issue a modified audit report.

Material misstatements arise from:

- *inappropriate* accounting policies;

- policies not properly *applied,* i.e. applied inconsistently to similar items or across accounting periods;

- inadequate *disclosure* of policies, which must be complete, in accordance with the framework, and sometimes more in order to achieve fair presentation.

---

[12] In many jurisdictions listed entities are not permitted to file financial statements on which a modified audit opinion has been issued.

Audit opinions are modified at two levels. *Potential* misstatements in the case of limitations in audit scope, and *actual* misstatements in the case of disagreements can both be either:

- *material* but not pervasive; or

- *pervasive*.

*Pervasive* means affecting or potentially affecting the view given by the financial statements as a whole, i.e. pervading the financial statements, either because it is a matter, such as a going concern problem, that affects many elements of the financial statements, or because even if it affects only one or a few, it affects a substantial proportion of the financial statements. Material matters may or may not also be pervasive but, by definition, anything that is pervasive is also material.

If property is materially overstated but represents only 10% of the balance sheet, even if it were properly stated, it is probably not pervasive. If it represents 90% of the balance sheet, it probably is pervasive. If inventories, receivables and payables are all materially misstated, it is possible that the view given by the financial statements as a whole is affected.

For disclosures, pervasive means fundamental to users' understanding of the financial statements. If properties represent a substantial proportion of the balance sheet and there is no accounting policy note, or the note is inappropriate, or only refers to properties in a certain jurisdiction, the matter may be pervasive.

*Modified opinions* are as follows:

- *except for* opinions where the matter is either a material misstatement that is not pervasive, or a *possible* material misstatement that is not pervasive in the case of insufficient appropriate audit evidence.

  Except for opinions state either that *except for the matters described* in the basis for qualification paragraph, the financial statements give a true and fair view or are presented fairly in all material respects . . . or *except for the possible effect or effects of the matters described* . . . . ;

- *adverse* opinions where the matter is *misstatement that is material and pervasive.*

  Adverse opinions state that *the financial statements do not give a true and fair view* or are not presented fairly in all material respects;

- *disclaimers* of opinion in the case of insufficient appropriate audit evidence such that the possible effects on the financial statements could be material and pervasive, including the extremely rare circumstances involving the cumulative effects of multiple uncertainties on the financial statements.

  Disclaimers of opinion state that *because of the significance of the matters described* in the basis of disclaimer of opinion paragraph, auditors have not been able to obtain sufficient appropriate audit evidence, and that *auditors do not express an opinion.*

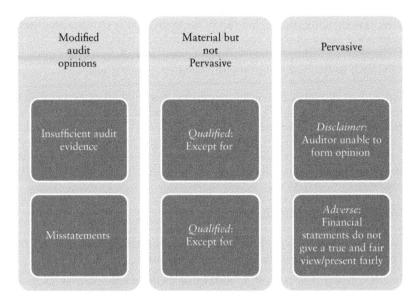

**Figure 6.4**   Modified audit opinions

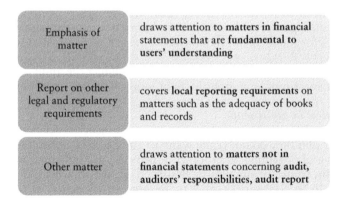

**Figure 6.5**   Additional paragraphs in audit reports, not constituting
modifications to the opinion

### *Basis for modification paragraph*

Where auditors issue a modification of opinion, a basis for modification paragraph entitled *Basis for Qualified/Adverse/Disclaimer of Opinion* paragraph appears immediately before the opinion paragraph. It describes the issue(s), quantifies the effects if possible or makes a statement to the effect that quantification is not possible.

Where the modification relates to non-disclosures by the entity which auditors are able to make, when all else fails, they should include the omitted disclosures unless prohibited by law or regulation. This rarely happens, not least because directors are unlikely to provide auditors with access to information which they are not prepared to disclose themselves, although legislation in some jurisdictions may prescribe it in specific areas, such as the non-disclosure of directors' remuneration.

Where an adverse or disclaimer of opinion is given, it is still necessary to provide details of any other matters that would have required a modification in their own right, i.e. one modification should not be used to hide another.

Disclaimers of opinion also require an amendment to the description of auditors' responsibilities paragraph that refers to auditors having obtained sufficient appropriate audit evidence.

There are *three types of limitations in audit scope*:

- limitations *outside the control of the entity*, such as the loss of books and records in a fire or their expropriation by a foreign government;

- limitations relating to the *timing or nature of audit work*, such as auditors being appointed after the period-end inventory count, or substantive procedures being insufficient at the same time as internal controls are ineffective;

- *limitations imposed by management*, such as refusing to allow auditors to attend an inventory count or to perform a circularisation where there is no alternative audit evidence, or refusing to provide certain mandatory written representations regarding responsibilities for the financial statements.

Limited resources such as a short time available to conduct the audit or a small budget generally do not constitute limitations in audit scope, whoever imposes the limitation.

### Imposed limitation in audit scope

From time to time, auditors are asked to accept appointments in which the client implies or makes it clear that they do not really want an audit to be conducted at all, that they have no intention of providing auditors with the necessary information, and that they fully expect a disclaimer of opinion to be issued. If auditors believe a disclaimer of opinion is likely to be necessary because of an *imposed* limitation of audit scope, they should not accept the engagement unless required to do so by law or regulation.[13]

If management imposes limitations likely to result in a disclaimer of opinion *after* the engagement starts and refuses to remove them, auditors have less choice. They inform those charged with governance and withdraw from the engagement if possible. In many jurisdictions, including the UK, legislation forces withdrawing auditors to make a statement regarding the circumstances of their withdrawal. If the audit is substantially complete, withdrawal might not be practical and a reference to the issue in an *other matter* paragraph in addition to the disclaimer of opinion might be appropriate.

---

[13] ISA 210 on engagement terms, paragraph 7. This does not apply to limitations in audit scope *outside the control of management*, such as destruction of accounting records by fire, flood, electrical failure or other catastrophe.

*Example modified audit report extracts*

## EXAMPLE 1: MATERIAL MISSTATEMENT OF
## INVENTORIES: *EXCEPT FOR* OPINION

*Basis for Qualified Opinion*

The company's inventories are carried in the statement of financial position at $XXX.

Management have not stated the inventories at the lower of cost and net realizable value but have stated them at cost, which constitutes a departure from International Financial Reporting Standards. The company's records indicate that had management stated the inventories at the lower of cost and net realizable value, an amount of $YYY would have been required to write the inventories down to their net realizable value. Accordingly, cost of sales would have been increased by $YYY, and income tax, net income and shareholders' equity would have been reduced by $ZZZ, $AAA and $BBB, respectively.

*Qualified Opinion*

In our opinion, except for the effects of the matter described in the Basis for Qualified Opinion paragraph, the financial statements give a true and fair view of [or present fairly, in all material respects] the financial position of ABCCO as at December 31, 20XX, and (*of*) its financial performance and its cash flows for the period then ended in accordance with International Financial Reporting Standards.

## EXAMPLE 2: MATERIAL AND PERVASIVE NON-CONSOLIDATION OF
## SUBSIDIARY: MATERIAL AND PERVASIVE, ADVERSE OPINION,
## NOT POSSIBLE TO QUANTIFY EFFECTS

*Basis for Adverse Opinion*

As explained in Note X, the company has not consolidated the financial statements of subsidiary XYZCO it acquired during 20XX because it has not yet been able to ascertain the fair values of certain of the subsidiary's material assets and liabilities at the acquisition date. This investment is therefore accounted for on a cost basis. Under International Financial Reporting Standards, the subsidiary should have been consolidated because it is controlled by the company. Had XYZ been consolidated, many elements in the accompanying financial statements would have been materially affected. The effects on the consolidated financial statements of the failure to consolidate have not been determined.

*Adverse Opinion*

In our opinion, because of the significance of the matter discussed in the Basis for Adverse Opinion paragraph, the consolidated financial statements do not give a true and fair view of [or do not present fairly, in all material respects] the financial position of ABCCO and its subsidiaries as at 31 December 20XX, and (*of*) their financial performance and their cash flows for the period then ended in accordance with International Financial Reporting Standards.

## EXAMPLE 3: UNABLE TO OBTAIN SUFFICIENT APPROPRIATE AUDIT EVIDENCE: MATERIAL INVESTMENT IN FOREIGN AFFILIATE, EXCEPT FOR OPINION

*Basis for Qualified Opinion*

ABC Company's investment in XYZCO, a foreign associate acquired during the period and accounted for by the equity method, is carried at $XXX in the statement of financial position as at December 31, 20XX, and ABCCO's share of XYZCO's net income of $XXX is included in ABCCO's income for the period then ended. We were unable to obtain sufficient appropriate audit evidence about the carrying amount of ABC's investment in XYZCO as at December 31, 20XX and ABCCO's share of XYZ's net income for the period because we were denied access to the financial information, management, and auditors of XYZCO. Consequently, we were unable to determine whether any adjustments to these amounts were necessary.

*Qualified Opinion*

In our opinion, except for the possible effects of the matter described in the Basis for Qualified Opinion paragraph, the financial statements give a true and fair view of [or present fairly, in all material respects] the financial position of ABCCO as at December 31, 20XX, and (*of*) its financial performance and its cash flows for the period then ended in accordance with International Financial Reporting Standards.

## EXAMPLE 4: UNABLE TO OBTAIN SUFFICIENT APPROPRIATE AUDIT EVIDENCE: MULTIPLE ISSUES, I.E. INVENTORIES AND ACCOUNTS RECEIVABLE, POSSIBLE EFFECTS MATERIAL AND PERVASIVE, DISCLAIMER OF OPINION

*Auditors' Responsibility*

Our responsibility is to express an opinion on these financial statements based on conducting the audit in accordance with International Standards on Auditing. Because of the matters described in the Basis for Disclaimer of Opinion paragraph, however, we were not able to obtain sufficient appropriate audit evidence to provide a basis for an audit opinion.

*Basis for Disclaimer of Opinion*

We were not appointed as auditors of the company until after December 31, 20XX and did not observe the counting of physical inventories at the beginning and end of the period. We were unable to satisfy ourselves by alternative means concerning the inventory quantities held at December 31, 20XY and 20XX which are stated in the statement of financial position at $XXX and $YYY, respectively. In addition, the introduction of a new computerized accounts receivable system in September 20XX resulted in numerous errors in accounts receivable. As of the date of our audit report, management were still in the process of rectifying the system deficiencies and correcting the errors. We were unable to confirm or verify by alternative means accounts receivable included in the statement of financial position at a total amount of $ZZZ as at December 31, 20XX. As a result of these matters, we were unable to determine whether any adjustments might have been found necessary in respect of recorded or unrecorded inventories and accounts receivable, and the elements making up the statement of comprehensive income, statement of changes in equity and statement of cash flows.

---

*Disclaimer of Opinion*

Because of the significance of the matters described in the Basis for Disclaimer of Opinion paragraph, we have not been able to obtain sufficient appropriate audit evidence to provide a basis for an audit opinion. Accordingly, we do not express an opinion on the financial statements.

---

### National differences

Audit reporting is one area in which there are significant national divergences that are difficult to narrow, partly because reporting requirements are often set out in national legislation. ISA 700 on audit reports has not been adopted in the UK, for example, but this is only partly because of legislation. The UK standard on audit reporting notes that the main effect of the non-adoption of the ISA is that the form of UK auditors' reports may not be exactly aligned with the precise format required by ISA 700 issued by the IAASB. The most obvious difference between the UK standard and the ISA lies in the fact that the UK standard permits cross-references to statements:

- of directors' responsibilities to statements that appear elsewhere in the annual report; and

- on the scope of the audit to statements maintained on the UK standard-setter's web-site.

The UK standard also has a paragraph that refers to the 'respective responsibilities of the directors and auditors' instead of two separate paragraphs referring to them separately. The rubric accompanying the UK standard notes it has been drafted such that compliance with it does not preclude auditors from asserting compliance with the ISAs issued by the IAASB.

UK legislation and other reporting regimes require auditors to make certain *statements by exception* as follows:

- adequate accounting records have not been kept;

- adequate returns have not been received from branches not visited;

- the financial statements are not in agreement with the accounting records and returns;

- certain disclosures of directors' remuneration required by law are not made;

- auditors have not received all the information and explanations they require for the audit.

These are examples of the types of information that could be covered by paragraphs on other legal and regulatory matters. In the UK, these statements are made in a paragraph entitled *Matters on Which we are Required to Report by Exception* that immediately follows a paragraph entitled *Opinion on Other Matter prescribed by the Companies Act 2006*, which states that:

- for quoted companies, the part of the Directors' Remuneration Report to be audited has been properly prepared in accordance with the Companies Act 2006;

- for all companies, the information given in the Directors' Report for the financial year for which the financial statements are prepared is consistent with the financial statements.

### The Future of Audit Reporting

Proposals for changes to audit reports have been made recently by the IAASB, the PCAOB and the EC and are dealt with in more detail in Section 5.

### Section essentials: what you need to remember

- *The types of modified audit opinion, i.e. qualified (two types), adverse and disclaimer.*

- *What gives rise to modified audit opinions, i.e. limitations in the scope of the audit resulting in auditors being unable to obtain sufficient appropriate audit evidence, and the two levels of modification, material and pervasive.*

- *The main headings and broad content of all audit reports.*


## 6.3   EMPHASIS OF MATTER AND OTHER MATTER PARAGRAPHS, GOING CONCERN

**Covering:** ISA 706, *Emphasis of Matter Paragraphs and Other Matter Paragraphs in the Independent Auditor's Report*, ISA 570 *Going Concern*.

### Why do I need to read this section?

*Emphases of matter are a versatile tool. They have been used, over-used, under-used and abused over the years. Auditors have sometimes failed to use them where they should have been used to draw attention to important matters, they have sometimes used them indiscriminately, and there has always been a temptation to use them in place of modified opinions.*

*Other matter paragraphs are not often used. Whereas modifications deal with things that are wrong in the financial statements, or situations in which auditors simply do not know whether they are right or wrong, and whereas emphases of matter draw the readers' attention to important matters in the financial statements, other matter paragraphs deal with audit issues not dealt with in the financial statements at all. It is also important to distinguish them from reports on other legal and regulatory requirements.*

*Going concern reporting is as important in practice as it is in theory. Auditors' procedures in the area are extensive and there are several different types of report dealing with doubts over the going concern status of an entity. It is important to understand though, that the going concern assessment is primarily the responsibility of management and not auditors, and that auditors can expect management to have performed a going concern assessment which they can then audit.*

**What is important in this section?**

- *The definition of an emphasis of matter.*

- *How emphases of matter differ from other matter paragraphs and where they are used.*

- *The different types of audit report that can be used where there are doubts about the going concern status of the entity and the audit procedures auditors are required to perform on the going concern status of an entity.*

**What sort of questions come up in this area?**

- *Short questions asking for definitions or descriptions of the various types of report used to communicate doubts about the going concern status of an entity.*

- *Questions on the audit work performed where there are going concern problems.*

- *Questions on where it would be appropriate to use an emphasis of matter.*

- *Questions asking students to draft elements of audit reports referring to going concern issues, and to draft emphases of matter.*

**How do I stand out from the crowd?**

- *Use examples demonstrating the purpose of and difference between emphases of matter and other matter paragraphs.*

- *Explain what management are expected to do as part of their going concern review.*

- *Explain what can be expected of smaller entities, and what is required in the audit of entities that clearly do not have going concern problems;*

- *Be clear about which audit report is appropriate where there are going concern problems.*

### 6.3.1   EMPHASIS OF MATTER AND OTHER MATTER PARAGRAPHS

We have seen in the introduction to this section that ***emphases of matter*** are used to draw users' attention to matters either on the face of the financial statements or in the notes, i.e. *matters presented or disclosed*, where they are of such importance that they are ***fundamental to users' understanding of the financial statements.***[14]

We have also seen that ***other matter paragraphs draw users' attention to matters concerning the audit, auditors' responsibilities or auditors' report,*** i.e. matters that are not dealt with in the financial statements.

---

[14] ISA 706 on emphases of matter and other matters, paragraph 1.

*Emphases of matter* appear after the opinion paragraph and indicate that the opinion is not modified in that respect, although opinions may be modified in other respects. Examples include drawing users' attention to:

- disclosures of uncertainties surrounding litigation;

- early application of new accounting standards;

- certain significant subsequent events such as catastrophic losses.

An example emphasis of matter concerning litigation might read as follows:

---

*Emphasis of Matter*

We draw attention to Note X to the financial statements which describes an uncertainty related to the outcome of litigation against the company involving XYZCO. Our opinion is not qualified in this respect.

---

*Other matter paragraphs* relevant to the audit might appear in the rare circumstances in which auditors were unable to withdraw from an engagement despite a limitation in the scope of the audit imposed by management, resulting in a disclaimer of opinion. Such a paragraph might also be used where two sets of financial statements were prepared and reported on under two different financial reporting frameworks,[15] or to restrict the distribution or use of the audit report.

Other matter paragraphs also need to be clearly distinguished from reports on other legal and regulatory requirements. The former deals with audit-related matters that do not appear in the financial statements, the latter deals with local legal and regulatory reporting requirements that are sometimes referred to in the financial statements.

Emphases of matter and other matter paragraphs should not be used to avoid issuing a modified opinion, or in an attempt to rectify inadequate or barely adequate disclosures in the financial statements, nor should they be used indiscriminately.

### Examples of Emphases of Matter and Other Matter Paragraphs

Other matter paragraphs may deal with situations in which:

- prior period financial statements were audited by other auditors or were not audited;

- when reporting on prior period financial statements in connection with the current period and the opinion on the prior period differ from the opinion originally expressed.[16]

---

[15] This is not the same as using one audit report to report on a set of financial statements that comply with two frameworks.
[16] ISA 710 on comparative information, paragraphs 13–19.

Where there are material inconsistencies in other information issued with audited financial statements and management refuses to make a necessary revision to the other information the issue is referred to in an other matter paragraph.[17]

If revised financial statements are issued as a result of facts which become known after the financial statements were issued, the new or amended auditors' report includes an emphasis of matter paragraph or other matter paragraph referring to the issue.[18]

If the financial reporting framework prescribed by law is unacceptable, auditors may only accept the engagement if, among other things, an emphasis of matter paragraph refers to the issue.[19]

### 6.3.2   GOING CONCERN

The term *audit failure* is often applied, rightly or wrongly, to a large entity that collapses, i.e. it goes out of business, becomes insolvent or has to be sold, shortly after the issue of an unmodified audit opinion. Sales of businesses before they become insolvent are often described as sales *as a going concern.*

*Corporate failure and audit failure:* commentators often confuse corporate failure with audit failure and appear to imply that the cause of corporate failure is an audit failure. Auditors do not cause companies to fail. It is often argued, though, that auditors contribute to corporate failure by neglecting to warn those who might have taken action to prevent the failure that there is a problem. The issues are not straightforward. Auditors are no better able to predict the future than anyone else and market conditions and shareholder sentiment can change very rapidly. Auditors report on the truth and fairness or fair presentation of historical financial statements. It would be quite another matter to report on the financial viability or health of a business, or on fraud, even though many believe that auditors either already do these things, or should do them.

*Going concern and the limitations of an audit:* going concern is one of the trickiest areas facing the profession. Auditing standards have always made it abundantly clear that a properly conducted audit will not necessarily detect material fraud, or a going concern problem. An audit report is not a guarantee of financial health. Nor is the audit fee an insurance policy that pays out when a company fails without much warning. Audit risk is the risk that an unmodified report is issued where a modified report should be issued and it cannot be eliminated because of human error. Entities can and do fail very quickly. This, however, calls into question the value of an audit: if audits cannot be relied on to detect material fraud and error or going concern problems that become apparent within months of the period-end, why bother performing them? Should they not be improved so that they can be relied on to do these things?

---

[17] ISA 720 on other information, paragraph 10a.
[18] ISA 560 on subsequent events, paragraph 16.
[19] ISA 210 on engagement terms, paragraph 19b.

*Audit as a hygiene factor:* auditors and clients agree that without challenge by auditors, the quality of reported information would be a great deal poorer than it is. Auditors do raise objections to disclosures and accounting treatments proposed by clients behind closed doors and entities comply with the auditors' suggestions in order to avoid modified audit opinions. The value and extent of this are not easy to measure though. Audit is a hygiene factor, meaning that people only notice it if it goes away, as with routine cleaning, and policing. It may only be possible to appreciate the value of an audit by removing it. That would be risky for public interest entities such as pension funds, banks, entities with a high proportion of small shareholders, and entities providing monopoly services or very high levels of employment. To that extent auditing is similar to policing, in that a great deal of policing is about prevention, no-one expects police forces to detect all crime, nor does anyone seriously contemplate doing away with policing just to find out if it is actually effective in preventing crime.

*Reporting on going concern problems:* issuing an audit report that makes any reference at all to the going concern status of an entity is fraught with difficulty. To issue such a report on a bank, for example, even an unmodified report with an emphasis of matter paragraph, might cause a run on the bank, precipitating its collapse. A modified audit opinion would become a self-fulfilling prophecy in that by highlighting a potential going concern problem, the report might cause a problem.[20]

Corporate governance regimes often require listed entities to make statements in a prescribed format about their going concern status and for auditors to review or report on those statements in the audit report either in an other matter paragraph or in a report on other legal and regulatory requirements. There are proposals to require all entities to report on their assessment of the going concern assumption.

## Definitions

The going concern assumption is ***the assumption that an entity will continue in business in the foreseeable future***. General purpose financial statements are prepared on this basis ***unless there is an intention to liquidate operations or cease operations or the entity has no realistic alternative but to do so***. The difference between financial statements prepared on the going concern basis and the *break-up* basis is that on the break-up basis assets and liabilities are valued at what they can be sold for.

Some financial reporting frameworks require specific disclosures about the going concern status of an entity and for management to make specific statements about what they have done to satisfy themselves that the going concern basis of preparation is appropriate. Even in the absence of such requirements, the going concern basis is a fundamental accounting concept that underlies the preparation of financial statements.

---

[20] Similar difficulties sometimes arise at the opposite end of the scale. Auditors of smaller entities may find themselves in the difficult position of being asked to provide banks with audited financial statements to help the bank to consider whether to renew facilities on which the entity is reliant, but they cannot provide the unmodified report the bank is looking for unless the bank confirms that it will renew facilities.

Whether an entity is a going concern is a matter of judgement that requires the entity to take account of all information available, and the fact that:

> *The auditor cannot predict future events or conditions. Accordingly, the absence of any reference to going concern uncertainty in an auditor's report cannot be viewed as a guarantee as to the entity's ability to continue as a going concern.*
>
> ISA 570 *Going Concern* paragraph 7

### Risk Assessment and Evaluating Management's Assessment

Auditors are required to assess the risk that the going concern assumption is not appropriate. The risk assessment requirement is positive, though, in that auditors are required to consider *whether there are events or conditions that cast significant doubt* on the going concern status of the entity[21]. A large part of the risk assessment involves evaluating management's assertions in that area, because it is the responsibility of those who prepare the financial statements to ensure that the underlying assumptions are appropriate.

Three terms are used in the context of going concern:

- *assumptions*, as described in ISA 570 above;
- *assessments* performed by management and the risk assessment performed by auditors;
- *assertions* in the financial statements which are statements made by management concerning the going concern status of the entity and the work it has performed to justify those assertions.

ISA 570 on going concern refers to management's going concern assertions and assessments. Even in jurisdictions in which those charged with governance take responsibility for the financial statements, such as the UK, in practice management performs the assessment and drafts the relevant assertions for inclusion in the financial statements.

Auditors discuss management's going concern assessment if it has performed one, including plans to address any potential problems. Auditors simply discuss the matter with management if there has been no assessment. Auditors clearly need to remain alert throughout the audit for evidence of going concern problems.

#### The auditors' risk assessment
Situations and events casting doubt on the going concern assumption, some of which are also fraud risk factors, include the following.

---

[21] ISA 570 on going concern, paragraph 10.

## Financial

- Net liabilities;

- fixed-term borrowings approaching maturity without prospect of renewal or repayment;

- short-term borrowings such as overdrafts used to finance long-term, i.e. non-current, assets;

- inability to pay creditors when due or comply with terms of loan agreements;

- adverse key financial ratios and substantial operating losses;

- suppliers requiring cash on delivery rather than credit.

## Operating

- Loss of key management without replacement;

- loss of a major customer, supplier, or franchise;

- loss of a licence to operate in a regulated industry such as banks and airlines;

- emergence of competitors;

- labour difficulties;

- shortage of supplies.

## Regulatory and legal

- Changes in legal or regulatory requirements affecting operations or profits, such as restrictions on ingredients in foodstuffs, or on exports or imports, or caps on charging;

- non-compliance with legal or regulatory requirements such as capital requirements in the financial services sector and requirements for electronics retailers to provide recycling facilities for used equipment;

- litigation that may result in claims the entity cannot meet, and uninsured catastrophes.

Many entities experience several such difficulties from time to time, but there is no significant doubt about their ability to continue as going concerns, because of mitigating factors. An inability to meet financial difficulties, for example, can be mitigated by rescheduling payments, factoring debts and disposing of assets such as properties, provided they have no significant effect on operations. The scale of operations can sometimes be reduced and diversification can accommodate changes in the business environment.

Smaller entities are particularly vulnerable to the loss of a single supplier, customer, franchise, contract or licence.

*Evaluating management's assessment*

---

Auditors are required to

*... evaluate management's assessment of the entity's ability to continue as a going concern.*

ISA 570 *Going Concern* paragraph 12

---

The primary responsibility for considering going concern issues lies with management, and it is not the auditors' responsibility to rectify any lack of consideration of the issue by management.[22] However, it is not possible for auditors to *demand* that management performs a formal going concern assessment where neither the financial reporting framework nor any other regulatory requirement demands it. Management may rightly refuse to perform one where there is little or no doubt about the matter because the entity has plenty of cash and a healthy order book, for example. In such cases, provided other audit procedures are adequate, the auditors' evaluation of management's assessment does not involve a detailed evaluation of a formal assessment.

*The period considered*
When looking to the future, auditors consider the same period as that considered by management. The period management considers is determined by the regulatory framework.

*If management's assessment covers less than twelve months from the date of the financial statements, auditors request management to extend the assessment period to at least twelve months.*[23]

Most financial reporting frameworks specify a period and it is normally 12 months, as under IAS 1,[24] for example, although start dates vary: under some frameworks it is from the balance sheet date, under others it is from the audit report date. It is important to remember that management and auditors *take into account anything already known about the period beyond* the 12-month period. Major problems on the horizon outside the 12-month time period cannot be ignored and auditors are specifically required to ask management about this period.

ISA 570 on going concern does not specify how to perform the evaluation of management's assessment. One of the few areas in which the UK has *pluses*, i.e. additions to ISAs, of any substance, is in this area. Firstly, the assessment starts from the date of the approval of the financial statements, which may be some time after the date of the financial statements. Secondly, going concern problems are very often cash flow problems which determine the extent of audit procedures in this area.[25] For these reasons, management often uses cash flow forecasts and budgets to perform the going concern assessment and auditors often look at the same in performing their evaluation. While such forecasts

---

[22] ISA 570 on going concern, paragraph A8.
[23] ISA 570 on going concern, paragraph 13.
[24] IAS 1 *Presentation of Financial Statements*.
[25] ISA (UK and Ireland) 570 *Going Concern*, paragraph A10-4.

and budgets provide the most persuasive evidence, alternative sources may be acceptable, particularly for smaller entities that are unlikely to produce them.

### Audit Procedures Where Significant Doubt Arises

Events or conditions that *may* cast significant doubt on the entity's ability to continue as a going concern require investigation. Additional audit procedures include:

- considering mitigating factors;
- asking for a going concern assessment from management if one has not already been prepared;
- considering whether management plans, such as selling assets, increasing borrowings or capital or reducing expenditure, are feasible;
- evaluating data underlying any cash flow forecast that is significant to management plans;
- determining whether there is support for the assumptions used;
- requesting written representations;
- considering whether past management plans proved reliable;
- reading minutes of shareholders', directors' and other meetings for references to difficulties;
- inquiring of the entity's lawyers about the prospects for litigation;
- discussing budgets, cash flow forecasts, interim and management information;
- confirming the terms and considering the adequacy of arrangements for financial support from third parties.

Third parties providing financial support include group companies, banks and others but support must actually be available if necessary. A guarantee from an insolvent holding company is not worth much and problems may arise if terms of loan agreements have been breached. Obtaining written confirmation of support from group companies, banks and other lenders is important, as is obtaining evidence of their ability to provide support. Such confirmations are sometimes known as comfort letters.

### Smaller Entities

Smaller entities often rely substantially on loans from owner-managers, or on bank loans. Banks will not always confirm that they will renew facilities and other evidence may be hard to find. However, management of smaller entities is more likely to have an in-depth knowledge of the business and its future prospects than to have prepared cash flow forecasts, budgets or any detailed going concern assessment, and simple discussions of the medium and long-term prospects may be sufficient. Documentary evidence is required, though, to support what management say about the likely level of future orders, for example.

Smaller entities are often supported by loans from owner-managers that are critical to the continued existence of the business. Such loans may sometimes be subordinated to, i.e. rank behind, loans from banks. Banks also sometimes seek personal guarantees from owner-managers or use their personal assets, such as their homes, as collateral for loans. Written representations regarding the continuation of owner-manager loans to entities and the terms and conditions of loans from banks may be relevant.

### Reporting

- *Going concern basis is appropriate but a material uncertainty exists* that casts significant doubt on the entity's ability to continue as a going concern.

  Provided the *financial statements adequately disclose* the issue, management's plans to deal with it and the fact that there is a material uncertainty and what this means, auditors may issue an *unmodified opinion with emphasis of matter* highlighting the material uncertainty and by drawing attention to the note disclosure.

  If the *financial statements do not adequately disclose* the issues, auditors give a *qualified or adverse* opinion, depending on the severity of the situation.

- *Going concern basis is inappropriate* but financial statements still prepared on the going concern basis.

  Auditors give an *adverse opinion*, regardless of disclosures. Disclosure does not compensate for inappropriate accounting.

- *Financial statements prepared on a liquidation basis*

  It may be possible to perform an audit and issue an opinion with an *emphasis of matter* but this happens rarely as reporting by insolvent entities is usually subject to insolvency legislation.

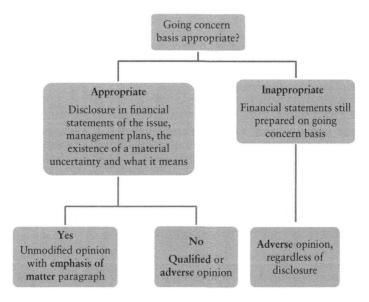

**Figure 6.6**   Going concern reporting

*Example emphasis of matter paragraph following unmodified opinion paragraph*

---

*Emphasis of Matter*

Without qualifying our opinion, we draw attention to Note X in the financial statements which indicates that the Company incurred a net loss of £ZZZ during the year ended 31 December 20X1 and, as of that date, the Company's current liabilities exceeded its total assets by £YYY. These conditions, along with other matters as set forth in Note X, indicate the existence of a material uncertainty that may cast significant doubt on the Company's ability to continue as a going concern.

**ISA 570** *Going Concern* **paragraph A21**

---

*Example basis for qualified opinion and qualified opinion paragraphs*

---

*Basis for Qualified Opinion*

The Company's financing arrangements expire and amounts outstanding are payable on 19 March 20X1. The Company has been unable to re-negotiate or obtain replacement financing. This situation indicates the existence of a material uncertainty that may cast significant doubt on the Company's ability to continue as a going concern and therefore the Company may be unable to realize its assets and discharge its liabilities in the normal course of business. The financial statements (and notes thereto) do not fully disclose this fact.

*Qualified Opinion*

In our opinion, except for the incomplete disclosure of the information referred to in the Basis for Qualified Opinion paragraph, the financial statements give a true and fair view of [or present fairly in all material respects], the financial position of the Company as at 31 December 20X0, and of its financial performance and its cash flows for the year then ended in accordance with . . .

**ISA 570** *Going Concern* **paragraph A23**

---

A similar format would be used for an ***adverse opinion*** that might be given where the company's financing arrangements had actually expired and the entity was considering filing for bankruptcy. The headings would be *Basis for Adverse Opinion* and *Adverse Opinion* and the opinion would state that because of the omission of the information the financial statements ***do not*** give a true and fair view.

If management are unwilling to make or extend their assessment where necessary, a qualified or disclaimer of opinion may be appropriate.

Auditors need to inform those charged with governance about events or conditions that give rise to a material going concern uncertainty, whether the going concern assumption is appropriate and the adequacy of relevant disclosures.

**Section essentials: what you need to remember**

- *Emphases of matter draw attention to matters already in the financial statements.*

- *Other matter paragraphs draw attention to audit-related issues.*

- *Management is responsible for providing auditors with evidence regarding the appropriateness of the going concern status of the entity.*

- *Most references to significant uncertainties regarding going concern in audit reports are within emphasis of matter paragraphs.*

## 6.4 COMMUNICATIONS WITH MANAGEMENT AND THOSE CHARGED WITH GOVERNANCE

Covering: ISA 260 *Communication with Those Charged with Governance*, ISA 265 *Communicating Deficiencies in Internal Control to Those Charged with Governance and Management.*

### Why do I need to read this section?

*Communications with those charged with governance and communication of deficiencies in internal control are both areas that have changed in recent years and continue to develop. The management letter used to consist largely of a routine statement of issues that had come to light during the audit, the actual and potential consequences and how the situation was resolved or suggestions as to how it could be further improved.*

*The development of corporate governance and oversight by audit committees have widened the whole area out from communications with management, mostly on internal control over financial reporting, to communications with those charged with governance on matters of governance interest. These encompass the auditors' responsibilities, the scope of the audit, independence, significant findings and the financial reporting process. Developing areas such as these are always of interest to examiners. There are many who would like auditors to make public reports on matters they currently only report to management and those charged with governance.*

### What is important in this section?

*Understanding who those charged with governance are, how and why they are different to management, what needs to be communicated and what auditors can expect in return. Understanding what needs to be communicated in writing and what can be discussed is also important, particularly for smaller audits where the cost of and irritation caused by formal communications can be a problem.*

### What sort of questions come up in this area?

*Practical questions on communicating deficiencies in the internal control are set frequently and it is worth practising them for that reason. Knowledge-based questions on what needs to be communicated and when are also set.*

How do I stand out from the crowd?

*Few students show that they really understand the difference between management and those charged with governance or why it is important, which makes students who do, stand out. Students who make imaginative suggestions as to the potential consequences of control deficiencies and focus on suggested improvements, rather than merely reiterating the problem that is presented in the question, also stand out.*

### 6.4.1  COMMUNICATION WITH THOSE CHARGED WITH GOVERNANCE

**Management and Those Charged with Governance**

We have already seen that corporate governance in practice varies internationally. For the purposes of ISA audits:

- *management* has *executive responsibility* for the conduct of the entity's operations which usually, but not always, includes the preparation of the financial statements;
- *those charged with governance* are those *with responsibility for overseeing the strategic direction of the entity and its obligations regarding accountability, including the financial reporting process.*[26]

This means that those charged *with governance include those with responsibility for approving the financial statements, regardless of whether they are classed as those charged with governance or management, and regardless of who actually prepares the financial statements.*

In practice, auditors often communicate in detail with a sub-group of those charged with governance such as an audit committee and report in summary form only to the main governing body.

In some jurisdictions, those charged with governance include persons who would be classed as management in other jurisdictions, such as executive members of a governance board. In the UK, those charged with governance include both executive and non-executive directors.

*Governance is usually the collective responsibility of a governing body* whether a board of directors, a supervisory board, a management committee, council of governors or similar. It is important to remember that *the purpose of appointing non-executives, members of a governing body and charging them with governance is for them to oversee or supervise the work of management.*

In smaller entities, management and those charged with governance are often the same people. Many of the required communications with those charged with governance are in areas that have already been reported to management. To avoid duplicating communications, requirements to report matters are sometimes prefaced

---

[26] ISA 260 on communications with those charged with governance, paragraph 10.

with the words, 'Unless all of those charged with governance are involved in managing the entity . . .'.

**What is Communicated and Two-Way Communication**

Auditors are required to:

- communicate the *auditors' responsibilities* and the *planned scope and timing* of the audit;

- *obtain relevant information*;

- *provide significant observations* about the audit as they arise;

- communicate *a statement on auditor independence* for listed entities;

- *promote effective two-way communication*.

Most of the information reported is from auditors to those charged with governance, but two-way communication is required to establish a constructive working relationship, to help auditors obtain the information they need for the audit and to help those charged with governance fulfil their oversight responsibilities.

There is an overlap between what auditors and management are required to report to those charged with governance, particularly concerning internal controls and the financial reporting process. Communications by auditors are not a substitute for communications by management, nor vice versa; however, the timing and extent of what is reported are influenced by what has already been reported. Those charged with governance may not need the same level of detail from both parties, or at the same time.

Many ISAs have specific communication requirements such as the requirement to communicate:

- an unreasonable management refusal to allow auditors to send a confirmation request;[27]

- events or conditions that may cast significant doubt on the entity's going concern status;[28]

- non-compliance with laws or regulations that come to the auditors' attention.[29]

*Auditors' responsibilities and planned scope and timing*
*Providing a copy of the engagement letter* effectively communicates many of the auditors' responsibilities. It might highlight the requirement for auditors to form an opinion on the financial statements but not to perform procedures specifically for the purposes of reporting to those charged with governance. Care is needed not to compromise the effectiveness of the audit when providing an overview of the planned scope and timing

---

[27] ISA 505 on specific procedures for selected items, paragraph 9.
[28] ISA 570 on going concern, paragraph 23.
[29] ISA 250 on laws and regulations, paragraph 22.

of the audit, especially where those charged with governance also manage the entity. Audit procedure should not be too predictable. Matters that might be communicated include an overview of:

- how significant risks are to be addressed;
- the approach to internal control;
- the application of materiality.

It is not necessary to re-communicate the same matters every year if nothing has changed.

Other planning matters it might be appropriate to discuss include any work with internal audit, the entity's objectives, strategies and business risks, communications with regulators, and the attitude of management towards internal control.

### Significant findings

Auditors may wish to discuss significant findings simply to make sure that those charged with governance have the same understanding of relevant facts. The following categories of findings, all of which are very sensitive, need to be communicated:

- *significant difficulties* encountered during the audit including:
  - *delays* in the provision of financial information for audit;
  - a very *short time* to complete the audit;
  - unexpected *difficulties in obtaining audit evidence* or the unavailability of evidence;
  - *restrictions imposed* by management;
- *significant matters discussed* with management including:
  - *business condition and strategies* affecting the risk of material misstatement;
  - *discussions about the appointment of the firm* concerning fees, auditing or accounting matters or discussions with other firms because entities sometimes try to pressurise auditors into accepting an accounting treatment this way;
- *written representations requested*;
- *other significant matters* relevant to the financial reporting process such as inconsistencies between the financial statements and other information in the annual report.

While it is generally acceptable to discuss matters with management before communicating them to those charged with governance, not least to ensure that they are right, in some areas, such as significant difficulties arising during the audit, this may not be appropriate.

### Auditor independence

Auditors of *listed entities* are required to make a statement to those charged with governance that the firm, network and engagement team *have complied with independence requirements*. They must also *disclose all relationships* that might reasonably be thought to have a bearing on independence *together with related safeguards* so that those charged with governance can make up their own minds.

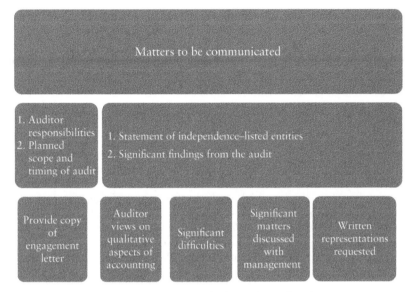

**Figure 6.7** Communications with those charged with governance

## The Communication Process

Not everything needs to be in writing which is important for smaller firms whose clients may not appreciate the need to incur the cost of written communications. What is to be communicated, when and how, all need to be discussed but there are only three areas that need to be communicated *in writing*:

- *significant audit findings*;
- the auditor *independence* statement for listed entities;
- anything for which *oral communication would be inadequate*.

Despite this, where matters are communicated orally, there still needs to be a record in the working papers. In practice, this means more is included in the written communication than might otherwise be the case. Furthermore, if for a smaller entity there are no significant audit findings to report and no other matters communicated orally, auditors need to consider whether they communicate the fact that nothing is to be communicated!

On larger audits communications are likely to take place throughout the audit. It is better for significant difficulties arising to be dealt with on the spot rather than at the end of the audit.

Auditors may attempt to restrict distribution of written communication and include caveats to the effect that communications have been prepared for the sole use of the entity, should not be relied on by third parties, and include disclaimers to the effect that no responsibility is assumed to third parties.

*Two-way communication*

Auditors are required to evaluate whether the two-way communication has been adequate for audit purposes. The willingness, ability and extent to which those charged with governance respond to matters raised by auditors are relevant to this evaluation. Poor two-way communications may indicate a weak control environment.

## 6.4.2   COMMUNICATING DEFICIENCIES IN INTERNAL CONTROL

ISA 265 on communicating deficiencies in internal control was developed partly because of international confusion about the meaning of terms such as *material deficiency* and *significant weakness* in the context of internal control. The Public Company Accounting Oversight Board (PCAOB) in the USA requires auditors of SEC registrants to conduct *integrated audits* in which auditors form an opinion on internal control effectiveness as well as on the fair presentation of financial statements. The PCAOB refers to *material deficiencies* and *significant weaknesses* in internal control. Neither of these two terms is used in ISA 265 to avoid confusion with terms used by the PCAOB and because ISA audits are not integrated audits. ISA 265 instead refers to *significant deficiencies* in internal control.

### Deficiencies and Significant Deficiencies

In any audit, auditors are required to obtain an understanding of internal control by examining their *design* and *implementation* as part of the risk assessment, regardless of whether they intend to test controls. Auditors identify deficiencies in internal control at this stage of the audit as well as when controls are tested.

A *deficiency* in internal control is *a missing control or one that* is designed, implemented or operated such that it *fails to prevent, detect or correct misstatements.*

A *significant deficiency* is one or a combination of deficiencies that *in the auditors' judgement is of sufficient importance to merit the attention of those charged with governance.*[30]

Some significant deficiencies may lead to material misstatements in the financial statements but the existence of a significant deficiency does not necessarily mean that a misstatement has arisen. Clearly, the bigger the potential error arising from the deficiency, the greater the likelihood of it occurring, and the weaker other controls are, particularly monitoring controls, the more likely auditors are to judge it significant. It is important to remember that controls are normally layered so that if one control fails, such as the failure to approve a transaction, another might catch it, such as an exception report.

Indicators of significant deficiencies include an ineffective control environment, management fraud, a failure to remedy weaknesses previously communicated, an ineffective or missing risk assessment process, or misstatements detected by auditors not detected by management.

---

[30] ISA 265 on deficiencies of internal control, paragraph 6.

## Communicating Deficiencies and Significant Deficiencies

Auditors are required to *communicate significant deficiencies to those charged with governance in writing* on a timely basis. Provided the relevant deficiency does not relate to management, auditors also communicate them to management, but not necessarily in writing. If they warrant management attention, auditors also communicate non-significant deficiencies to management if they have not already been reported by internal audit or regulators, for example.

Deficiencies need to be communicated sooner rather than later, orally in the first instance if necessary, so that they can be corrected.

It may be necessary to repeat the communication in the case of significant deficiencies if management takes no remedial action, particularly if those charged with governance or management change, but auditors should consider why there has been no action and whether the deficiency is genuinely significant.

## Content of Communications

In addition to a *description of deficiencies* and a *caveat* to the effect that the audit is not designed to identify deficiencies and that what is reported is limited to matters identified during the audit, reporting often includes:

* the *potential consequences* of deficiencies;
* *recommendations* for improvement;
* *management's response,* and whether auditors have verified that responses have been implemented.

Reporting to smaller entities needs to be realistic. Smaller entities do not have formal control systems or enough staff to segregate duties, but the involvement of the owner-manager in the day-to-day running of the business can both compensate for these weaknesses, or exacerbate them, particularly if the owner-manager has a habit of over-riding controls. Management's approval of credit to customers and of all significant purchases may remove the need for more detailed control activities, but the common lack of differentiation by some owner-managers between personal and business assets may represent a deficiency.

## Section essentials: what you need to remember

* *The need to communicate auditors' responsibilities, the planned scope and timing of the audit, significant observations about the audit, and a statement on auditor independence for listed entities.*
* *The need to consider two-way communication.*
* *When to report to those charged with governance but not management.*
* *Significant deficiencies are those that auditors consider warrant the attention of those charged with governance.*

# 6.5   OTHER INFORMATION

**Covering:** ISA 720 *The Auditor's Responsibilities Relating to Other Information in Documents Containing Audited Financial Statements.*

### Why do I need to read this section?

*Dealing with other information is an increasingly important and difficult part of audits. Annual reports are much longer than they used to be and, despite numerous initiatives by standard-setters and professional bodies to cut clutter, they show little sign of becoming shorter.*

*One survey of narrative reporting noted that the average UK report length almost doubled from 56 pages in 2000 to 101 pages in 2010, not least because entities feel they need to include everything their competitors have in their reports, and then have some more.*

*Financial statements still tend to appear at the back of annual reports but, in most cases, this is the only element of the annual report that has been subject to audit. Regulatory requirements for auditor comment or assurance on corporate governance disclosures that are scattered around the annual report, such as statements on risk management, directors' remuneration and the board nomination process, make many audit reports complex and lengthy. It is not always easy to navigate what auditors have done to different bits of the annual report. This represents a risk to auditors, as does any conflict between what appears in the audited information and what appears elsewhere. The main issue is for auditors not to be associated with misleading information.*

### What is important in this section?

*Understanding what other information consists of and what auditors are required to do with this information.*

### What sort of questions come up in this area?

*Knowledge-based questions on the auditors' responsibilities often come up in lower level papers but higher level papers sometimes ask students to discuss the problems associated with different types of other information, the risks it presents to auditors and how auditors can manage those risks.*

### How do I stand out from the crowd?

*By explaining why other information is important to auditors as well as knowing what auditors are required to do with it.*

## 6.5.1   OTHER INFORMATION IN DOCUMENTS CONTAINING AUDITED FINANCIAL STATEMENTS

The smallest of entities often issue the audited financial statements together with unaudited information, usually because legislation requires it. The following often accompany audited financial statements in annual reports:

- reports of the management board;
- directors' reports;

- financial summaries or highlights;

- quarterly data;

- operating and financial reviews (OFRs);

- management discussion and analyses (MDA);

- corporate governance reports;

- reports on internal control;

- reports on directors' remuneration;

- reports on social, environmental or community matters.

The audit opinion does not cover these reports even though local legislation often requires auditors to perform procedures or provide assurance on them. For the purposes of an ISA audit, the only consideration is *whether the other information, which can be financial or non-financial, undermines the credibility of the audited financial statements.*

The credibility of financial statements is undermined if any of the other information *contradicts* information in the audited financial statements, or if other information unrelated to the audited financial statements is *incorrectly stated or presented* because such *material misstatements of fact call into question the credibility of the audited information by association.*

A contradiction might involve financial statements showing a gross profit but a loss before tax, and the accompanying information referring to profits for the year without further explanation.

A statement that the entity performs thorough supply chain audits when in fact it only does so for less than half of its suppliers has nothing to do with the financial statements, but if that fact appears in a document containing the audited financial statement, it might cast doubt on the credibility of the audited financial statements.

ISA 720 on other information only deals with other information provided by the entity. It does not deal with additional reports by auditors on significant audit findings, internal control or other matters.

Auditors are required to make arrangements to obtain the other information before the date of the audit report, or as near as possible thereto, even though they may have no automatic right of access to it. Some jurisdictions, such as the UK, prohibit auditors from signing audit reports until they have performed the work they consider necessary on the other information.

The basic requirement is for auditors to *read* the other information *in order to identify material inconsistencies with the audited financial statements and any apparent misstatement of fact*. Reading is in the light of the auditors' knowledge of the business, but there is no requirement to verify anything.

### Inconsistencies between the other information and the financial statements

If inconsistencies come to the auditors' attention as a result of reading the other information, it is possible that the audited financial statements are at fault, in which case auditors request the necessary changes or, if the changes are not made, modify the audit report. If, however, as is more likely, it is the other information that requires amendment and management refuses to do so, auditors either:

- include an *other matter* paragraph in the audit report *describing the inconsistency*; or
- *withhold the audit report*; or
- *withdraw* from the engagement.

The last two options might not be possible under local legislation.

If auditors do not obtain the other information until after the annual report has been issued, and it becomes apparent that inconsistencies require amendment to the financial statements, consideration needs to be given to their revision. If management refuses, auditors need to inform those charged with governance and take legal advice. Where management will not make necessary changes for subsequent events, resignation or speaking at the AGM are possibilities in some jurisdictions.

### Material Misstatements of Fact

Factual misstatements unrelated to the audited financial statements will never require changes to the audited financial statements but they should be discussed with management, who should be advised to take legal advice if the matter cannot be resolved.

In some jurisdictions such as the UK, an *other matter* paragraph is permitted. Again, in practice there is not much auditors can do if the client refuses to take legal advice or act on advice it has obtained, apart from, as for inconsistencies, informing those charged with governance, taking legal advice, resigning or speaking at the AGM.

### Section essentials: what you need to remember

- *Auditors read other information to ensure that the credibility of the financial statements is not undermined by either inconsistencies between the audited financial statements and the other information, or material misstatement of fact in the other information.*

- *Where management refuses to make necessary amendments to financial statements, there is not much auditors can do apart from taking legal advice, exercising any rights to speak at AGMs and withdrawing from the engagement.*

# SECTION 6, SHORT-FORM QUESTIONS

**SFQ 1:** List and briefly describe the main contents of an unmodified audit report. (4 marks)

**SFQ 2:** List and describe the three main types of modified audit report. (3 marks)

**SFQ 3:** Define and provide examples of 'emphasis of matter' paragraphs. (3 marks)

**SFQ 4:** Define and provide examples of 'other matter' paragraphs and 'other legal and regulatory requirements' paragraphs. (3 marks)

The going concern assumption is a fundamental principle in the preparation of financial statements. ISA 570 on going concern requires auditors to consider whether there are events or conditions casting significant doubt on the entity's ability to continue as a going concern throughout the audit.

**SFQ 5:** Describe the procedures undertaken by auditors where they discover events or conditions that cast significant doubt on an entity's going concern status. (3 marks)

**SFQ 6:** Describe the circumstances in which different types of audit report can be issued where there are significant doubts about the going concern status of an entity. (4 marks)

Alfco is a family-owned company that has the franchise to operate a nationally branded fast food restaurant in a small town. It borrowed a large sum from the bank to fund the franchise and while it is making repayments on time, declining profitability and an economic downturn mean that it is unlikely to continue to do so. The directors consider that the only realistic option is to sell the franchise. They are refusing to disclose the matter in the financial statements.

Murfco operates a small stud farm that breeds and trains racehorses. It is unprofitable because it has been poorly managed and the owner-managers have taken too much in salaries and dividends. It owes a substantial amount of money to a wealthy foreign backer who has expressed increasing dissatisfaction at the way the business is run. Repayment terms are uncertain. The proprietors have told you that they are in the process of installing experienced new managers, have decided to cease paying themselves dividends and are going to sell the land on which the farm operates to a local property company and lease it back, however, they have to date been unable to provide you with any evidence showing that these plans have been put into action.

**SFQ 7:** On the basis of the information provided above, describe the audit report or reports that you consider might be issued in the case of Alfco and Murfco, giving reasons. (5 marks)

Total (25 marks)

# 7 FRAUD, MONEY LAUNDERING, FORENSIC ACCOUNTING, FINANCIAL INSTRUMENTS

Covering: ISA 240 *The Auditor's Responsibilities Relating to Fraud in an Audit of Financial Statements*, ISA 250 *Consideration of Laws and Regulations in an Audit of Financial Statements*, Money Laundering, Forensic Accounting, IAPN 1000 *Special Considerations in Auditing Financial Instruments*.

**Why do I need to read this section?**

*Technology, globalisation and the complexity that goes with them can facilitate sophisticated frauds. Audits of financial statements conducted in accordance with ISAs are not fraud investigations, but increasing regulation and expectations of auditors mean that auditors now probably spend more time on fraud, laws and regulations than they used to. Money laundering regulations in particular worry practitioners. The development of forensic accounting techniques and the demand for forensic accounting services have also grown to the extent that forensic auditing expertise is now a recognised specialism in its own right.*

*The auditors' responsibilities in relation to fraud, laws and regulations are well established and easy to examine. Money laundering is a relatively new area but sufficiently well established to be examined, regularly. Forensic accounting is generally examined in higher level papers. Very complex financial instruments are outside the scope of many syllabuses. Auditing guidance on financial instruments covers all but the simplest of financial instruments.*

**What is important in this section?**

- *The auditors' basic responsibilities for:*
  - *the detection of fraud and error and the presumed risk of fraud in revenue recognition;*
  - *specific procedures aimed at detecting material misstatements due to fraud including risk analyses, discussions among the engagement team and discussions with the client;*
  - *considering the three different types of laws and regulation.*
- *Understanding client due diligence procedures and suspicious transaction reports in the context of money laundering.*
- *The similarities and differences between financial statement audits and forensic engagements, the specialist skills required of forensic accountants and the*

*techniques they use to gather evidence, the 'chain of custody' and the contents of forensic reports.*

- *Understanding the basic audit issues associated with observable and unobservable inputs to valuation models for financial instruments.*

**What sort of questions come up in this area?**

*Knowledge-based questions and questions based on simple scenarios are common methods of examining auditor responsibilities relating to fraud, error, laws and regulations.*

*Money laundering is examined at all levels and while it is important for students to display an understanding of the requirements that firms and their clients should put in place to combat money laundering, many questions also ask students to give examples of what money laundering is, and to demonstrate their understanding of how it happens and why it is important.*

*Forensic accounting is a relatively new area in which a limited number of questions have been set. However, it is likely that the number of questions will increase over time because it is a relatively straightforward area to examine. Questions covering students' knowledge of the area and simple questions on the application of techniques in investigations of common frauds are possible.*

*The guidance on auditing financial instruments is relatively new but the basic principles and difficulties associated with auditing different levels of inputs are easily examined.*

**How do I stand out from the crowd?**

*There is an overlap between the risk factors for material misstatements arising from fraud and non-compliance with laws and regulations, going concern problems and money laundering. Questions on money laundering or fraud may well have going concern implications, and vice versa. Few students make these connections in answers to exam questions and those who do stand out.*

*Forensic auditing may be viewed as peripheral and students who attempt questions in this area stand out. Students also stand out if they display an understanding of the wide range of forensic services available, the necessary safeguards associated with providing forensic services to existing audit clients and the commercial and routine planning aspects of forensic engagements.*

# 7.1   FRAUD: AUDITORS' RESPONSIBILITIES

## 7.1.1   DEFINITIONS

Newspapers write about fraud with a degree of certainty that belies the complexity of the issue. Fraud is not a defined legal term. Certain types of fraud, such as the many different types of theft, are often dealt with in legislation or have been established by the courts. The courts determine whether an act is in fact fraudulent and *fraud for audit purposes might not involve an illegal act.*

For the purposes of ISA 240[1] fraud is:

> *An intentional act by one or more individuals . . . involving the use of deception to obtain an unjust or illegal advantage*
>
> ISA 240 *The Auditor's Responsibilities Relating to Fraud in an Audit of Financial Statements* paragraph 11

The individuals concerned may be management, employees, those charged with governance or third parties, who may collude with management or employees. The risk of auditor non-detection of fraud is greater for management fraud than for employee fraud.[2] The extent to which auditors are likely to detect fraud depends on the extent of manipulation, the skill of the perpetrators, the degree of collusion and the inherent limitations of an audit.[3] This means that there is an unavoidable risk that material misstatements due to fraud go undetected, even in a properly conducted audit.[4]

It is important to remember that auditors are not engaged to identify or report on fraud; they are engaged to report on the truth and fairness or fair presentation of the financial statements.

Most significant frauds do affect the view given by the financial statements but if they do not, they do not concern auditors except to the extent that they may be under a general or specific legal obligation to report the fraud. Auditors also need to consider the implications of the fraud for the integrity of those charged with governance and management. For example, where audited entities[5] hold client money, there are many ways in which clients can be defrauded. Client money accounts can also be used for money laundering. Client money regulations exist in many jurisdictions to prevent this and auditors are often required to report on compliance with such regulations. However, even if there are serious problems with the way client money has been handled, client money does not usually appear in the financial statements. The only potential effects on the audited financial statements in such cases might be the need to accrue for any fine or penalty levied by the regulatory body for the mishandling of client money. If the matter were sufficiently serious, regulators could of course remove the operating licence of the entity, in which case auditors would need to consider disclosures about its going concern status.

---

[1]  ISA 240 on fraud.
[2]  ISA 240 on fraud, paragraph 7.
[3]  ISA 200 on overall objectives, paragraph A45 notes that the inherent limitations of an audit arise from the limitations of financial reporting, the limitations of audit procedures and time and cost constraints. All of this means that audit evidence is persuasive rather than conclusive.
[4]  ISA 240 on fraud, paragraph 5.
[5]  Entities that hold client money include lawyers, accountants and entities dealing in real estate or providing financial services.

## 7.1.2  TYPES OF FRAUD

*Misstatements in financial statements only arise from fraud or error.* Fraud is intentional, error is not and any misstatement that is not a fraud is, by definition, an error. In practice, the distinction between error and fraud is fuzzy. Two auditors might look at a situation where management have taken a 'very optimistic' view on a valuation. One may think that is fraudulent manipulation, the other may think that is just within the boundary of acceptable judgement. Similarly, errors can become frauds. A client may make a genuine mistake and underpay sales taxes. This is an error. The client then notices the error but does nothing, despite the legal obligation to do so promptly. At what point is a fraud committed?

Misstatements arising from fraud involve either:

- *the **misappropriation of assets**,*[6] where assets that appear in the balance sheet have been misappropriated, i.e. taken without authority; or

- *fraudulent financial reporting*, such as the fabrication of revenue or assets that do not exist.

### Asset misappropriation
Asset misappropriation, including theft, can be of cash, inventories, fixtures and fittings, machinery and intellectual property, among other things. Common frauds include the following:

- cash receipts from accounts written off being diverted to personal bank accounts;

- trade secrets being sold to competitors;

- employees being bribed by vendors to approve contracts at inflated prices;

- personal use of the entity's assets;

- employees in entity A setting up fictitious accounts payable and colluding with employees in entity B who either produce fictitious sales invoices that are then approved by other entity A employees also involved in the fraud, or many sales

---

[6] The word 'theft' is usually a defined legal term, or at least a term of art recognised in law. Until a court determines that an asset has been stolen, it is usually more accurate to describe it as 'misappropriated', i.e. taken without authority. Misappropriation can be innocent. The definition of theft in most legal systems involves the intention to steal. If I simply make a mistake and take someone else's suitcase off the carousel in an airport because it looks very similar to mine, I am unlikely to have committed a crime. On the other hand, the fact that I have not committed a crime does not mean that I have not engaged in fraud under ISA 240 because fraud may involve obtaining *unjust* financial advantages that may not be illegal. Some may take the view that even though tax avoidance is legal (tax evasion is not), it represents an unjust financial advantage to those who can afford to buy tax planning advice. Others disagree. Auditors rarely have the inclination or resources to challenge arrangements that are apparently legal on the basis that they might involve deception and are 'unjust'.

invoices for relatively small amounts that fall below the limit required for approval.[7] All of those involved split the proceeds between them;

- staff working in payroll departments colluding with IT and other staff to set up fictitious employees on the payroll, pay them and split the proceeds among those involved.

The last two examples involving fraudulent collusion circumvent internal controls involving segregation of duties.

Where assets are simply stolen, there may be no effect on the financial statements, particularly if the theft is discovered and proper adjustments are made in the records. More often, records are falsified in an attempt to hide the theft, resulting in misstatements in the financial statements.

### Financial reporting fraud

Financial reporting fraud involves international misstatements achieved by the non-application of accounting standards, omissions of disclosures or the falsification of accounting records.

The purpose of financial reporting fraud is usually to make the financial position and performance appear better than they are. Meeting and exceeding targets for profits may trigger bonuses and may justify extracting a higher price in take-over bids. Banking covenants and other loan agreements may require the maintenance of certain liquidity or gearing ratios and financial reporting fraud may be designed to cover up the fact that the requirements have not been met. Sometimes the objective is to present the position as worse than it is to avoid tax, particularly in smaller entities, or to smooth profits, or take all of a 'hit' in one year to improve the appearance of the position or financial performance the following year.

The mechanics of fraud are many and varied but generally fall under three headings:

- falsifying or fabricating records such as invoices and journal entries;
- omitting or concealing transactions;
- engaging in complex transactions to hide their true nature.

The main requirements of auditors in respect of misstatements arising from fraud are that they:

---

[7] A common variation of this fraud is for entities to be set up solely to raise fictitious sales invoices for entries in non-existent or poor quality directories or registers where no order for the entry was made by the entity receiving the invoice. Unfortunately, such invoices are sometimes paid because they are for small amounts and look plausible. No collusion among staff is required.

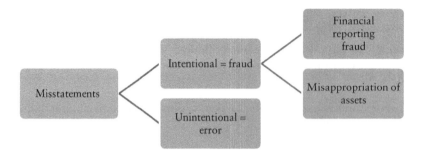

**Figure 7.1**    Fraud and error

- maintain an attitude of professional *scepticism;*

- investigate inconsistencies in audit evidence, particularly responses to inquiries of management and those charged with governance, and consider whether unusual or unexpected relationships identified during analytical procedures might be indicative of fraud;

- discuss among the engagement team the *susceptibility* of the financial statements to misstatements due to fraud;

- make *inquiries* of management, internal audit and those charged with governance regarding fraud;

- *evaluate* fraud risk factors;

- *identify, assess and respond to the risk* of material misstatement due to fraud.

### 7.1.3   AUDITOR SCEPTICISM: IS THIS DOCUMENT FORGED?

Auditors *may* accept documents as **authentic** unless there is reason to believe otherwise, in which case they *must* investigate. It would not be practical to conduct an audit on any other basis. If doubts arise as to the authenticity of documents, confirmations with third parties or the use of experts may be necessary. Forged documentation provided to auditors, particularly forged certificates or confirmations from third parties, is a feature of many frauds.[8]

Scepticism in this context means recognising that a material misstatement could exist, regardless of the auditors' experience of the honesty and integrity of management and those charged with governance. While auditors cannot be expected to disregard their past experience, circumstances change and auditors cannot assume that because management have been honest in the past, this will continue. This is not the same as assuming that management are dishonest, but if management integrity is suspect, auditors

---

[8]   The Parmalat case involved a forged bank confirmation purportedly confirming balances of some $5.5bn with the Bank of America. It was alleged that the confirmation request was sent using Parmalat's internal mail and that the forged confirmation was put together by Parmalat employees using scissors and a scanner.

will presumably be more on their guard, and if it is very suspect, auditors need to consider whether they should continue to act as auditors at all.

## 7.1.4   ENGAGEMENT TEAM DISCUSSION

The discussion among the engagement team required by ISA 315[9] requires particular emphasis on the susceptibility of the financial statements to misstatements due to fraud. The discussion should cover, for example, potential indicators of earnings management, incentives, opportunities and possible rationalisations for fraud, unusual or unexplained changes in behaviour, allegations of fraud, and the need for unpredictability in testing.

---

Fraud requires an *incentive* to commit it, i.e. pressures or motivations such as difficult personal circumstances, the pressure or temptation to meet targets, or simple greed. Fraud also requires the *opportunity* to commit it and some *rationalisation* of why the fraud is justified, such as being denied a deserved promotion or pay rise after many years of service. Anyone in a position of power or trust has the opportunity to abuse their position, and it is very easy even for otherwise honest people to rationalise fraud when under pressure.

---

## 7.1.5   INQUIRIES

Auditors make inquiries of management, internal audit and those charged with governance regarding:

- any actual, suspected or alleged frauds;
- management's assessment of the susceptibility of the financial statements and different locations and business segments to fraud, and their processes for dealing with fraud;
- management's communications of their expectations regarding ethical requirements to employees;
- how those charged with governance oversee management's actions;
- internal audit's approach to fraud, including whether management have responded satisfactorily to findings.

## 7.1.6   EVALUATING FRAUD RISK FACTORS

General indicators of fraud include:

- last-minute *adjustments* to the financial statements;
- *allegations* of fraud made by entity staff to auditors;

---

[9]   ISA 315 on risk assessment.

- missing *documents* and documents that appear to have been altered;

- significant unexplained items in large *suspense accounts*;

- inconsistent, vague or contradictory *explanations* from management;

- a large number of *credit entries* and other adjustments to receivables records;

- poor documentation of *changes to IT systems*;

- excessive *time pressure or delays* in providing information;

- frequent *changes to accounting policies* or estimates;

- a history of *disputes with auditors*.

Incentives to commit fraud are among the fraud risk factors auditors are required to evaluate. Incentives might include alcohol or gambling problems, individuals living beyond their means, the loss of income in divorce cases and pressure to meet earnings or other targets, particularly if they trigger bonuses or prevent inquiries as to why targets have not been met.

Features of financial reporting fraud include:

- threats to financial stability such as increased competition, rapid changes in technology, declines in demand, rapid growth and new legislation or regulation;

- pressure from analysts and investors to maintain and increase profitability and growth and sometimes pressure on management by management where evidenced by excessively optimistic profit forecasts;

- excessively complex transactions or group structures, the use of business intermediaries for no apparent reason, assets being held in tax havens;

- a poor control environment, poor monitoring of controls, ineffective IT systems;

- a high turnover of and low morale among management and accounting staff;

- a record of agreeing to unrealistic targets;

- owners making no distinction between personal and business assets.

Legitimate business practices can degenerate into financial reporting fraud. In the UK, the Financial Reporting Council issued a consultation paper in 2001 entitled *Aggressive Earnings Management* that described an entity that met analysts targets during a slow-down in business by authorising overtime and making shipments early. This unfortunately led to even higher targets that were again met by additional overtime, greater discounting, early invoicing and a reduction in provisions for returns and bad debt. By the third year, provisions were eliminated altogether, invoices from the subsequent period were brought forward and false journal entries were made.

Asset misappropriation and related misstatements are more likely where:

- there are anticipated layoffs or pay cuts;

- there are easily stolen assets, particularly if controls such as physical controls and segregation of duties are poor;

- there is poor record-keeping and reconciliations are not performed;

- there is a poor attitude to controls and petty theft is tolerated.

## 7.1.7   RISK ASSESSMENT AND RESPONSES

Auditors identify, assess and respond to the risk of material misstatement due to fraud. This includes a *presumption that there are risks of material misstatement due to fraud in revenue recognition.*[10] If auditors conclude that this is not the case, i.e. that there is little risk of material misstatement due to fraud in revenue recognition, as will sometimes be the case, they are required to document that fact.

*Any assessed risk of material misstatement due to fraud is a significant risk.*[11] As with all significant risks, this means that auditors need to obtain an understanding of relevant controls.

### *Overall responses and responses at the assertion level*
Overall responses to a *heightened risk of misstatement* resulting from fraud are very similar to responses to a heightened risk of misstatement in any area. They include:

- assigning more experienced staff and/or supervising them more closely, and considering whether forensic or IT experts are needed;

- paying particular attention to accounting policies;

- incorporating an element of unpredictability into testing using different sampling methods, and performing procedures at different times and places;

- being more sceptical by paying more attention to documentation and corroborating management explanations;

- considering whether the balance of procedures might be weighted away from controls and towards more substantive procedures at the period-end;

- obtaining more and better quality evidence by, for example:

  - attending more inventory counts and performing more test counts;

  - analysing inventory shortages by location, discounts or returns for unusual trends;

  - using computer assisted audit techniques to test controls over and the ageing of inventory;

  - increasing sample sizes;

  - performing analytical procedures at a more detailed level.

---

[10] ISA 240 on fraud, paragraph 26.
[11] ISA 240 on fraud, paragraph 27.

Paying more attention to management explanations where management are expected to meet earnings targets might involve not just confirming outstanding balances, but confirming details of the terms of trade, such as rights to return goods, and checking dates to detect any invoicing before delivery.

### Management override and journal entries

Management override of controls is always a risk factor and the abuse of journal entries and accounting estimates are the commonest ways in which management override controls. For these reasons, irrespective of the assessed risk, auditors are required to:

- test the *appropriateness of period-end journal entries and other adjustments* particularly for equal and opposite entries just before and after the period-end, and consider the need to test entries throughout the period;

- make *inquiries* about inappropriate or unusual journal entries;

- *review estimates for bias* and even if individual estimates are reasonable, evaluate whether collectively they could represent possible bias and, if so, whether it could be material;

- *retrospectively review management judgements* and assumptions;

- *evaluate the business rationale of unusual transactions* and those outside the normal course of business. These may be suspect if management is overly concerned with presentation, if transactions involve related parties, particularly non-consolidated related parties in a group situation, or if they have not been properly reviewed or approved.

Fraudulent journal entries may involve little-used accounts and be made by people who do not usually make such entries. Such entries may have little or no explanation and may be round numbers.

### Analytical procedures and written representations

When used properly, analytical procedures are a very powerful audit tool that can be used to highlight fraud as well as error. If fabricated sales are put through using invoices and reversed out with credit notes, rather than using journals, the fabrication will not show up in a review of journal entries. Analytical procedures might highlight such a problem, though, provided sufficient attention is paid to unusual changes at the period-end.

Written representations are needed stating that management have disclosed to auditors:

- the results of management's assessment of material misstatement due to fraud;

- management's knowledge of actual or suspected fraud involving management and certain senior employees;

- management's knowledge of any allegations of frauds affecting the financial statements made by employees, former employees, regulators, analysts or others.

Management also need to acknowledge their responsibility for internal controls that deal with fraud.

## 7.1.8 REPORTING

Auditors must not be associated with misleading financial statements. In exceptional circumstances, a material misstatement due to fraud might mean that continuing the engagement is no longer possible because of the significance of the issue, particularly if it might give rise to the need for a disclaimer of opinion or has serious implications regarding the integrity of management. In such circumstances, auditors need to consider whether it is possible to withdraw from the engagement, except where it is prohibited, and to whom they need to report. Jurisdictions such as the UK have mechanisms in place to ensure that auditors do not resign simply to avoid having to deal with a fraud, usually by requiring them to make public statements about whether there is anything that needs to be brought to the attention of members or creditors when they resign, are removed or are not re-appointed.

Where actual or suspected frauds involving management come to the auditors' attention, auditors clearly need to report them to the next highest level of management. This is problematic where the fraud involves the most senior levels of management or those charged with governance, i.e. where there is no clear 'next highest level of management' to report to. In all such cases, auditors also need to consider any statutory reporting responsibilities and any obligation to report in the public interest.

### *Reporting in the public interest*

In many jurisdictions, law and regulation provide auditors with specific and general rights and duties to report matters in the 'public' or 'national' interest, or in the interests of 'national security'. Reporting is to individuals or bodies outside the audited entity. Matters to be reported are likely to include some significant frauds or non-compliance laws and regulations. There are more likely to be specific reporting requirements for auditors of banks and others in the financial services sector.

Auditors may have either a ***legal right or duty*** to report to bodies that might include financial intelligence units responsible for dealing with reports of money laundering, authorities dealing with serious financial fraud, financial services, banking and securities regulators, bodies regulating charities and pension funds, competition authorities, government departments, the police or tax authorities. A duty to report is usually clear, a right requires auditors to make a judgement as to whether reporting is appropriate and in practice taking legal advice is essential.

Where auditors have a right to report to third parties, unless they have lost confidence in the integrity of those charged with governance because they are involved, it is generally appropriate for the audited entity to report matters in the first instance. Before exercising their own right or duty to report auditors should normally urge clients, in writing, to make any necessary reports. Only if the client fails to provide evidence that it has done so, should auditors consider doing it themselves.

Jurisdictions differ, but auditors reporting because they have a right rather than a duty are often protected from claims of ***defamation*** or that they have ***breached their duty of confidentiality*** if they act reasonably and in ***good faith*** and report to a ***proper authority*** in their capacity as auditors.

In deciding what is in the public interest and whether to report, auditors consider:

- the likely extent of *damage,* any *corrective action* taken by the entity, and the *extent to which the public is affected;*
- the general *ethos* within the entity of disregarding the law, the *weight of evidence* and the likelihood that the fraud or non-compliance will be *repeated;*
- the *seriousness* (gravity) of the matter.

If the decision to report is questioned later, auditors are likely to be judged based on what they:

- knew at the time;
- should have known;
- should have concluded;
- should have done.

The fact that reported matter subsequently turns out *not* to have constituted an offence, does not of itself mean that auditors should not have reported.

## 7.2   LAWS AND REGULATIONS: AUDITORS' RESPONSIBILITIES

Fortunately, the principles of auditors' responsibilities in relation to fraud are very similar to those applying to laws and regulation. Several references are made below to money laundering, which is dealt with in Section 7.3.

A fraud under ISA 240 may or may not involve an illegal act. Illegal acts defined as 'frauds' or described as 'fraudulent' in legislation or case law may include *fraudulent trading, fraudulent misrepresentation* or a *fraud on the public.*

Frauds that may also be illegal acts because of specific legal provisions include:

- *bribery,* such as making illicit payments in exchange for the award of contracts;
- *extortion,* such as seeking illicit payments to avoid threats of business interruption;
- *blackmail,* such as threatening the revelation of something injurious to the business or someone within it to extract payment or a particular course of action.

In many jurisdictions[12] bribery is now subject to legislation. It may constitute a criminal offence committed by companies as well as individuals, wherever in the world the bribe takes place. The only defence for a company may be that adequate procedures were in place to prevent bribery, which include making company policy known to staff and having proper reporting lines and sanctions in place. These provisions often apply to firms of accountants as well as to their clients.

---

[12] The UK implemented the Bribery Act 2010 in July 2011.

## 7.2.1   TYPES OF LAWS AND REGULATIONS

Three categories of laws and regulations are relevant to the audit. Laws and regulations may:

- have *a direct effect on the financial statements* such as companies, tax and pensions legislation and accounting standards, all of which affect the format, amounts and disclosures in financial statements. Companies legislation often includes specific requirements for auditors to report non-compliance with requirements for accounting records or non-disclosure of directors' remuneration, for example. Such laws or regulation may be industry specific. Auditors are expected to obtain *sufficient, appropriate audit evidence* regarding compliance with such laws and regulations;

- be *fundamental to the operation of the business*, i.e. those that could result in material penalties or that affect business continuation, such as operating licences in the aviation industry, solvency, capital or investment requirements in the financial services sector, or environmental regulations for entities involved in minerals extraction or manufacturing involving toxic waste. Auditors are required to perform *specified audit procedures* to identify any non-compliance that might have a material effect;

- relate to the *operation of all businesses* such as health and safety and employment legislation. Auditors are only expected to *respond appropriately* to instances of non-compliance with such laws and regulations if they come to their attention. Such laws and regulations may include money laundering legislation and legislation on bribery in many jurisdictions.

The category depends on the client. Food hygiene regulations apply to all businesses but they may be fundamental to the operation of a restaurant chain.

As with fraud, auditors cannot be expected to detect all non-compliance with laws and regulations, because of the inherent limitations of an audit, because of materiality considerations and because there are so many laws and regulations that may apply to an entity but are far removed from the financial statements and are very unlikely to have a material effect. Financial reporting systems cannot normally be expected to capture information about parking fines incurred by sales staff driving their own vehicles, for example, even if legislation or case law does make the employer responsible.

---

Auditors cannot prevent fraud or non-compliance with laws and regulations but their presence and activities may deter both.

---

Non-compliance may be by those charged with governance, management or employees. Indicators are similar to the indicators for fraud and going concern problems and include:

- regulatory investigations;
- payments for unspecified services;

- purchases at above or below market value;
- unusual transactions with entities in tax havens.

## 7.2.2 AUDITOR PROCEDURES

Auditors obtain a ***general understanding of the legal and regulatory framework*** and of how the entity ensures that it complies. The simplest way to do this is ask management. Larger entities are likely to ensure compliance by maintaining and enforcing a code of ethics and by means of risk management or compliance and internal audit functions. For larger entities it is likely that auditors will make ***inquiries of lawyers,*** internal or external and ***inspect correspondence with regulators***.

Entities in regulated industries of all sizes are likely to be required to maintain internal control systems to ensure compliance with regulations such as client money regulations. Auditors may need to evaluate the design and implementation of such systems and test them for regulatory purposes, but not necessarily for audit purposes where the output of the system does not directly affect the financial statements.

Auditors obtain ***written representations*** to the effect that management have disclosed to auditors all known non-compliance with laws and regulations relevant to the financial statements. This is not, of course, sufficient evidence regarding compliance with laws and regulations.

### *Investigating non-compliance and reporting*
Even if auditors are not looking for non-compliance, it may arise during inquiries about other matters, or when reading minutes, or in discussions with employees, for example.

Auditors investigate identified and suspected non-compliance, no matter how it comes to their attention. This includes ***discussing*** the issue with management or those charged with governance, to confirm the auditors' understanding, and to obtain sufficient information to form a view as to whether there is any material effect on the financial statements. This is not straightforward. An immaterial matter may result in adverse publicity, fines or litigation, all of which could have a material effect. If the information is not forthcoming, auditors may need to take legal advice and there may be a limitation in the scope of the audit. There may be further reporting implications when there are legal requirements for auditors to make statements as to whether they have received all of the information and explanations they require.

Auditors need to be careful if the non-compliance involves money laundering. Legislation in many jurisdictions makes 'tipping-off' an offence, i.e. warning an individual that a money laundering investigation may take place. This means that auditors and others may even be prohibited from discussing suspected non-compliance with management or those charged with governance, particularly if auditors have already reported suspected money laundering activity to financial intelligence units, which is often required by legislation. Subject to these requirements, auditors report all apparently intentional instances of non-compliance, other than clearly inconsequential matters,[13] to the next highest level of management and those charged with governance, as soon as possible. If those charged with governance are involved or auditors believe that the communication may be ignored, legal advice may be needed. As with fraud, withdrawal from the engagement may be possible but only in exceptional circumstances and there may be a need to consider reporting in the public interest, as described above in the context of fraud.

*Reporting*

The reporting implications of non-compliance with laws and regulations can be extensive.

To summarise the requirements above, auditors may need to report to:

- management and those charged with governance as described above, unless this would constitute 'tipping off' in the context of money laundering;

- shareholders in the audit report where:

  - there is a limitation in the scope of the audit because management have failed to provide sufficient information for auditors to form an opinion and, as is often the case,

  - there is also a requirement for auditors to report, by exception or otherwise, on whether all information and explanations necessary for the audit have been received from management;

- regulators, such as those in the banking and financial services sectors where there are specific legal requirements to report on matters such as client monies, solvency or capital;

- third parties in the public interest.

## 7.3 MONEY LAUNDERING

### 7.3.1 WHAT IS MONEY LAUNDERING?

Money laundering is the process by which the proceeds of crime, such as stolen cash, are made to appear as if they come from somewhere else.

The proceeds of crime can include a very wide variety of assets. The proceeds of drug dealing or extortion can include property, vehicles or jewellery. Relatively small amounts such as the 'proceeds' arising from a failure to buy a train ticket or put money into a parking meter, both of which are a form of theft, may also be the proceeds of crime.

---

[13] Non-payment of parking fines is likely to be clearly inconsequential in many cases.

*How money can be laundered*

It may be difficult for a criminal to buy a house with a large amount of cash that has been obtained by extortion. One way of hiding the origin of the cash might be to bribe a lawyer to place the money in a client account, and for the lawyer to pay the property seller by cheque or bank transfer. Such a lawyer is thereby helping the criminal benefit from the crime, which is itself a crime in many jurisdictions. The lawyer is also committing a further crime by accepting a bribe.

In many jurisdictions, helping a criminal commit or benefit from a crime is known as *aiding, abetting,* or *being an accessory* to a crime and money laundering is an example. These, together with *concealing or counselling* (advising) on money laundering are often specific crimes which accountants and lawyers may be involved in.

Money laundering is the means by which the origins of the money earned from criminal activities are disguised so that the money can be used for legitimate activities. 'Dirty' money is thereby 'laundered', i.e. washed and made 'clean'. It enables criminals to use the proceeds of crime for legal activities, such as buying property, paying school fees or setting up legitimate businesses. If criminals cannot spend the money they earn, crime becomes less attractive. It has always been difficult for criminals to spend the cash proceeds of crime without inviting questions or attracting the sort attention they would rather avoid. The price of money laundering is very high, for this reason.

Criminals laundering money from the proceeds of cigarette smuggling might systematically feed cash into a restaurant business. This helps the restaurant keep its prices low, which attracts business. The suspicions of the tax authorities are not aroused because the addition of the 'dirty' money to the cash taken from customers makes the profit margins look normal, despite the low prices. If questioned, the restaurant owner explains this by saying that he has good relationships with suppliers who give good discounts because of the high volume of purchases. The restaurant's profits can then be paid to the money launderer, apparently as legitimate earnings from a restaurant. The cost of this may be very high, but there may be no alternative.

Any business involving the movement of high volumes of cash is at risk of becoming a victim of money launderers. Financial intelligence units often target such businesses because they are sometimes set up simply to launder money. Such businesses vary from jurisdiction to jurisdiction but they can include casinos, car dealers, dealers in precious metals and real estate agents.

Money laundering generally involves acts which conceal, disguise, convert, transfer, remove, use, acquire or possess property resulting from criminal conduct.

*Placement, layering and integration*
The three stages of the money laundering process are:

- *placement:* involves getting money into the financial system, through bank accounts, travellers cheques, through lawyers' or accountants' client accounts, or through life insurance policies, pensions or other financial products.[14]

---

[14] Anti-money laundering regulations recognise that large cash transactions may be the proceeds of crime and require banks, accountants, lawyers and others to investigate large cash transactions, and make appropriate reports where the source is suspect.

- *layering:* creates a series of further, often complex, offshore transactions so that the original source of funds is obscured and difficult to trace;

- *integration:* converts the proceeds of money laundering into a legitimate form.

A lawyer may be instructed to buy a life insurance policy by a criminal client who gives the lawyer a large amount of cash. The lawyer banks the cash in a client account and executes the transaction (placement). The insurance company receives a cheque or bank transfer from the lawyer and has no cause to suspect the origin of the funds. The criminal client then sells the insurance policy to further obscure the origins of the transaction (layering). The proceeds of the sale of the policy are then used by the criminal for investment in a legitimate business, school fees for children, or real estate (integration).

Anti-money laundering procedures are most effective at the placement stage.

### 7.3.2 INTERNATIONAL EFFORTS TO COMBAT MONEY LAUNDERING

A key source of money laundering legislation internationally is the *FATF Recommendations.*[15]

The recommendations cover the need for:

- money laundering *policies,* laws and regulations;

- *countries to confiscate* the proceeds of crime;

- the criminalisation of the *financing of terrorism* and the *proliferation* of weapons of mass destruction;

- the *prevention* of money laundering by means of, among other things, customer due diligence;

- transparency regarding the beneficial *ownership of legal entities;*

- competent authorities, i.e. *financial intelligence units* such as the Serious Organised Crime Agency in the UK;

- *international co-operation.*

---

[15] The *International Standards of Combating Money Laundering and the Financing of Terrorism and Proliferation,* Revised February 2012, previously known as the 'FATF 40', is issued by the Financial Action Task Force (FATF). FATF is an inter-governmental body that promotes international policies to combat money laundering, the financing of terrorism and the proliferation of weapons of mass destruction. It seeks to generate the necessary political will to bring about legislative and regulatory reforms in these areas. It currently comprises 34 member jurisdictions and 2 regional organisations, representing most major financial centres. It originally established a series of Recommendations in 1990 that have been endorsed in over 180 countries. www.fatf.org.

### Money laundering policies

Countries should undertake money-laundering *risk assessments* and ensure that national agencies are co-ordinated. Appropriate action to mitigate risks includes requiring financial institutions (such as banks) and designated non-financial businesses and professions, including accountants, to conduct risk assessments. Agencies responsible for dealing with money laundering, including financial intelligence units (FIUs) set up to deal with reports of money laundering, should be able to co-operate with each other, which is often a problem in practice.

### Designated non-financial businesses and professions

(DNFBPs) are those that are used, or can be used, knowingly or otherwise, in money laundering. They are often businesses that have a high volume of cash transactions: casinos, car dealers, dealers in precious metals and real estate agents. Professions include lawyers and other independent legal professionals such as notaries, and accountants, if their activities could involve money laundering. Lawyers, notaries, accountants and company service providers often manage client money or other assets arising from real estate transactions or from creating, buying and selling businesses.

### Confiscation

Countries should criminalise money laundering based on international conventions and enable competent authorities to *freeze or seize and confiscate assets* used in connection with money laundering or terrorism. Countries should consider whether a criminal conviction should be needed for this to happen.

### Financing of terrorism and the proliferation of weapons of mass destruction

Countries should *criminalise terrorist financing* and implement financial sanctions regimes in accordance with UN Security Council resolutions requiring asset freezing. *Charities* are easily used as conduits for terrorist financing and countries should review the adequacy of laws designed to deal with this.

### Prevention

### Customer due diligence (CDD)

Many of the irritating security measures imposed by banks and others requiring proof of identity with several different types of documentation when new customers try to open accounts or establish business relationships, derive from customer due diligence requirements.

*Customer due diligence measures are required of financial institutions and DNFBPs, including accountants, when:*

- *establishing business relations;*
- *for certain high value occasional transactions;*[16]
- *when their suspicions are aroused.*

---

[16] US $15,000 as at 2013.

Measures include:

- *customer identity verification* using reliable third party documentation such as bank statements, utility bills and photo ID such as passports, driving licences and identity cards for individuals, and incorporation documents or certificates of the registered address for legal entities;

- identifying and verifying the *beneficial owners* of legal entities, which involves understanding group structures;

- understanding the *purpose of the business relationship,* hence the question 'why are you opening this bank account?';

- conducting *on-going* due diligence.

*Records* should be kept for at least *five years.* It may be necessary to rely on third parties in remote locations to perform some of these measures but some work needs to be performed to ensure that the third party is actually doing the work properly. Enhanced procedures are required for higher risk countries. The money laundering risks associated with *new technologies* should be assessed.

*Financial institutions* need to *implement controls on a group-wide basis.* Financial institutions should assess the extent of compliance with the recommendations of any correspondent banks they deal with. They should not deal with 'shell' banks.

Additional measures are required for 'foreign politically exposed persons' and their close family members, including taking measures to establish the source of funds, and obtaining senior management approval for establishing or continuing such relationships.

Similar considerations apply to money and wire transfer services.

Accountants need to perform customer due diligence procedures for new and existing clients. They may also need to advise their clients of them.

*Suspicious transaction reports (STRs)*
Financial institutions and designated non-financial businesses and professions with *reasonable grounds to suspect that funds are the proceeds of criminal activity should be required to report it to a financial intelligence unit, i.e. make suspicious transaction reports.*

Financial institutions and designated non-financial businesses and professions should be protected by legislation from any liability arising from any breach of duty of confidentiality provided that they report suspicions in good faith, even if they are not sure of the precise details. Considerations here are similar to the provisions in many jurisdictions covering reporting in the public interest.

Financial institutions and designated non-financial businesses and professions should be *prohibited from 'tipping off',* i.e. disclosing to the client the fact that a suspicious transaction report has been made, regardless of who has made the report.

### Transparency and beneficial ownership

Countries should take steps to prevent the misuse of legal persons, including companies, for money laundering and terrorist financing. The issue of bearer shares, i.e. shares belonging to whoever happens to have them at any given point in time, and the use of nominee shareholders can be problematic.

### Competent authorities

Countries should establish properly co-ordinated regulation and enforcement mechanisms for dealing with money laundering and terrorist financing. Casinos, for example, should be subject to comprehensive regulatory measures including licensing. *Countries should establish financial intelligence units that serve as national centres for the receipt and analysis of suspicious transaction reports and other relevant information.*

### International co-operation

Countries should implement international conventions on money laundering and terrorist financing and respond promptly to requests for extradition. They should not prohibit or restrict the provision of cross-border legal assistance. Requests from overseas competent authorities are often in conflict with local confidentiality requirements, unfortunately.

---

*National Requirements: Money Laundering and Accountants*

*Offences under money laundering legislation*[17] may include:

- handling the proceeds of crime through client accounts or accepting payment of fees that are the proceeds of crime;

- non-compliance with customer due diligence requirements;

- a failure to make suspicious transaction reports to financial intelligence units;

- 'tipping off'.

National requirements often go into more detail on how firms should go about ensuring that they comply with relevant legal requirements. Legislation may extend the scope of the requirements to all activities the firm engages in, not just those listed in the FATF recommendations such as real estate transactions and buying and selling businesses. Suspicious transactions are similar to the types of transaction giving rise to concerns about fraud, non-compliance with laws and regulations and going concern problems, such as large unspecified cash transactions, transactions with entities in tax havens, excessively complex transactions and transactions with shell companies.

*Money laundering plans for a firm* might include:[18]

- *customer due diligence,* on-going monitoring of business relationships and *record-keeping;*

- *training* for all relevant employees;

---

[17] The relevant UK legislation includes the Proceeds of Crime Act 2002, the Terrorism Act 2000 and the Money Laundering Regulations 2007.
[18] In the UK, the Financial Reporting Council's Practice Note 12 on money laundering deals with this in more detail.

- the implementation of systems and **controls** to ensure compliance with money-laundering regulations;

- the appointment of a **money laundering reporting officer** whose role is to take responsibility for the requirements, to receive reports from staff regarding suspected money laundering and to decide whether to make a report to a financial intelligence unit.

**The need for ethical requirements** in different jurisdictions arises from:

- the fact that firms of accountants may be used to launder money without knowing it;

- severe penalties often associated with money laundering and non-compliance with the regulations;

- the need to deal with the conflict between a firm's general duty of confidentiality and the need to report suspicious transactions and make other reports to regulators and to shareholders arising from money laundering. Legislation normally states that those making reports are not in breach of any other duty, such as the duty of confidentiality, if reports are made in good faith.

# 7.4   FORENSIC ACCOUNTING

## 7.4.1   FORENSIC ACCOUNTING AND HOW IT IS USED

The word *forensic* simply means *pertaining to legal proceedings* and many firms now have forensic accounting divisions or specialise in the area.

The term **forensic accounting** refers to the skills employed by forensic accountants. Forensic skills are mostly called for in disputes rather than in criminal proceedings but all forensic activity involves investigations. Forensic accountants may be engaged to:

- appear as expert witnesses or provide evidence in **legal or disciplinary** proceedings, often in professional negligence cases;

- help conduct investigations into **corporate collapses and alleged frauds** such as theft, tax evasion and insider trading on behalf of government, regulators, tax authorities or the police;

- provide support to **insurers** in claims for business interruption, property losses, personal liability and wrongful dismissal;

- help **investigate** management or employee fraud and computer misuse;

- provide evidence in **business disputes** between shareholders, management and partners and in **matrimonial disputes**.

Much of the above can be categorised as litigation support or insurance work.

In many jurisdictions, forensic audits are a common part of government investigations into the abuse of public money, or the abuse of public process for personal benefit, such as the misallocation of state assets during privatisations and the misuse of public assets built or operated by private contractors.

The different types of fraud which forensic accountants investigate in the private sector include:

- conflicts of interest, such as managers inappropriately authorising the expenses of a friend;
- asset misappropriation and theft including fraudulent payments to suppliers and payments to fictitious employees.

*Computer or digital forensics* involve *data recovery* and rebuilding computer records lost through malfunction or sabotage, *systems analysis* to detect the existence of network intrusions or fraudulent transactions, using data mining tools to analyse unusual patterns or repeat transactions, for example, *data storage,* and advice on computer security.

*Investigations of employee and management frauds and computer misuse* on behalf of companies cover the misuse of IT by employees and breaches of workplace IT policy. Frauds might include identity theft. Misuse might include email harassment, circulation of offensive material, disclosing confidential information or conducting a private business. The methods used by forensic accountants in these areas include tracing the source of threats sent electronically and the surveillance and recording of computer use, keystroke-by-keystroke.

### 7.4.2   FORENSIC ACCOUNTING, FORENSIC INVESTIGATIONS, FORENSIC AUDITING

*Forensic accounting* refers to the areas covered by forensic accountants. Forensic accounting requires specialised accounting, auditing and investigation skills including the ability to:

- investigate and analyse financial evidence, often using traditional auditing skills or similar;
- develop computerised applications for the analysis and presentation of financial evidence;
- communicate findings in the form of reports, exhibits and collections of documents.

While single individuals may have all of these skills, they are more likely to exist within a team.

*Forensic investigations* are the practical steps that forensic accountants take, similar to the steps taken in a financial audit, i.e. planning, evidence gathering, review and reporting.

The purposes of an investigation, in the case of an alleged fraud, for example, might be to:

- discover if a fraud had *actually* taken place;
- *identify* those involved;

- *quantify* the monetary amount;
- *present findings* to the client and in legal proceedings.

*Forensic auditing* is the set of procedures and techniques used in forensic investigations. Forensic auditing also requires broader skills and experience to:

- recognise the motives and opportunities to commit fraud;
- determine whether there has been collusion between several persons involved in the fraud or attempts to destroy evidence;
- use comments made during interviews effectively.

### 7.4.3   ETHICAL AND COMMERCIAL CONSIDERATIONS: ENGAGEMENT ACCEPTANCE

*Competence:* does the firm have the necessary skills and experience? Forensic accounting is a specialist area in its own right and the communication and interrogation skills required, together with the required knowledge of legal process, mean that not all auditors are suitable candidates.

Forensic investigations are not simply extended audits. If auditors are not aware of legal processes, they may inadvertently compromise evidence that may later be required in court proceedings. The safe custody of evidence gathered in forensic investigations is even more important than it is in ordinary audits.

*Independence and conflicts of interest:* is an existing client requesting the investigation? If an audit client asks for help, the firm is exposed to self-review, advocacy and management threats and strong safeguards are needed. While there is no absolute prohibition on the provision of forensic services to audit or other clients, auditors need to manage the threats. Conflicts of interest can be a bar if the dispute or litigation is with another of the firm's clients.

*Commercial considerations:* does the fee reflect the risks and costs involved? Forensic work is by nature specialised despite the fact that many firms provide such services now and the risks to the firm include risks to reputation. Senior and more highly paid staff are likely to be involved in forensic investigations and training costs need to be taken into account. Forensic accounting services cannot be provided cheaply.

### 7.4.4   CONDUCTING FORENSIC ENGAGEMENTS

*Planning*
The routine planning considerations for forensic audits are similar to planning considerations in financial audits. They include engagement timing, the availability of staff, scheduling site visits and interviews, and liaison with others involved in the investigation such as technical experts.

Detailed technical planning involves consideration of the objectives of the investigation including specific requirements for any reports, presentations or evidence to be presented in court. Planning includes identifying, for example, the nature of the fraud investigated, how long it has been going on, how it has been concealed, how those responsible are to be identified and quantifying the client's financial loss. The balance of techniques used, such as computer-assisted audit techniques and interviews with staff, are key considerations. Timing can be critical because without sufficient 'hard' evidence, it is unlikely that an interview with a suspected fraudster will be helpful. Poor timing may compromise the whole case.

### Evidence gathering

Evidence in fraud cases needs to provide proof of the identity of the fraudster, how the fraud was conducted and the extent of financial loss. A clear chain of custody of evidence is essential until the evidence is presented in court, because gaps in the chain can be challenged in court and can render evidence inadmissible. A key difference between forensic investigations and financial statement audits is that while in both cases auditors must be alert for the possibility of falsified documentation, in an audit auditors are entitled to assume that documents are genuine, unless evidence suggests otherwise. This assumption cannot be made in forensic investigations.

Evidence gathering techniques are otherwise similar to those used in financial statement audits. They include:

- *tests of control effectiveness* to identify the weaknesses which allowed the fraud to be perpetrated;

- *analytical procedures* to compare trends over time or to provide comparisons between different segments of the business;

- applying *computer assisted audit techniques*, to identify the timing and location of relevant details being altered in a computer system, for example;

- *discussions and interviews* with employees;

- *substantive techniques* such as reconciliations, cash counts and reviews of documentation.

If a fraud actually occurred, the ultimate goal of the forensic investigation team is to obtain a confession by the fraudster. For this reason, investigators are likely to avoid deliberately confronting the alleged fraudster(s) until they have gathered sufficient evidence to extract a confession. The interview with the suspect and the evidence it can provide are critical parts of any fraud investigation.

### The chain of custody

If a defendant accused of an attack questions the *chain of custody* of evidence in a court case, he is asking for proof that the knife used as evidence against him is the knife used in the crime. Evidence capable of use in court to convict criminals must be handled scrupulously to avoid allegations of tampering, which can compromise the case.

*Maintaining the integrity of the chain of custody establishes that evidence presented in court relates to the crime rather than having been 'planted' or tampered with to make someone appear guilty.* This requires documentation of every transfer of the evidence, from person to person, starting with its collection, and proof that nobody else could have accessed the evidence. It is best to minimise the number of transfers. If evidence such as falsified invoices in a fraud case has at some point been left open in an office overnight or in a briefcase in the back of a car, for example, questions may legitimately be asked about whether it has been interfered with.

### Reporting

Forensic reports do not provide assurance. They are often lengthy and provide the client with a summary and details of the *findings* of the investigation, a *summary of evidence,* and a conclusion as to the *amount of loss.* Reports may also explain:

- the mechanics of the fraud;

- how poorly designed or operated controls were circumvented;

- how to prevent the re-occurrence of the fraud.

### 7.4.5   COURT PROCEEDINGS

If the investigation culminates in legal proceedings, the evidence gathered may be presented in court and members of the forensic accounting team working on the engagement may be called to explain the evidence. The ability to present the work performed clearly and professionally, which may involve simplifying complex accounting issues, is clearly a key skill for anyone intending to pursue a career in this area.

# 7.5   FINANCIAL INSTRUMENTS

### 7.5.1   WHAT ARE FINANCIAL INSTRUMENTS?

Financial instruments encompass nearly all receivables and payables, loans and bank balances. They are nearly all stated at amortised cost rather than fair value and the audit issues are straightforward. This section deals with all but the simplest financial instruments.

Rightly or wrongly, complex financial instruments are associated with excessive risk-taking and fraud. While the business environment requires sophisticated tools in the form of financial instruments, it is clear that excessive complexity in the design of some financial instruments has served, sometimes intentionally, to hide their true nature. Accounting standard-setters have sought to ensure that financial statements show the substance of transactions, including the substance of financial instruments, but with mixed success. Developers of some complex financial instruments continue to engineer them to keep liabilities off the balance sheet or to present or value them in a more favourable light than is warranted. While the vast majority of financial instruments are used for legitimate purposes, usually to reduce an entity's exposure to any external factors it cannot control such as interest or exchange rates, complexity always increases audit risk.

Most complex financial instruments are valued, at least in part, at fair value but the disclosure of risks and uncertainties associated with financial instruments is just as important as the valuation.

Among other things, complex financial instruments are used:

- to *reduce exposure* to currency, interest rate or commodity price risk, through *hedging*. Hedging usually reduces risk by, for example:

  - *forward currency purchases or sales* in anticipation of the need to pay or convert a receipt in foreign currency in the future,

  - *swaps* that convert future floating interest rates into fixed rates and vice versa,

  - *options* against price movements which often involve embedded derivatives;

- for *trading and investment*.

Entities of all sizes use financial instruments, not just larger entities. IAPN 1000[19] applies to a broad range of financial instruments auditors are likely to encounter. IAPN 1000 applies to all except the simplest of financial instruments, such as cash or trade accounts receivable.

### 7.5.2   AUDIT ISSUES

Auditors are concerned with:

- the *risks* associated with and *controls* over financial instruments;

- financial statements *assertions* such as completeness, accuracy and valuation;

- *valuation* methods, processes and controls, the use of models and the role of third parties such as experts and third-party pricing sources;

- financial *reporting* requirements, especially the disclosure of risks and uncertainties.

Auditing guidance does not normally deal with valuation methods but IAPN 1000 provides an outline because it serves an educational purpose in a complex area, and it is not possible to audit these areas without that understanding.

Entities often use third parties to value complex financial instruments where management do not have the required expertise or market data, or simply when they need to value a large portfolio in a short space of time.

### 7.5.3   RISKS ASSOCIATED WITH FINANCIAL INSTRUMENTS

Unlike more straightforward assets and liabilities where valuation methods are well-established, risks associated with financial instruments arise from the valuation techniques themselves, as well as from controls over them.

---

[19] IAPN 1000 on financial instruments is the first *International Auditing Practices Note*. It constitutes non-authoritative guidance that provides practical assistance and does not create requirements beyond those already in ISAs. It does not have the authority of ISAs or other International Standards issued by the IAASB.

The main risks associated with complex financial instruments are:

- *credit risk*: the risk that the counterparty will default, i.e. fail to pay;

- *market risk*: the risk that the instrument's value will fluctuate because of changes in, for example, currency, interest rate and commodity values;

- *liquidity risk*: the risk the instrument cannot be sold because there is no market for it, i.e. no-one wants to buy it;

- *operational risks*: these include a lack of understanding of financial instruments, poor documentation or control, over-reliance on third party valuations, the risk of fraud, inappropriate valuation methods and the risks associated with financial instruments rapidly changing from assets to liabilities and back again.

*Significant risks* associated with financial instruments requiring special audit consideration arise where:

- there is high *measurement uncertainty*;

- there is a *lack of evidence to support valuations*;

- there are *significant valuation adjustments*;

- *management do not understand* the instruments or reporting requirements.

### 7.5.4 CONTROLS OVER FINANCIAL INSTRUMENTS

Controls over financial instruments are no different to controls in any other area. However, focus on the following control elements is important:

- the *control environment*, particularly if management or those charged with governance *do not understand* the instruments they are dealing with and are relying on third parties for advice, which is common;

- *risk management processes* including the entity's *appetite* for risk and the extent to which it *understands* and *manages* its exposure to risk;

- *IT controls* which are more likely to be automated in entities engaging in a high volume of transactions;

- control procedures such as:

  - *segregation of duties between dealing room specialist traders* or those with responsibility for pricing, buying and selling instruments, *and the back office*, or those who process the transactions,

  - *authorisation* of transactions,

  - *reconciliation of dealing room trades and traders' profits with back office settlement records*, and the use of trade confirmations and clearing houses which monitor the exchange of trade confirmations,

  - *reconciliation of records held by banks and custodians* to entity records of bonds and shares held within financial instruments.

### 7.5.5    VALUING FINANCIAL INSTRUMENTS

IFRS and some other financial reporting frameworks have a three-tier fair value hierarchy supporting valuations:

* *level 1 inputs: quoted prices in active markets* for identical assets and liabilities at a given date, which are straightforward to audit;
* *level 2 inputs*: largely *observable* inputs other than level 1 inputs including *quoted prices for similar assets in active markets*, for identical or similar assets in inactive markets, and other observable inputs such as interest rates, yield curves and credit spreads;
* *level 3 inputs: unobservable inputs* usually involving discounted cash flow *models*. Auditors evaluate the soundness of these models by testing controls such as documentation, regular calibration of the models and the use of observable inputs within the model.

*Third party pricing sources, pricing models and inactive markets*
Third-party pricing sources providing inputs include:

* *pricing services* which provide entities with prices, market and other data for a variety of financial instruments, often performing daily valuations of large numbers of financial instruments;
* *consensus pricing services* which use information sent in by subscribers to calculate an average price for instruments such as exotic derivatives;[20]
* *brokers* who provide quotes to their clients without detailing how the price was calculated. They have access to information on transactions that take place outside the markets. Such quotes may be indicative of offers to purchase. Broker quotes can be problematic because they do not provide sufficient information for audit purposes and there may well be no other source of evidence, hence the need for a quote in the first place. Financial instruments are often purchased from the broker providing the quote which compounds the problem.

The *reputation and objectivity of third party pricing services* affect the auditors' risk assessment, as does the extent to which the *entity controls valuations involving third party pricing services*, by actively considering the information provided rather than simply accepting it, for example.

As with other accounting estimates, where models are used, auditors need to evaluate the underlying assumptions and data and have confidence in the model. Well-established models such as the Black-Scholes option pricing model are widely used, but the underlying data and assumptions applied to them about volatility, and the value of a private company's shares, for example, may be highly subjective. It is even more

---

[20] Exotic derivatives are derivatives such as futures, options and swaps with features that make them more complex than commonly traded derivatives.

difficult where broker quotes are the only source of information, and the ability of auditors to develop their own point estimates or ranges is limited.

Inactive markets also cause auditors problems because they are often the principle source of valuation evidence. When they become inactive, significant judgements are required as to:

- whether the lack of activity is temporary or permanent;
- the effect of inactivity on liquidity risk;
- the need for valuation adjustments to reflect the change in liquidity.

### 7.5.6 OTHER AUDIT CONSIDERATIONS

Other audit considerations include:

- the need to maintain and document professional scepticism;
- whether it is efficient to test the effectiveness of controls over the processing and valuation of financial instruments, which may be poor, or whether to adopt a wholly substantive approach;
- use of internal audit work and the entity's correspondence with regulators;
- communications with those charged with governance;
- presentation and disclosure of risks and uncertainties, which are often highly judgemental.

### Section essentials: what you need to remember

- *A properly conducted audit will not necessarily detect a material fraud.*
- *The risk factors for fraud and non-compliance with laws and regulations are similar to the risk factors for money laundering and going concern problems.*
- *Practitioners have a duty of confidentiality to their clients and generally have no right to report fraud to any third party; however, national laws and regulations may permit or require auditors to report matters, such as suspicions of terrorism or money laundering to various authorities and regulators.*
- *The details of customer due diligence requirements and suspicious transaction reports in the context of money laundering.*
- *The ethical and commercial considerations involved in taking on a forensic engagement.*
- *What is involved in the 'chain of custody' and why it is important in court cases.*
- *Forensic engagements use techniques similar to audit techniques but with more emphasis on the possible falsification of records and weaknesses in controls.*
- *Forensic reports do not provide assurance: they detail the identity of the fraudster, the mechanics of the fraud, the length of the fraud, the extent of financial loss and recommendations to prevent similar frauds in future.*

# SECTION 7, SHORT-FORM QUESTIONS

Your firm has been approached by a company, Dabco, requesting that you act as its auditors. It is a new company that has not prepared financial statements in the past.

It becomes clear during initial meetings with directors that the company has engaged in a series of property transactions in remote overseas jurisdictions. Your firm has no expertise in this area. It is also made clear that few if any accounting records will be made available to you. It is not clear whether records have been kept or whether the company simply does not want to make them available to you. The directors indicate that the financial statements will be prepared by the company's accountant but that they are likely to be brief, and unlikely to comply fully with legislation or accounting standards.

The directors say that they know that this may result in a qualified audit opinion, but that they think it should be possible to avoid a disclaimer or adverse opinion. Your offer to help with preparing the financial statements is politely but firmly declined. The directors indicate that they realise the situation is unusual, and that because of this they are unlikely to question your audit fee, within reason.

**SFQ 1:** **Describe the factors that you will take into account that will determine your course of action for Dabco.** (7 marks)

Accountants and auditors have specific responsibilities in relation to money laundering activities.

**SFQ 2:** **Explain your understanding of the term 'money laundering', and give examples of money laundering offences.** (4 marks)

**SFQ 3:** **Describe the money laundering offences that may be committed by firms of professional accountants.** (3 marks)

**SFQ 4:** **Describe the policies and procedures that a firm of professional accountants should establish to meet its money laundering responsibilities.** (5 marks)

From time to time, external auditors during the course of an audit engagement come to suspect that senior management lack integrity and may be engaging in illegal activities, other than money laundering.

**SFQ 5:** **Explain the actions auditors should consider when they have strong suspicions that senior management lack integrity and may be engaging in illegal activities.** (5 marks)

A common fraud involves collaboration between a purchase ledger controller or person with a similar level of authority, and a person outside the company. The person outside the company raises false invoices for small amounts that are authorised by the purchase ledger controller. The proceeds are then split between the purchase ledger controller and the party outside the company. Your audit client suspects that this might have been happening at a low level with a number of identified suppliers for a long time, but is very concerned that no allegations should be made against the purchase ledger controller, who has worked for the company for a long time, unless there is very strong evidence. The annual audit showed strong controls and no substantive errors in this area.

**SFQ 6:** Describe the objectives of a forensic investigation into a fraud and describe the steps that might be undertaken in a forensic investigation into the fraud described before the purchase ledger controller is interviewed. **(6 marks)**

Total **(30 marks)**

# 8 THE WIDER FRAMEWORK: ASSURANCE, OTHER ENGAGEMENTS, AUDIT QUALITY AND QUALITY CONTROL

**Covering**: *International Framework for Assurance Engagements*, ISA 200 *Overall Objectives of the Independent Auditor and the Conduct of an Audit in Accordance with International Standards on Auditing*, ISAE 3000, *Assurance Engagements Other than Audits or Reviews of Historical Financial Information.*

Standard-setting and the *Preface to the International Quality Control, Auditing, Review, Other Assurance, and Related Services Pronouncements.*

ISQC 1 *Quality Control for Firms that Perform Audits and Reviews of Financial Statements, and Other Assurance and Related Services Engagements*, ISA 220 *Quality Control for an Audit of Financial Statements.*

### Why do I need to read this section?
*Understanding how auditing standards are developed and the overall framework for assurance and non-assurance engagements really does help students understand how they work. Examiners are gaining confidence in setting questions on assurance outside audits and reviews of historical financial statements, because it is a rapidly growing area.*

*Terms such as 'subject matter information' and 'suitable criteria' are not very friendly but the area is not really so complicated and the terms can be legitimately applied to all assurance engagements, including audits of historical financial information. For these reasons it is worth learning them.*

*Quality control is often relevant to questions dealing with areas such as engagement acceptance, direction, supervision and review and it is often examined in its own right.*

*Some syllabuses only examine these areas in higher-level papers. Check this before you read this section.*

### What is important in this section?

*The five elements of assurance engagements[1] are worth learning because they apply to all assurance engagements and can help structure answers to questions in areas in which there are no IAASB standards.*

---

[1] A three party relationship, appropriate underlying subject matter, suitable criteria, evidence and an assurance report.

*Quality control can be brought into answers to many questions. ISQC 1 and ISA 220 cover the same areas from the different perspectives of requirements for firms and engagement partners. Learning them together saves time.*

## What sort of questions come up in this area?

*Questions on the benefits of audit have been set for a long time.*

*Questions contrasting the level of assurance obtained in reasonable and limited assurance engagements, such as audits and reviews, are easy to set, straightforward to answer and very relevant to practice because of the increase in audit exemption levels in many jurisdictions, which means that practitioners can offer a choice of services.*

*Questions sometimes cover the different services offered by internal and external auditors, their relative merits and the relationship between auditors and audit committees.*

*Questions are rarely set on the standard-setting process in isolation, but control of the standard-setting process is very relevant to current issues questions in higher-level papers about the independent regulation of the profession and the future of audit, for example.*

*General questions on assurance engagements for which there is no specific standard other than ISAE 3000 are increasingly likely. Questions presenting a request for assurance on a mixture of financial and non-financial information such as key performance indicators on the capacity of a manufacturing facility have been set in the past. Examiners are sometimes looking for students to demonstrate their understanding of the fact that assurance cannot be provided in some cases, particularly where there are no suitable criteria. Agreed-upon procedures engagements may be more suitable in such cases.*

*Knowledge-based questions are set in lower level papers requiring an explanation of how quality control is organised within firms, and on individual engagements. More interesting questions on the quality control implications of things that have gone wrong on an audit are also possible. Questions are set on:*

- *the need for engagement quality control reviews;*
- *the difference between engagement quality control reviewers and engagement partners;*
- *how smaller firms can apply quality control requirements.*

## How do I stand out from the crowd?

- *Demonstrate clarity about the five elements of all assurance engagements and have the confidence to apply them to the scenario in the question.*
- *Demonstrate a broad understanding of why quality control is important to practitioners, regulators and audit clients.*

- *Suggest, where appropriate, the need to consider whether an engagement quality control review is called for under the firm's own policies.*

- *Bring quality control issues, such as observations about the firm's reviews of its staff development and training policies into answers to questions about planning or engagement team composition, for example.*

- *Bring overarching matters such as professional judgement and scepticism, and the requirement to comply with quality control and ethical requirements, into general questions about engagement acceptance and planning.*

## 8.1 INTERNATIONAL STANDARDS

### 8.1.1 WHAT IS IFAC?

The International Federation of Accountants (IFAC) is a federation of accountancy bodies.[2] IFAC's mission is to serve the public interest by, among other things, contributing to the development of international standards and to strong professional accountancy associations and firms. Founded in 1977, IFAC now has over 160 member bodies in 120 countries.[3] A large number of jurisdictions in which those member bodies operate, and some others, have adopted standards set by IFAC's independent standard-setting boards.[4]

Membership of IFAC is conditional and not all professional bodies who apply for membership succeed. Among other things, IFAC members and associate bodies must comply with Statements of Membership Obligations (SMOs). These require members and associates to use their best endeavours to implement standards set by IFAC's independent standard-setting boards as well as the International Financial Reporting Standards (IFRSs) set by the International Accounting Standards Board (IASB).[5] Member bodies are also required to monitor compliance with those standards through quality assurance, investigation and discipline programmes.

The quality of standards issued by IFAC's standard-setting boards has improved greatly in recent years. Its standards were once thought of as lowest common denominator standards, best suited to developing countries that did not have sufficient resources to develop their own standards. ISAs in particular are now much more demanding and are held in much higher regard internationally.

IFAC has improved its governance structures in recent years and regulators and other stakeholders now have a very significant role in standard-setting, but there remains

---

[2] Member bodies include the Institut der Wirtschaftsprüfer (IDW) in Germany, the Institute of Certified Public Accountants in Hong Kong (HKICPA), the Institute of Chartered Accountants in India (ICAI), Chartered Accountants Ireland (CA Ireland), the Institute of Chartered Accountants in England and Wales (ICAEW) and the Association of Chartered Certified Accountants (ACCA). A full list can be found at www.ifac.org/about-ifac/membership/members.

[3] Many countries have more than one professional accountancy body that is a member of IFAC.

[4] www.ifac.org/about-ifac/membership/compliance-program/basis-isa-adoption.

[5] The IASB does not operate under the auspices of IFAC. IFAC is based in New York. The IASB is based in London.

a perception in some quarters that the output of IFAC's four independent standard-setting boards would be improved if there were less practitioner involvement. IFAC is partly funded by contributions from the profession, albeit indirectly through member bodies.

The four independent standard-setting boards are:

- the International Auditing and Assurance Standards Board (IAASB);
- the International Ethics Standards Board for Accountants (IESBA);
- the International Accounting Education Standards Board (IAESB);
- the International Public Sector Accounting Standards Board (IPSASB).

IFAC also supports:

- a Small and Medium Practices Committee (SMPC);
- a Professional Accountants in Business Committee (PAIB);
- a Professional Accountancy Organisation Development Committee (PAODC);
- a Transnational Auditors Committee (TAC).

The TAC is the executive arm of the *Forum of Firms*, an association of international networks that perform *transnational audits*. The TAC identifies issues for consideration by the standard-setting boards, candidates to sit on them and facilitates interaction among transnational firms and among regulators and financial institutions with regard to audit quality and audit firm transparency. Membership of the Forum is open to networks and firms of all sizes willing to promote the *consistent application of high-quality practices worldwide,* to support convergence of national auditing standards with ISAs and commit to meeting the Forum's membership obligations. This includes compliance with or conforming to standards such as ISQC 1, ISAs, IESBA's *Code,* and performing internal *quality control* reviews. It has over 20 members including the Big 4.

The *International Forum of Independent Audit Regulators* (IFIAR) was set up in response to concerns about firms operating internationally but regulators operating nationally. Members of IFIAR share knowledge of the audit market and practical experience of audit regulation, promote collaboration in regulatory activity and provide a focus for contacts with other international organisations interested in audit quality.

### Standards set by the IAASB

Auditing, like all practical disciplines, started with people doing things that later became known as audits. National and international auditing standards came much later. ISAs are sometimes inaccurately described as 'theoretical', despite the fact that auditing theory remains the preserve of academics. ISAs are in part developed on the basis of what the better resourced and innovative firms do, but this does not make auditing standards 'best practice', because some firms will always be ahead of standards, and because all firms performing ISA audits must comply with them. Auditing standards are what they say they are: standards with which auditors must comply, upheld by the profession as a whole and enforced by regulators in jurisdictions in which they apply.[6]

Auditing involves obtaining assurance and the International Auditing and Assurance Standards Board (IAASB) has developed a *Framework* for all assurance engagements. *Ethical requirements* apply to all engagements, *and quality control requirements* apply to all engagements to which IAASB's standards apply, including some non-assurance engagements.

ISAs are used,[7] often with local variations to accommodate legal, regulatory and other requirements, in Canada, Australia, South Africa and a number of major Asian and European jurisdictions. The UK adopted ISAs in 2005 with a few 'pluses'. UK auditing standards are now known as ISAs (UK and Ireland).[8]

*Auditing standards in the USA*
Two sets of auditing standards operate in the USA. For listed entities,[9] auditing standards issued by the Public Company Accounting Oversight Board (PCAOB) apply.[10] The differences between IAASB and PCAOB standards are complex and the extent to which they will converge in future is not clear.

The Auditing Standards Board (ASB) of the American Institute of Certified Public Accountants (AICPA) sets auditing standards for the audit of other entities.[11] It undertook a 'clarity project' to make generally accepted auditing standards in the USA (GAAS) easier to read, understand and apply, similar to the project undertaken by the IAASB. Again, the differences between IAASB and AICPA standards are complex. The AICPA has developed a plan to converge US GAAS with the ISAs, while avoiding unnecessary conflict with PCAOB standards, in the light of the increasingly widespread acceptance of ISAs. It has aligned its standard-setting agenda with that of the IAASB, and now develops its standards based on ISAs, permitting it to consider projects at the same time as the IAASB and to provide more effective input. The commitment of *Forum of Firms* members to use ISAs on transnational audits has also helped embed ISAs in audits all around the world.

---

[6] Regulators enforcing the application of auditing standards include, for example, the Audit Quality Review team of the Financial Reporting Council (FRC) in the UK for auditors listed and other major public interest entities, and some professional bodies such as ICAEW and ACCA for auditors of other entities.

[7] ISAs are used because they are required by law or regulation, or because the national auditing standard-setter has adopted them, or because the national standard-setter has used ISAs as a basis for local standards.

[8] UK auditing standards were aligned with ISAs in the mid-1990s.

[9] Entities whose securities are registered with the Securities and Exchange Commission (SEC).

[10] The PCAOB also enforces compliance with those standards by inspection of audit firms, including overseas firms.

[11] Entities whose securities are not registered with the SEC.

*Principles and rules*

Auditing standards have become longer and more detailed. It is not always clear whether the supposed benefits of this, including improved audit quality, are proportional to additional costs of compliance. Many practitioners assert that high level principles are better than detailed rules in auditing standards, but the issue is complex.

Is it better to tell a driver to:

- open the car door, put the key in the ignition, engage the gear shift and drive *slowly* into the parking space etc.; or

- park the car?

On the fact of it, the latter seems preferable. Only if the driver consistently runs the car into the kerb or obstructs the highway are detailed driving lessons in order. The situation with audits is not so straightforward.

Auditors probably prevent a substantial number of corporate collapses and scandals by applying pressure to their clients to use appropriate accounting policies. No-one can see how many, though, or how much pressure is applied. To an extent, this has to be taken on trust.

Even if auditors do not cause corporate collapses, there is a deeply held belief in some quarters that auditors could probably do quite a lot more to prevent them, or at least warn those the audit is supposed to benefit that there are problems, or provide more information so that stakeholders can make their own minds up. Some regulators and investors believe that:

- the requirements of auditing standards need to be improved; and/or

- even if auditing standards are adequate and auditors know how to conduct audits, they are not doing it properly.

If practitioners have to abide by very detailed rules, it is argued that they will cease using their judgement, develop a compliance mentality and audits will be reduced to box-ticking. High calibre people will no longer wish to enter the profession and audit quality will suffer. All of this may be true to some extent but:

- there is no clear distinction between principles and rules. Standards set in the USA are similar in their level of detail to IAASB standards but are often described as 'rules-based';[12]

- principles-based standard-setting has to be accompanied by principles-based regulation because audit inspectors drive the behaviour of auditors. Many regulators

---

[12] Formally, US auditing standards are principles-based and some believe that US auditing standards are in fact no more or less rules- or principles-based than ISAs. Others assert that US standards operate in an environment that does not and cannot tolerate a high level of judgement in accounting and auditing matters, and that standards are therefore necessarily rules-based.

cannot or will not adopt such an approach, particularly in the USA and parts of continental Europe where lawyers sometimes play an important role in standard-setting and where a compliance-based approach to audit regulation is well established. This seems unlikely to change anytime soon;

- it is arguable that the more detailed rules there are, the more judgement is required, not less, and that the quality of entrants to the profession relates to status and potential rewards, not to the work itself.

### The IAASB

Like IFAC, the IAASB has a public interest mandate. It is an independent standard-setting body that serves the public interest by setting high-quality international standards for auditing, quality control, review, other assurance and related services, and by facilitating the convergence of international and national standards. In doing so, it enhances the quality and consistency of auditing practices and strengthens public confidence in the profession.

IAASB's due process ensures that the views of those affected by its standards are considered while the standards are being written. The process includes the presentation of the proposed standard as an *agenda paper* for discussion and debate at an IAASB meeting open to the public, followed by *exposure for public comment*. Widely distributed exposure drafts appear on the IAASB's website. At least 120 days are ordinarily given for comment. Comments received are considered at an open IAASB meeting and re-exposure is sometimes required. Approval of exposure drafts and the final standard requires a *two-thirds majority of IAASB members*.

The IAASB has a full-time chairman and 17 volunteer members from around the world. The board is balanced between *practitioners in public practice* with significant auditing and assurance experience (no more than nine members), *individuals not in public practice* and at least three *'public' members*. Members are appointed by the IFAC Board based on recommendations from the IFAC Nominating Committee and are approved by IFAC's independent Public Interest Oversight Board (PIOB).[13]

---

[13] IFAC's Public Interest Activity Committees (PIACs) are currently three of the independent standard-setting boards, IAASB, IESBA and IAESB, covering standard-setting for auditing, ethics and education. They all have their own Consultative Advisory Group (CAG) comprising a broad range of international stakeholders whose participation helps guarantee the public interest focus of the standard-setting process. The IAASB's CAG comprises representatives of regulators, business and international organisations, and users and preparers of financial statements with an interest in the development of high-quality international standards. It advises IAASB on its agenda, project timetable, priorities and technical issues. The PIACs are also overseen by the PIOB. The PIOB exists to increase investor confidence that IFAC's public interest activities are properly responsive to the public interest. The PIOB is in turn accountable to a Monitoring Group, which is composed of bodies such as the Basel Committee on Banking Supervision, the International Association of Insurance Supervisors, the World Bank, the European Commission and the Financial Stability Board.

*The IAASB's clarity project*

The IAASB completed a comprehensive programme to enhance the clarity of ISAs (the clarity project) in 2009. Before, much of the material in ISAs was expressed in the present tense: auditors *conduct* confirmations, auditors *perform* tests of controls, etc. It became clear to regulators that auditors in different jurisdictions took very different views on how important the present tense statements were. The clarity project restructured ISAs and each ISA now has:

- an *objective* that auditors *must achieve*;

- *mandatory requirements*, denoted by the word *'shall'*;

- *non-mandatory application material* and appendices.

The project also developed *overall objectives* for the audit and for auditors, and improved the *readability* of the standards.

The IAASB brought the deadline for the clarity project forward to enable the European Commission to propose legislation to mandate use of the clarified ISAs for all statutory audits within the European Union. This legislation has yet to take effect and may be restricted to the audit of large or listed entities.

All ISAs are approved by IFAC's PIOB to ensure that they reflect the public interest. The use of ISAs is supported by the Basel Committee on Banking Supervision, the World Bank, the World Federation of Exchanges, the International Organisation of Securities Commissions (IOSCO) and the United National Commission on Trade and Development (UNCTAD). At least 22 of the largest firms' methodologies are now aligned with ISAs and many such firms, particularly those that are members of the *Forum of Firms,* have used ISAs as a basis for their global methodologies for several years.

## The *Preface*

The *Preface*[14] sets out the scope authority and status of IAASB pronouncements (International Standards). It does not override local requirements.

IAASB pronouncements include:

- *International Standards on Quality Control (ISQCs)* applying to **all** engagements covered by IAASB Standards;

- *International Standards on Auditing (ISAs)* applying to the audit of historical financial information;

- *International Standards on Review Engagements (ISREs)* applying to the review of historical financial information;

---

[14] *Preface to the International Quality Control, Auditing, Review, Other Assurance, and Related Services Pronouncements*

- *International Standards on Assurance Engagements (ISAEs)* applying to assurance engagements other than audits or reviews of historical financial information;

- *International Standards on Related Services (ISRSs)* applying to compilation engagements, engagements to apply agreed-upon procedures and other related services engagements;

- *International Auditing Practice Notes (IAPNs)* that do not impose additional requirements but instead provide practical assistance to auditors. They are intended for dissemination by national standard-setters, use in developing corresponding national material and they provide material that firms can use in developing their training programmes and internal guidance.

The IAASB may also issue International Review Engagement Practice Notes (IREPNs), International Assurance Engagement Practice Notes (IAEPNs), and International Related Services Practice Notes (IRSPNs), although as yet there are none.

International Standards have an effective date but, unless otherwise stated, they may be applied before that date.

International Standards are relevant to public sector engagements and additional *Public Sector Perspectives* are sometimes included.

International Standards are applied as follows:

- *Ethical requirements* apply to *all* engagements;

- International Standard on Quality Control 1 (*ISQC 1*) applies to *all engagements for which there are IAASB standards*, which include assurance and non-assurance engagements;

- The International *Framework* for Assurance Engagements (the Framework) applies to *all assurance engagements*, i.e. audits, reviews and other assurance engagements;

- International Standards on Auditing (*ISAs*) apply to *audits of historical financial information*;

- International Standards on Review Engagements (*ISREs*) apply to *reviews of historical financial information*;

- International Standards on Assurance Engagements (*ISAEs*) apply to *other assurance engagements*, i.e. all assurance engagements that are not audits or reviews of historical financial information, such as audits of greenhouse gas statements. ISAE 3000 *Assurance Engagements Other than Audits or Reviews of Historical Financial Information* is the overarching standard in this area and other ISAEs falling under it cover areas such as ISAE 3400 on *prospective financial information*, ISAE 3402 on controls at service organisations and ISAE 3410 on *greenhouse gas statements*;

- International Standards on Related Services (*ISRSs*) apply to *non-assurance* engagements and include ISRS 4400 on *agreed-upon procedures* and ISRS 4410 on *compilation engagements*.

The full title of ISAE 3000 *Assurance Engagements Other than Audits or Reviews of Historical Financial Information* is off-putting but it is worth understanding its

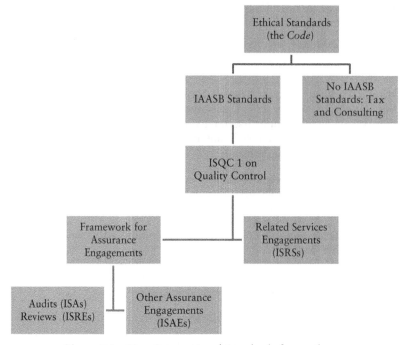

**Figure 8.1**    How International Standards fit together

scope. *The* Framework *applies to all assurance engagements.* Assurance engagements can be reasonable or limited assurance engagements and include audits and reviews.[15] Information assured can be historical or forward looking, and financial or non-financial. *ISAE 3000 applies to assurance on:*

- *anything that is forward looking, whether financial or not,* such as projections of profits, forecasts or cash flows, and prospective financial information included in prospectuses; and

- *anything historical provided it is not financial information,* such as audits and reviews of greenhouse gas statements and reports on controls at service organisations.

For some such engagements there are already IAASB standards. For example, prospective financial information is covered by the *Framework*, ISAE 3000 *and* ISAE 3400[16] on that subject. For others, such as engagements to provide assurance on physical characteristics such as the projected capacity of a facility, for example, or compliance with

---

[15] Audits are reasonable assurance engagements and reviews are limited assurance engagements. Not all reasonable assurance engagements are audits and not all limited assurance engagements are reviews, although they may incorrectly be described as such.

[16] ISAE 3400 on prospective financial information.

corporate governance codes or on the effective functioning of internal controls,[17] only the *Framework* and ISAE 3000 apply.

## 8.2 OVERALL OBJECTIVES OF AUDITS, THE FRAMEWORK FOR ASSURANCE ENGAGEMENTS, ISAE 3000

### 8.2.1 ISA 200: OVERALL OBJECTIVES OF THE AUDIT

*Definitions*
*The overall objectives of auditors* in performing audits are *to obtain reasonable assurance* about whether the financial statements are free from material error and have been prepared in accordance with the financial reporting framework, and *to report* on the financial statements.[18]

---

Auditors' objectives need to be distinguished from the purpose of the audit:

*The purpose of an audit is to enhance the degree of confidence of intended users in the financial statements.*

ISA 200 *Overall Objectives of the Independent Auditor and the Conduct of an Audit in Accordance with International Standards on Auditing* paragraph 3

---

The audit opinion enhances confidence. In order to express an audit opinion, auditors obtain a reasonable level of assurance, which means reducing audit risk[19] to an acceptably low level.

*Reasonable assurance is a high but not absolute level of assurance.* The inherent limitations of an audit, for example, mean that absolute assurance can never be obtained.[20] Reasonable assurance involves reducing engagement risk to an acceptably low level.

In *limited assurance engagements, such as reviews,* engagement risk is also reduced to an acceptable level but risk is greater than for reasonable assurance engagements. Assurance is nevertheless meaningful to intended users.

The nature of audit and non-audit assurance is not a settled area and it is clear that practitioners and non-practitioners are not always clear about the meaning of terms such as

---

[17] There is no standard as yet on audits or reviews of internal control statements but it is probably only a matter of time before one is developed, not least because internal control audits are mandatory for entities with US listings.

[18] ISA 200 on overall objectives paragraph 11.

[19] Audit risk is the risk of expressing an inappropriate audit opinion when the financial statements are misstated.

[20] The inherent limitations of an audit are the inherent limitations of financial reporting, the limitations of audit procedures and time and cost constraints, which mean that audit evidence is persuasive rather than conclusive.

reasonable and limited assurance. ISAs require auditors to obtain reasonable assurance and ISREs require practitioners performing reviews to obtain limited assurance.

---

### Components of ISAs: objectives, requirements, application material

ISAs comprise:

- *objective(s)*: each ISA has at least one objective that auditors *must achieve*. Achievement of ISA objectives facilitates the achievement of the overall objectives of auditors, i.e. to obtain reasonable assurance about whether the financial statements are free from material error, etc. Failure to achieve one objective may mean failure to achieve the overall objective;[21]

- *requirements:* auditors *must comply with all requirements* in ISAs, denoted by the use of the word '*shall*' unless:

  - *the entire ISA is not relevant*, such as the ISA on internal audit where there is no such department;

  - *the requirement is conditional and the condition does not exist*, such as the requirement to report significant deficiencies in internal control to those charged with governance, where there are no such deficiencies;

  - *very exceptionally*, alternative procedures are required to achieve the aim of requirement but only where the requirement is for a specific procedure that would be ineffective in achieving the aim.

- *application material*, including appendices, providing explanations of requirements and examples.

---

An ISA audit requires compliance with the entire text of all ISAs that are relevant to the audit.

---

*Auditors must also consider what additional requirements are necessary to achieve the objectives of the ISA and the audit beyond the requirements in ISAs.*

---

### The premise of an audit

Audits are conducted on the premise that management and those charged with governance acknowledge their responsibility:

- for the *preparation of financial statements* in accordance with the financial reporting framework and for the *internal controls* necessary to do so;

- to provide auditors with *access to all information* that management are aware of that is necessary for financial statement preparation, and with any additional information that auditors request;

---

[21] Some of the objectives of ISAs amount to little more than requirements to comply with the requirements of ISAs, unfortunately. This makes them difficult to distinguish from the requirements themselves. For example, the objective of ISA 230 on audit documentation is . . . *to prepare documentation that provides: (a) a sufficient and appropriate record of the basis for the auditor's report; and (b) evidence that the audit was planned and performed in accordance with ISAs and applicable legal and regulatory requirements.*

- to provide auditors with ***unrestricted access to people*** within the entity as auditors consider necessary.

### 8.2.2 THE *FRAMEWORK* AND ISAE 3000

*Considerations applying to all assurance engagements*
There are substantial similarities between audits and reviews of historical financial information conducted under ISAs and ISREs, and the way other assurance engagements are conducted under ISAE 3000. The following documents cover much common ground:

- the *Framework* covering all assurance engagements;

- ISA 200 covering the overall objectives of an independent audit;

- ISAE 3000 covering assurance engagements other than audits or reviews of historical financial information.

The ***Framework*** is not a standard but it facilitates understanding of ***all assurance engagements*** including ISA audits, review engagements conducted under the ISRE 2400 series and other assurance engagements conducted under the ISAE 3000 series.

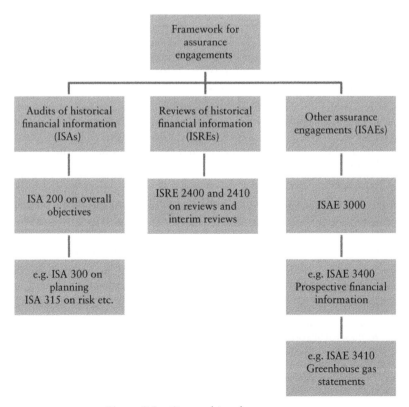

**Figure 8.2** Overarching documents

It does not cover non-assurance engagements such as agreed-upon procedures and compilation engagements.

*ISAE 3000* deals with assurance engagements *other than audits and reviews of historical financial information.* It is a 'how to' standard for all assurance engagements, both reasonable and limited, not covered by ISAs[22] or ISREs,[23] including reports on greenhouse gas statements, controls at service organisations and prospective financial information. For some such engagements, IAASB standards already exist, such as ISAE 3410 on greenhouse gas statements. For others, such as assurance on the effectiveness of internal control statements, no standard exists yet, and ISAE 3000 applies directly to them.

*Elements common to all assurance engagements*   All assurance engagements have some common elements and it is probably easier to learn these together than it is to deal with them separately for each type of engagement. In many cases, the requirements in assurance standards other than ISAs, i.e. ISAEs, are very similar to the requirements in ISAs for audits of historical financial information. For example:

- the description of materiality when providing assurance on greenhouse gas statements[24] is very similar to the description of materiality for ISA purposes;

- ISAE 3000 deals with the need for practitioners to achieve the objectives and comply with the requirements of standards in much the same way as ISA 200 requires practitioners to achieve objectives by complying with requirements in the context of ISA audits;

- the ISAE 3000 requirements concerning engagement acceptance and continuance, independence and competence, the need for written engagement terms, justification of changes to those terms, and provisions concerning what to do when law or regulation prescribes the layout or wording of assurance reports, are close to the requirements of ISA 210 on engagement terms;

- the broad requirements of ISAE 3000 regarding the engagement partner's responsibilities for the engagement and the engagement team, for planning and performing the engagement, working with experts and internal audit, obtaining written representations and considering subsequent events are also similar to the requirements of the ISAs dealing with those areas.

---

Both of the following issues are almost always relevant to questions on accepting and conducting assurance engagements, regardless of the type of engagement:

- *ethical requirements:* the ethical requirements of IESBA's *Code* apply to all engagements;

- *quality control: ISQC 1* deals with firm level quality control policies and procedures and applies to all engagements for which there are IAASB standards.

---

[22] ISAs apply to audits of historical financial information, a type of reasonable assurance engagement.
[23] ISREs apply to reviews of historical financial information, a type of limited assurance engagement.
[24] The description of materiality in ISAE 3410 on greenhouse gas statements is the same regardless of whether the engagement is a reasonable assurance engagement or a limited assurance engagement.

Some engagement level quality control procedures similar to the requirements of ISA 220.[25] Other assurance engagements apply to particularly those relating to reviews of working papers and engagement level quality control reviews.

### Reasonable and limited assurance engagements

> ***Assurance engagements*** are engagements in which practitioners aim to obtain sufficient appropriate evidence to express a conclusion designed to enhance the confidence of intended users about the outcome of the measurement or evaluation of an underlying subject matter against criteria.[26] The 'outcome' is also known as the 'subject matter information'.

NB: 'Measurement or evaluation' in this context refers to the measurements and evaluations performed in preparing the information auditors report on, such as the financial statements prepared by management. It does not refer in this context to auditors' or practitioners' measurements and evaluations performed in arriving at an audit opinion or review conclusion.

*Examples of assurance engagements*

- For **ISA audits:**
  - financial statements = outcome/subject matter information;
  - underlying financial information about position and performance, i.e. the accounting systems and other information = underlying subject matter;
  - financial reporting framework such as IFRS = criteria.

Auditors enhance users' confidence in the financial statements by providing an audit report on the preparation of the financial statements (the outcome/subject matter information) prepared by management from the accounting systems and other information (the underlying subject matter) with reference to (against) the financial reporting framework (criteria).

- For **statements on the effectiveness of internal controls:**
  - management's statement on the effectiveness of controls = outcome/subject matter information;
  - entity's internal control processes = underlying subject matter;
  - a recognised control framework such as COSO[27] = criteria.

Assurance providers enhance users' confidence in management's statement of their compliance with an internal control framework by providing an assurance report on the preparation of the statement prepared by management (outcome/subject matter

---

[25] ISA 220 on quality control.
[26] ISAE 3000, paragraph 8 and *Framework*, paragraph 10.
[27] Committee of Sponsoring Organizations of the Treadway Commission (COSO), which issues a great deal of guidance on internal control in the USA.

information) from internal control system information (underlying subject matter) with reference to (against) the internal control framework (criteria).

- For **key performance indicators** such as earnings per share (EPS):
    - management's calculation of EPS = outcome/subject matter information;
    - earnings and number of shares information from the entity's systems = underlying subject matter;
    - IFRS method of calculating EPS = criteria.

Assurance providers enhance users' confidence in the calculation by providing an assurance report on the calculation prepared by management (outcome/subject matter information) from information about earnings and the number of shares within the entity's systems (underlying subject matter) with reference to (against) IFRS EPS calculation requirements (criteria).

- For **greenhouse gas (GHG) statements**:
    - management's GHG statement = outcome/subject matter information;
    - information about the entity's greenhouse gas emissions = underlying subject matter;
    - national reporting requirements for the disclosure of GHG emissions = criteria.

Assurance providers enhance users' confidence in the GHG statement by providing an assurance report on the statement prepared by management (outcome/subject matter information) from information about emissions from within and outside the entity, perhaps from independent inspectors (underlying subject matter) with reference to (against) national reporting requirements (criteria).

- For **statements on compliance with laws and regulations**:
    - management's statement of compliance = outcome/subject matter information;
    - information about compliance from the entity's systems and other information = underlying subject matter;
    - laws and regulations = criteria.

Assurance providers may enhance users' confidence in the statement of compliance by providing an assurance report on the statement prepared by management (outcome/subject matter information) from information about compliance from the entity's systems and other information, perhaps from external lawyers (underlying subject matter) with reference to (against) national reporting requirements (criteria).

> **Reasonable assurance:** the practitioners' conclusion is expressed in a positive form as an *opinion* on the outcome of the measurement/evaluation of the underlying subject matter;[28]
>
> Opinions are expressed in terms such as *in our opinion the financial statements give a true and fair view in accordance with IFRS,* or, *in our opinion internal controls are effective in all material respects based on XYZ criteria.*

---

[28] *Framework*, paragraph 17.

*Limited assurance engagement*: the practitioners' *conclusion*, which is not an opinion, and is expressed in a negative form is that *based on procedures performed, nothing has come to the practitioners' attention* to cause the practitioner to believe that the *subject matter* information is *materially misstated*.[29]

Conclusions are expressed in terms such as:

- for fair presentation frameworks: . . . *based on our review*/the procedures performed, *nothing has come to our attention to cause us to believe that the financial statements do not give a true and fair view/present fairly in all material respects the financial position, performance and cash flows in accordance with IFRS;*

    - for compliance presentation frameworks: . . . *based on our review*/the procedures performed, *nothing has come to our attention to cause us to believe that the financial statements have not been prepared in all material respects in accordance with [the national accounting standards of X country].*

Reasonable and limited assurance engagements both involve reducing engagement risk to an acceptable level but for limited assurance engagements, the residual risk is greater than for reasonable assurance engagements. The difference lies in the work effort, *not* in the underlying subject matter, or in the suitability of the criteria. If a financial reporting framework or the underlying financial records are not good enough for a reasonable assurance true and fair or fair presentation opinion, they are not good enough for a limited assurance conclusion either.

*If it is not possible to perform a reasonable assurance engagement because of shortcomings in the subject matter or criteria, it is not possible to perform a limited assurance engagement on the same subject matter or using the same criteria.*

Both reasonable and limited assurance engagements require an understanding of the business, however:

- reasonable assurance engagements require a *full risk assessment and response;*

- limited assurance engagements require a *limited set of procedures* by comparison with those for a reasonable assurance engagement, and *consideration of the risks of material misstatement*[30] as a basis for determining the nature and extent of procedures required to obtain a level of assurance that is meaningful to users.

Generally, limited assurance engagements require a combination of inquiries, analytical procedures and sometimes other procedures. There is much less emphasis on controls.

---

[29] *Framework*, paragraph 18.
[30] This is sometimes described as a risk assessment, but it is not a full assessment.

## Attestation and direct engagements
Assurance engagements can also either be:

- *Attestation engagements*: a party other than the practitioner measures/evaluates the underlying subject matter against criteria resulting in an outcome/subject matter information.[31] Practitioners express a conclusion that can either be:
  - on the outcome/subject matter information, such as *in our opinion the directors' statement that internal control is effective is fairly stated in all material respects*; or
  - in terms of the underlying subject matters such as *in our opinion internal control is effective in all material respects*.

Attestation engagements were previously known as assertion engagements. Audits of financial statements are attestation engagements.

- *Direct engagements*: practitioners measure/evaluate subject matter against criteria and present the outcome/subject matter information in or with the assurance report. The work on assurance is often performed at the same time as the work on the outcome/subject matter information.

Attestation engagements are the most widely understood in practice. Direct engagements can, at first sight, appear to involve practitioners reporting on their own work.

In attestation engagements, modified conclusions are possible because there is some defect in the application of the criteria (such as IFRS) to the underlying subject matter (accounting systems), i.e. management do not prepare the financial statements properly. This seems less probable with direct engagements because practitioners are unlikely to criticise their own work, but modified conclusions are possible if, for example, there is some defect in the underlying subject matter for which practitioners are not responsible, such as where there is a limitation in the scope of an engagement resulting from a lack of records. Practitioners are also independent of the engaging party, intended users and the party responsible for the underlying subject. This independence and the performance of assurance procedures distinguish direct engagements from mere compilation engagements.[32]

## Preconditions for assurance engagements
The preconditions for acceptance of assurance engagements under the *Framework* are essentially the same are those required under ISAE 3000. At first sight, they may appear to be different to those required for an ISA audit. It is probably fairer to say that they are simply expressed differently. ISA audits are, after all, reasonable assurance engagements and the *Framework* applies to all assurance engagements.

---

[31] The outcome/subject matter information can be presented in a report, such as a greenhouse gas statement prepared by an entity, but it can be presented by the practitioner in the assurance report, even though the practitioner is not responsible for it.

[32] A practitioner compiling a greenhouse gas statement would not test controls over the calibration of emissions measuring equipment. A practitioner providing direct assurance on such an engagement might do so.

Under ISA 210[33] preconditions for the acceptance of an ISA audit include requirements for:

- the financial reporting framework to be acceptable;

- management[34] to accept their responsibility for the financial statements and internal control, and to provide auditors with whatever they need for the audit.

These requirements are not dissimilar to the *Framework* and ISAE 3000 preconditions that include establishing whether:

- the responsible party, the measurer/evaluator and the engaging party, who may be different people or who may simply be management, have *appropriate responsibilities;*

- the underlying *subject matter is appropriate;*

- the *criteria* to be applied are suitable and *available to intended users;*

- the *practitioner has access* to the evidence needed;

- the *practitioner expresses a conclusion* in a written report;

- there is a rational purpose for the engagement, and for limited assurance engagements, a meaningful level of assurance can be obtained.

*Five elements of assurance engagements*

The five elements of assurance engagements are:

- a *three party relationship;*

- an appropriate underlying *subject matter;*

- suitable *criteria;*

- *evidence;*

    - an *assurance report.*[35]

These elements are dealt with in detail below.

*Three party relationship*
The three party relationship involves:

- a *practitioner,* such as an auditor;

- a *responsible party,* such as management, who is responsible for the underlying subject matter, such as the financial information in the accounting records and, in attestation engagements such as audits, for the outcome/subject matter information, i.e. the financial statements;

- *intended users* for whom the practitioners' report is prepared, such as shareholders.

---

[33] ISA 210 on engagement terms.
[34] Where appropriate, management or those charged with governance.
[35] *Framework*, paragraph 4.

The responsible party, such as management, may be from the same entity as intended users, such as a supervisory board. Practitioners cannot be the responsible party or an intended user, i.e. practitioners cannot report on or to themselves.

The responsible party is responsible for the underlying subject matter, such as accounting records, and the outcome/subject matter information, such as financial statements. However, the responsible party may not actually do the preparation (measurement/ evaluation) of the financial statements from the underlying records. An external consultancy preparing a greenhouse gas statement might do that, for example.

In a direct engagement, the practitioner is the measurer/evaluator (i.e. the preparer).

The responsible party may also be the *engaging party*, but may not be, such as where regulators (the engaging party) appoint practitioners to report on statements of compliance prepared by management (the responsible party). Management are often both measurer/evaluator and the engaging party, such as in an ISA audit.

To claim compliance with an assurance standard, practitioners, who may or may not be professional accountants, must comply with ISQC 1 and ethical requirements. Practitioners, with help if necessary, need the requisite competencies to perform the engagement.

*Engagement terms* should be in writing wherever possible, but clients sometimes have difficulty with this, particularly smaller entities that may consider a written engagement letter an unnecessary expense. If laws and regulations cover engagement terms, their existence may suffice but for ISA audits, ISA 210[36] requires in all cases written confirmation of the premise on which an audit is conducted, i.e. management's responsibility for the financial statements, internal control and for the provision of information to auditors.

A *change to engagement terms*, particularly if it involves a change from a reasonable to a limited assurance engagement (such as from an audit to a review), or a limited assurance engagement to a non-assurance engagement (such as a review to a compilation engagement), *needs reasonable justification*. A reasonable justification would be a misunderstanding about the level of assurance required. It would not be appropriate to make the change to avoid a modified conclusion and, in any case, practitioners are not permitted to disregard information they have already obtained.

*Appropriate underlying subject matter*
The underlying subject matter can be:

- *historical* financial information for which the outcome/subject matter information might be financial statements, *or future* financial information for which the outcome/ subject matter information might be financial forecasts or projections;

- *non-financial information* where the outcome/subject matter information might be historical or forecast key performance indicators, greenhouse gas statements,[37] value

---

[36] ISA 210 on engagement terms, paragraph A22.
[37] Forecast greenhouse gas statements might cover expected emissions reductions as a result of planting trees.

for money statements, corporate social responsibility statements, descriptions of systems as implemented at a point in time, or physical characteristics such as the size of a leased property;

- *systems or processes* such as control or IT systems, for which the outcome/subject matter information might be a description of them, a statement of their operating effectiveness or on the adequacy of their design, or on the design of proposed controls;

- *behaviour* such as compliance with corporate governance requirements, banking covenants or regulatory requirements for which the outcome/subject matter information might be a statement of compliance or a statement on the effectiveness of an audit committee.

*Suitable criteria*
Criteria are the benchmarks used to measure/evaluate the underlying subject matter, such as IFRS for financial statements and COSO for internal controls. To be suitable, they must be:

- *relevant* to the decision making of intended users;

- *complete*, by not omitting factors that could reasonably be expected to affect the decisions of intended users;

- *reliable,* to allow consistent measurement/evaluation of the underlying subject matter;

- *neutral,* i.e. free from bias;

- *understandable.*

These characteristics resemble the qualitative characteristics of useful financial information as outlined in the IASB's *Conceptual Framework for Financial Reporting*. They are the criteria applied to determine the acceptability of the financial reporting framework for audits of historical financial information.[38]

Suitable criteria, including acceptable financial reporting frameworks for audits of historical financial information, may be *embodied in laws or regulations or issued or authorised by recognised bodies of experts that follow a transparent due process. It is assumed that such established criteria are suitable* in the absence of indications to the contrary.

For assurance engagements other than audits or reviews of historical financial information, though, criteria are more likely to be developed by a private industry group that does not follow (and has no need to follow) a transparent due process, developed for a private sale between contracting parties, or specifically designed for the engagement in some other way. There is nothing wrong with such criteria but practitioners cannot assume they are suitable, and assurance cannot be provided, unless they can be shown to be relevant, complete, reliable, etc.

---

[38] ISA 210 on engagement terms, Appendix 2, paragraph 3.

Practitioners can work alongside experts to provide assurance on complex technical criteria on matters such as greenhouse gas statements where the criteria have been established through due process. Where they are not established, it will often be beyond the capacity of practitioners, even with the help of experts, to determine whether the criteria are complete, reliable and neutral, etc.[39]

Intended users are important. If the user group is restricted to regulators and others within the industry, and the information reported on is unlikely to be made widely available, it and the criteria it is based on are more likely to be regarded as understandable, even if highly technical, than if it is aimed at the investing public. Where there is substantial estimation uncertainty, as there always is in greenhouse gas statements, for example, there are difficult trade-offs between completeness, understandability and bias. The greater the level of required disclosure, i.e. completeness, the less likely the criteria are to appear biased. However, for general users, the additional disclosures are not likely to aid understandability, whereas they are likely to do so for regulators and industry insiders. It is therefore more important where the statement is made widely available that any questions regarding bias and completeness are addressed.

Criteria need to be *available to intended users* either publicly, such as IFRS which are available to anyone, or within the assurance report or the information reported on where the criteria are developed privately for a specific purpose. Where criteria are designed for a specific purpose, such as for regulatory purposes in the banking sector, the assurance report states that fact.

*Evidence: reasonable and limited assurance engagements*

The important distinction to make regarding evidence in assurance engagements is between the evidence required for reasonable assurance engagements, such as ISA audits, and the evidence required for limited assurance engagement, such as reviews conducted under ISRE 2400.

---

Very broadly, *reasonable assurance engagements* including ISA audits require a *full risk assessment and response, and corroboration of explanations*. Considerable time and effort are spent on internal control. Evidence required for all reasonable assurance engagements is similar to the evidence required for audits of historical financial information.

---

A *reasonable assurance engagement* is based on *an understanding of the underlying subject matter and other engagement circumstances including internal control* over the preparation of the underlying subject matter (such as accounting records) and involves:

- *identifying and assessing risks* of material misstatement;
- *responding to assessed risks* overall and to specific risks;

---

[39] Due process always involves consultation with a wide range of technical experts and others who collectively, are less likely than just one or two experts to agree on criteria that are incomplete or biased, for example.

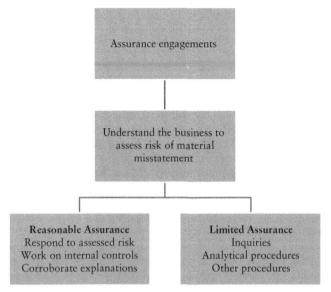

**Figure 8.3**  Evidence: reasonable and limited assurance engagements

• *evaluating whether the risk assessment remains appropriate* before completing the engagement.

A *limited assurance engagement* is also based on *an understanding of the underlying subject matter and other engagement circumstances* but does not involve detailed consideration of internal control. It does involve *consideration of the risks of material misstatement that determine the nature, timing and extent of procedures performed to obtain a level of assurance that is meaningful to intended users.* Additional procedures are required if matters arise causing practitioners to believe the subject matter information may be materially misstated. The procedures performed in *limited assurance engagements* including reviews vary, but they usually consist of *inquiries, analytical procedures and sometimes other procedures* based on an understanding of the underlying subject matter and the risks of material misstatements, but not a full risk assessment. Unless problems arise, corroboration is not required and internal controls are not necessarily central to the engagement.

**The procedures for limited assurance engagements are deliberately limited relative to reasonable assurance engagements.** Any specific pronouncement, such as an ISRE covering the subject, will provide requirements and guidance on procedures. Under ISRE 2400,[40] for example, reviews of financial statements consist primarily of inquiries and analytical procedures. In the absence of standards, procedures for limited assurance

---

[40] ISRE 2400 on review engagements.

engagements are likely to consist of inquiries, analytical procedures and other procedures that vary with the circumstances of the engagement, the underlying subject matter and the information needs of the intended users and the engaging party, and time and cost constraints.

*All assurance engagements* involve consideration of materiality, risk, evidence and reporting in a similar manner to that required by ISAs. In many cases, identical wording is used except that the term *audit* is replaced by more appropriate terms. Requirements dealing with *audit risk* in ISAs, for example, become requirements to deal with *assurance engagement risk* or simply *engagement risk*. All assurance engagements are likely to involve reconciling the information reported on to the underlying records and obtaining written representations. Many involve going concern and subsequent events reviews.

Written representations are likely to cover management's responsibility for the information reported on, the controls facilitating its production, particularly for reasonable assurance engagements, the completeness of the information reported on, the appropriateness of the criteria, such as the financial reporting framework, and for the provision of information to practitioners.[41] Specific representations may be required concerning the identity of related parties and transactions with them, fraud and non-compliance with laws and regulations, as well as the going concern assumption and subsequent events, for example.

Understanding the underlying subject matters involves understanding the business including industry and external regulation as well as the business itself, its ownership and governance, objectives, strategies, systems and accounting policies. This is as for an ISA audit and other reasonable assurance engagements, but only *in sufficient detail to identify areas where material misstatements are likely to arise* and *to design appropriate procedures* in order to report. This is considerably less than a full, formal risk assessment, which requires an understanding of the design and implementation of controls, tests of controls and designing procedures to respond to assessed risks at the financial statement and assertion level. The main procedures required are *inquiry* and *analytical procedures focusing on areas in which material misstatement may arise.*

*Required for all assurance engagements.* *Professional scepticism* is a *questioning attitude of mind* that includes being alert to, for example:

- evidence that is *inconsistent* with or *contradicts* other evidence;

- information that *calls into question* the reliability of documents and responses to inquiries;

---

[41] In the case of an audit, these representations constitute the premise on which the audit is conducted and they are required in writing. For other assurance engagements, if public written statements to the same effect are required by law or regulation, written representation may not be required.

- circumstances that suggest the *need for additional procedures*;
- conditions that may indicate *fraud*.

Auditors and practitioners apply *professional scepticism* throughout assurance engagements to reduce the risk of:

- overlooking unusual circumstances;
- over-generalising when drawing conclusions from observations;
- using inappropriate assumptions in determining engagement procedures.

Scepticism is necessary for a critical assessment of the sufficiency and appropriateness of evidence. *Records and documents can be accepted as genuine* unless practitioners have reason to believe otherwise, and while practitioners cannot be expected to disregard their past experience of the honesty and integrity of those providing evidence, or otherwise, this should not prevent them from exercising professional scepticism.[42]

*Professional judgement* is the application of relevant knowledge and experience to facts and circumstances. Its key feature is its exercise by practitioners whose training, knowledge and experience have resulted in the necessary competencies to make reasonable judgements. It is particularly important in making informed decisions about courses of action regarding:

- materiality and risk;
- the nature and extent of assurance procedures;
- evaluating whether appropriate evidence has been obtained;
- evaluating management's judgements in applying the financial reporting framework;
- drawing conclusions, on the reasonableness of estimates, for example.

The test is whether the judgements reflect a competent application of auditing and accounting principles, appropriate in the light of, and consistent with, the facts and circumstances known to auditors at the reporting date.

Professional judgement should not be used to justify decisions that are not otherwise supported by the facts and circumstances or supported by evidence. In other words, it is not acceptable for practitioners to state that despite most of the evidence pointing, for example, to the need to discontinue an engagement because of doubts about the integrity of the client, in their professional judgement the firm may continue with the engagement. For this reason, among others, the exercise of judgement needs to be documented.

---

[42] Auditors have been called upon to display increased scepticism in recent years and IAASB issued Staff Q & A on the subject in February 2012.

*Materiality* in assurance engagements is similar to materiality in the context of an ISA audit. A matter is material if it *could reasonably be expected to influence relevant decisions of intended users* based on the subject matter information, such as a greenhouse gas statement, a statement on the effectiveness of internal controls, or financial statements in the context of an audit.

The assessment is affected by practitioner perceptions of the common information needs of intended users as a group. Intended users of a greenhouse gas statement are likely to have a broad range of interests. They may include market participants where the statement is used in an emissions trading scheme, regulators where the statement is produced for regulatory purposes, but also investors, management, customers and suppliers and others in the broader community where voluntary disclosures are made. The decisions they are likely to be making are to invest in, make representations to,[43] buy from, sell to or be employed by the reporting entity. As in an ISA audit, though, practitioners can assume that intended users understand materiality and have a reasonable knowledge of the underlying subject matter and a willingness to study the subject matter information with reasonable diligence.

Materiality is considered in the context of qualitative factors and, when applicable, quantitative factors. Whereas in an audit of financial statements the main considerations for materiality may be quantitative, in an audit or review of greenhouse gas statements, for example, it is much likely that qualitative factors will be prominent. Qualitative factors may include:

- the nature of misstatements, such as the nature of observed deviations from controls when the subject matter information is a statement that the control is effective;

- whether a misstatement affects compliance with laws or regulations;

- whether a misstatement is an error or the result of an intentional act.

It may seem counter-intuitive but *materiality is not affected by the level of assurance* auditors seek. Materiality is based on the information needs of intended users so for the same intended users, materiality for a reasonable assurance engagement is the same as for a limited assurance engagement.

Reporting criteria such as IFRS and reporting guidelines for greenhouse gas emissions usually cover materiality and provide a frame of reference. Some criteria for the preparation of greenhouse gas statements[44] describe materiality in similar terms to those used in IFRS.

*Written assurance reports*
For *reasonable assurance engagements,* practitioners' conclusions are expressed in the form of an *opinion* on the outcome (such as the financial statements) of the measurement/evaluation of the underlying subject matter (such as the accounting records). For an ISA audit, the practitioner is the auditor and the conclusion is an opinion on the truth and

---

[43] Decisions may include decisions to make representations to others, such as politicians.

[44] Criteria are developed or promoted by bodies such as the International Integrated Reporting Council (IIRC), the Global Reporting Initiative (GRI) and The Prince's Accounting for Sustainability Project (A4S).

fairness or fair presentation of the financial statements in accordance with the financial reporting framework.

For *limited assurance engagements*, the practitioners' *conclusions* are that, based on the procedures performed, *nothing has come to the practitioners' attention* to cause the practitioner to believe the subject matter information has not been prepared in all material respects in accordance with the applicable criteria.

In both types of engagement a summary of the procedures performed is also required in the assurance report. This summary is more extensive for limited assurance engagements because the procedures are less likely to be prescribed and are more likely to be engagement-specific than they are in a reasonable assurance engagement. A statement is also required for limited assurance engagements that the procedures are limited by comparison with a reasonable assurance engagement and that practitioners therefore might not become aware of all significant matters that might be identified in a reasonable assurance engagement.

Assurance reports can be long form or short form. Despite their increasing length, most reports, including those required under ISA 700, are short form reports containing basic elements that are usually prescribed in detail by standards and/or legislation. Long form reports include other information that does not affect the practitioners' conclusion, such as the qualifications and experience of practitioners and engagement teams, materiality levels, recommendations and sometimes the fine detail of the work performed and the findings. This might be the case for an assurance report on the effectiveness of internal control, for example.

The detailed contents of assurance reports for:

- audits of historical financial information appear in ISAs 700, 705 and 706;

- reviews of historical financial information and interim reviews appear in ISREs 2400 and 2410, respectively;

- other assurance engagements appear in ISAE 3000 and other ISAEs.

All of the standards above recognise that reporting requirements may be prescribed by law or regulation. Where this is the case, the prescribed wording can be used provided it is unlikely to result in misunderstandings regarding the level of assurance obtained. Additional wording may be necessary. If misunderstandings cannot be avoided, the engagement should not be accepted.

Third parties such as lenders seeking audits or reviews of information sometimes look for 'certifications' and similarly inappropriate wording that either cannot be provided at all, or can only be provided at a cost that is greater than the provider is willing to bear. It is common to explain in these cases that agreed-upon procedures may be more appropriate.

*Under ISAE 3000, all assurance reports include the following:*

- a *title*: independent assurance report;

- an *addressee;*

- an *introductory paragraph identifying the information reported on,* i.e. the outcome/subject matter information, and a summary of the accounting/reporting policies.[45] For a greenhouse gas statement, for example, this paragraph would include a reference to any exclusions or deductions from the statement;

- *criteria:* the reporting criteria, such as the COSO framework for internal controls when reporting on internal control effectiveness, where they can be accessed, and any significant inherent limitations associated with the measurement/evaluation of the underlying subject matter, which may be the case with certain elements of greenhouse gas statements. Where appropriate, reports alert readers to the fact that the criteria are for a special purpose such as a private transaction, or for regulatory purposes and may not be suitable for other purposes;[46]

- the *responsibilities* of the *responsible party* such as the responsibilities of management for the preparation of greenhouse gas information, and of the measurer/evaluator if different;

- the *responsibilities* of the *practitioner* for performing a reasonable or limited assurance engagement in accordance with the *relevant ISAE*, for applying *ISQC 1*, and the independence and other ethical requirements of IESBA's *Code*;

- an *informative summary of the work performed*: the wording may be set out in the relevant ISAE or ISRE. In a limited assurance engagement this includes a statement that procedures are more limited than for a reasonable assurance engagement and do not enable the practitioner to become aware of all significant matters that might be identified in a reasonable assurance engagement;

- a *conclusion:* in reasonable assurance engagements, a positive *opinion* on the truth and fairness/fair presentation of the subject matter information in accordance with the relevant reporting framework (criteria);

- in limited assurance engagements, a *conclusion* expressed in negative terms as to whether anything has come to the practitioner's attention to cause the practitioner to believe that the subject matter information is materially misstated (i.e. is not true and fair/fairly presents the position in accordance with the relevant reporting framework (criteria));

- a clear description of the matter(s) giving rise to any modification;.

- the practitioners' *signature*

- *date*: no earlier than the date on which the practitioner has obtained the relevant evidence, which must include evidence that those with the recognised authority have asserted that they have taken responsibility for the subject matter information (i.e. signed or approved for release the information reported on, such as a greenhouse gas statement);

- *location:* the address(es) of the practitioners' office(s) in the jurisdiction where the practitioner practices.

---

[45] The corresponding paragraph in an ISA audit, to which ISAE 3000 does not apply, would refer to the financial statements.

[46] For the corresponding criteria in an ISA audit, to which ISAE 3000 does not apply, the reference would be to the applicable financial reporting framework such as IFRS.

## 8.3 AUDIT QUALITY AND QUALITY CONTROL

### 8.3.1 AUDIT QUALITY AND QUALITY CONTROL

Audit quality is important to practitioners. Firms are increasingly using audit quality as a marketing tool and audit regulators take an interest in the area not least because they come under pressure during financial crises to be seen to be taking action to improve audit quality.

The overall quality of audits is not easy to describe or measure. A high quality audit is not as obvious as a high quality car, for example because establishing whether an audit is of high quality requires, among other things, a review of the audit files.

Quality control and audit quality are not the same thing but they are related. A high quality audit can only be conducted if ISQC 1[47] and ISA 220[48] have been applied. Quality control should lead to higher overall audit quality but audit quality is not just a function of quality control. Factors such as the quality of people entering the profession that in turn depends on the status of the profession in different jurisdictions, for example, have an effect on audit quality, as do auditor training, remuneration and the quality of audit regulation. Auditing standards cannot deal with all of these matters.

The IAASB's developing framework for audit quality covers matters such as:

- inputs to audit quality, such as audit firm culture, the knowledge, skills, experience and quality of auditors and the effectiveness of audit processes, including methodologies and auditing standards;

- outputs, such as the reliability and usefulness of audit reports and other auditor communications;

- the audit quality effects of the relationship between auditors and management and those charged with governance, financial statements and users;

- environmental factors, such as business practices, the legal and regulatory framework, the educational environment and broader cultural factors.

### 8.3.2 ISQC 1 AND ISA 220 OBJECTIVES

*All engagements conducted in accordance with IAASB standards*, including audits and reviews of historical financial information, other assurance engagements, compilation engagements and agreed-upon procedures engagements *are subject to International Standard on Quality Control No 1 (ISQC 1) which deals with quality control at the firm level.*

*ISA 220 Quality Control for an Audit of Financial Statements* deals with *quality control at the engagement level for ISA audits only.*

---

[47] ISQC 1 on firm level quality control.
[48] ISA 220 on engagement level quality control.

*ISQC 1 deals with the quality control systems that need to be in place at the firm level. ISA 220 mirrors these requirements at the engagement level for ISA audits.* ISA 220 makes the engagement partner responsible for ensuring that the firm level policies and procedures have been properly applied and sets out the responsibilities of the engagement quality control reviewer.

The objectives of ISQC 1 are for the *firm* to establish and maintain quality control systems providing it with reasonable assurance that:

- staff comply with professional standards, legal and regulatory requirements;

- reports issued are appropriate.

The objectives of ISA 220 are to implement quality control procedures at the *engagement level* to provide auditors with the same assurance. ISA 220 deals largely with the responsibilities of the engagement partner and the engagement quality control reviewer.

The six main areas broadly covered by both ISQC 1 and ISA 220 are:

- *leadership responsibilities;*
- *ethical requirements;*
- *acceptance and continuance of client relationships;*
- *human resources;*
- *engagement performance;*
- *monitoring.*

ISQC 1 also deals with documentation of quality control systems.

### 8.3.3   LEADERSHIP RESPONSIBILITIES

*Leadership: ISQC 1*

The *tone at the top* matters. Quality control policies and procedures[49] communicated to firm personnel include the message that each individual has a personal responsibility for quality. Training, mission statements and newsletters recognise that the firm's

---

[49] *Policies* guide strategic decision-making and accommodate managerial discretion. *Procedures* are tactical tools to drive actions, are detailed and relatively inflexible. ISQC 1 requires policies and procedures designed to provide a firm with reasonable assurance that it deals appropriately with complaints and allegations. The policy will be to provide reasonable assurance to the firm's partner that the objective has been achieved. Procedures might include requirements for all complaints and allegations to be documented, for them all to be referred to the ethics partner, and for a quarterly meeting of partners to consider and approve how each one has been dealt with. Policies for the retention of engagement documentation might include keeping all documentation for a minimum of six years. The objective would be to keep it for a period sufficient to meet the needs of the firm or as required by law or regulation. Procedures might include all completed files, including electronic documentation, being kept at a central location.

business strategy comes second to the overriding requirement for quality in all engagements. *Compensation and promotion criteria* should encourage and reward quality and management responsibilities should be assigned so that *commercial considerations do not override audit quality.*

Ultimate responsibility for quality lies with the firm's chief executive officer or managing board. Those to whom they may delegate responsibility must have sufficient seniority, authority and experience to assume the responsibility. When concepts of audit quality were first developed, they threatened the aggressive commercial culture of some firms. They attempted to deal with the issue by assigning responsibility to a relatively junior partner who had neither the experience nor authority to implement the requirements effectively.

### *Leadership: ISA 220*
Engagement partners take responsibility for the overall quality of audits they are assigned to and, where problems arise under any of the headings below, they take the necessary action to resolve them, which may include putting in place safeguards or recommending withdrawal from the engagement.

### 8.3.4   ETHICAL REQUIREMENTS

#### *Ethical requirements: ISQC 1*
Leaders setting an example, training, monitoring and processes for dealing with non-compliance reinforce the fundamental ethical principles of integrity, objectivity, competence, confidentiality and professional behaviour.

Firms are required to have policies and procedures that provide reasonable assurance that independence requirements have been met and to:

- *communicate those requirements* to staff;

- *identify and evaluate threats to independence, and take appropriate action to reduce them* to an acceptable level by applying safeguards, or withdrawing from the engagement where appropriate, if possible.

Engagement partners should be required to present the firm with enough information about the services provided to the client to enable the firm to evaluate the overall impact on independence. Personnel should be required to notify the firm where threats to independence arise. Criteria should be established covering:

- safeguards to reduce the familiarity threat when using the same senior personnel over a long period of time;

- for listed entity audits, the rotation of key audit engagements partners including engagement quality control reviewers. IESBA's *Code* requires rotation every seven years but national requirements may be more stringent;

- annual written confirmations of compliance with the firm's policies and procedures on independence that should be obtained from all relevant firm personnel. Confirmations might be provided electronically.

*Ethical requirements: ISA 220*
Engagement partners remain alert for evidence of non-compliance with relevant ethical requirements and do what is necessary to form a conclusion on independence. This includes reviewing the application of all of ISQC 1's requirements.

### 8.3.5    ACCEPTANCE AND CONTINUANCE OF CLIENT RELATIONSHIPS

*Acceptance and continuance: ISQC 1*
A firm's policies and procedures should provide it with reasonable assurance that it will only undertake or continue engagements where:

• it is competent and has the time and resources to do so;

• it can comply with relevant ethical requirements; and

• it has considered the client's integrity and does not consider it a problem.

The identity and reputation of the client's owners, management and related parties, their business practices and attitude towards fees, accounting standards and internal control, their reasons for changing auditors, any attempts to limit the scope of audit work, and any indication of money laundering or other criminal activities are all relevant.

Where the firm obtains information that would have caused it to decline the engagement had that information been available at the outset, the firm has to consider the option of withdrawing from the engagement, although in some jurisdictions this is not possible.

Continuing a client relationship may be inappropriate where the client outgrows the auditors or expands into areas where firms do not have expertise.

*Acceptance and continuance: ISA 220*
Engagement partners have to be satisfied that appropriate acceptance and continuance procedures have been applied and that the conclusions reached are appropriate.

Information coming to light that would have caused the firm to decline the audit engagement had it been known at the time must be communicated within the firm so that the necessary action, such as making additional resources available, can be taken.

### 8.3.6    HUMAN RESOURCES

*Human resources: ISQC 1*
HR policies and procedures, including those on recruitment, performance evaluation, competence, career development and compensation, should provide reasonable assurance that the firm has personnel who comply with ethical requirements and have the competencies and capabilities it needs.

Competence is achieved through professional education and continuing professional development (CPD, sometimes referred to as CPE, i.e. continuing professional education), work experience (or 'on-the-job' training), coaching and mentoring by more experienced staff and specific training on independence requirements.

Firms of all sizes sometimes use external consultants when internal resources are unavailable or in short supply. Smaller firms tend to look outside the firm for specialist technical training; larger firms sometimes do this but increasing use is made of external consultants for coaching, mentoring and soft skills development.

The most difficult aspect of policy for HR is balancing commercial considerations and audit quality. Audit quality must ultimately prevail but firms have to make a profit to stay in business. In the short run, the two objectives are in conflict: more profit can be made if corners are cut on audit quality. In the longer term, the objectives of audit quality, audit efficiency and profitability need to be aligned if profits are to be sustainable.

Performance evaluation, compensation and promotion procedures should reward competence and commitment to ethical requirements, but to be effective they also need to penalise non-compliance. Some firms will not promote or pay bonuses to partners who fail audit quality reviews, for example, or allow them to continue signing audit reports.

### *Human resources: ISA 220*
Firms assign an appropriately experienced engagement partner to each engagement. The responsibilities of the engagement partner need to be clearly distinguished from those of the firm to prevent partners blaming the firm when things go wrong and vice versa. The firm is also responsible for the policies and procedures that assign appropriate personnel to engagements, but the engagement partner is responsible for ensuring that this actually happens on individual audits.

## 8.3.7 ENGAGEMENT PERFORMANCE

### *Engagement performance: ISQC 1*
This is a wide area and covers:

- consistency of engagement performance;
- supervision;
- review;
- consultation;
- engagement quality control reviews (EQCRs);
- differences of opinion;
- documentation.

*Consistency of engagement performances* is achieved through properly integrated policies covering procedures and technology, manuals, software and other forms of standardised documentation, and industry and subject matter guidance.

*Supervision and review* involve more experienced engagement team members reviewing the work of the less experienced.

*Consultation* must be required for difficult or contentious matters. This may take time and cost money. Sufficient resources must be available and conclusions acted on, which does not always happen. Effective consultation on significant technical or ethical requirements includes providing those consulted with all the relevant facts. Those consulted must have appropriate knowledge, seniority and experience. Smaller firms may need to employ suitably qualified external consultants or refer to the technical help-lines of professional bodies for these purposes.

An *engagement quality control review (EQCR)* is a review before the audit report is signed that provides an objective evaluation of the significant audit judgements made and conclusions reached in forming the audit opinion. It is required for:

- listed entity audits; and
- other entities that need such a review, as determined by the firm.

A firm's policy for other entities needing an EQCR might include:

- *large private* entities;
- *higher risk* entities such those involved in oil, gas or mining;
- entities with some *public interest element* such as entities involved in financial services or charities, even if they are small;
- entities where there is the possibility of issuing a *non-standard audit report* or where the *engagement partner has a poor history, or for new partners*.

It is possible for the firm to determine that there are no such entities within its client base.

The firm's policies should ensure that Engagement Quality Control (ECQ) *reviewers are technically competent* in relevant areas, *objective* and have appropriate *experience and authority*. They should also cover the extent to which EQC reviewers can be consulted during the audit without compromising their objectivity, the idea being that a limited amount of consultation is better than discovering significant differences of opinion late in the day.

To be objective, reviewers should not be selected by the engagement partner and should not otherwise participate in the engagement. IESBA's *Code* also subjects them to many of the objectivity requirements applying to key audit partners and members of the engagement team, including the seven-year key audit partner rotation requirement for public interest entities and the two-year cooling off period.

It is important to distinguish between ECQRS and the type of review that used to happen, in which a second partner would act as a consultant during the audit and he or she would be available to answer technical questions and questions on the conduct of the audit overall. Such partners had often been the engagement partner on a client for some time and the review was regarded as a way of smoothing the transition to a new partner. It is the relative lack of objectivity of such partners that distinguishes them from EQC reviewers.

*Smaller firms* and sole practitioners have problems with applying these requirements because there are insufficient appropriately experienced senior people to go round. It may not be practicable for the engagement partner not to be involved in selecting the reviewer, for example, and suitably qualified external consultants may be needed. Such firms sometimes group together or employ training consortia to facilitate EQCRs. The same standards apply whether the reviewer is from within the firm or from outside.

EQCRs consist of:

- discussing significant matters with the engagement partner;
- reviewing the financial statements and considering whether the proposed report is appropriate;
- reviewing selected engagement documentation in areas where significant judgments have been made and evaluating the conclusions reached.

For listed entities EQCRs also cover:

- the assessment of the firm's independence;
- whether appropriate consultation has taken place and been acted on;
- whether appropriate documentation has been selected for review.

*Differences of opinion* can arise between the engagement partner, the engagement quality control reviewer and those who have been consulted. Clear policies and procedures are needed to determine how such differences are to be resolved, and whose opinion ultimately prevails. Again, for smaller firms in particular, procedures to resolve differences may include consulting with a suitably qualified external consultant or professional body. Conclusions must be documented and audit, review and other reports cannot be issued until such matters are resolved.

*Engagement documentation* policies should require completion of the files within *60 days*. Policies and procedures covering the *confidentiality and safe custody of documentation* commonly include requirements not to leave laptops in cars. Policies and procedures covering the retention of working papers may refer to local laws and regulations but, subject to any such requirements, ISQC 1 suggests that the retention period should ordinarily be no shorter than *five years* from the date of the report. Problems in practice arise where there are changes in systems. Electronic documentation must be readable. Documentation should enable regulators to review documentation for quality control or other purposes. Engagement documentation is generally the property of the firm and clients cannot demand to see it, although the firm may make some of it available to clients in some cases. Systems for dealing with hard copy and electronic documentation need to cover:

- data protection legislation that might affect information about client staff on audit files as part of the payroll audit, for example;
- the need to determine when and by whom engagement documentation was created, changed or reviewed;
- the prevention of unauthorised changes by means of passwords, for example;
- appropriate back-up routines.

*Engagement performance: ISA 220* Engagement partners take responsibility for the direction, supervision, review and performance of the audit in accordance with the firm's policies and procedures. They must satisfy themselves, by reviewing documentation and by discussing the audit with the engagement team, that sufficient appropriate audit evidence has been obtained, before the audit report is signed. They:

- take responsibility for the engagement team undertaking appropriate consultation;

- determine that an engagement quality control reviewer has been appointed where relevant;

- discuss significant audit matters with the engagement quality control reviewer.

### 8.3.8 MONITORING

*Monitoring: ISQC 1*

Monitoring involves ongoing evaluation of the firm's system of quality control, including a periodic inspection of a selection of completed engagements, i.e. cold file reviews, designed to provide evidence that the quality control system is operating effectively. Monitoring is essentially a control process designed to determine whether the quality control system has been *appropriately designed and implemented* and is *operating effectively*.

As with controls testing for audit clients, the design and implementation of controls require evaluation, but determining whether controls have been applied requires testing. Testing in this context involves inspection of audits on a cyclical basis, of at least one completed engagement for each engagement partner. ISQC 1 suggests that inspection cycles may span three years, depending on the number of partners, staff and offices, their location, the client base, the results of previous monitoring procedures and the way monitoring is conducted, either by individual offices or by head office, or both. Critical in practice to the inspection process is how individual engagements are selected. Some audits might be selected for review without prior notice.

Responsibility for the monitoring process should be assigned to persons with appropriate experience and authority. Those performing EQCRs should not be involved in inspecting their own engagements, although, once again, there are issues for smaller firms who may need to employ suitably qualified external consultants.

As with any system of internal control, there will be exceptions. Where deficiencies are noted, they are either isolated or indicate more serious systemic or significant problems. Remedial action may include communication of the findings to those responsible for training and professional development, changes to the quality control system and disciplinary action against those who fail to comply with firm policies.

If the deficiencies are sufficient to indicate that an engagement has not been performed in accordance with ISQC 1, ISAs or ethical requirements, the firm needs to consider the implications. Audit files, for example, can only be re-opened after the audit report has been issued in very limited circumstances, usually where new information has come to light about the audited entity, not the audit. This prevents auditors from changing their minds about their opinion when it becomes clear that something has gone wrong.

The results of monitoring are communicated at least annually to those with responsibility for quality control within the firm so that appropriate firm-wide changes can be made.

Policies and procedures are needed covering *complaints and allegations* about the quality of the firm's work, including those from firm personnel, i.e. there need to be whistle-blowing procedures.

### *Monitoring: ISA 220*
Engagement partners consider the results of the firm's monitoring process and whether deficiencies noted may affect the audit being performed.

## 8.3.9   DOCUMENTING THE QUALITY CONTROL SYSTEM

### *Documentation: ISQC 1*
Policies and procedures should cover the retention of documentation for a period long enough to permit monitoring. Audit firm methodologies and quality control systems require a lot of maintenance because of constant changes to accounting and auditing standards, and companies, money laundering and other legislation. Documentation needs updating regularly to address all of this.

### *Documentation: ISA 220*
Audit-specific documentation covers compliance with ethical requirements, conclusions on independence, acceptance and continuance and consultations.

## 8.3.10   SMALLER FIRMS AND ISQC 1

Smaller firms can find it particularly difficult to comply with the requirements of ISQC 1, which is one of the reasons that some jurisdictions have not implemented it. In many jurisdictions, there is no tradition of quality control for firms that do not provide regulated services such as audit. ISQC 1 attempts to deal with this by making it clear that national standards at least as demanding as ISQC 1 are an acceptable alternative to ISQC 1, because some sort of firm monitoring for such firms is in place in most jurisdictions. The main reason that smaller firms have problems is because of the requirements for a number of independent roles performed by different people. These roles are necessarily combined in smaller firms. They include:

- the person(s) with ultimate responsibility for quality control within the firm;

- the engagement partner;

- the engagement quality control reviewer;

- the person(s) responsible for monitoring;

- the person(s) responsible for dealing with complaints and allegations;

- the person(s) to be consulted on technical or ethical requirements.

Some of these roles are mutually exclusive, such as the engagement quality control reviewer and the engagement partner. Others are not but in most cases the individual must have appropriate experience and authority. In many cases experienced staff can fulfil the roles. Sole practitioners with no staff are likely to be forced to rely on third parties to fulfil some of these roles.

### Section essentials: what you need to remember

- *Reasonable assurance engagements such as audits require a full risk analysis and response, and a conclusion that is an opinion on truth and fairness or fair presentation.*

- *Limited assurance engagements such as reviews involve inquiries, analytical procedures and sometimes other procedures, and a conclusion that is not an opinion but that states whether anything has come to the practitioners' attention to cause them to believe that the information may be materially misstated.*

- *Assurance is only possible where the five criteria for assurance engagements are present, i.e. a three party relationship, an appropriate subject matter, suitable criteria, evidence and an assurance report.*

- *The six key areas covered by quality control, i.e. leadership, ethical requirements, acceptance and continuance, human resources, engagement performance and monitoring.*

- *The qualities needed of an engagement quality control reviewer and the circumstances in which such a review is needed.*

# SECTION 8, QUESTION

Implementing quality control procedures can be difficult in firms of all sizes but they can be particularly difficult for smaller firms. ISQC 1 deals with quality control at the firm level, ISA 220 deals with quality control at the engagement level.

Required:

(a) Explain the overall objectives of quality control, how they can be balanced among themselves, and how they interact with commercial pressures. (3 marks)

(b) Describe the particular difficulties faced by smaller firms implementing quality control requirements and suggest how they can be overcome. (8 marks)

You have just joined a 10-partner firm, Danco, with 4 offices and 60 staff, as a partner with responsibility for quality control.

You are aware that the firm uses a good quality audit methodology, performs some file reviews and has basic HR policies and procedures in place, but there are no other formal policies or procedures relevant to quality control.

You have been asked to prepare a report for the next partners' meeting making recommendations for cost-effective policies and procedures to ensure compliance with ISQC 1 and ISA 220 on quality control.

The practice's client base is mostly SMEs, including several financial services providers and local pension funds. There are no listed clients yet. The firm is keen to grow, by acquiring other practices in the area if necessary. Another firm with a similar profile and ambitions also operates in your area.

The partners are aware that growth means that more attention must be paid to systems and compliance and that the professional body is likely to perform a monitoring visit on the firm soon, because it has not recently visited, and because of the firm's growth.

Required:

(c) Prepare a short report for the next partners' meeting outlining the main areas the firm is obliged to deal with under ISQC 1 and ISA 200 on quality control, with particular reference to the current and likely future circumstances of the firm. (9 marks)

Total (20 marks)

# 9  SMALLER ENTITY AUDITS, REVIEWS, COMPILATIONS, AGREED-UPON PROCEDURES ENGAGEMENTS, NOT-FOR-PROFIT ENGAGEMENTS

**Covering:** *Smaller Entity Audits,* ISRE 2400 *Engagements to Review Historical Financial Statements,* ISRE 2410 *Review of Interim Financial Information,* ISRS 4410 *Compilation Engagements,* ISRS 4400 *Engagements to Perform Agreed-Upon Procedures Regarding Financial Information, Not-for Profit Engagements.*

## Why do I need to read this section?

*Smaller entities provide most of the work that keeps smaller firms in business and a great deal of the work that supports larger firms. Often described as the backbone of the economy, smaller entities provide a large proportion of national employment in many jurisdictions. Smaller entities grow into larger entities. For accounting and auditing purposes, smaller entities are often defined by their turnover, total assets and number of employees. Numerically, the vast majority of companies or other business entities registered in many jurisdictions are officially smaller or medium-sized. While practitioners have always provided tax services to their smaller entity clients, they increasingly provide business advice and assistance, often in connection with accounting software. Even so, smaller entities have always needed and will probably always need help with their accounts; furthermore, compilation services as well as audits and reviews remain an important revenue stream for many smaller auditing firms.*

*Not-for-profit engagements, including work for charities, are an enduring feature of professional life. Many practitioners do not charge charities for their work or apply reduced rates.*

*Many securities exchanges and regulators require listed entities to prepare and publish interim financial information. Such information, like the preliminary financial information released at the period-end before the full audited financial statements become available, is price sensitive. Practitioners are sometimes required or asked to review it.*

## What is important in this section?

*Understanding:*

- *the characteristics of a smaller entity;*
- *the fundamental differences between audits and reviews, where assurance is obtained, and compilation and agreed-upon procedures engagements, where it is not;*

- *the value of compilation and agreed-upon procedures engagements;*
- *the characteristics of not-for-profit entities and how they might be audited or reviewed, their accounts compiled or agreed-upon procedures engagements performed.*

**What sort of questions come up in this area?**

*Simple questions are sometimes set on:*

- *the characteristics of smaller entities and the audit approach to a smaller entity audit;*
- *audit and review procedures for a small charity;*
- *analytical procedures to apply to the review of interim financial information;*
- *the difference between audits and reviews;*

*Questions are also set on:*

- *the appropriate type of engagement for a given set of circumstances;*
- *what procedures might be performed, such as a request for assurance on the completeness and accuracy of a finance application made to a bank or a grant-making body or a request for assurance on key performance indicators.*

*In questions in which the client requests an assurance engagement it is perfectly legitimate to suggest that an agreed-upon procedures engagement is more appropriate where that is the case.*

**How do I stand out from the crowd?**

*Students who have the confidence to tackle questions in areas such as not-for-profit engagements stand out simply because so few students attempt such topics. Questions set in such areas are often very straightforward and, with a little knowledge of the topic, the principles of mainstream audits are easily adapted. Sometimes students do not attempt such questions simply because they think that they do not have the critical knowledge the examiner is looking for. In the vast majority of cases, examiners are satisfied with limited knowledge, as long as it is accompanied by a lot of imagination in applying that knowledge to a given scenario, i.e. making up tests!*

## 9.1   SMALLER ENTITY AUDITS

Smaller entity audits are not going away any time soon. Despite rising levels of audit exemption, a very large number of small audits will continue to be performed in many jurisdictions for the foreseeable future.

ISAs are designed to work for audits of entities of all sizes, but IFAC's Smaller and Medium Practices Committee (SMPC), national standard-setters and professional bodies have all found it necessary to produce guidance to help practitioners perform smaller entity audits.[1] Some argue that there should be a different, less demanding set of auditing standards for smaller entity audits. Others counter that an audit is an audit and that to lower standards or reduce requirements for smaller entity audits by establishing some sort of 'limited audit' or 'light' audit might:

- lead to confusion about the level of assurance obtained;

- diminish the value of all audits;

- deter growth in smaller businesses lacking the discipline provided by a full audit;

- result in a two-tier profession in which some auditors were only qualified to perform smaller entity audits.

It is suggested that those seeking a less expensive process, with a lower level of assurance, not requiring the same level of documentation or attention to internal controls, should look to review, agreed-upon procedures or compilation engagements rather than asking for the credibility conferred by an audit opinion to be provided at lower cost. This debate is a long-standing one.

### 9.1.1   WHAT IS A SMALLER ENTITY?

There is no generally accepted definition of a smaller entity for audit purposes. The EU and other jurisdictions have quantitative definitions for accounting and auditing purposes, generally based on turnover, assets and number of employees.[2] Nevertheless, the turnover of a smaller entity in North America is considerably larger than that of a smaller entity in Africa. The same applies to practitioners in that the Big 4 in some jurisdictions are the same size in terms of partner and staff numbers, as smaller firms

---

[1]  IFAC's SMPC has issued a guide to quality control for small and medium practices, a guide to practice management and a guide to using ISAs in the audit of SMEs at www.ifac.org. IAASB has issued short videos and slides on some ISAs at www.ifac.org/auditing-assurance/clarity-center/support-and-guidance and guidance on applying ISAs proportionately to the size and complexity of an audit, highlighting the considerations for the audit of smaller entities within ISAs. ICAEW's *Right First Time* publications at www.icaew.com provide guidance on ISAs relevant to smaller entity audits.

[2]  For example, the 4th EC Directive is implemented in national company law throughout the EU. Broadly, it permits member states to exempt from audit requirements companies that qualify as small. Accounting exemptions also apply to such companies. Current EC proposals are for small companies to be defined as those that satisfy two or more of the following criteria in a given year: average no. of employees: no more than 50; balance sheet total: no more than €5 million; turnover: no more than €10 million. Transitional arrangements apply and public, insurance and banking companies and certain others are excluded from audit exemption. Minority shareholders are protected by arrangements permitting shareholders holding at least 10% of the share capital to demand an audit. Current UK limits are: employees: 50; balance sheet total £3.26 million; turnover £6.5 million at www.gov.uk/audit-exemptions-for-private-limited-companies.

in other jurisdictions. Wherever they practise, firms of all sizes have smaller clients. Just as important in this context is complexity. Some large entities, such as those that exist simply to hold a property, may have similar characteristics for audit purposes to smaller entities, in that they are relatively simple to audit and have unsophisticated systems. Some smaller entities may engage in complex transactions, be subject to complex regulation or have other complex features, such as those in the financial services sector or in biotechnology.

Most ISAs contain a section entitled *additional considerations for smaller entities*. Smaller entities for these purposes are characterised as entities in which there is *concentration of ownership and management* in a small number of individuals[3] *and* one or more of the following:

- straightforward uncomplicated transactions;

- simple record keeping;

- few lines of business or products within lines;

- few internal controls;

- few management tiers responsible for many controls, or few staff with a range of duties.

Few listed entities have these characteristics.

### Applying ISAs Proportionately

IFAC believes that ISAs can be applied proportionately to the size and complexity of an entity.[4] ISAs are sometimes also described as being 'scalable'. Significant considerations for smaller entities in ISAs include the following:

### General

- the objectives are the same for all audits but this does not mean that they are all planned and performed in the same way;

- interim or management accounts many not exist in smaller entities so an early draft of financial statements may be used for analytical procedures;

- ISAs that may not be relevant to smaller audits include ISA 610 on internal audit, ISA 402 on controls at a service organisation, and ISA 600 on group audits;

- required engagement team discussions are not relevant if there is only one person in the team, such as a sole practitioner with no staff, as are most requirements regarding supervision and pre-issuance reviews;

---

[3]  ISA 200 on overall objectives paragraph A64.
[4]  IFAC Staff Question and Answers, *Applying ISAs Proportionately to the Size and Complexity of an Entity.*

- applying professional judgement does not mean that auditors may decide not to apply an ISA or its requirements if circumstances indicate that they are relevant, or apply it in a way that was not intended.

*Internal controls and documentation*

- further audit procedures in response to assessed risks may be primarily substantive procedures, although this may not be efficient. All audits involve an evaluation of the design and implementation of controls. This work can be used as a basis for testing the operational effectiveness of controls that have not previously been tested, and may be efficient even where in the past, an almost entirely substantive approach has been taken;

- smaller entities are usually less structured than larger ones and typically have simpler processes to achieve their objectives. Their information systems and financial reporting processes are relatively unsophisticated;

- controls requiring effective communication between management and staff in smaller entities may be less formal and easier to achieve than in larger entities;

- documentary evidence on the control environment may not be available in smaller entities and the attitude, awareness and actions of management may either increase control risk, or reduce it;

- the nature and extent of documentation for smaller entity audits is determined in part by the approach taken by audit inspectors. Documentation for smaller entity audits should be less extensive and simpler than for larger audits. Auditors need not necessarily document the entirety of their understanding of the business,[5] and a brief memorandum may serve as an audit strategy document;[6]

- engagement letters: engagement terms should always be in the form of a written engagement letter where possible but owner-managers of smaller entities may struggle with the content of such letters,[7] the need for them and their cost. In such cases, as a minimum, there needs to be a written agreement covering the responsibilities of management for financial statements and the provision of information to auditors.

## 9.2 OVERVIEW OF REVIEWS, AGREED-UPON PROCEDURES AND COMPILATION ENGAGEMENTS

It is not possible to say with any certainty whether, in general, more reviews are performed than compilation engagements or vice versa. The issue is complicated by the use of different terminology for the same thing in different jurisdictions, and the performance of hybrid engagements.

It has been suggested that review-type engagements will fill the gap created by rapid increases in audit exemption levels in Europe and other jurisdictions in recent years.

---

[5] ISA 315 on risk assessment, paragraph A132.
[6] ISA 300 on planning, paragraph A11.
[7] Owner-managers may not understand the content of engagement letters and/or object to the fact that they make it very clear that auditors are not responsible for the financial statements.

This has yet to happen, partly because not all entities that are audit exempt take advantage of the exemption.

One obstacle to the adoption of IAASB standards for review, compilation and agreed-upon procedures engagements, is the need for practitioners performing them to have implemented ISQC 1-style quality control arrangements at firm level. In many jurisdictions, practitioners who do not perform audits are not subject to ISQC 1. For this reason, some professional bodies and national standard-setters have developed and promoted review and compilation engagements based on, but not entirely compliant with, IAASB standards particularly in respect of ISQC1, instead of simply adopting IAASB standards.

Compilation-type engagements, in which practitioners issue a report simply stating that they have compiled the financial statements that are the responsibility of the entity, have existed in many jurisdictions for a long time. Along with tax, these engagements continue to constitute a major income stream for many smaller practitioners. Even so, the automation of accounts preparation software and the accuracy of accounting packages have eroded the value of smaller practitioner services in this area. Companies no longer need practitioners to spend so much time preparing their accounts for them, but they do need more advice on which packages to buy, and how to customise and use them. Some firms specialise in this type of advice, others specialise in maintaining accounting records for clients.

Compilation and review engagements are commonly performed in jurisdictions in which there are no mandatory audit requirements for unlisted entities, such as the USA, or high levels of audit exemption, such as the EU. Compilation engagements are currently more common than review engagements in the UK and it remains to be seen whether review-type engagements[8] fill the gap created by audit exemption, or whether compilation engagements remain the main way in which practitioners are associated with the financial statements prepared by their clients.

Table 9.1   Overview of overarching IAASB requirements applying to audits, reviews, compilations and agreed-upon procedures

|  | Code of Ethics | ISQC 1 | Framework | Assurance |
|---|---|---|---|---|
| Audits | ✓ | ✓ | ✓ | **Reasonable**: true and fair/fair presentation auditor opinion |
| Reviews | ✓ | ✓ | ✓ | **Limited**: nothing has come to the practitioners' attention to indicate material misstatement |
| Compilations | ✓ | ✓ | ✗ | **None**: we have compiled the financial statements from information  supplied |
| Agreed-upon procedures | ✓ | ✓ | ✗ | **None**: we have performed procedures, these are the findings |

---

[8]   An example of review-type engagement is the *Assurance Service* developed by ICAEW based on IAASB standards www.icaew.com.

### 9.2.1  COMMON FEATURES: COMPILATION AND AGREED UPON PROCEDURES ENGAGEMENTS

Unlike review engagements in which limited assurance is obtained, assurance is not obtained in compilation and agreed-upon procedures engagements, but they are conducted under IAASB standards. Common features include the following:

- no assurance is obtained;

- the value of the engagement lies in the practitioners' specialist skills being brought to bear on the relevant financial information using professional standards within the framework of ethical requirements;

- the firm must be subject to the requirements of ISQC 1 or national or other standards that are at least as stringent;

- independence is not required.

## 9.3   REVIEW ENGAGEMENTS

Reviews or review type engagements may be performed:

- for smaller audit-exempt entities;

- on interim or other financial information for larger entities;

- to support contractual arrangements;

- for regulators, although agreed-upon procedures are often more appropriate to the specific areas regulators are interested in.

The purpose of review engagements, as for all assurance engagements, is to enhance the degree of confidence of intended users in the information reported on.

---

Review engagements are *limited assurance* engagements. Review reports state that *nothing has come to the practitioners' attention to cause them to believe that:*

- *the financial statements do not present a true and fair view of / present fairly in all material respects the financial position, performance and cash flows, in accordance with the financial reporting framework (for fair presentation frameworks);*

- *are not prepared in all material respects with the applicable financial reporting framework (for compliance frameworks).*

---

In other words, practitioners state that *based on the review, nothing has come to their attention to cause them to believe that the financial statements may be materially misstated.*

---

Review procedures consist *primarily of inquiry, analytical procedures and evaluating evidence.* The work performed is substantially less than it would be for an audit. If matters do come to the practitioners' attention indicating a possible material misstatement, they perform additional procedures.

---

General purpose frameworks are designed to meet the common financial needs of a wide range of users. Special purpose frameworks are designed to meet the needs of specific users.

### 9.3.1    REQUIREMENTS FOR REVIEW ENGAGEMENTS

As with all assurance engagements, practitioners are subject to the relevant ethical requirements of IESBA's *Code*. They are also subject to the requirements of *ISQC 1*[9] or other requirements that are at least as demanding and they apply engagement level quality control procedures similar to those stipulated under ISA 220.[10] This means, for example, that the engagement partner must be satisfied that the engagement team collectively has the right skills set to perform the engagement and that the firm's quality control monitoring procedures have not highlighted anything untoward regarding compliance with ethical requirements. Practitioners also exercise *professional scepticism* and *professional judgement* throughout the engagement.

ISRE 2400[11] only deals with engagements in which practitioners who are *not* auditors of an entity, review historical financial information. It would be a rare and probably pointless exercise for auditors to review information they also audit. ISRE 2400 can, however, be applied by auditors of component entities for the purposes of group audits in certain circumstances. Reviews of interim financial information performed under ISRE 2410[12] *are* performed by auditors.

#### Acceptance of Review Engagements
Practitioners should not accept review engagements if management lack integrity or independence requirements cannot be satisfied, if the information needed to perform the engagement will not be available or if imposed limitations in audit scope are likely to result in a disclaimer of opinion. There needs to be a rational purpose for the engagement. This means that, among other things, if an audit were likely to produce a modified opinion, a review engagement should not be performed. The appropriate response to a material misstatement is to correct the material misstatement, not to perform a lower level assurance engagement in order to avoid a modified conclusion!

The *preconditions* for accepting review engagements, aligned with those in ISAE 3000 and the *Framework* require that:

- the responsible party (the reviewed entity) has appropriate responsibilities *and acknowledges and understands its responsibility:*
  - *for the preparation of financial statements in accordance with the relevant financial reporting framework* and for internal control, as is necessary to achieve this;
  - to provide the *practitioner with access* to the evidence needed and unrestricted access to persons within the entity;
  - the underlying *subject matter is appropriate,* i.e. the financial records of the entity;

---

[9]  ISQC 1 on firm-level quality control.
[10]  ISA 220 on engagement-level quality control.
[11]  ISRE 2400 on review engagements.
[12]  ISRE 2410 on interim financial information.

- the *suitability of the criteria* to be applied, i.e. those embodied in the financial reporting framework such as IFRS,[13] and their *availability to intended users,* which would not be an issue with IFRS given that they are widely available.

*Agreed engagement terms* should cover:

- the intended use and distribution of the financial statements;
- the financial reporting framework to be used;
- the responsibilities of both practitioners and entity and the scope of the engagement;
- likely content of the report;
- a statement that the engagement is not an audit and will not satisfy audit requirements.

Terms should also cover any necessary arrangements with predecessor practitioners and any other practitioners or experts involved.

As with an audit, review engagement terms should always be in the form of an engagement letter if possible, to avoid misunderstandings. This is particularly important where review engagements are voluntary arrangements and are not required by law or regulation.

A change to the terms of the agreement, particularly if it involves a downgrade to an agreed-upon procedures engagement, needs reasonable justification. A reasonable justification would be a misunderstanding about the nature of assurance to be provided.

Communication of significant findings from the review to those charged with governance is required much as it is for an audit, including significant qualitative aspects of accounting policies and estimates and difficulties in obtaining information.

### 9.3.2 PERFORMING REVIEW ENGAGEMENTS

While full risk assessments are not required for review engagements, *an understanding* of the entity, its environment, and the applicable financial reporting framework is *sufficient to identify areas in the financial statements where material misstatements are likely to arise,* and to be able to design procedures to address those areas.

Performing review engagements involves considering *materiality* and *understanding the business,* including the industry and external regulation, as well as the business itself, its ownership and governance, objectives, strategies, systems and accounting policies. This is as for an audit or other reasonable assurance engagement, but needs

---

[13] In the absence of indications to the contrary, practitioners can generally assume that financial reporting frameworks prescribed by legislation, such as IFRS, are likely to be suitable for general purpose financial statements.

to be carried out only *in sufficient detail to identify areas in which material mis-statements are likely to arise* and *to design appropriate procedures*. This is considerably less than a full, formal risk assessment, which requires an understanding of the design and implementation of controls, tests of control effectiveness and designing procedures to respond to assessed risks at financial statement and assertion level. The main procedures required are *inquiry* and *analytical procedures focusing on areas in which material misstatement may arise.*

As for audits, matters are material if individually or together they can be reasonably expected to influence the economic decisions of users taken on the basis of the financial statements.

### Inquiry

Inquiries cover areas similar to those covered in an audit or other reasonable assurance engagement. The difference lies in how they are followed up. Inquiries cover, among other things:

- significant changes in the business environment, operations, group structure, accounting policies, customers or suppliers, conditions of loans or other financing arrangements;
- significant transactions with related parties, journal entries, transactions either side of the period-end, accounting estimates;
- suspected or actual fraud or non-compliance with laws or regulations;
- the going concern status of the entity and subsequent events.

Inquiries about actions decided on at meetings of owners, management and those charged with governance provide information about all of these issues. For future-oriented issues such as the going concern assessment, evaluating past management actions and discussing the entity's prospects may be relevant. Formally comparing budgets with outcomes and assessing the feasibility of cash flow forecasts, which might be appropriate for an audit, are not.

It is inevitable that responses to inquiries will sometimes give rise to doubts about whether the information reviewed is in fact materially misstated, and lead to further inquiries. Generally, practitioners will accept responses to inquiries that appear reasonable provided they are not inconsistent with other evidence or the practitioners' knowledge of the business. Generally, practitioners will *not* seek to test controls or corroborate explanations with reference to documentary evidence or evidence from third parties. If inquiries about related parties, for example, highlight previously undisclosed related parties or transactions, reasonable responses to further enquiries about the full extent of transactions and any other related parties may be accepted without further investigation. This would not be the case in an ISA audit. Similarly, if there is significant doubt about an entity's going concern status, practitioners may accept management explanations about plans to deal with it, and will consider the feasibility of those plans, but they will not necessarily seek to examine the relevant budgets, forecasts, cash flow statements or correspondence with lenders, as they might in an ISA audit.

*Analytical procedures*

Analytical procedures performed in review engagements are also similar to those performed in ISA audits. *The difference lies in the required level of precision in predictions about expected relationships, and in follow up.* In an ISA audit or other reasonable assurance engagement, the analysis needs to be sufficiently detailed for practitioners to form a view as to whether the financial statement is materially misstated.

In a review engagement, less precision and less follow up are required. Information might be aggregated at a higher level, for example, and practitioners would not seek to corroborate explanations that appeared reasonable. Receivables might be analysed on a quarterly basis and by division, rather than on a monthly basis by jurisdiction, and practitioners might consider an explanation regarding an unexpected decrease in revenue in the light of their overall understanding of the business, rather than seeking documentary evidence. Practitioners do, however, need to consider the adequacy of the source of the information used in analytical procedures, such as a receivables ledger, but they do not need to test controls over that information as they might in an ISA audit.

*Additional procedures where the financial statements may be materially misstated*

In practice, determining when additional procedures are required can be difficult because many errors or inconsistencies, even small ones, may point to a misstatement, and the question then becomes whether they are pointing to a material misstatement.

The additional procedures should in any case enable practitioners to conclude either that the matter is not likely to have caused a material misstatement, or that it has. Procedures consist of additional inquiry and analytical procedures and possibly substantive procedures and external confirmations. If, for example, procedures on receivables show deteriorating debtor days, and a number of long overdue large balances, practitioners might ask why. They might also consider confirming some of the large balances and reviewing cash received. If as a result of these procedures practitioners still have concerns and management refuses to make appropriate provisions, practitioners might conclude that the financial statements are in fact materially misstated, or that there is insufficient evidence to support a conclusion that nothing has come to their attention to indicate that the financial statements are not materially misstated.

*Written representations and subsequent events*

As with all assurance engagements, the written representations required cover the preconditions for the engagement and other matters. In particular, they cover management's responsibility for the information reviewed, for the controls underlying that information, its completeness, the appropriateness of the applicable financial reporting framework and the provision of information to practitioners.

As with ISA audits, if public statements to the same effect are required by law or regulation, written representations are not required. Specific representations are required concerning the identity of related parties and transactions with them, in relation to fraud and non-compliance with laws and regulations, the going concern assumption and subsequent events. As always, if management does not provide the representations or the representations are unreliable because of a lack of management integrity, a disclaimer of opinion or withdrawal from the engagement may be necessary, although this is rare.

### 9.3.3   REPORTING

Practitioners need to ensure that the financial information reconciles to the underlying records, to avoid reporting on information that is not based on what they have reviewed.

As with audit and other assurance engagements, law and regulation sometimes prescribe the wording of review reports. This is acceptable provided the wording is unlikely to result in misunderstandings about the level of assurance obtained, but additional wording may be necessary.[14]

Third parties such as lenders seeking audits or reviews of information often ask for *certifications or guarantees* that either cannot be provided at all, because the criteria for assurance engagements are not met,[15] or can only be provided at a substantially greater cost than the client is willing to bear. It is common to explain in these cases that agreed-upon procedures or compilation engagements may be more appropriate.

Modified conclusions for review engagements are similar to modified audit opinions. They can be qualified because of a limitation in the scope of the review, or because the financial statements are materially misstated. Adverse conclusions and disclaimers of conclusion are also possible where the effects are pervasive. Emphases of matter drawing readers' attention to matters fundamental to the understanding of the financial statements and other matters paragraphs relating to the audit are also possible.

### 9.3.4   CONTENT OF REVIEW REPORTS

Review reports, which are very similar in format to audit reports, have the following elements:

- *title*: independent review report to . . .
- *addressee;*
- *paragraph identifying the financial statements reviewed,* stating that they have been reviewed and referring to significant accounting policies;
- the *responsibilities of management for the preparation* of the financial statements, internal controls, judgements and assumptions;

---

[14] If misunderstandings are unavoidable because of the prescribed wording and additional wording cannot rectify this, the engagement should not be accepted unless required by law or regulation, in which case practitioners cannot claim compliance with the ISRE.

[15] The five criteria for assurance engagements are a three party relationship, suitable criteria, an appropriate underlying subject matter, the existence of evidence that will not result in a disclaimer or adverse opinion, and an assurance report.

- the *responsibilities of practitioners* to perform the limited assurance engagement in accordance with *ISRE 2400,* to obtain evidence, to apply *ISQC 1* and the independence and other ethical requirements of IESBA's *Code*;

- a *summary of the inquiries, analytical and other procedures performed* and a statement that the review procedures do not enable the identification of significant matters that would be identified in an audit;

- *conclusion,* i.e. nothing has come to practitioners' attention to cause them to believe that the financial statements do not give a true and fair view of/present fairly in all material respects the financial position performance and cash flows, in accordance with the financial reporting framework (i.e. are not materially misstated);[16]

- practitioner(s)' *signature*

- *date:* not before all of the evidence on which the conclusion is based has been obtained;

- *location:* the address(es) of the practitioners' office(s) in the jurisdiction where the practitioner practises.

An example review report might appear as follows:

---

INDEPENDENT PRACTITIONERS' REVIEW REPORT to the DIRECTORS OF ABCCO

We have reviewed the financial statements of ABCCO, which comprise the statement of financial position as at 31 December 20XX, and the statement of comprehensive income, statement of changes in equity and statement of cash flows for the year then ended, and a summary of significant accounting policies and other explanatory information.

*Management's Responsibility for the Financial Statements*

Management are responsible for the preparation and fair presentation of these financial statements in accordance with International Financial Reporting Standards, and for such internal control as management determine necessary to enable the preparation of financial statements that are free from material misstatement, whether due to fraud or error.

*Practitioners' Responsibility*

Our responsibility is to express a conclusion on the accompanying financial statements based on our review. We conducted our review in accordance with International Standard on Review Engagements (ISRE) 2400, *Engagements to Review Historical Financial Statements.* ISRE 2400 requires us to conclude whether anything has come to our attention that causes us to believe that the financial statements, taken as a whole, are not prepared in all material respects in accordance with the applicable financial reporting framework. This Standard also requires us to comply with relevant ethical requirements.

---

[16] For compliance frameworks, the conclusion is that nothing has come to practitioners' attention to cause them to believe that the financial statements have not been prepared in all material respects in accordance with the identified financial reporting framework.

A review of financial statements in accordance with ISRE 2400 is a limited assurance engagement. Practitioners perform procedures, primarily consisting of making inquiries of management and others within the entity, applying analytical procedures and evaluating the evidence obtained.

The procedures performed in a review are substantially less than those performed in an audit conducted in accordance with International Standards on Auditing. Accordingly, we do not express an audit opinion on these financial statements.

*Conclusion*

Based on our review, nothing has come to our attention that causes us to believe that these financial statements do not give a true and fair view of [or do not present fairly, in all material respects] the financial position of ABCCO as at 31 December 20XX, and *(of)* its financial performance and cash flows for the year then ended, in accordance with International Financial Reporting Standards.

**Report on Other Legal and Regulatory Requirements**

*[Form and content depend on local reporting responsibilities]*

Signature(s):

Date of review report:

Address(es):

As with audit reports, the paragraphs above that are most likely to change are the conclusion and the report on other legal and regulatory requirements. A qualified conclusion might appear as follows:

*Basis for Qualified Conclusion*

The company's inventories are carried in the statement of financial position at $XXX. Management have not stated the inventories at the lower of cost and net realizable value but have stated them at cost, which is a departure from the requirements of International Financial Reporting Standards. The company's records indicate that, had management stated the inventories at the lower of cost and net realizable value, an amount of $YYY would have been required to write the inventories down to their net realizable value. Accordingly, cost of sales would have been increased by $YYY, and income tax and net income, and shareholders' equity, would have been reduced by $ZZZ.

*Qualified Conclusion*

Except for the effects of the matter described in the Basis for Qualified Conclusion paragraph, based on our review, nothing has come to our attention that causes us to believe that the financial statements of ABCCO are not prepared, in all material respects, in accordance with International Financial Reporting Standards.

Where special purpose financial statements are prepared, a note on the basis of accounting and a restriction on distribution and use might appear as follows:

---

**Basis of Accounting, and Restriction on Distribution and Use**

Without modifying our conclusion, we draw attention to Note X which describes the basis of accounting. The financial statements are prepared to assist ABCCO to comply with the financial reporting provisions of the contract referred to above.[17] As a result, the financial statements may not be suitable for other purposes. Our report is intended solely for ABCCO and DEFCO and should not be distributed to or used by parties other than them.

---

### 9.3.5 REVIEW OF INTERIM FINANCIAL INFORMATION

Securities exchanges and regulators often require listed entities to prepare interim financial information on a half-yearly basis. In the USA, it is commonly prepared on a quarterly basis. The capital markets react to this information and there may be mandatory review requirements or auditors may be asked to perform a review. In some jurisdictions such as the UK, if a review is performed, the report must be published.

Unlike ISRE 2400 on review engagements, ISRE 2410 on the review of interim financial information requires that those performing reviews on interim information are the entity's auditors. This is because the interim financial information only makes sense in relation to the prior period financial information.[18]

Reviews conducted under ISRE 2400 and ISRE 2410 are both limited assurance engagements stating that nothing has come to the practitioners'/auditors' attention to indicate that the financial statements/interim financial information do not give a true and fair view of/fairly present in all material respects the position, performance and cash flows, in accordance with the financial reporting framework. In additional to the requirements of ISRE 2400 to make inquiries and perform analytical procedures, ISRE 2410 requires auditors to perform other review procedures and there is more focus on internal control and risk analysis.

Auditors *update their understanding of the business, including its internal control,* from the previous audit by reading the prior period interim and final financial information and performing analytical procedures on the current information with reference to both. They consider:

- whether significant risks have changed;
- materiality and any corrected misstatements;

---

[17] The reference would be the paragraph dealing with management's responsibilities for the financial statements. Instead of being prepared in accordance with IFRS, they would be prepared in accordance with the contract.
[18] Practitioners who are not also auditors perform the review of interim information under ISRE 2400 on review engagements.

- the results of any audit procedures which may be conducted concurrently with the interim review;

- any significant changes in the business, internal control or the preparation process for the interim financial information.

*Inquiries and analytical procedures* normally cover changes in accounting principles, complex transactions, related party transactions, transactions around the reporting date and any known or suspected frauds. Procedures include reading the interim financial information.

The analytical procedures, as for other review engagements, would be similar to those performed in an audit but:

- the comparisons would be made between current information, prior period interim information and full prior period information;

- the quality of interim information may be affected by the lack of cut-off controls that are applied at the period end. While auditors do not test controls over the underlying information in a review, the nature and extent of evidence they require to support their conclusion is nevertheless affected by their assessment of the quality of interim information;

- in all review engagements, less precision and less follow up are required than they would be for an audit.

Requirements to reconcile the information with the underlying records, relating to subsequent events, the going concern review, the evaluation of misstatements and written representations, communications with those charged with governance, are similar to those required under ISRE 2400 and ISAs.

# 9.4   COMPILATION ENGAGEMENTS

In many jurisdictions such as the UK, all incorporated entities, regardless of size, and some unincorporated entities, are required to prepare and file basic financial information in accordance with reporting criteria such as IFRS, the IFRS for SMEs or national standards, at a public registry. The responsibility sometimes lies with management, sometimes with those charged with governance. Practitioners help their clients by compiling the information in the required formats. Many practitioners also help extract the relevant information from the underlying accounting records and produce a trial balance, particularly for very small entities.

It is important to note at this point that compilation engagements are not assurance engagements. Many of the 'rules' applying to assurance engagements do not apply to compilations. ISAs, ISAE 3000, the five criteria for assurance engagements[19] and the

---

[19]   The five criteria for assurance engagements are a three party relationship, appropriate subject matter, suitable criteria, evidence and an assurance report.

*Framework* do not apply. Practitioners are not required to assess the suitability of the reporting criteria. But this does not mean the compilation engagements are a free-for-all. ISQC 1 on firm-level quality control applies to compilation engagements. While the independence requirements of the IESBA's *Code* do not apply, there is an overriding requirement for practitioners not to be associated with misleading information.[20]

The applicable financial reporting framework mandated by national laws and regulations may be a fair presentation framework, meaning that the financial statements must give a true and fair view or fairly present the position, or a compliance framework, meaning that the financial statements are only obliged to comply with the framework's requirements. Even if practitioners are not required to assess the suitability of these criteria, they are required to ensure that they are not misleading.

Most reporting frameworks mandated by laws and regulation are general purpose frameworks serving the needs of a wide range of users. Special purpose frameworks, such as the tax or cash bases of accounting, are sometimes appropriate. A special purpose framework appropriate for a particular entity might be a combination of the cash basis with selected accruals, depending on the purpose of the information, but it is important to distinguish between what is appropriate and what is desired to provide the best presentation, which may be misleading. Where financial statements have been compiled in accordance with a financial reporting framework that has been modified, attention needs to be drawn to that fact.

Special purpose information, such as information prepared by a bank for regulatory purposes, may not be suitable for other purposes and the distribution or use of the compilation report may be restricted.

### 9.4.1 NATURE AND PURPOSE OF COMPILATION ENGAGEMENTS

Compilation engagements, as the name implies, involve the practitioner compiling financial information.[21]

> *In a compilation engagement, the practitioner applies accounting and financial reporting expertise to assist management in preparing financial information in accordance with an applicable financial reporting framework and reports in accordance with ISRS 4410.*[22]

Practitioners are hired to prepare financial statements but they do not take any responsibility for that information because their role is to **assist management**. As with

---

[20] If practitioners are unwilling or unable to comply with ISQC 1, they may still perform compilation engagements, but they may not assert compliance with ISRS 4410 on compilation engagements.

[21] ISRS 4410 on compilation engagements applies to compilations of historical financial information but the principles can be applied to compilations of other information including prospective financial information such as budgets and forecasts.

[22] ISRS 4410, paragraph 17 (b).

agreed-upon procedures engagements, *practitioners obtain no assurance* and there is no requirement for the practitioner to be independent.[23]

The value of compilation and agreed-upon procedures engagements lies in bringing practitioners' specialist skills to bear on the records supplied, using professional standards, within the framework of ethical requirements and ISQC 1.[24]

Compiled financial information may be needed:

- because an entity is required to file financial statements with a public registry;
- for periodic financial reporting under a loan or similar agreement;
- for a funding or grant-awarding body;
- to support a transaction such as a merger of acquisition.

### 9.4.2   ACCEPTING COMPILATION ENGAGEMENTS

As always, engagement terms need to be agreed. They should cover the:

- intended use and distribution of the compiled information;
- financial reporting framework, the objective and scope of the engagement and the responsibilities of the practitioner;
- responsibilities of management for the preparation of the financial information and the completeness and accuracy of the records and the judgements made.

A written agreement is needed. If management or those charged with governance will not accept responsibility for the information compiled, the practitioner cannot take the engagement on, at least not under the ISRS.

### 9.4.3   PERFORMING THE COMPILATION

Practitioners *obtain an understanding, sufficient to perform the engagement,* of the:

- business and operations including its accounting system and records (but there is no requirement to understand internal control);
- applicable financial reporting framework.

The compilation is performed using documents, records, explanations, other information and judgements, *all supplied by management*. Practitioners are likely to advise on judgements for smaller entities, particularly with regard to accounting estimates such

---

[23] Unlike agreed-upon procedures engagements, where practitioners are not independent, there is no requirement to state that fact in the report.
[24] Quality control requirements similar to those in ISA 220 on engagement-level quality control also apply to compilation engagements.

as provisions for depreciation or inventory write-downs, for example, but they remain management judgements.

Practitioners *read* the information they have compiled in the light of their understanding of the business. They obtain an acknowledgement of responsibility from management or those charged with governance for the final version of the financial information.

If practitioners become aware that:

- anything provided by management is incomplete, inaccurate or unsatisfactory;
- what they have compiled does not adequately disclose the financial reporting framework;
- requested amendments are not made;
- the compiled financial information is otherwise misleading

they attempt to resolve the matter with management. If this is not possible, they withdraw from the engagement where possible, and take legal advice otherwise.

Documentation is required for much the same reasons as it is in any other type of engagement, i.e. to provide a record of continuing relevance to future engagements and to enable the engagement team to be accountable within the firm and to external inspectors for their work. Audit inspectors in many jurisdictions review the quality of work performed in unregulated areas, including compilations. Documentation is specifically required for:

- significant matters arising and how they were addressed;
- the reconciliation of the information with the underlying records.

### 9.4.4 REPORTING

There are no modified reports or emphases of matter in reports on compiled financial information. This is because there is no opinion or conclusion to modify. Practitioners simply state what they have been instructed to do, and what they have done. If they are not able to do what they are instructed to do, because it would be misleading, they do not take on the engagement and do not report.

An example compilation report might appear as follows:

---

PRACTITIONERS' COMPILATION REPORT to the DIRECTORS OF ABCCO

We have compiled the accompanying financial statements of ABCCO based on information provided by management. These financial statements comprise [*name the financial statements prepared under the basis of accounting specified in the contract (or the IFRS for SMEs) and the period/date to which they relate*].

---

We performed this compilation engagement in accordance with International Standard on Related Services 4410, *Compilation Engagements*.

We have applied our expertise in accounting and financial reporting to assist management in the preparation and presentation of these financial statements on the basis of accounting described in Note X.

We have complied with relevant ethical requirements, including principles of integrity, objectivity, professional competence and due care.

These financial statements and the accuracy and completeness of the information used to compile them are management's responsibility.

Since a compilation engagement is not an assurance engagement, we are not required to verify the accuracy or completeness of the information provided to us by management to compile these financial statements. Accordingly, we do not express an audit opinion or a review conclusion on whether these financial statements are prepared in accordance with the basis of accounting described in Note X.

As stated in Note X, the financial statements are prepared and presented on the basis described in Clause Y of the provisions of ABCCO's contract with XYZCO dated XX/YY/20XX and for the purpose described in Note Y to the financial statements. Accordingly, these financial statements are intended for use only by the parties specified in the contract and may not be suitable for other purposes. Our compilation report is intended solely for the parties specified in the contract, and should not be distributed to other parties.[25]

Signature(s):

Date:

Address(es):

## 9.5   AGREED-UPON PROCEDURES ENGAGEMENTS

Agreed-upon procedures engagements, as the wording implies, involve practitioners performing procedures agreed with the client and sometimes a third party. Where agreed-upon procedures engagements are performed for regulators, regulators often specify that auditors must perform the procedures, but there is no requirement in ISRS 4400[26] for this and, in principle, any practitioner can perform agreed-upon procedures engagements. For example:

---

[25] A similar paragraph drawing attention to a departure from accounting standards might appear as follows:
*As stated in Note X, the financial statements are prepared and presented in accordance with IFRS for SMEs, excluding property. Property is revalued in the financial statements rather than being carried at historical cost. The financial statements are prepared for the purpose described in Note Y to the financial statements. Accordingly, these financial statements may not be suitable for other purposes.*

[26] ISRS 4400 on agreed-upon procedures engagements.

- it is common for regulators in many sectors to need some form of report from auditors on financial matters for which the regulator has responsibility. Many entities hold money on behalf of their clients, as deposits for goods or services such as holidays, in the financial services sector, and when facilitating property transactions. Regulators of travel agents, regulators in the financial services sector and regulators of accountants, lawyers and real estate agents, are all required to ensure that systems and controls are in place to guarantee that that money is not misused. One way of doing that is by commissioning a report from auditors on systems, controls or money held. Regulators generally specify that client money is to be held in separate accounts, for example, that such accounts must not be overdrawn, that interest on the money must be accounted for to the client unless agreed otherwise, and that deductions from client monies for fees cannot be made without informing the client in writing. In many cases, the procedures to be performed and the report to be issued are agreed between the regulator and professional bodies representing auditors. For example, auditors might perform an external confirmation of amounts held on behalf of customers and report on who was circularised, how many responses there were and what percentage were agreed or reconciled;

- the circulation figures for newspapers and magazines are a key issue for advertisers and practitioners might be commissioned by an advertiser or by a regulator to recalculate circulation levels from information provided by publishers;

- an entity might simply want an auditor to confirm all bank balances held at an interim period if it has concerns over the control or recording of cash balances.

Regulators often want a high level of assurance on such matters but assurance is expensive by comparison with agreed-upon procedures, and the conditions required for assurance engagements, such as suitable criteria, are often absent. Agreed-upon procedures engagements are often more suitable.

### 9.5.1 REPORTING ON AGREED-UPON PROCEDURES

*No assurance is obtained in agreed-upon procedures engagements.* The report provided is restricted to those agreeing the engagement because others who are unaware of the reasons for the procedures might misinterpret the results. Users of the *report of factual findings* assess the report for themselves and draw their own conclusions. The value of the engagement, as with compilation engagements, lies in bringing the practitioners' specialist skills to bear on the relevant financial information, using professional standards, within the framework of ethical requirements and ISQC 1.

The fundamental principles of IESBA's *Code* apply[27] to agreed-upon procedures engagements as they do for all engagements. Independence is *not* a requirement for non-assurance engagements although independence may be required by the terms of the engagement or local requirements. Despite this, if practitioners performing agreed-upon

---

[27] The fundamental principles of the IESBA's *Code* are integrity, objectivity, professional competence and due diligence, confidentiality, professional behaviour and technical standards.

procedures engagements are not independent, a statement of that fact should be made in the report of factual findings.[28]

The firm must be subject to the requirements of ISQC 1 or national or other standards that are at least as stringent.

### 9.5.2   AGREEING THE PROCEDURES

As with any other engagement, practitioners ensure that there is a clear understanding with the entity and whoever else will receive a copy of the report regarding:

- the fact that there will be no audit or review and that no assurance will be obtained;
- the purpose of the engagement;
- the financial information to which the procedures will be applied;
- the procedures to be applied;
- the anticipated form of the report;
- the limitations on the distribution of the report.

Where the engagement terms are determined by an agreement between a regulator and representatives of auditors, it is particularly important that auditors discuss these matters with management.

A *written engagement letter*, as always, prevents misunderstandings and confirms the practitioners' appointment. In addition to matters such as the scope, objectives and the form of report to be issued, the letter should list the procedures to be performed and any restrictions on the distribution of the report.

### 9.5.3   PERFORMING THE PROCEDURES

Planning and documentation are essential parts of any engagement. The procedures to be performed include techniques recognisable from audits and include inquiry, analysis, re-computation, observation, inspection and obtaining confirmations.

### 9.5.4   REPORTING

As with all reports, the report of findings should contain:

- a title and addressee;
- identification of the information to which the procedures have been applied;
- a statement that the engagement was performed in accordance with ISRS 4400;

---

[28]  This requirement is now anomalous and is not replicated in ISRS 4410 on compilation engagements.

- a list of the procedures performed and the findings;

- a statement that the procedures do not constitute an audit or review and that had either been performed, additional matters might have come to light.

An agreed-upon procedures report might appear as follows:

---

PRACTITIONERS' REPORT OF FACTUAL FINDINGS to the DIRECTORS OF ABCCO

We have performed the procedures agreed with you and enumerated below with respect to the accounts payable of ABCCO as at (date), set forth in the accompanying schedules. Our engagement was undertaken in accordance with the International Standard on Related Services 4410 applicable to agreed-upon procedures engagements. The procedures were performed solely to assist you in evaluating the validity of the accounts payable and are summarised as follows. We:

- obtained and checked the addition of the trial balance of accounts payable as at XX/YY/20XX prepared by ABBCO, and we compared the total to the balance in the related general ledger account;

- compared the attached list (not shown in this example) of major suppliers and the amounts owing at XX/YY/20XX to the related names and amounts in the trial balance;

- obtained suppliers' statements or requested suppliers to confirm balances owing at XX/YY/20XX;

- compared such statements or confirmations to the amounts referred to above.

For amounts that did not agree, we obtained reconciliations from ABCCO. For reconciliations obtained, we identified and listed outstanding invoices, credit notes and outstanding checks, each of which was greater than $XXX. We located and examined such invoices and credit notes subsequently received and checks subsequently paid and we ascertained that they should in fact have been listed as outstanding on the reconciliations.

We report our findings below. With respect to:

- item 1, we found the addition to be correct and the total amount to be in agreement;

- item 2, we found the amounts compared to be in agreement;

- item 3, we found there were suppliers' statements for all such suppliers;

- item 4, we found the amounts agreed, or with respect to amounts which did not agree, we found ABBCO had prepared reconciliations and that the credit notes, invoices and outstanding checks over $XXX were appropriately listed as reconciling items with the following exceptions:

[List exceptions]

Because the above procedures do not constitute either an audit or a review made in accordance with International Standards on Auditing or International Standards on Review Engagements, we do not express any assurance on the accounts payable as of XX/YY/20XX.

Had we performed additional procedures or had we performed an audit or review of the financial statements in accordance with International Standards on Auditing or International Standards on Review Engagements (or relevant national standards or practices), other matters might have come to our attention that would have been reported to you.

Our report is solely for the purpose set forth in the first paragraph of this report and for your information and is not to be used for any other purpose or to be distributed to other parties. This report relates only to the accounts and items specified above and does not extend to any financial statements of ABBCO taken as a whole.

Signature(s):

Date:

Address(es):

# 9.6   NOT-FOR-PROFIT ENGAGEMENTS

## 9.6.1   TYPES OF NOT-FOR-PROFIT ENTITIES

The operation of not-for-profit organisations is very jurisdiction-specific. With a few notable exceptions, most not-for-profit organisations are small and operate within national boundaries. The laws and regulations governing such entities differ widely but not-for-profit entities generally do not make profits for distribution to shareholders or other private owners, but instead apply or reinvest the funds they raise and profits they make to further the entity's objectives.

Not-for-profit entities include organisations that promote education, science, culture, religion, medical research, amateur sport, the protection of the environment and animal welfare, the saving of lives, the relief of poverty, particularly among the young, the elderly and the disabled, women, children, widows and war veterans. In some jurisdictions, entities such as these enjoy exemptions from certain taxes because their activities are considered to be for the public rather than private benefit. Other not-for-profit organisations include credit unions, mutuals and thrifts, trade or labour unions, co-operatives, and housing associations which exist (in theory) to benefit a specific group of people such as a particular trade or profession or people who live in a particular location. Such entities may or may not enjoy tax privileges.

Entities that enjoy tax privileges are referred to in some jurisdictions as having charitable status and they are often more heavily regulated than for-profit entities of a similar size to ensure that the money they raise is used in the manner that the donors intended.

Not-for-profit entities may be constituted as companies but they often have a different legal status and may operate, depending on jurisdiction, as trusts, industrial and provident societies, building societies or savings and loans associations, for example. Those charged with the governance of not-for-profit entities therefore include directors where entities are constituted as companies and trustees where they are constituted as trusts, or a management board.

This section applies to the generality of not-for-profit entities, however they are constituted. Many of the issues relating to such entities identified in this section arise from the fact that they are usually smaller entities, rather than from their not-for-profit status.

## 9.6.2 OBLIGATIONS OF NOT-FOR-PROFIT ENTITIES

Some entities engaged in not-for-profit activities enjoy a variety of tax-related and other privileges and exemptions that are not available to for-profit entities. Obligations accompany the privileges and exemptions and include requirements to:

- register with government or government appointed bodies that oversee the activities of such entities;[29]

- apply funds raised strictly in accordance with the objectives of the entity;

- prepare accounts and annual returns and, often subject to size criteria, to have those entities audited, reviewed, inspected, examined or reported on in some way by a person who may or may not need to be a professional accountant or qualified as an auditor.[30]

## 9.6.3 FEATURES OF NOT FOR PROFIT ENTITIES

*Features of not-for-profit entities* include:

- *management by trustees* or a management board rather than directors, if entities are not constituted as companies;

- strictly defined *objectives* that restrict how revenue is to be distributed;

- requirements for an *annual report and annual returns by trustees or the management board under relevant legislation* rather than, or in addition to, a directors' report and accounts under companies legislation;

- *preparation of statements of financial performance,* i.e. income and expenditure or receipts and payments accounts, *and statements of financial assets* or balance sheets in accordance with the requirements of relevant legislation[31] and the requirements of regulatory bodies, combined with, the profit and loss accounts and balance sheets prepared under companies legislation where appropriate;

- depending on the size of the entity, an *audit, review, inspection, examination or report* by a person, not necessarily a professional accountant or an auditor;[32]

---

[29] The Charity Commission, for example, oversees the activities of charities in England and Wales.

[30] The Charities Act 2011 in England and Wales, for example, exempts charities with an income of under £5,000 from the requirement to prepare accounts.

[31] Such as Statement of Recommended Practice (SORP 2005) in the UK.

[32] Inspections, examinations and reports on accounts can sometimes operate as agreed-upon procedures engagements. They were common in practice before IFAC and national standard-setters came into existence and they exhibit characteristics that do not fit easily within the IFAC *Framework*. When legislation is changed, there is sometimes an opportunity for professional accountancy bodies to try to persuade regulators to bring their requirements into line with up-to-date thinking, although the status quo is sometimes difficult to change.

- *internal controls and accounting records* may be *unsophisticated, trustees* and staff keeping records may be *unpaid volunteers.*

### 9.6.4    AUDITS AND REVIEWS OF NOT-FOR-PROFIT ENTITIES

*Engagement acceptance and continuance*

The requirements for audits and reviews of not-for-profit entities conducted under ISAs are the same as those for profit-making entities. Practitioners sometimes erroneously believe that because the audited or reviewed entity is not-for-profit, or because reduced fees are charged, or fees are not charged at all, lower auditing standards can be applied. Not-for-profit entities are increasingly regulated and in some jurisdictions are becoming a specialist area in their own right.

The rise in audit exemption levels in many jurisdictions has resulted in some practitioners only retaining their registration as auditors in order to conduct the audit of a few small local charities, which they have performed for many years and which they conduct on a *pro bono* basis, i.e. fees are waived (not charged). At the same time, the documentation, quality control and other requirements for audits have expanded and practitioners sometimes have to make a difficult choice between giving up an audit that represents a contribution to the local community, and continuing with it at increasing expense to themselves, not least in terms of keeping up with changes in standards.

*Understanding the entity's activities and risk assessment*

Understanding the entity, its environment, and the applicable financial reporting framework for the purposes of an audit risk assessment involves consideration of:

- constitutional documents, the entity's legal nature and the tax and other exemptions and privileges it enjoys;
- the entity's governance structure and the qualifications, experience, competencies and training of its trustees and any paid or volunteer staff;
- its activities, assets and performance in terms of trading or fund-raising in the context of the prevailing economic climate;
- the entity's financial reporting obligations and track record and its accounting systems and internal controls.

Not-for-profit entities can be large and have global operations, necessitating systems, controls, and paid staff and trustees who run the entity in many ways as if it were a business. Many larger not-for-profit entities have trading operations that do make a profit, all of which is transferred to the main not-for-profit entity. The risks associated with trading operations are similar to the risks associated with trading in for-profit entities. The vast majority of not-for-profit entities that most practitioners are likely to encounter, however, are smaller entities.

The particular *risks associated with the activities of all not-for-profit entities,* but particularly smaller entities that have few, if any, paid staff, include:

- non-compliance with the entity's objectives, including conditions relating to restricted funds[33] that can only be used for specific purposes within the entity's wider objectives;

- uncertainty over the completeness of income arising from voluntary donations;

- misappropriation of funds and fraud;

- lack of experience, qualifications and competencies among volunteer staff, directors, trustees or management boards;

- poor control procedures, such as a lack of segregation of duties between volunteer staff handling assets, records and master files;

- a poor control environment involving little or no oversight of day-to-day activities and infrequent trustees' meetings, for example;

- production of poor quality financial information or information produced late;

- limited access to professional advice and training, because of the perceived expense.

While *a full risk assessment is not required for a review engagement, an understanding of the entity,* its environment and the applicable financial reporting framework *is needed to identify areas in the financial statements where material misstatements are likely to arise.* Areas to understand are similar to those noted above for audits, but not in as much depth or detail.

*Substantive procedures, tests of control effectiveness, inquiries and analytical procedures For an audit, tests of control effectiveness and substantive procedures* are likely responses to assessed risks of material misstatements in:

- a statement of financial activities, i.e. income and expenditure, or receipts and payments for smaller entities, including movements of and transfers between funds, and related notes;

- assets in a balance sheet or statement of assets, and related notes.

Auditors also read the trustees' and/or directors' or combined report, depending on what is required, for consistency with the financial statements.

For *review engagements, appropriate procedures include inquiries and analytical procedures* in areas practitioners assess as likely to be subject to material misstatement.

---

[33] General funds can be applied to all of the entity's objectives. An entity's objective might be the education of orphans. Restricted funds are those granted or donated to the entity for specified purposes and subject to conditions which may include the repayment of all or part of the grant/donation if it is not spent as specified.

Practitioners will not seek to corroborate explanations or develop such precise expectations for analytical procedures as they would for an audit.

*Income*

The main risk associated with income for not-for-profit entities is often of understatement (or incompleteness) associated with fraud, and errors arising in connection with poor accounting systems and internal controls, branches, fundraising groups and professional fund-raisers.

In addition to any income from trading divisions, not-for-profit income often includes:

- *cash donations*: where cash is collected at events such as carnivals, fairs or street parties, at private events or in public places such as shopping centres, sealed, numerically identified collections buckets or tins are often used and two persons should be present when they are issued, returned, opened, the money counted and amounts recorded;

- *postal donations*: the post should also be opened by two persons to ensure that cheques, cash and postal orders are correctly recorded and banked. Tests of control effectiveness might check the signatures of both people dealing with the cash received, and the signature of an accountant or other person reviewing amounts received in a larger entity. Substantive procedures might include checking that the amounts recorded in the cash book and paying in slips agree with the bank statement, and vice versa. Surprise checks might be appropriate for some entities.

- *on-line donations made into bank accounts*: important controls here are the controls imposed by banks when accounts are set up. There should be proper authorisation of the account by trustees or directors, for example, and the entity needs to exercise controls ensuring that donors can be identified and receipts matched to promises. Tests of control effectiveness and substantive procedures might involve reconciling bank income with recorded receipts;

- *deeds of covenant:* in many jurisdictions the donor as well as the entity benefit from tax advantages and deeds of covenant are the legal documents which facilitate this. Tests of control effectiveness might involve ensuring that there has been a review to ensure that deeds are properly signed, substantive procedures might include checking that the promise to pay has actually resulted in payment and that the relevant tax has been claimed and received;

- *legacies:* not-for-profit entities are usually informed by persons wishing to leave them money or assets that they intend to do so, and such entities often ask for a copy of the will and details of the executors and relevant professional advisers. The entity needs mechanisms to ensure that it learns when the donor has passed away and to ensure that the money or assets are then collected. Tests of these controls and substantive procedures checking that money and assets are received may be performed.

- *donations in kind*: these include books and clothes and more valuable assets such as property, furniture and works of art, some of which need to be valued for inclusion in the balance sheet or statement of assets. Controls over the security of such assets can be tested and substantive procedures can be performed on valuation reports provided by experts whose independence and competence need to be assessed, as they would be in the audit of a for-profit entity;

- *grants*: controls should exist so that applications for grants are properly authorised and approved, the receipt of grants is checked and conditions attached to how grants are to be spent are complied with. If controls exist in these areas, as they should do even in smaller entities, practitioners may conduct tests of control effectiveness. Checking a simple calendar of when receipts from grants are due might serve as a control. Substantive procedures, such as checking that monies have actually been received and that disbursements have been made in accordance with the relevant conditions, should always be performed, not least because grants often become repayable if conditions are not complied with. Grants for regional and youth funds are often paid on condition that the money is spent within the region or on facilities that are predominantly used by people under the age of 30, for example, and records proving that these conditions have been met are important.

*Expenditure and balance sheets or statements of assets*
The expenditure, balance sheets and statements of assets of not-for-profit and for-profit entities are similar, except that expenditure incurred in generating income and expenditure on the objects of the entity need to be clearly distinguished. The main risk is that funds are misused and/or that the recorded funds are misstated. Controls within accounting systems to ensure the correct use and recording of funds can be tested and substantive procedures can be performed on individual funds and expenditure accounts within the general ledger.

Tests of assets and liabilities such as cash, receivables and payables, tests on leases, which are often held by sports clubs, and on assets that require valuation, are the same as those that would be performed for for-profit entities.

*Movements on funds*
Transfers between funds need to be authorised and properly disclosed. They may or may not require actual transfers of money between bank accounts.

*Analytical procedures*
Practitioners can perform analytical procedures on a weekly, monthly, quarterly, half-yearly or annual basis, as appropriate, comparing the following relationships:

- income to fund-raising expenditure, which is a key ratio for regulators;

- investment income to investments;

- charitable expenditure to income: many not-for-profit entities specify that a certain percentage of income must be used for the objects of the entity during a given period.[34]

---

[34] Many not-for-profit entities struggle to spend their income because the amounts raised are larger than needed to cover routine activities, but too small for the major projects they might wish to undertake.

The effectiveness of analytical procedures depends on the quality of the systems producing the information on which it is based and practitioners need to be wary of over-reliance on small, poorly controlled systems. Larger systems producing management accounts may be more reliable and comparisons with forecasts and budgets may be possible.

*Trustees' and directors' reports*
Trustees' and directors' reports cover matters such as entities':

- structure, governance and management;

- aims and objectives and activities;

- achievements and performance;

- performance and reserves policy;

- future plans;

- volunteer and administrative information.

As always, it is important that the credibility of the financial information is not undermined by other information issued with it and auditors should read that information for inconsistencies with the financial statements and material misstatements of fact,[35] as well as for any other purposes.


## 9.6.5    REPORTING AUDIT AND REVIEW CONCLUSIONS

Reporting requirements for not-for-profit entities remain highly jurisdiction-specific, simply because most not-for-profit entities are small and operate within national boundaries. For audit engagements, the ISA 700, 705 and 706 reporting requirements apply, as do the requirements of ISAs dealing with written representations, going concern and subsequent events, for example.

For review engagements, ISRE 2400 reporting requirements apply.

Local reporting requirements may be added to IAASB requirements, or take their place. If practitioners wish to claim compliance with IAASB standards, the locally prescribed wording for reports may be used, provided it is unlikely to result in misunderstandings about the level of assurance. Additional wording may be necessary to clarify the situation. Local requirements to report on the *accuracy* or *correctness* of financial information prepared by not-for-profit entities may well lead to misunderstandings. Agreed-upon procedures or compilation engagements may be more appropriate in some cases.

**Section essentials: what you need to remember**

- *The characteristics of smaller entities, including uncomplicated transactions and record keeping, few internal controls, few product lines, a limited number of staff and/or management.*

---

[35] As required by ISA 720 on other information.

- *The importance of the attitude, awareness and actions of an owner-manager to the control environment in a smaller entity.*

- *The difference between audits and reviews in terms of the procedures performed, the assurance obtained and reporting requirements.*

- *Compilation and agreed-upon procedures engagements do not involve assurance. Their value lies in bringing the practitioners' specialist skills to bear on the relevant financial information using professional standards in the context of ethical requirements and ISQC 1.*

- *The characteristics of not-for-profit entities, how they are managed, sources of income, how it is controlled, and restrictions on the distribution of funds.*

# SECTION 9, QUESTION

Professional accountants provide a very wide range of services to their clients, including:

- audit engagements;
- review engagements;
- agreed-upon procedures;
- compilation engagements.

The work performed and any assurance obtained when providing such services vary significantly. It is particularly important that users of reports understand the different levels of assurance.

You are a new partner in Danco. Following a meeting with a potential new client Mattco, you have agreed to write a letter to the company helping them decide which of your services they need.

Mattco operates a chain of three dry cleaning shops. It is seeking to raise funds from the bank to acquire two more local shops. The bank has indicated that among other things, it would like a certification of the next set of financial statements, quickly, to enable it to decide whether to provide funding.

Mattco's bookkeeper has prepared financial statements in the past but there have been problems with non-compliance with IFRS, which are applicable in your jurisdiction.

Required:

Write a letter to Mattco outlining for audit engagements, review engagements, agreed-upon procedures and compilation engagements the:

- nature of the work performed;
- level of assurance obtained if any, and the content of the report provided;
- type of information produced or reported on.

Explain to Mattco which of the services you think might be suitable in the circumstances.

There is no statutory audit requirement in your jurisdiction. You are not required to deal with prospective financial information. You should assume that the required criteria for assurance engagements have been met.

(20 marks)

# 10 OTHER ASSURANCE ENGAGEMENTS

**Covering:** *Types of Other Assurance Engagement, Key Performance Indicators, Social and Environmental Reporting and* ISAE 3410 *Assurance Engagements on Greenhouse Gas Statements,* ISAE 3400 *The Examination of Prospective Financial Information,* ISAE 3420 *Assurance Engagements to Report on the Compilation of Pro Forma Financial Information Included in a Prospectus.*

## Why do I need to read this section?

*Prospective financial information, social and environmental reporting, greenhouse gas statements and pro-forma financial information are areas that are neither as obscure nor as complex as their names might appear. Students who become general practitioners are likely to encounter at least some of them more often than they might think. Prospective financial information, in the form of financial forecasts and projections, is particularly common in applications for loans and funding. Understanding how specific examples of this type of assurance engagement work makes it much easier to comprehend assurance engagements generally.*

*Social and environmental reporting is a rapidly developing area and, while it is still largely confined to very large companies, it is likely to become the norm for smaller entities over time.*

## What is important in this section?

- *Understanding that in all cases, auditors and practitioners report on information that is the responsibility of management.*

- *Understanding that reasonable and limited assurance engagements can be performed on the same information, such as greenhouse gas statements, and that if it is not possible to perform a reasonable assurance engagement, it will not be possible to perform a limited assurance engagement either.*

- *Understanding how an entity might develop key performance indicators and how assurance might be provided on them.*

- *The difference between forecasts and projections, and the nature of pro-forma financial information.*

## What sort of questions come up in this area?

*ISAE 3400 on prospective financial information is well established and relatively straightforward questions are sometimes set on procedures to be applied to cash flow projections and forecasts, and on the contents of reports on such information.*

*Questions sometimes ask for examples of suitable key performance indicators in a given set of circumstances. Social and environmental reporting is likely to be examined more now that ISAE 3410 on greenhouse gas statements has been issued. The ISAE very clearly demonstrates the differences between reasonable and limited assurance engagements.*

*Prospective financial information, greenhouse gas statements and pro-forma financial information tend to be included in the syllabuses of higher-level papers. Check this before reading this section.*

**How do I stand out from the crowd?**
*Display an understanding of:*

- *the relative merits of reasonable and limited assurance engagements in the context of social and environmental reporting, and which might be better in a given situation;*

- *the purpose of prospective financial information and the limitations of the assurance that can be provided on it.*

# 10.1   INTRODUCTION TO OTHER ASSURANCE ENGAGEMENTS

## 10.1.1   TYPES OF ASSURANCE ENGAGEMENT CURRENTLY PERFORMED

Many practitioners have never performed an assurance engagement other than an audit, and some never will, but this is changing.

Prospective financial information includes budgets, forecasts and financial projections and practitioners are increasingly asked to provide assurance on such information, often in support of applications for loan finance. Prospective financial information has been examined in auditing papers for a long time.

The issue of ISAE 3000 on assurance engagements other than audits or reviews of historical financial information has given examiners the scope to examine students' understanding of key performance indicators. Examiners also test students' understanding of the limited ability of practitioners to provide assurance on such figures. Practitioners cannot provide reports on KPIs for which there is no suitable reporting framework, i.e. no suitable criteria, but they can perform agreed-upon procedures engagements.

It remains to be seen how reporting on greenhouse gas emissions and similar social and environmental reporting requirements develop, particularly for smaller entities. Entities of all sizes that produce such information are likely to need or want some practitioner involvement, either with its preparation or with the provision of assurance on it to enhance its credibility. Governments and securities regulators everywhere are requiring or encouraging larger entities to produce such information.

Other assurance services on internal controls and on compliance with regulations and codes of conduct such as corporate governance codes are being developed as larger companies broaden the scope of their reporting beyond financial reporting. In the long term, this will have an effect on the way smaller entities report.

Only a few practitioners are likely to be asked to report on the compilation of pro-forma financial information included in a prospectus but the area is well established and more straightforward, at least from an exam point of view, than might be expected.

## 10.1.2 REVISION OF THE BASIC ELEMENTS OF ASSURANCE ENGAGEMENTS

We have seen that ISAE 3000[1] covers assurance engagements other than audits and reviews of historical financial information. It applies to all forward-looking information such as prospective financial information, and any historical information that does not amount to a set of financial statements, such as greenhouse gas statements, key performance indicators (KPIs), the effectiveness of internal controls, and statements of compliance with laws and regulations or corporate governance codes. Such information can be provided voluntarily, as part of a contract, in applications for funding or for regulatory purposes as may be the case for statements on internal control effectiveness or compliance with corporate governance codes.

We have also seen that all assurance engagements require:

- a *three party relationship*;
- an appropriate underlying *subject matter*;
- suitable *criteria*;
- *evidence*;
- an *assurance report*.[2]

Suitable *criteria* are often a problem. Where there is no established framework, such as COSO for internal controls, or IFRS for financial information, or any corporate governance codes, criteria need to be developed that are *relevant, reliable, complete, neutral and understandable*. The cost of this development may be prohibitive and, in such cases, agreed-upon procedures, rather than an assurance engagement may be more appropriate.

The type of *evidence* required depends on whether the engagement is a reasonable or limited assurance engagement. Reasonable assurance engagements require a full risk assessment and response. Limited assurance engagements require inquiries, analytical procedures and sometimes other procedures depending on the requirements of any relevant ISAE. Both require an analysis of the risk of material misstatement in order to design appropriate responses, in the case of reasonable assurance, and appropriate procedures, in the case of limited assurance.

---

[1]  ISAE 3000 on assurance engagements other than audits and reviews of historical financial information.
[2]  *Framework,* paragraph 4.

Finally, we have seen that assurance reports contain the following elements:

- *title and addressee;*

- *introductory paragraph* identifying the information reported on and the criteria used;

- *responsibilities of the party* responsible for the information;

- *responsibilities of the practitioner* to conduct the engagement in accordance with ethical requirements, ISQC 1 and ISAEs, and an informative summary of the work performed;

- *a conclusion* in the form of an opinion on truth and fairness/fair presentation in a reasonable assurance engagement, and in a limited engagement, a conclusion as to whether anything has come to the practitioners' attention to indicate that the subject matter information is materially misstated;

- *signature, date* and *location.*

## 10.2   ASSURANCE OR AGREED-UPON PROCEDURES: KEY PERFORMANCE INDICATORS

*Key performance indicators (KPIs) are often reported* and analysts pay a great deal of attention to them, but they cannot be the subject matter of an assurance engagement unless there is some sort of framework, either specifically developed or referring to established industry benchmarks, that can be used by practitioners to evaluate them. KPIs need to be specific, measurable, achievable, realistic and timely.

KPIs often appear in information issued with audited financial statements that auditors need to read for consistency with the audited financial statements and for material misstatements of fact,[3] but not audited or reviewed. KPIs also often appear in applications for funding or capital and there is sometimes an expectation that practitioners will be able to 'certify' them, however, in the absence of a framework, agreed-upon procedures may be the best that can be achieved.

The basic problem with KPIs for which there is no framework, is that they can be calculated in many different ways. Even if there is full disclosure of how they have been calculated, there is still ample scope for incompleteness or bias that will not necessarily be apparent from the disclosure. Simple operational KPIs such as the percentage of orders despatched within 24 hours are subject to many variables such as orders only being counted if they are in inventory, or are national rather than international deliveries, or are sales to established customers where it takes time to set up an account. A framework would also need to deal with potential distortions arising from high volumes of returns because of incorrect despatches. Similarly, operational KPIs regarding the time taken to answer calls are distorted if, for example, callers are regularly cut off immediately after the phone is answered, or are immediately put on hold.

---

[3]  ISA 720 on other information.

KPIs can be categorised as operational, financial, and social and environmental.

*Operational KPIs* might include the:

- percentage of repeat business for holiday companies;
- percentage of orders despatched within 24 hours of receipt;
- percentage of orders returned;
- percentage of calls answered within 7 minutes;
- percentage of calls completed within 20 minutes;
- number of visitors to an attraction and the number of educational visits;
- occupancy rates for hotels;
- percentage of arrivals and departures on schedule for airlines and train companies.

*Agreed-upon procedures* for such operational KPIs might include:

- reading summaries of orders and checking their extraction from the system on a sample basis;
- reading internal audit or external consultants' reports on the quality of design and effective implementation of internal controls systems that produce call centre data, or aggregated occupancy data for chains of hotels;
- observing the arrivals and departures of planes and trains and checking to ensure that the arrival/departure concerned is correctly recorded;
- performing test counts on the number of visitors;
- performing analytical procedures on the levels of calls answered, timing of calls, returns of goods, occupancy rates, visitor numbers and arrivals and departures information.

*Financial KPIs* include gross profit margins, sales per square metre, growth rates for particular product sales, growth rates in a particular region, and return on capital employed for particular investments.

The financial element of some financial KPIs can effectively be extracted from the audited financial statements, but this does not mean that assurance can be provided on them in the absence of a framework. The audit opinion is on the truth and fairness or fair presentation of the financial statements as a whole, not on individual elements.

Agreed-upon procedures on parts of such KPIs would nevertheless involve procedures similar to audit procedures that may have already been performed during the audit. The denominator in some such KPIs, such as the square metres in sales per square metres calculations, and the calculation of the growth rates, however, are not part of the audited financial statements. Procedures such as checking that growth rates are calculated consistently across regions and that figures have been extracted accurately from regional data on a sample basis might be appropriate in such cases.

*Social KPIs* might include absolute figures and percentage changes in:

*Staff*

- The proportion of female and ethnic minority employees;
- employee satisfaction rates;
- employee evaluation of in-company training;
- staff turnover;
- accident/hospitalisation/fatality rates, particularly in heavy industries;

*Customers and Community*

- Customers indicating that they are at least satisfied with the goods/services that they have purchased, or the cleanliness of the hotel room they stayed in;
- repeat bookings at a hotel;
- staff hours dedicated to company sponsored community activities;
- sporting/artistic/charitable events, exhibitions or programmes sponsored and the value of donations such as staff time, know-how, goods and services and facilities;
- charitable donations in cash.

*Agreed-upon procedures* in respect of social KPIs might include:

- examination of HR and payroll records to check the extraction of data;
- arithmetical checks on percentages and other calculations performed;
- reading internal audit or external consultants' summaries of employee and customer satisfaction surveys and checking on a sample basis the extraction of information from the underlying data.

*Environmental KPIs* include absolute figures and percentage changes in:

- waste produced, energy and water consumed;
- cardboard, plastic and paper recycled;
- environmentally friendly consumables used such as paper, light bulbs and cleaning materials;
- environmentally friendly materials used in the construction of buildings;
- carbon emissions.

ISAE 3410 on greenhouse gas statements provides guidance on reasonable and limited assurance engagements on greenhouse gas statements dealing with carbon emissions where they are part of an established reporting framework.

*Agreed-upon procedures* for environmental KPIs other than carbon emissions might include:

- comparisons of actual to target reductions in the use of electricity or water in total and per unit of output;

- inspection on a sample basis of the type of paper, bulbs, cleaning materials and other consumables used at various sites and facilities;

- inspection of recycling facilities to confirm their existence;

- reading or commissioning reports prepared by internal or external experts on the calibration of instruments used to measure the consumption of electricity and water, noting reports of any material errors;

- checking the arithmetical accuracy of schedules supporting the KPIs and their extraction from underlying records;

- checking on a sample basis from source documentation recording of volumes of cardboard, plastic and paper recycled through to the KPIs, and vice versa.

## 10.3 SOCIAL AND ENVIRONMENTAL REPORTING AND ISAE 3410 ASSURANCE ENGAGEMENTS OF GREENHOUSE GAS STATEMENTS

Social and environmental reporting, sustainability reporting and triple-bottom-line reporting overlap. The area is developing rapidly and the terminology changes regularly. There are numerous projects to codify best practice in reporting and social attitudes, regulations outlawing the use of toxic materials, customer preferences and the behaviour of competitors all continue to increase pressure on larger companies in particular to provide information on:

- employment practices, including child labour;

- health and safety records;

- the ethical sourcing of raw materials, supply chain materials management and supply chain audits;

- charitable donations and social engagement, by providing health and educational facilities for the use of staff and the communities in which entities operate, for example;

- reductions in the use of energy, water and waste materials;

- increases in recycling and the use of recycled materials for fuel and packaging, for example;

- reductions in the use of packaging;

- the use of energy-efficient building materials and consumables such as paper, light bulbs and cleaning materials;

- carbon emissions, targets for their reduction and targets for spills and fugitive emissions (leaks from pipes).

Targets can be set internally or correspond to external targets set by government, industry groups or market leaders.

Assurance report providers for social and environmental reports include large firms of accountants who employ non-accountant specialists in the area and some very small specialist providers. In all cases, the report requires the combined expertise of practitioners and experts in the field reported on. There is little regulation of assurance reporting on greenhouse gas statements and there are many consultancies offering assurance services that do not employ professional accountants. The competence of these consultancies varies. Large firms of accountants emphasise the fact that, where they provide assurance reports on greenhouse gas statements, their services are offered within the context of quality control requirements, compliance with ethical requirements and the framework of IAASB standards. Other consultants may not be subject to these requirements, although they may adopt them voluntarily.[4]

Reporting on greenhouse gas statements is still mostly by larger entities[5] but over time, reporting methodologies will become established and smaller entities are more likely to follow suit. Assurance reports presented with these statements enhance their credibility.

Obtaining evidence to provide an assurance report on greenhouse gas statements is not difficult. To do so, it is necessary to understand the rudiments of greenhouse gases but beyond that, the principles that apply to any assurance engagement apply. ISAE 3000 on assurance engagements applies to this type of assurance engagement and together with ISAE 3410 on greenhouse gas statements they cover *acceptance, planning, evidence, documentation and reporting.*

### 10.3.1   GREENHOUSE GASES

Every business emits greenhouse gases such as carbon dioxide, nitrous oxide and fluorinated gases. Greenhouse gas emissions can be:

- direct (Scope 1) emissions from sources owned or controlled by the entity, such as emissions from *factories, vehicles used for transporting goods, boilers and incinerators* including fugitive emissions (leaks);

- indirect (Scope 2) emissions associated with energy from sources owned or controlled by another entity but transferred to and consumed by the reporting entity, such as *electricity, heat or steam*;

---

[4]   ISAE 3410 on greenhouse gas statements can be used by anyone provided they comply with all of its requirements, including those relating to quality control and ethical requirements, or their equivalents.

[5]   Reporting on greenhouse gas emissions is required for entities listed on the London Stock Exchange's main market as of 2013.

- indirect (Scope 3) emissions, such as emissions arising from *employee air travel*, emissions arising from outsourced activities, emissions arising from the use of the entity's products which may be substantial for any manufacturer of electronic equipment, and emissions arising from the extraction of the raw materials purchased from third parties.

Many entities in the service sector with no scope 1 emissions may only have scope 2 emissions that are relatively easy to measure and convert using supplier invoices and widely available conversion factors. Scope 3 emissions can be difficult to deal with because of the variation in calculations of emissions factors by airlines, the need to draw a line at the operational boundary at which point an entity's responsibility for emissions stops and the fact that many such emissions will also be counted by other entities.

### Greenhouse gas statements

Greenhouse gas statements quantify emissions. They are produced in connection with emissions trading schemes,[6] for regulatory purposes in many jurisdictions or voluntarily as part of a larger sustainability report, for example. Government and other bodies[7] provide measurement and reporting guidelines and in some industries, some KPIs involving greenhouse gases have become critical. The weighted average emissions per kilometre of vehicles have a direct impact on the manufacture and taxation of those vehicles in many jurisdictions.

> Greenhouse gases are either physically measured at source, or emissions are estimated by multiplying activity data, such as the amount of fuel used, by emissions conversion factors. There are many greenhouse gases and, to facilitate comparison, gases other than carbon dioxide are often quantified using carbon dioxide equivalents.

Greenhouse gas statements often include:

- *removals* of gases through biological sinks such as trees, or geological sinks underground;

- *deductions* such as purchased offsets, in which *an entity pays another entity* to:

  - reduce emissions;

  - increase removal by planting trees, for example;

  - not increase emissions, by not undertaking deforestation, for example.

Deductions can also arise from jurisdiction-specific credits unrelated to changes in emissions.

---

[6] Emissions trading schemes are sometimes known as 'cap-and-trade' schemes, such as the EU Emission Trading Scheme (EU ETS). Firms are required to hold permits known as 'carbon credits' representing their emissions which may not exceed the cap. Firms needing to reduce their emissions must buy permits from those who require fewer permits. The trading of permits means that buyers pay for polluting and sellers are rewarded for reducing emissions. Carbon credits are traded on several exchanges including the European Climate Exchange (EXC). Carbon has become one of the world's leading traded commodities.

[7] Bodies such as the Department for Environment, Food and Rural Affairs (DEFRA) in the UK provide conversion factors and reporting templates.

*Reasonable and limited assurance*

> Assurance on greenhouse gas statements can be either reasonable or limited assurance.
>
> An agreed-upon procedures engagement might be more suitable than an assurance engagement for an entity with little or no greenhouse gas reporting experience.
>
> As with all assurance engagements, if it is not possible to obtain reasonable assurance, it will not be possible to obtain limited assurance as the five criteria for assurance engagements are the same, regardless of whether reasonable or limited assurance is obtained.

## 10.3.2   ACCEPTANCE, PLANNING AND UNDERSTANDING THE ENTITY

The engagement partner is responsible for ensuring the right blend of competencies to perform the engagement. Multi-disciplinary teams are normally required combining assurance skills and greenhouse gas competencies, which may include scientific, engineering and IT skills. Someone needs to understand the calibration of equipment measuring emissions, for example.

The engagement partner must also be satisfied that preconditions for engagement acceptance are met and in particular that:

- the greenhouse gas statement and the engagement are at least capable of being *useful to intended users,* taking account of the *exclusion of any significant emissions* and the *inclusion of deductions,* both of which may represent significant risks;
- *criteria are suitable,* i.e. that the *quantification methods* and *reporting policies including disclosures* are complete, relevant, reliable, neutral and understandable and enable users to understand the significant judgements made, including the organisational boundary,[8] the categorisation of emissions and the quantification methods used, for example;[9]
- the entity *acknowledges its responsibilities* for the *preparation* of the greenhouse gas statement in accordance with suitable criteria and the maintenance of *internal controls* to facilitate this.

Engagement terms agreed need to cover the objective and scope of the engagement, the respective responsibilities of the entity and practitioners, the criteria to be used, the form and content of the assurance report and an agreement by the entity to provide written representations.

The definition of materiality is very similar to the definition for the purposes of financial statement audits: matter(s) are material if they could reasonably be expected to influence

---

[8]   The reporting boundaries in a large group of entities with many subsidiaries, associates and joint ventures need to be clear.
[9]   Criteria are developed or promoted by bodies such as the International Integrated Reporting Council (IIRC), the Global Reporting Initiative (GRI) and The Prince's Accounting for Sustainability Project (A4S).

relevant decisions of users taken on the basis of greenhouse gas statements. Users are likely to include regulators and market participants in emissions trading schemes. A percentage applied to a benchmark such as gross reported emissions may need to be adjusted for volatility in emissions, and qualitative matters to be taken account of include whether intended users are likely to focus on a particular type of emission.

The procedures required to understand the entity, its internal control and to assess risks for obtaining reasonable assurance on a greenhouse gas statement are very similar to those required for an audit. Practitioners need to understand the industry, the regulatory environment in which the entity operates, its operations and emissions, changes from the prior period, the entity's climate change objectives and who is responsible for emissions information and the applicable criteria.

### 10.3.3   RISK ASSESSMENTS, RESPONSES AND PROCEDURES PERFORMED

Both reasonable and limited assurance engagements involve, as with a financial statement audit, a *risk assessment* through *understanding the entity* and its environment *including its internal control and performing procedures to address risks*. The main differences between reasonable and limited assurance engagements are that for limited assurance:

- practitioners do *not require an understanding of internal control components*, and they do *not need to evaluate the design and implementation* of controls *or test controls*, which means that they are likely to focus on the control environment and high level controls such as the entity's own risk assessment process;

- the *risk assessment* requires *inquiries only* and is *at the overall financial statement level and for material types of emissions*, it is *not* at the assertion level (completeness, accuracy, occurrence, etc.) as it would be for a reasonable assurance engagement. Practitioners determine their own responses to risks, which are not prescribed;

- for *analytical procedures, expectations* of emissions quantities or ratios do not need to be developed as precisely as they do for reasonable assurance engagements, and *inquiries rather than investigations* are required where differences arise;

- for *estimates,* practitioners only need consider whether *further procedures* are necessary whereas for reasonable assurance engagements, as with audits of financial information, one or more specific procedures is required including testing controls,[10] developing a point estimate or a range for comparison with that of the client, and testing how the entity made the estimate.

Analytical procedures are not *required* for either type of engagement but either analytical procedures or tests of details (i.e. some substantive procedures) are required for reasonable assurance engagements. Expectations may link the relationship between scope 2 emissions, production levels and energy costs, for example.

---

[10] Tests of controls might involve testing instruments used in measuring emissions.

For all engagements, as with all financial statement audits, practitioners make inquiries regarding fraud, and discuss the susceptibility of the greenhouse gas statement to material misstatement due to fraud or error within the engagement team. Where internal audit or other external experts are involved, as will often be the case, practitioners need to consider whether they are sufficiently independent and competent for practitioners to use their work. As always, the practitioners' responsibility is not reduced by use of this type of work and no reference is made to it in the assurance report. The greenhouse gas statement needs to be reconciled to the underlying records but less work on adjustments is required for limited assurance engagements.

*Risks of material misstatement* arise from complexity, quantification methods, fraud, omission of significant emissions and non-compliance with laws and regulations, particularly where there are changes in the business. An entity with significant scope 1 emissions that only reported scope 2 emissions would create a risk as would a situation in which practitioners were only asked to report on a small part of the greenhouse gas statement. An entity's objectives are important if public statements are made, undertakings are given or imposed, or compensation is dependent on the achievement of specific reductions targets or dates for becoming carbon neutral, for example, as this increases the pressure to manipulate results to show that targets have been met. Risks at the greenhouse gas statement level are higher where there is a poor control environment and in the first years of reporting.

*Responses to risk* for reasonable assurance engagements, but not limited assurance engagements, include tests of control and consideration of whether external confirmations, such as confirmations of air travel from travel agents or the results of third party analysis of the calorific value of samples, for example, might be necessary.

Requirements for all greenhouse gas engagements covering the accumulation of misstatements, written representations, subsequent events, comparative information, other information and documentation are similar to those required in financial statement audits. 'Other information' may include emissions information recalculated on a different basis to that calculated in the greenhouse gas statement and it is important that any inconsistent information that might undermine the greenhouse gas statement is removed.

Site visits to significant facilities are important, particularly when performing an engagement for the first time, to establish whether data collection procedures and estimation techniques are appropriate. A suggested benchmark to determine what is significant is a facility exceeding 15% of total production.

## 10.3.4    ASSURANCE REPORTS ON GREENHOUSE GAS STATEMENTS

Assurance reports on greenhouse gas statements require, as for all assurance reports:

- a *title* and *addressee*;
- identification of the *information reported on* and the *criteria*, i.e. the reporting framework used;
- the *preparer's responsibilities*;

- the *practitioners' responsibilities* to conduct the engagement in accordance with ethical requirements, ISQC 1 and ISAE 3410 on greenhouse gas statements, and an *informative summary of the work performed*;

- *conclusion, signature, date* and *location*.

In practice, the summary of the work performed can be extensive, particularly for limited assurance engagements where the procedures prescribed by ISAE 3410 are not as detailed as they are for reasonable assurance engagements. It often constitutes a substantial proportion of the report. The summary should not be overstated or imply a higher level of assurance than was actually obtained.

In addition, all assurance reports on greenhouse gas statements:

- state that the greenhouse gas quantification is subject to *inherent uncertainty* as a result of *scientific uncertainty* about the nature and effects of greenhouse gases[11] and *estimation/measurement uncertainty*.[12] Where the combined uncertainty is *very high*, practitioners do not accept engagements to report on greenhouse gas statements;

- state that the engagement was carried out by a *multi-disciplinary team* where that is the case, as it usually is.

*Reasonable assurance* engagement reports:

- give the practitioners' *opinion* on whether the greenhouse gas statement *has been prepared in all material respects in accordance with applicable criteria;*

- contain a *standardised list of procedures* that are always performed.

*Limited assurance* engagement reports:

- give the practitioners' *conclusion* on whether anything has *come to their attention to make them believe that the greenhouse gas statement has not been prepared in all material respects in accordance with the applicable criteria;*

- *summarise the procedures performed* and *not performed* and state that the procedures are *less than* those that would have been performed in a reasonable assurance engagement.

Emphases of matter in reports on greenhouse gas statements operate as they do for financial statements audits, to draw the readers' attention to matters that are fundamental to understanding the greenhouse gas statement where, for example, the reporting criteria have been revised or updated since the prior period. Similarly, 'other matter' paragraphs operate to draw readers' attention to matters relating to the assignment,

---

[11] There is scientific uncertainty about the rate of removal in biological sinks and the global warming potential of various amounts and combinations of greenhouse gas, for example.

[12] Measurement/estimation uncertainty can arise from the calibration of measurement equipment and where estimation techniques are used, particularly if they are specific to the entity.

perhaps where the scope of the engagement has changed from prior periods to include or exclude a new category of emissions.

## 10.4   PROSPECTIVE FINANCIAL INFORMATION

Prospective financial information (PFI) consists of *forecasts* and *projections* based on assumptions about *events that may occur and possible actions* by an entity.[13]

*Forecasts,* like weather forecasts are based on assumptions about events that are *expected to take place,* and *actions management expects to take,* collectively known as *best estimate assumptions.* Forecasts can be prepared part way through a period and combine unaudited historical information with best estimate assumptions about the remainder of the period.

*Projections* are prepared based on *hypothetical assumptions* about future events and management actions that are *not necessarily expected to take place,* during times of uncertainty such as *start-ups,* or when there are major changes in operations. They can be mixed with best-estimate assumptions and enable management to demonstrate what might happen in various different circumstances.

PFI includes forecast or projected financial statements, which can be used internally to evaluate projects or investments, using different assumptions about revenue, return on capital, and interest and exchange rates, for example. PFI also includes information made public or provided to third parties in prospectuses or for potential lenders, for example. As always, management is responsible for the preparation and presentation of the information including the assumptions on which it is based and auditors may be asked to report on it, or may be required to report on it by securities regulators, for example.

Reporting is *not* on whether the forecast or projection will be achieved.[14] Conclusions are expressed on whether:

- *anything has come to the auditors' attention* that causes the auditors to believe that the assumptions do not provide a reasonable basis for the PFI, i.e. *limited assurance on the assumptions underlying the PFI;*
- the PFI is *properly prepared* on the basis of the assumptions in accordance with the financial reporting framework, i.e. *reasonable assurance on the PFI itself.*

### 10.4.1   ENGAGEMENT ACCEPTANCE

As always, engagement terms should be agreed, preferably in writing, to avoid misunderstandings and should cover the provision of information by the entity to auditors,

---

[13] ISAE 3400 on prospective financial information.

[14] Auditors rarely, if ever, report on *outcome* rather than *process,* unless compelled to do so by law or regulation. Law in many jurisdictions *requires* reporting on the truth and fairness or fair presentation of financial statements.

the responsibility of the entity for the PFI, the intended use and distribution of the information, the type of assumptions to be used and the format and period to be covered.

If assumptions are clearly unrealistic or the information inappropriate for its intended use, auditors do not accept the engagement. The longer the period covered, the less management is able to make best estimate assumptions; therefore, the period should not extend beyond that for which management has a reasonable basis for the assumptions, taking account of operating cycles and the needs of users. Auditors also need to comply with ethical requirements and ISQC 1.

### 10.4.2 UNDERSTANDING THE BUSINESS

The auditors' understanding of the business needs to:

- be sufficient to *evaluate whether management has identified all significant assumptions;*
- cover the *process* for preparing the information, including the internal controls, the experience of staff, the methods used to develop and apply assumptions and the accuracy of PFI prepared in prior periods.

To some extent PFI is always based on historical financial information and should be consistent with it. Auditors have more confidence in the process if the historical information was audited or reviewed.

### 10.4.3 PROCEDURES

Procedures are not prescribed but will be developed on the basis of the:

- auditors' consideration of the risk of material misstatement, although no formal risk assessment is required;
- auditors' experience of management's competence and past record in this area;
- extent to which the information is affected by management's judgement;
- adequacy and reliability of the underlying information.

Specific procedures focus on:

- whether best estimate or hypothetical assumptions seem at least feasible, i.e. the entity appears capable of them, and they are not clearly unrealistic in the case of hypothetical assumptions;
- the reliability of best-estimate assumptions in the light of past experience;
- where hypothetical assumptions are issued, whether all *significant implications* have been considered, such as the need for investment to support sales growth, and whether such assumptions are internally consistent between the various elements of the PFI, such as the need for consistency between assumptions about revenues and cash flows;

- re-computation and other clerical checks on the accuracy of calculations;
- areas that are particularly sensitive to variation, such as small changes in assumptions about growth, interest or exchange rates that would have a material effect on the PFI.

*Written representations* are needed covering management's responsibility for the PFI, its intended use and for the completeness of assumptions.

*Presentation and disclosure* need to comply with the financial reporting requirements. Auditors also need to consider:

- whether the PFI is misleading;
- whether assumptions, their type, sensitivity and associated uncertainties have been adequately disclosed;
- any changes in accounting policy since the most recent historical financial information.

### 10.4.4 SPECIFIC PROCEDURES FOR INCOME, EXPENDITURE, CASH FLOWS AND WORKING CAPITAL

PFI typically includes income, expenditure, cash flows, working capital requirements and capital expenditure.

Projected or forecast *income* is likely to be the most subjective and contentious figure. Procedures might include checking:

- *assumptions* about growth in markets, market share, the effects of advertising, marketing and changes in foreign exchange rates. These need to be reasonable and internally and externally consistent, in the light of the practitioners' understanding of the business and the environment in which the entity currently operates, and has operated in historically;
- the entity's *track record* regarding assumptions by performing *analytical procedures* comparing actual to budgeted exchange rates, for example;
- projected or forecast sales prices per unit to existing *market rates* for similar items;
- the *calculation* of income on the basis of assumptions used.

Projected or forecast *expenditure* is easier to deal with as it is under the control of the entity. Procedures might include checking the:

- entity's *track record* of over-spending or under-budgeting;
- relationships between current expenditure and income such as *established relationships* between marketing spend and income, as a basis for predicting future trends;
- *calculation* of expenditure on the basis of the assumptions used.

Good *working capital management* can be critical in industries such as fast moving consumer goods, food and clothing, and forecasts and projections are highly sensitive to the timing of cash flows, small changes in exchange rates, interest rates, inflation and other macro-economic factors which can affect supply and demand. Procedures might include:

- performing analyses sensitivity to changes in interest or exchange rates on working capital, income and expenditure;
- establishing the extent to which working capital requirements depend on external financing and the terms and conditions attached thereto;
- checking the reasonableness of assumptions about the balance of inventory levels, receivables and cash in the light of the practitioners' knowledge of the business and its past performance.

*Capital expenditure* projections and even forecasts may be prone to higher levels of misstatement than other types of expenditure because of the lengthy periods covered, the specialised nature of the expenditure and unanticipated problems on large projects. Procedures might include:

- reading any contracts, quotations or other documentary evidence of negotiations with suppliers and comparing assumptions about terms and conditions with existing terms and conditions;
- considering the entity's track records of accurate capital expenditure forecasting and projections;
- checking the calculations of schedules supporting the information and the extraction of that information from supporting documentation.

### 10.4.5  REPORTING

Once again, as with all assurance reports, reports require:

- a *title* and *addressee*;
- identification of the *PFI reported on* and the *criteria*, i.e. the reporting framework used such as IFRS;
- the *preparer's responsibilities* for the PFI and the assumptions on which it is based;
- the *practitioners' responsibilities* to conduct the engagement in accordance with ethical requirements, ISQC 1 and ISAE 3400 on prospective financial information;
- *conclusions, signature, date* and *location*.

Conclusions are on whether:

- *anything has come to the auditors' attention* that causes them to believe that the *assumptions do not provide a reasonable basis for the PFI;*[15]

---

[15] A conclusion expressed in negative terms conveying limited assurance.

- the PFI is *properly prepared* on the basis of the assumptions and *in accordance with the financial reporting framework*.[16]

In addition, assurance reports on PFI:

- refer to the purpose and/or restricted distribution of the PFI where relevant;
- contain caveats (warnings) concerning the achievability of the results.[17]

Report of ABCCO to the Directors of XYZCO:

---

We have examined the forecast set out on pages x to y for the period 31 December 20X0 to 30 June 20X1. This forecast has been prepared for [describe purpose] and is not suitable for any other purposes. Actual results may be materially different from the forecast.

Management are responsible for the forecast including the assumptions on which it is based set out in Note X.

We conducted our examination in accordance with International Standard on Assurance Engagements 3400 *The Examination of Prospective Financial Information*. That standard requires us to [insert summary of procedures performed].

### Conclusions

Based on our examination of the evidence supporting the assumptions, nothing has come to our attention which causes us to believe that these assumptions do not provide a reasonable basis for the forecast.

In our opinion the forecast is properly prepared on the basis of the assumptions and is presented in accordance with International Financial Reporting Standards.

---

Modified conclusions are similar to modified audit conclusions. If the presentation or disclosure regarding assumptions is inadequate, qualified or adverse conclusions are appropriate.

If the assumptions are simply not reasonable, adverse conclusions or withdrawal from the engagement may be appropriate.

If auditors are unable to perform the necessary procedures, a disclaimer of conclusions or withdrawal may be appropriate.

---

[16] A conclusion expressed as a positive opinion on compliance with the financial reporting framework.

[17] The warning might be that the PFI is being prepared for a particular purpose such as to support an application for finance, using a set of hypothetical assumptions about future events and actions that are not necessarily expected to occur.

## 10.5   ISAE 3420 REPORTING ON THE COMPILATION OF PRO-FORMA FINANCIAL INFORMATION IN PROSPECTUSES

Pro-forma financial information is prospective financial information. It is required by securities regulators in prospectuses to illustrate the effect of proposed events and transactions that have not yet happened, so that investors can decide whether to support them. An event might be a significant investment that the entity is seeking funds for through the prospectus. A transaction might be a proposed takeover or sale of a business.

The financial effects of a proposed takeover of one entity by another cannot be illustrated simply by bolting together two sets of financial statements. The reporting dates and accounting policies are likely to be dissimilar, and the purpose of the transaction is usually to create value through synergies that also need to be taken into account. The compilation of this type of pro-forma financial information is performed where several businesses are acquired prior to a public offering of securities, and a pro-forma net asset statement and income statement are prepared to show what the business would look like.

It is important to distinguish this type of engagement, in which auditors report on management's compilation, and compilation engagements performed by practitioners.

A *three-column format* is normally used:

- unadjusted information such as audited or interim financial statements in column 1;

- pro-forma adjustments in column 2 illustrate the effect of the event or transaction and reconcile accounting policies;

- the resulting information in column 3 does not show the actual transaction, but only how the proposed transaction might appear had it been undertaken at the reporting date.

---

The practitioners' conclusion is an **opinion on whether the pro-forma information has been compiled in all material respects in accordance with the applicable criteria.**

---

In many jurisdictions securities regulators prohibit the issue of modified opinions and where an unmodified opinion cannot be issued, practitioners are presented with a difficult choice between withholding a report and withdrawing from the engagement. It may be necessary to seek legal advice.

### 10.5.1   ENGAGEMENT ACCEPTANCE

As with all assurance engagements, compliance with ethical requirements and ISQC 1 is required.

Before accepting an engagement, practitioners consider issues such as:

- the *competence* of those performing the compilation;

- whether the *criteria* to be used, as determined by the securities regulator, are likely to be suitable and whether the information produced is likely to be misleading;

- the *wording required* and whether it will be appropriate based on procedures performed;

- whether the *sources of unadjusted information* have been audited or reviewed. If the unadjusted information has never been audited or reviewed, auditors obtain an adequate understanding of that information including information about the entities to be acquired;

- the need for the reporting entity to agree to *provide practitioners with access* to all information they consider necessary for the engagement and to others within the acquired entities and their advisers, such as their auditors.

## 10.5.2 PRACTITIONER PROCEDURES

Practitioners need to obtain an *understanding of the event, transaction and compilation process* including, for example, the nature of the acquirer or disposer, and of the entities to be acquired, merged or disposed of, their operations, assets and liabilities, how they are structured and financed and the financial reporting frameworks they use. Where the information relates to a proposed investment, practitioners need an understanding of the assumptions used and the bases on which revenue and expenditure are allocated.

*Suitable criteria* are usually determined by the securities regulator requiring the information and as a minimum must include requirements that:

- the *unadjusted information* should come from an *appropriate source,* such as audited financial statements;

- *adjustments must be directly attributable* to the transaction rather than arising as a result of it. The closure of redundant sites might be a key effect of a transaction but closure is rarely part of the transaction itself;

- *adjustments must be consistent* with the financial reporting framework, appropriate for intended users, unlikely to result in misleading information and *factually supportable* by reference to, for example:

  - sale and purchase agreements;

  - financing arrangements;

  - valuations;

  - employment agreements.

*Materiality* is determined by the size and nature of the transaction and the purpose of the information compiled, which is usually to enable investors to decide whether to support the proposed event or transaction.

As in an audit of financial statements, practitioners ensure that calculations are accurate and that information has been properly extracted. They obtain appropriate external confirmations, particularly from lawyers where appropriate, obtain written representations and read other information presented with the information reported on for consistency and material misstatements of fact, as they would under ISA 720 on other information.

### 10.5.3 REPORTING

Finally, as with all assurance reports, reports require:

* a *title* and *addressee*;

* identification of the ***compiled information reported on*** and the ***criteria***, i.e. the reporting framework required by the securities regulator, the purpose of the information in connection with the transaction or event, the *source of unadjusted information* and whether it was audited or reviewed, and the period covered;

* the *preparer's responsibilities* for the compilation of the information and the assumptions on which it is based;

* the *practitioners' responsibilities* to conduct the engagement in accordance with ethical requirements, ISQC 1 and ISAE 3410,[18] that neither an audit nor a review have been conducted, that no assurance is provided and that historical information has not been updated;

* a *conclusion, signature, date* and *location*.

The conclusion is on whether the information has been compiled in all material respects in accordance with the applicable criteria, i.e. the reporting requirements of the securities regulator.

**Section essentials: what you need to remember**

* *The different types of PFI including budgets, forecasts and projections and how they are used.*

* *Different types of KPI and the agreed-upon procedures that can be performed on them.*

* *Situations in which it is not possible to provide assurance because suitable reporting criteria do not exist.*

* *The types of information appearing in social and environmental reports and greenhouse gas statements, the issues associated with providing reasonable or limited assurance on them and the need for appropriate expertise.*

---

[18] ISAE 3420 on pro-forma financial information in prospectuses.

# SECTION 10, QUESTION

Professional accountants are able to provide a very wide range of assurance engagements other than audits and reviews of historical financial information. They are not able to provide any level of assurance on any information though, as there are certain criteria that must be fulfilled if assurance is to be provided under ISAE 3000 *Assurance Engagements Other than Audits or Reviews of Historical Financial Information*.

Reporting on social and environmental matters is mandatory for large entities in many jurisdictions. Professional accountants may be asked to report on such matters. ISAE 3410 *Assurance Engagements on Greenhouse Gas Statements* deals with one particular type of environmental report.

**Required:**

(a) Give five examples of the type of information on which professional accountants can provide assurance, other than audits or reviews of historical financial information. (5 marks)

(b) Define an assurance engagement and describe the conditions that must be present for an assurance engagement to be performed. (10 marks)

(c) Describe the different types of information that appear in social and environmental reports, including information on greenhouse gases, and briefly state the problems associated with providing assurance on such reports. (10 marks)

Total (25 marks)

# IAASB STANDARDS AND RELATED GUIDANCE COVERED IN THIS PUBLICATION

The following is the list of IAASB pronouncements covered in this publication. It is not a comprehensive list and excludes, for example, the ISA 800 series on specialised areas.[1]

*Preface to the International Quality Control, Auditing, Review, Other Assurance, and Related Services Pronouncements,* often referred to as the *'Preface'*

*International Framework for Assurance Engagements,* often referred to as the *'Framework'*

## International Standards on Quality Control (ISQCs)

ISQC 1, *Quality Control for Firms that Perform Audits and Reviews of Financial Statements, and Other Assurance and Related Services Engagements*

## ISAs

ISA 200, *Overall Objectives of the Independent Auditor and the Conduct of an Audit in Accordance with International Standards on Auditing*
ISA 210, *Agreeing the Terms of Audit Engagements*
ISA 220, *Quality Control for an Audit of Financial Statements*
ISA 230, *Audit Documentation*
ISA 240, *The Auditor's Responsibilities Relating to Fraud in an Audit of Financial Statements*
ISA 250, *Consideration of Laws and Regulations in an Audit of Financial Statements*
ISA 260, *Communication with Those Charged with Governance*
ISA 265, *Communicating Deficiencies in Internal Control to Those Charged with Governance and Management*

ISA 300, *Planning an Audit of Financial Statements*
ISA 315, *Identifying and Assessing the Risks of Material Misstatement through Understanding the Entity and Its Environment*
ISA 320, *Materiality in Planning and Performing an Audit*
ISA 330, *The Auditor's Responses to Assessed Risks*

ISA 402, *Audit Considerations Relating to an Entity Using a Service Organization*
ISA 450, *Evaluation of Misstatements Identified during the Audit*

ISA 500, *Audit Evidence*

---

[1] Auditing standards and related guidance are always work in progress. A comprehensive list of IAASB pronouncements at any point in time can be established by adding recent publications to the indexes in IAASB's most recent handbooks, both of which can be found at www.ifac.org/auditing-assurance/publications-resources. UK auditing standards can be found at www.frc.org.uk/Our-Work/Codes-Standards/Audit-and-assurance/Standards-and-guidance/Standards-and-guidance-for-auditors.aspx.

ISA 501, *Audit Evidence – Specific Considerations for Selected Items*
ISA 505, *External Confirmations*
ISA 510, *Initial Audit Engagements – Opening Balances*
ISA 520, *Analytical Procedures*
ISA 530, *Audit Sampling*
ISA 540, *Auditing Accounting Estimates, Including Fair Value Accounting Estimates, and Related Disclosures*
ISA 550, *Related Parties*
ISA 560, *Subsequent Events*
ISA 570, *Going Concern*
ISA 580, *Written Representations*

ISA 600, *Special Considerations – Audits of Group Financial Statements (Including the Work of Component Auditors)*
ISA 610, *Using the Work of Internal Auditors*
ISA 620, *Using the Work of an Auditor's Expert*

ISA 700, *Forming an Opinion and Reporting on Financial Statements*
ISA 705, *Modifications to the Opinion in the Independent Auditor's Report*
ISA 706, *Emphasis of Matter Paragraphs and Other Matter Paragraphs in the Independent Auditor's Report*
ISA 710, *Comparative Information – Corresponding Figures and Comparative Financial Statements*
ISA 720, *The Auditor's Responsibilities Relating to Other Information in Documents Containing Audited Financial Statements*

**International Standards on Review Engagements (ISREs)**

ISRE 2400, *Engagements to Review Financial Statements*
ISRE 2410, *Review of Interim Financial Information Performed by the Independent Auditor of the Entity*

**International Standards on Assurance Engagements (ISAEs)**

ISAE 3000, *Assurance Engagements Other than Audits or Reviews of Historical Financial Information*
ISAE 3400, *The Examination of Prospective Financial Information*
ISAE 3402, *Assurance Reports on Controls at a Service Organization*
ISAE 3410, *Assurance Engagements on Greenhouse Gas Statements*
ISAE 3420, *Assurance Engagements to Report on the Compilation of Pro-Forma Financial Information Included in a Prospectus*

**International Standards on Related Services (ISRSs)**

ISRS 4400, *Engagements to Perform Agreed-Upon Procedures Regarding Financial Information*
ISRS 4410, *Compilation Engagements*

**International Auditing Practices Notes (IAPNs)**

IAPN 1000, *Special Considerations in Auditing Financial Instruments*

# ANSWERS

## SECTION 1   ANSWER

### (a)   Nature, differences and similarities between audit and compilation engagements

- Audit engagements are reasonable assurance engagements in which auditors perform a risk assessment on historical financial information, and perform audit procedures to reduce the assessed risk of material misstatement to an acceptable level. This provides auditors with reasonable assurance about whether the financial statements are free from material misstatement.

- The audit opinion states that in the auditors' opinion the financial statements give a true and fair view of (or present fairly, in all material respects) the financial position, performance, cash flows, etc., in accordance with an identified financial reporting framework such as IFRS.

- Compilation engagements do not involve assurance. The practitioner compiles the financial information from information supplied by the client. Users benefit from the knowledge that the practitioner has been involved.

- Similarities between audit and compilation engagements include the fact that in both cases:
  - the financial statements, including the underlying assumptions and the significant judgements made, remain the responsibility of the client;
  - the financial information benefits from being associated with the practitioner, who brings expertise, and an obligation to comply with professional, ethical, regulatory and disciplinary arrangements;
  - agreement of engagement terms is required and practitioners are not permitted to be associated with misleading information.

### (b)   Benefits of an audit and its limitations

The benefits of an audit include:

- enhancing the confidence of intended users in the financial statements, i.e. adding credibility to the financial statements as a result of the auditors' independence and expertise. Users include customers, suppliers, lenders and investors;

- reducing the risk of fraud, error and management bias to an acceptable level;

- the recommendations auditors make for improvements to internal control;

- the discipline imposed by the audit process, which helps businesses grow.

The limitations of an audit include:

- human error in the selection, performance and evaluation of audit procedures and the fact that even if every transaction, balance and disclosure could be tested, human error would still mean that no guarantees could be given;
- time and cost budgets, which mean that audit evidence is persuasive rather than conclusive;
- the inherent limitations of internal controls, including the possibility of management override of controls, and fraudulent collusion between employees to misappropriate assets and falsify the related records;
- the inherent limitations of financial reporting, which include subjectivity and the need to exercise judgement in calculating estimates such as depreciation.

(c)    **the main stages of the assurance process**

Audits and other assurance engagements involve the following overall stages:

- *acceptance and planning,* involving:
  - compliance with ethical requirements for independence and competence and the avoidance of conflicts of interest;
  - quality control requirements, ensuring that audits are conducted in accordance with professional standards, including proper supervision and review;
  - compliance with the protocols for changes in professional appointment including inquiries of the previous practitioner and the agreement of engagement terms in an engagement letter;
  - liaison with third parties such as internal auditors, group auditors and any experts;
  - commercial considerations such as whether the client is able to pay.
- *risk assessment by understanding the business* involving extensive analysis of the risks associated with the client's activities and an evaluation of the design and implementation of internal control, where appropriate;
- *evidence-gathering* by responding to the assessed risks with substantive procedures, i.e. tests of details and analytical procedures, and tests of controls;
- *finalisation* including obtaining written representations confirming that management acknowledges its responsibility for the information reported on, and subsequent events reviews for matters that should be adjusted for or disclosed in the financial statements;
- *reporting* including the auditors' opinion on the truth and fairness or fair presentation of the financial statements. Auditors also report on weaknesses in internal control that have come to their attention during the course of the audit.

**SECTION 2   ANSWER**

(a)   **Independence**

- Audit partners and staff working on an audit for a long time create familiarity and self-interest threats to independence.

- *Familiarity threat:* while the partners and staff who have worked on a client for a long time have a thorough understanding of the business, they are less likely to question an accounting treatment or disclosure than partners and staff who are not so familiar with the client.

- *Self-interest threat:* a long-standing relationship with senior audit staff often suits clients, who are understandably irritated if asked the same basic questions by different audit staff every year. They appreciate the understanding of long-standing audit staff knowing that such staff are unlikely to ask awkward questions on an accounting treatment in years 2–4 when they accepted it in year 1. Such staff are in a good position to brief other staff from the firm efficiently when the client commissions further non-audit services. The client's continued positive feedback to the firm about the performance of such staff is valuable to the staff.

- *General safeguards* against these threats to independence include:

  - rotating senior staff off the audit team;

  - having staff who are not audit team members review their work;

  - independent internal or external quality reviews.

- *Key audit partners:* should not work on public interest audit clients for more than 7 years. After that they should not be a member of the engagement team or act as engagement quality control reviewer, provide consultation or otherwise influence the audit, for 2 years. An additional year is permissible in the case of unforeseen circumstances outside the firm's control such as the incapacity of the intended engagement partner.

- When an audit client becomes a public interest entity, if the key audit partner has served the client for 5 years or less they may continue to serve for 7 years, less the years already served. If they have served 6 or more years, they may continue for a maximum of 2 further years.

- It is acceptable for key audit partners to serve for more than 7 years if an independent regulator permits it because of lack of people to rotate, provided the firm applies additional safeguards required by the regulator, such as external reviews.

- In jurisdictions such as the UK, firms may be required to monitor the length of time senior staff serve on each audit and assess the relevant threats and safeguards. They may also have further limitations such as requiring that for listed entities:

  - engagement partners serve for 5 years with 5 years off;

  - engagement quality control reviewers serve for 7 years with 5 years off;

  - other key audit partners serve for 7 years with 2 years off.

Safeguards are needed for senior staff and other partners in place for more than 7 years.

(b)  **6 high-level prohibitions on non-assurance services: PIEs**

- Prohibited services include:
  - assuming a management responsibility;
  - accounting and bookkeeping services, except in an emergency.
- Services prohibited if amounts are material to the financial statements include:
  - valuation services and calculations of current or deferred taxes;
  - internal audit services relating to internal controls over financial reporting, accounting systems, or financial statement amounts or disclosures;
  - designing or implementing financial reporting IT systems;
  - estimating damages as part of litigation support services.

---

Other examples of prohibited services might include:

- payroll services;
- preparing the financial statements and related financial information;
- promoting, dealing in, or underwriting client shares;
- negotiating for the client;
- recruiting directors, officers or senior management for the client with significant influence over accounting records or financial statements.

Other examples of services prohibited if material include:

- tax or corporate finance advice that depends on a particular accounting treatment or presentation where there is reasonable doubt about appropriateness;
- acting as advocate before a public tribunal or court to resolve a tax matter or to resolve a dispute.

---

(c)  **Barco and Malco**

- The situation described involves a potential conflict of interest between two clients, outside the control of the firm, and threats to the firm's objectivity and to confidentiality.
- The firm cannot act for both clients without both clients being aware of the situation, but it is highly unlikely that either client will be willing to accept this.
- If Barco's request for help has already been accepted, the firm should inform Malco that it is not able to act in the matter, but it will not be possible to explain why without breaching the firm's duty of confidentiality to Barco.

Malco is likely to find it odd or annoying that the firm is unable to act, and unable to explain why.

- If Barco's request for help has not already been accepted but the firm wants to accept the work, it will be necessary to explain to Barco that the firm is acting for another bidder in another capacity (i.e. as auditor). The firm will not, however, be able to disclose to Barco the fact that Malco is the other bidder without Malco's permission, which is unlikely to be forthcoming, given that the firm will decline to act on Malco's behalf. The same applies if the position is reversed, i.e. if the firm wants to act for Malco rather than Barco.

- It may therefore be better to decline the offer to help either entity. However, if the firm does act for one entity, safeguards might include:

  – the use of separate engagement teams to work on Barco and Malco;

  – physical and other procedures to prevent information about Barco being passed to Malco and vice versa, such as secure data filing and prohibiting partners and staff on the two teams discussing their respective clients with each other.

## SECTION 3   ANSWER

(a)   **Key elements of materiality and performance materiality**

A matter is material if it is likely to affect the decisions of users of financial statements.

- Users are expected to have a reasonable knowledge of business and be willing to study the financial statements, to understand the concept of materiality and to recognise the inherent uncertainties in the measurement of estimates.

- Some misstatements in financial statements will always remain undetected and some detected misstatements are not corrected because they are clearly trivial. Together, there is a risk that they will exceed materiality. Performance materiality is lower than overall materiality and is designed to reduce that risk to an acceptable level.

- Performance materiality is the amount set by auditors at less than materiality for the financial statements as a whole, to reduce to an appropriately low level the probability that the aggregate of uncorrected and undetected misstatements exceeds materiality.

- In practice, performance materiality can be set as a percentage of materiality, somewhere between, say, 50% of materiality in relatively high risk situations such as for complex financial instruments and, say, 90% in lower risk situations such as cash.

(b)   **Common benchmarks and their use**

Common benchmarks for the calculation of materiality include:

- 0.5 – 1% of total revenue and gross profit;
- 5 – 10% of profit before or after tax;
- 0.5 – 2% of total assets.

It is common to determine materiality with reference to an average of several different benchmarks and/or an average of the same benchmark over several periods.

Unusual or exceptional items can be stripped out before applying benchmarks and some benchmarks are more appropriate for some entities than others. For example, a not-for-profit entity with substantial income and expenditure may have few if any assets. Asset-related benchmarks will not be appropriate for such entities.

(c)   **Rodco**

- $15m revenue represents 1.15% of revenue in the prior period and 1.2% of revenue in the current period. The benchmark of 1% for materiality for revenue makes the matter marginal.

- The provision for a write-down of inventory represents a very small proportion of gross assets in both periods but 5% of profit before tax in the prior period and a slightly lower amount in the current period. A benchmark of 5–10% of profit before tax also makes the provision marginal.

- The directors clearly have some justification for their assessment of both items as immaterial. However, the matter is marginal in both cases and auditors should consider other factors that may affect the assessment of materiality such as performance materiality, i.e. the need to take account of undetected and uncorrected misstatements, and the view given by the financial statements as a whole.

- Have the directors taken an aggressive approach in other areas, for example, and are there other matters that are material that are likely to be of concern to users that directors do not wish to disclose? Is the competition likely to result in other discontinued product lines in future periods?

- The matter is likely to be negotiated with the client in the light of the auditors' understanding of the business as a whole.

(d) **Documentation: purpose and test applied**

The purposes of audit documentation are:

- to provide an adequate record of the basis for the audit report and evidence that the audit was conducted in accordance with ISAs;

- to facilitate planning, supervision, direction and review of the work, internal quality control reviews under ISQC 1 and external regulatory inspections;

- to ensure that the audit team is accountable.

Documentation must be sufficient to enable an experienced auditor, having no previous connection with the audit, to understand:

- the nature, timing, extent and results of the procedures and the evidence thereby obtained;

- significant matters, conclusions reached and significant professional judgements made.

## SECTION 4.1   ANSWER

**(a)   Audit risk, financial statement risk and detection risk**

- Audit risk is the product of financial statement risk, i.e. the risk of material misstatement in financial statements, and detection risk. It is the risk that there are material misstatements in financial statements, that audit procedures do not detect them, and that auditors issue an unmodified audit opinion where a modified one (qualified, disclaimer or adverse) is appropriate.

- The higher the assessed risks of material misstatement, the lower detection risk must be to keep audit risk at an acceptably low level. Audit risk must be reduced to an acceptable level by reducing detection risk, which can be altered by changing sample sizes, for example, and by altering the balance of tests of control effectiveness and substantive procedures.

- Financial statement risk, the risk of material misstatement, is the product of inherent risk and control risk. It is the risk that the financial statements do not give a true and fair view of, or present fairly the entity's financial position and performance. It is assessed by auditors and is outside their control.

- Inherent risk is the susceptibility of the overall financial statements, and of transactions, balances and disclosures, to material misstatement, regardless of controls. Some businesses and account areas are simply more risky than others. Food retailing is generally less risky than financial services, cash is generally less risky than complex financial instruments.

- Control risk is the risk that internal controls will fail to prevent, detect or correct material misstatements. Some areas, such as cash and inventory, are generally better controlled than others, such as payables.

- Control risk can never be eliminated because of the inherent limitations of internal control including human error, management override of controls and the avoidance of controls by collusion.

- Detection risk is the product of sampling risk and non-sampling risk. Unlike the risk of material misstatement, auditors can control it, although it cannot be eliminated altogether. It is the risk that audit procedures fail to detect a material misstatement.

- Detection risk is a function of the effectiveness of audit procedures, i.e. how well designed they are, and of how well they are applied by auditors.

- Sampling risk is the risk that samples are not representative of the populations from which they are drawn. Provided samples are selected properly, it is generally very low.

- Non-sampling risk includes human error in selecting the sample or in interpreting the results, for example, and auditor errors in other areas.

- In short, some misstatements will occur in financial statements. Controls will detect and misstatements some of them but some will always remain. Auditors will detect some of these outstanding misstatements but not all of them, because audit procedures and the people who apply them are not infallible. The residual risk, after all of these safety nets have been applied, is that auditors will issue an unmodified audit report on financial statements that are materially misstated.

(b)　**Reducing risks: receivables**

Dazco's receivables ledger is likely to be typical of many with a large number of small receivables and a small number of larger ones. Larger customers are likely to be slower in paying but may be less likely to default in this case. However, increased sales combined with an economic downturn, a high turnover of staff, poor credit control and poor systems mean that:

- there is an increased risk of bad debts in all categories of receivable;
- the receivables ledger may be overstated;
- there may be numerous errors in the receivables ledger;
- allowances for doubtful receivables may be understated;
- there is scope for fraud.

Frauds might include receipts from customers being diverted to the personal bank accounts of staff and the amounts written off, and staff colluding with customers to raise invoices with excessive discounts, for example.

To reduce heightened risk to an acceptable level, the audit approach may involve:

- taking account of the quality of controls over cash receipts and the results of testing in that area;
- performing detailed analytical procedures as part of the risk assessment to highlight overall trends in receivables, including any increase in receivables over say, 90 days old, and focusing audit effort in these areas;
- exercising professional scepticism by paying particular attention to any transactions, balances or series of transactions and balances that seem abnormal given the heightened risk of fraud;
- performing more substantive procedures, including tests of details as well as analytical procedures rather than seeking to rely on tests of control effectiveness;
- paying particular attention to the reconciliation of the sales ledger to the sales ledger control account;
- performing a direct confirmation of accounts receivable which will require the consent and co-operation of Dazco's management, which may not be forthcoming, given the poor controls and errors. It may or may not be effective in any case and, if not, attention to cash received after date and orders will be critical;
- paying particular attention to the basis of the calculation of the allowances for doubtful receivables, checking the calculation and considering it in the light of management's past experience of making such provisions, and in the light of cash received after the period-end;
- inquiring of Dazco's legal department, if there is one, as to the existence and nature of any disputes with customers.

## SECTION 4.2 ANSWER

(a) **Relationships**

(i) **Substantive procedures, tests of control effectiveness**

- If an account area is well controlled, it is less likely that it will contain errors. Auditors test the operating effectiveness of controls throughout the period with a view to reducing the level of substantive procedures they must perform to reduce audit risk to an acceptable level.

- There is a requirement to test controls relating to significant risks, and in areas where substantive procedures alone would be insufficient.

- Substantive procedures are designed to detect material misstatement and include tests of details and detailed analytical procedures.

- Tests of details are tests of individual transactions such as purchases, balances such as payables, and disclosures such as those relating to amounts payable within one year and amounts payable after one year.

- Substantive analytical procedures involve the analysis of relationships between financial and non-financial data. Direct relationships exist between fuel consumption and manufacturing levels, for example, and between payroll costs and the number of employees.

- Analytical procedures involve the evaluation of relationships on a weekly, monthly, quarterly or other appropriate basis, and comparisons with prior periods, budgets and expectations. Auditors investigate and substantiate significant variations.

(ii) **Internal control, design, implementation, operational effectiveness**

- There is little point in testing the effectiveness of a control that has not been properly designed or implemented. Controls that are not properly designed or implemented cannot be effective, except by chance.

- A poorly designed control might require a signature on all invoices over a certain amount by the credit controller, but not specify what sort of check the credit controller is expected to perform, or who is to perform the check in the credit controller's absence.

- A poorly implemented control in the same area might involve the credit controller delegating the requirement to check prices on invoices over a certain amount to a more junior person, but not checking that the more junior person has actually done so.

- Walk-through tests may provide evidence about the design and implementation of a control. They involve tracing transactions from source documentation through invoices and ledgers to the financial statements and vice versa, to establish what controls are being applied.

- Auditors evaluate the effectiveness of controls in preventing, detecting and correcting material misstatements by testing control effectiveness. This means checking to ensure that the control has been applied.

- Auditors may check that the credit controller has signed the sales ledger control account reconciliation each period to show that it has been reviewed. The signature provides audit evidence that the control has been applied. Auditors are not checking to ensure that the reconciliation is correct, which would be a substantive test.

(b) **Deviations from the application of control procedures**

- Deviations are departures from or non-application of control procedures.

- Some are simple errors of omission. Sampling takes account of an expected rate of deviation but auditors must assume that deviations in samples are not isolated unless they can prove otherwise by further testing. Isolated deviations are deemed rare.

- Deviations are either isolated and controls are in fact effective, or they are not isolated and the control is not working. If a control has broken down, unless there are compensating controls, auditors must re-assess risk and the audit approach.

- If there are no compensating controls, it may be necessary to take a wholly substantive approach to an area. This is unlikely because well-designed systems generally rely on several layers of controls to achieve an objective.

- Any significant change in audit approach is unlikely to have been budgeted for, which highlights the importance of getting the original risk assessment right.

(c) **Financial statement assertions and relevance**

Financial statement assertions include assertions about:

- completeness: all transactions, events and balances that should have been recorded have been recorded and all disclosures that should have been made, have been made;

- accuracy: the details of recorded transactions and events have been recorded appropriately;

- cut-off: transactions and events have been recorded in the correct accounting period;

- existence: assets, liabilities and equity interests actually exist;

- accuracy and valuation: financial and other information is disclosed fairly at appropriate amounts.

Many audit procedures relate to the completeness, existence and accuracy of transactions, balances and disclosures in the income statement, balance sheet and associated notes. Automated controls exist to ensure that the financial statements are complete and accurate and these are often easily tested. Controls over existence may not be automated but may be routine and include reconciling asset registers to assets, for example.

Controls over cut-off and valuation are less likely to be automated and are often less robust than automated controls. Significant errors and manipulation can occur because of this. Intentional movements of transactions into or out of the accounting period around the period-end, late adjustments and poorly supported valuations can make cut-off and valuation higher risk areas.

Controls over disclosures are often all manual and require the use of checklists, but they are increasingly important.

## SECTION 4.3   ANSWER

(a)   **Analytical procedures in risk assessment and limitations**

- Analytical procedures must be performed during risk assessments to help auditors develop an understanding of the entity and highlight matters of which auditors were previously unaware.

- Comparisons of performance and position with reference to prior periods, budgets and competitors' facilitates an understanding of where the business is going and whether its performance is good, bad, adequate, improving or deteriorating.

- Analytical procedures during risk assessment may also highlight misstatements arising from fraud or error and/or high risk areas. These may be indicated where ratios that can be expected to be stable are not, such as where gross margins change for no apparent reason, where they appear to be outside normal parameters, or where they are at variance with budgets or industry averages.

- Analytical procedures are often performed before the period-end based on draft financial statements, management accounts, interim information or budgets.

- The value of analytical procedures is limited if auditors do not work on information for the full period, particularly if a business is seasonal or volatile. It is also limited if they do not work on relevant information, i.e. information that ultimately appears in the financial statements. Management accounts may be produced by systems different to those underlying the financial statements.

- The quality of analytical procedures also depends on the quality of the information on which the procedures are performed. This in turn depends on the quality of internal controls over that information. Cut-off procedures will not have been performed and period-end adjustments may not have been made.

- The quality of analytical procedures also depends on how accurately relationships between the various items of financial and non-financial information can be predicted. This may be difficult where a business is growing, where markets are volatile or where auditors have little or no experience of a business.

**(b)** **List of questions and observations**

After wishing the existing manager well with the forthcoming hospital visit, and making apologies for needing to ask questions, I would indicate the amount of time I am likely to require and then cover as much as possible of the following:

*Risk assessment, control environment and prior year audits*

- What have been the overall results of risk assessment in prior years?

- What audit approach has been taken in prior years? Has it been possible to test internal controls?

- What is the quality of the control environment and have there been any significant changes during the year?

*Planning meeting*

- What other matters were covered at the planning meeting? Was the susceptibility of the financial statements to fraud discussed? What are the significant risks?

- What has been the effect in the current year of the rapid growth and increase in competition?

- Would the growth have been greater if there had been less competition, or is the overall market for software and hardware for schools growing?

*Figures provided*

- Have similar figures been extracted from management accounts in the past? Is it possible that the figures may be inaccurate?

- On the basis of past experience, when are draft financial statements likely to be available?

*Revenue and gross margins*

- Tonco has increased its sales by 17% in a competitive market but its gross margin has only increased by 5%. Might this be a result of increased inventory in the form of hardware?

- How does Tonco account for revenue from software? Have there been errors in the past in these areas? Have there been changes in accounting policies?

- What are the expected gross margins for hardware and software respectively? What is the contribution of each to the total?

*Expenses as a percentage of sales*

- Administrative expenses have increased by 30%, which is substantial by comparison with the increase in revenue.

- Despite the increase in revenue, distribution costs and selling expenses have actually reduced, quite substantially in the case of selling expenses. This does not really make sense and may indicate errors in posting to these accounts.

(c) **Additional information**

I would ask for:

- a detailed schedule of revenue, cost of sales, a breakdown of the cost of sales figure showing the opening and closing inventory figures, and a schedule of operating expenses, all on a monthly basis if possible;
- details of revenue recognition policies for software and hardware;
- an explanation of the disproportionate increase in administrative expenses and for the decrease in distribution costs and selling expenses;
- the results of any inventory counting during the period;
- details of any known errors, of any cost reclassifications, and of any changes in or known breakdowns in controls.

## SECTION 4.4   SHORT-FORM ANSWERS

### SFQ 1: Importance of inventory

- Inventories may be material to the balance sheet and income statement for manufacturers, retailers and others. Opening and closing inventory figures have a direct effect on profits.
- Valuable and easily portable inventories may be misappropriated and the records may therefore be overstated.
- Inventory valuation is sometimes subjective and easily manipulated.
- If costs are inappropriately included in inventory instead of expenses, they can turn losses into assets.
- Key performance indicators calculated with reference to inventory include inventory turnover, days sales in inventory and the current, quick and working capital ratios.

### SFQ 2: Audit tests, finished goods

- Auditors should check to ensure that only permissible costing methods, such as standard cost, FIFO and weighted average have been used.
- Costs to be checked include costs of purchase, taxes, transport and handling costs. Costs of conversion include fixed and variable overheads.
- Purchase costs for finished electrical goods will include the costs of components, adhesives, wire, plastics and packaging. Samples of purchase costs can be checked from inventory records through invoices, daybooks and ledgers.

- Variable costs directly related to production levels include direct labour costs (including tax and social insurance), energy costs for machinery and the cost of small tools and similar items.

- Direct labour costs can be checked to payroll and production records, timesheets, clock cards and payment records. Energy costs can be traced to invoices and accruals.

- Small tool cost can be checked to invoices ensuring that items that should be expensed are not capitalised.

- Fixed production overheads allocated on the basis of a normal level of activity include depreciation, energy for heat and light in the factory and factory administration overheads.

- Overheads unrelated to production such as abnormal waste, storage costs and administrative and selling costs are excluded.

- Depreciation should be checked to ensure that calculations are accurate, depreciation rates are reasonable and that the allocation is appropriate.

- Fixed overheads that have been allocated can be checked to invoices, as for variable overheads. Auditors also check the appropriateness and accuracy of the allocation.

- Analytical procedures on costs and gross profits may involve comparisons with prior periods, budgets, production levels, profits and factory capacity.

- Cut-off tests include checks just before and just after the period-end between inventory records, the inventory itself and purchase and sales records for the relevant period.

- Net Realisable Value (NRV) is the estimated selling price in the ordinary course of business, less selling costs and the cost of completion. It is only relevant if goods are likely to be sold below cost.

- Inventory count results and inventory records should be reviewed for old or slow-moving items and checked to any allowances made.

- Where a reduction to NRV has been made, it should be checked to post period-end sales or contracts, and any further costs such as advertising that may be included.

- Management's past performance in estimating allowances is relevant.

## SFQ 3: Provision for warranty claims

- These provisions are subjective estimates. Auditors need to test how management makes them and assess them for reasonableness in the light of previous provisions and subsequent claims.

- Auditors may also test controls over the calculation of claims or develop their own estimates.

- The provision should be checked to the level of claims and payments before and after the period-end. More work is necessary if provisions and claims have not matched in the past.

- If the entity has taken out insurance against claims it may require disclosure.

- Auditors should check the calculation of the provision and ensure it is made in line with the method prescribed.

- Any change in method must be for a reason, because of changed levels of claims or changes in the product mix, for example, and properly disclosed if material.

- Any write-back of prior period provisions in the current period because of over-provisions in previous periods must be reasonable and properly disclosed.

- Correspondence with customers may provide some evidence and a legal department, if it exists, may provide details of disputes over claims.

### SFQ 4: Judgement and statistical sampling

- Judgement sampling uses auditor judgement to select the items to test (how many items and which ones) and in interpreting results. No special conditions are required.

- Statistical sampling uses probability theory to do the same. To be effective, a large, homogeneous population in which each item has a quantifiable chance of being selected is required.

- Judgement is involved in statistical sampling, in the assessment of materiality and in the determination of what constitutes tolerable misstatement, for example.

### SFQ 5: Audit of 5-year bank loan

- The period-end bank confirmation should provide details of the capital and interest outstanding, amounts paid and payable during the period and details of any security held.

- Analytical procedures can be performed on interest paid and payable and the capital amounts outstanding.

- Evidence of authorisation for the loan should be in the minutes of board or other meetings.

- The contract for the loan and relevant correspondence should be checked to ensure proper disclosure of terms, including any conditions (covenants) relating to the use of any assets held as security.

- Where conditions have not been complied with, auditors need to consider the implications.

- Disclosure is required for amounts payable in 1 year, and over 1 year, and of assets held as security.

**SFQ 6: Substantive procedures: trade payables, purchase accruals and expense accruals**

- The nature and extent of substantive procedures depend on the results of tests of control effectiveness.

- Evidence regarding the completeness of trade payables and accruals is usually important.

- Direct confirmation of trade payables should be considered in the light of past experience although supplier statement reconciliations may be sufficient. Some combination can be considered.

- Client co-operation is required in direct confirmations to authorise requests and help reconcile differences between entity and supplier records.

- Analytical procedures can be performed on the age and amount of trade payables by comparison with purchases, production and prior periods.

- To test for completeness, a sample of 'potential' trade payables can be taken from a complete list of suppliers, and orders and invoices traced through the daybooks and ledgers to the schedules supporting the financial statements.

- A sample of trade payables can be traced in the opposite direction from the schedules supporting the financial statements to the ledgers, daybooks and source documentation to ensure that the amounts recorded are accurate.

- A schedule of purchase accruals can be checked for arithmetical accuracy and completeness by comparing them with prior periods and invoices received after the period-end.

- Cut-off for trade payables and purchase accruals can be tested with reference to invoices and inventory records before and after the period-end.

- There may be evidence of disputes with suppliers held by a legal department or in correspondence files.

- If expense accruals are not material, analytical procedures may be sufficient.

- A schedule of expense accruals should be obtained and checked for arithmetical accuracy. Individual accruals can compared with prior periods and budgets.

- Amounts paid after the period-end can be checked to bank statements and a sample of amounts payable can be checked to subsequent invoices.

### SECTION 4.5   ANSWER

(a)   **Reasons for, types of and drawbacks of outsourcing Jillco's accounting function**

  (i)   Jillco's reasons for outsourcing an accounting function may include a desire or need:

  - to focus business resources on growing the business rather than maintaining accounting records;

- to transfer some of the risks associated with the accounting function, which might be substantial for Jillco;

- for cost control, particularly as the business expands with the attendant strain on cash flow. This might include avoiding the need to invest in upgrades that may not last for long;

- to smooth the effect of any seasonal spikes which are likely in parcel distribution;

- to utilise the economies of scale and technological advantages offered by service organisations, and possibly to standardise or link with the service organisations used by partner organisations.

(ii) Jillco might use a service organisation for:

- data processing from records supplied, such as invoicing and payroll maintenance;

- maintenance of the accounting records, including the daybooks and ledgers;

- transaction execution such as order initiation, processing, billing and credit control.

In Jillco's case, it is very likely that systems will work best if they are tightly integrated. It may be possible to use the same organisations as those used by overseas partners.

(iii) Drawbacks for Jillco might include:

- underestimating the time and effort required to make the change, particularly management time;

- loss of quality of service, staff morale problems and unpopularity with customers resulting in increased costs;

- overestimating cost savings;

- the need for changes to operational arrangements to conform with the service organisation's requirements.

(b) **Problems for external auditors and risks arising from the use of service organisations**

*Problems*

- It is essential that auditors are able to access accounting records and evaluate systems and controls if they are to perform an effective risk assessment.

- Where a third party, with whom auditors have no direct relationship, controls systems and records, it is essential that the contract between the entity and the service organisation provides for appropriate auditor access and/or reports by the service organisation or its auditors to the user entity's auditors.

- In most jurisdictions, there are legal requirements to keep proper accounting records and the use of a service organisation makes no difference to this requirement. In many jurisdictions, company law requires auditors to make a statement in their audit report if they do not consider that adequate accounting records have been kept.

- It is essential that the audited entity exercises proper control over the service organisation. Management authorisation and review of the information provided to the organisation and the information that comes back is important. Information returned often summarises transactions processed and provides key metrics.

*Risks*

Auditors evaluate the risks associated with:

- the contractual arrangements and the controls exercised by the entity over the service organisation including entity and auditor rights of access to information;

- the risks associated with the service organisation including its reputation and the quality of its systems, controls and outputs;

- the risks associated with the level of service provided which will be lower where, for example, the service organisation only provides simple data processing, and the user entity keeps the records;

- controls operated at the service organisations, in order to decide whether to test their operational effectiveness;

- the extent to which internal or external auditors of the service organisation are prepared to perform specific procedures and provide reports on the design, implementation or operational effectiveness of the system.

(c) **Limits to external auditor use of internal audit work**

It may not be possible for external auditors to use relevant internal audit work if internal auditors:

- are insufficiently independent within the organisation, because they have insufficient operational freedom, or report to those who control the areas they work on, or report on their own work;

- are incompetent, inexperienced or unqualified;

- lack integrity;

- do not plan or document their work, or if management does not consider their recommendations.

(d)    **Internal and external audit reports**

Information in internal audit reports normally includes:

- a cover page dealing with the subject matter, the distribution list, date, and authors;

- an executive summary including an introduction, summary terms of reference, outcome of the work, key risks identified, key action points/recommendations and further work required;

- the main report contents including findings, potential action points together with recommendations for who might be responsible for executing them, costs and time-scales;

- appendices with, for example, the full terms of reference, questionnaires and tests performed.

Information in external audit reports includes:

- a title and addressee, the auditors' signature, location and date;

- details of the financial statements audited and the auditing and accounting standards applied;

- reference to the responsibilities of directors and auditors;

- a summary of audit procedures;

- an opinion paragraph;

- a paragraph on other legal and regulatory requirements, if relevant;

- an 'other matter' paragraph dealing with audit-related matters, if relevant.

Comparison:

- the wording and layout of external audit reports is determined by ISA 700 on audit reports and national requirements;

- external audit reports are generally highly summarised, and do not contain recommendations or action points;

- internal and external audit reports both state what has been done, the overall findings/opinion and the context, i.e. law and accounting standards in the case of external reports, and the terms of reference in the case of internal reports;

- external audit reports are often required by law and are regulated. Internal audit reports are usually required by management for control and corporate governance purposes.

## SECTION 4.6   ANSWER

### (a)   Importance of related parties and auditor responsibilities

Many related party transactions, including transactions with group companies, are in the normal course of business and are not high risk. Other transactions with parties such as directors, or companies and other entities they control, may be higher risk because:

- attempts may be made to avoid disclosure of the true nature of transactions with related parties through a complex web of relationships and transactions. There is often a heightened risk of fraud;

- information systems may not be designed to identify related party relationships and transactions, and management may be unaware of their existence, or of the accounting and disclosure requirements, or of the need to authorise such transactions;

- transactions may not be conducted at arms' length.

IFRS and other financial reporting frameworks specify accounting and disclosure requirements for related party relationships and transactions. Auditors therefore need to perform procedures to identify and respond to the risks of material misstatement in this area.

Even if the financial reporting framework establishes minimal or no requirements, auditors still need to obtain an understanding of related party relationships and transactions to ensure that the financial statements give a true and fair view or are presented fairly, or are not misleading where compliance frameworks are used.

Understanding related party relationships and transactions is also required by ISA 240 on fraud. ISA 315 on risk assessment and ISA 240 require an engagement team discussion about the susceptibility of the financial statements to material misstatement due to fraud or error arising from the entity's related party relationships and transactions.

Management is required to account for related party relationships and transactions. Auditors are required to inquire of management about the identity of the entity's related parties and transactions with them. This is particularly difficult for smaller entities that often require help in this area.

Auditors are required to remain alert during the audit for information that may indicate the existence of related party relationships or transactions that management have not previously identified or disclosed. They should inspect bank and legal confirmations, minutes of directors and shareholders' meetings and other relevant records.

Further enquiries and procedures are required if auditors identify significant transactions outside the normal course of business (which are treated as significant risks) or previously unidentified or undisclosed relationships or transactions. These include asking why the entity failed to identify them, reconsidering audit risk, including the risk of fraud, and considering whether transactions have been properly accounted for.

Assertions that related party transactions are conducted at arms' length, i.e. on normal commercial terms, need to be substantiated.

**(b)   Displaying comparative information and auditor responsibilities**

*Comparative information* is displayed either as:

- *corresponding figures*, i.e. for each figure for the current period, there is a corresponding figure for the prior year(s) and the auditors' opinion is on the current period only;
- *comparative financial statements*, in which two more sets of financial statements are displayed side by side and the auditors' opinion refers to each period for which financial statements are presented.

The basic requirement is for:

- the comparative information to agree with prior period amounts and disclosures, or to have been properly restated;
- accounting policies reflected in the comparative information to be consistent with current period policies, or for changes to be properly accounted for and disclosed.

*Corresponding figures*: if the audit opinion on the prior period was modified and the matter remains unresolved, the opinion on the current period's financial statements is modified because of the possible effects of the unresolved matter:

- on the current period's figures; or
- on the comparability of the current period's figures.

For example, if the audit opinion on the prior period was modified in respect of opening inventory for that period, the comparability of the current period's figures is affected. If the modification was in respect of closing inventory, the current period's profit figure is affected as well as comparability.

Evidence of material misstatements in prior period financial statements on which an unmodified opinion was issued requires a restatement of the corresponding figures. Where this has not been done, a modified opinion is expressed on the current period financial statements relating to the corresponding figures.

If the financial statements of the prior period were audited by another firm or unaudited, reference may be made to this in an 'other matter' paragraph in the auditors' report.

*Comparative financial statements:* where comparative financial statements are presented the audit opinion refers to each period presented. If the opinion on the prior period financial statements has changed, the reasons are disclosed in an 'other matter' paragraph.

If the financial statements of the prior period were audited by another firm this is also referred to in an 'other matter' paragraph. If auditors conclude that a material misstatement in the prior period financial statements exists but no modification was issued by the other firm, they inform management and those charged with governance and request that the predecessor auditor be informed. If the prior period financial statements are amended and the predecessor auditor issues a new report, current auditors only report on the current period financial statements.

If the prior period financial statements were not audited, it is referred to in an 'other matter' paragraph but evidence still needs to be obtained in relation to opening balances and comparatives.

## (c) Additional work for initial engagements

Evidence is required in initial engagements about whether:

- opening balances contain misstatements that materially affect the current period; and
- appropriate accounting policies have been consistently applied or changes accounted for and disclosed.

Auditors read the most recent financial statements and determine whether:

- the closing balances have been properly brought forward or restated;
- opening balances reflect the application of appropriate accounting policies.

Auditors perform one or more of the following on *opening balances*:

- an evaluation of the evidence provided by current period procedures relevant to opening balances;
- specific audit procedures to obtain evidence regarding the opening balances.

Additional procedures are required where there is evidence that the opening balances contain misstatements that could materially affect the current period's financial statements.

**SECTION 5   ANSWER**

(a)   **Internal audit: good corporate governance and risk management**

- A requirement to establish and maintain an internal audit function as part of an entity's risk management system is a key element of many corporate governance codes.

- There are many codes of corporate governance such as the OECD *Code on Corporate Governance* and the *UK Corporate Governance Code 2010*. Some are mandatory, others are applicable on a 'comply or explain' basis to companies listed on stock exchanges.

- Corporate governance is the way entities ensure they meet all of their objectives, which may related to financial performance, operations and products, the regulatory environment, and corporate social responsibility.

- Risk management is sometimes treated as an independent function and sometimes it is viewed as part of the wider corporate governance structure. The internal audit function should not itself perform risk management procedures because it needs to provide an independent appraisal of the adequacy and effectiveness of the entity's risk management policies and procedures.

- Internal audit reviews the risk management processes in place, provides constructive criticism, and audits those processes after they have been implemented and when they change.

- Internal auditors contribute to good corporate governance by considering the extent to which clear objectives have been set and communicated, the mechanisms for identifying, analysing and mitigating key risks, and the ability of the business to deal with internal and external change.

(b)   **Audit committees**

- Detailed guidelines on corporate governance task audit committees with monitoring the integrity of financial statements, internal control and the internal audit function, making recommendations for the appointment of auditors, their remuneration, other services that they may provide and monitoring their independence.

- Codes require that audit committees are properly resourced, adequately informed, permitted to ask questions, have access to independent legal advice and be comprised of competent non-executive directors with sufficient time to devote to the task.

- Despite apparent compliance with all requirements, corporate collapses have occurred unexpectedly. Even the best audit committees cannot prevent corporate collapses, but they may reduce the likelihood.

- Audit committees are not responsible for corporate collapses or for failing to be able to see into the future, but there may be weaknesses in the way audit committees operate that contribute to the lack of warning of corporate failure such as:

- recommendations that are not always complied with because there may be too few truly independent, competent and experienced persons to staff audit committees;

- excessive involvement of executive directors;

- in the past, audit committees may not have been provided with sufficient information or have been adequately resourced in terms of staff, legal advice or time. They may have been unable to challenge the main board effectively. Furthermore, some individuals may hold too many non-executive director-ships and not have sufficient time to devote appropriate attention to audit committee matters;

- despite strenuous, genuine efforts by some companies, it has sometimes been difficult to avoid giving the impression that those sitting on audit committees are people with very similar characteristics;

- the fact that in many cases, the main board retains ultimate control over appointments to the audit committee, which renders the committee vulner-able to the main board.

• It is very likely that some corporate collapses have been prevented by the efforts of properly constituted audit committees; this good work is rarely publicised and it is important not to assume that audit committees are valueless just because, in some cases, there have been failures.

(c) **Limiting liability**

• Contractual or statutory limitation of the auditors' liability to a fixed amount is forbidden in some jurisdictions and permitted in others. In some jurisdictions it is set by laws and regulation. It is common for the cap to be fixed, either at an absolute monetary amount regardless of circumstances, or as a multiple of audit fees, or it can depend on the size of the audited entity.

• Most common law jurisdictions apply the principle of joint and several liability to claims in negligence meaning that all of the defendants are responsible for all of the loss. The advantage of this is that it maximises the plaintiffs' chances of recovery. The principal disadvantage is that it encourages claims against the well-insured, and is clearly unfair to insured parties who are only responsible for a small amount of the loss.

• Auditors are required to carry professional indemnity insurance (PII) in most jurisdictions; directors are not.

• Proportionate liability restricts auditors' liability to that part of any loss caused by them. This is legislated for in many different ways and is sometimes only permitted when the defendants are accountable for a small proportion of the blame.

• The principal advantage of limiting auditor liability is that it protects firms from potentially catastrophic claims and discourages dysfunctional behaviour and resistance to change on the part of those potentially facing such claims.

- Other advantages of limiting liability include the creation of an environment which avoids a compliance mentality, attracts people to the profession and encourages audit innovation.

- Potential disadvantages of restricting auditors' liability in any way include:

  - audit quality: if the consequences of performing a negligent audit are limited, the likelihood of a negligent audit may increase;

  - the value of the audit opinion, and thereby the credibility of the financial statements, which may be diminished;

  - a race to the bottom if the limitation is calculated by reference to fees: if lower audit fees are associated with a lower level of liability, there is a risk that less work will be performed. This is relevant to providers of professional indemnity insurance who might seek to restrict maximum audit fees;

  - reduced competition in the audit market arising from larger caps being set by larger firms.

- Firms limit their exposure to litigation and claims generally by:

  - ensuring that client acceptance procedures are properly implemented so that the risks associated with clients are properly understood and managed;

  - implementing proper quality control policies and procedures at the firm and engagement level to ensure that all relevant standards and requirements are complied with;

  - paying particular attention to documentation requirements;

  - issuing audit and other reports with appropriate caveats about their use and limitations, such as the 'Bannerman' clauses used in some UK audit reports, where permitted;

  - carrying adequate professional indemnity insurance.

## SECTION 6   SHORT-FORM ANSWERS

### SFQ 1: Main contents of unmodified audit reports

These are:

- a *title:* indicating the auditors' independence;

- an *addressee:* usually shareholders or those charged with governance;

- an *introductory paragraph:* identifying the entity, stating that financial statements have been audited, identifying each statement audited, the dates or periods covered and the accounting policies used;

- a paragraph on *management responsibilities:* for the preparation of financial statements, for internal controls that facilitate this and for the selection of accounting policies;

- a paragraph on *auditors' responsibilities:* referring to compliance with ethical requirements, the risk of material misstatement, the use of judgement, testing internal controls, evaluating the appropriateness of accounting policies, the reasonableness of estimates and overall presentation;

- an *opinion* on truth and fairness or fair presentation;

- a *signature:* by the firm, the individual auditor or both;

- the *date:* of the report;

- an *address:* the location in which the auditors practice.

### SFQ 2: Modified audit reports

These are:

- *qualified* opinions: i.e. 'except for' opinions where there is either a:
  - material *lack of evidence* that is not pervasive;
  - material *misstatement* that is not pervasive.

- *disclaimers* of opinion: where there is a pervasive lack of evidence resulting in auditors being unable to form an opinion;

- *adverse* opinions: where there is a pervasive material misstatement.

*Pervasive* means affecting the view given by the financial statements as a whole.

### SFQ 3: Emphasis of matter paragraphs

- Emphasis of matter paragraphs draw users' attention to matters in the financial statements that are fundamental to their understanding of the financial statements. Their inclusion does not make the audit opinion a modified opinion.

- Such paragraphs can refer to matters such as going concern uncertainties, disclosures of uncertainties surrounding litigation, the early application of new accounting standards and certain significant subsequent events such as catastrophic losses.

### SFQ 4: Other matter paragraphs and reports on other legal and regulatory requirements

- Other matter paragraphs draw users' attention to matters that are not referred to in the financial statements but are relevant to the audit, the auditors' responsibilities or the audit report. The inclusion of such paragraphs does not make the audit opinion a modified opinion. They are sometimes used to restrict the distribution or use of audit reports.

- Reports on other legal or regulatory requirements are reports on local requirements such as reports or compliance with corporate governance requirements and reports, sometimes by exception, on adequate accounting records, the agreement of the financial statements with the underlying records and on auditors having received sufficient information and explanations for the purposes of the audit. Such reports are common, particularly where a modified opinion is given.

### SFQ 5: Procedures when events or conditions cast significant doubt

Auditors review management's plans for dealing with the problem by:

- reviewing cash flow, profit and other relevant forecasts with management;
- considering any restructuring plans;
- considering the reliability of the entity's system for generating forecasts and support for the underlying assumptions;
- comparing forecasts for prior periods with historical results;
- reviewing interim financial information;
- reading minutes of meetings of those charged with governance, shareholders and the board;
- making inquiries of the entity's lawyers about the reasonableness of management's assessments about the outcome of litigation;
- confirming the existence, legality and enforceability of arrangements with group companies or others to provide or maintain financial support, and assessing their ability to do so;
- reviewing subsequent events.

### SFQ 6: Possible audit reports and circumstances

- Where there is a material uncertainty that casts significant doubt on the entity's ability to continue as a going concern, but auditors do not disagree with the going concern basis and adequate disclosures are made, auditors include an 'emphasis of matter' paragraph highlighting the existence of the uncertainty and drawing attention to the relevant note.

- Where the period to which directors have paid particular attention is less than 12 months from the balance sheet date, auditors consider the need to modify the audit report resulting from the limitation in the scope of the audit.

- Where auditors disagree with the going concern basis, or there is a material uncertainty that is not properly disclosed, they issue an adverse opinion.

- If auditors are unable to form an opinion because of a limitation in the scope of the audit, they issue an 'except for', or disclaimer of opinion, but this is unusual.

## SFQ 7: Alfco and Murfco

- *Alfco*: there is a material uncertainty that casts significant doubt on Alfco's going concern status that should be disclosed in the financial statements. If no disclosure is made, a qualified or adverse opinion is required.

- Alfco probably does not want to disclose the matter because it may give competitors the upper hand in any negotiations for the sale, and it may cause the bank to call in the loan. References to going concern problems can be self-fulfilling prophecies.

- *Murfco*: there is a material uncertainty that casts significant doubt on the going concern status of Murfco.

- It is possible that the going concern assumption is *not* appropriate. It may be possible to delay the issue of the audit report while the directors action their plans but if they are unable or unwilling to do so, it is possible that the financial statements should be prepared on a liquidation basis, and that an emphasis of matter paragraph be issued, although this would be unusual.

- If directors do have evidence regarding the feasibility of their plans, disclosure of the material uncertainty should still be made and an emphasis of matter should refer to the disclosures.

## SECTION 7   SHORT-FORM ANSWERS

### SFQ 1: Factors determining the course of action for Dabco

- Paragraph 7 of ISA 210 on engagement terms requires that if auditors believe a disclaimer of opinion is likely to be necessary because of a limitation imposed by management, they should not accept the engagement unless required to do so by law or regulation.

- Dabco appears to be attempting to steer the course of the audit and the audit opinion. It also appears to be attempting to buy the right to do so by offering any fee, within reason. This is not normal behaviour and could be construed as attempted bribery, which is illegal in most jurisdictions.

- Unless the directors of Dabco can provide a good explanation for the non-availability or non-provision of accounting records, and for their refusal of help, there may be grounds for suspecting that management lacks integrity.

- The fundamental principles of professional ethics require that professional accountants:

  - act with integrity, which means, among other things, not knowingly being associated with misleading information;

  - perform their work competently, having regard to professional standards, and having, or being able to obtain, expertise in the relevant area, which may not be possible in this case;

  - display professional behaviour, which means complying with laws and regulations and avoiding behaviour that might discredit the profession.

- Dabco's request threatens all of these fundamental principles and it is likely that, even with safeguards, the threats cannot be reduced to an acceptable level.

- Further information about the company, its activities, its directors and those charged with governance will be necessary if the engagement is to be considered. Relevant expertise in this area will also be needed.

- Ethical considerations aside, the firm may consider the audit as potentially very high risk and may decide to decline it on commercial grounds.

### SFQ 2: Money laundering

- Money laundering is the concealment of the true origin of the proceeds of criminal activities. Money earned from criminal activities is laundered so that it appears to come from a legitimate source.

- Money laundering involves acts which conceal, disguise, convert, transfer, remove, use, acquire or possess property resulting from criminal conduct, such as tax evasion and the proceeds of drug trafficking and terrorism. Aiding, abetting, concealing or advising on such activities are usually criminal offences.

- Three stages of the money laundering process involve *placing* money in the system, often using accounts managed by lawyers, accountants, banks and real estate agents, creating *layers* of often complex transactions to conceal the source of the funds, and their *integration* into the mainstream financial system.

- A criminal may launder the proceeds of drug trafficking by placing small amounts of cash into a bank account every week or month, so as not to attract attention, eventually purchasing a property with that money and then selling the property to a third party and using the proceeds to set up a legitimate business.

## SFQ 3: Offences that accountants may commit

Offences that may be committed by accountants include:

- handling the proceeds of criminal activity, using client accounts or simply by accepting fees paid from the proceeds of criminal activity;
- advising on the use of such proceeds of crime;
- failing to make required suspicious transaction reports;
- 'tipping off', i.e. making disclosures likely to prejudice investigations into money laundering;
- failure to comply with customer due diligence and other specific regulatory requirements.

## SFQ 4: Money laundering policies and procedures

Policies and procedures required of firms include:

- the appointment of an appropriately senior Money Laundering Reporting Officer (MLRO). The MLRO receives and deals with reports of suspected money laundering from staff and decides whether to make reports to the appropriate external body;
- customer due diligence, or 'know your client' or 'customer identification' procedures to verify the identity of clients and potential clients. National identity cards, passports, driving licence, and evidence of addresses such as utility bills are often requested for individuals. For companies and other corporate entities, the certificate of incorporation and verification of the identity of key management personnel and those people in control of the entity are required;
- records of the clients' identity, the business relationship with the entity and details of transactions with it are kept for five years after the end of the business relationship. Any internal or external money laundering reports are also kept for five years;
- training on the requirements, the firms' policies and reporting lines for all relevant employees;
- internal control, risk assessment, management and monitoring of compliance with the obligations which include client screening, testing of the systems in place and regular reviews.

### SFQ 5: Strong suspicions, lack of integrity and illegal activities

Firms should consider:

- the sufficiency of audit evidence, its quality and extent, particularly where judgement is critical;
- the need to resist pressure to sign audit reports, even if there is a threat that significant transactions will be prejudiced, particularly if significant late adjustments are presented;
- reporting to those charged with governance;
- reporting to third parties where required or permitted by law or regulation, such as reporting in the public interest, or in the interests of national security, or suspicions of money laundering, to appropriate authorities. There are often specific requirements in the financial services sector.
- authorities include regulatory bodies such as stock exchanges or bank regulators, the police, serious fraud or tax authorities. In some cases it is appropriate to inform the client first and ask the client to report, and only to report if the client fails to provide evidence that they have done so. In some cases reporting is without reference to the client;
- the likely effect on the client relationship, which will often be destroyed. Reporting without client consent is a very serious step and legal advice is often taken.

### SFQ 6: Objectives of forensic investigation and steps and procedures

The objectives of an investigation into an alleged fraud might be to:

- discover if a fraud had *actually* taken place, rather than a series of errors;
- *identify* those involved;
- *quantify* the monetary amount;
- *gather evidence and present findings* to the client and in legal proceedings.

The procedures employed in conducting a forensic investigation are similar in some respects to those that might be used in an audit, and include planning, evidence gathering and reporting.

To investigate the purchase ledger fraud it might be appropriate to:

- establish the reasons for the suspicions, including any documentary evidence, covering any potential motive, such as difficult personal circumstances, opportunities to commit the fraud and attempts to conceal the fraud by altering records or documents;
- set out a formal plan covering the expected conduct of the investigation and establish whether, if a fraud has taken place, the client intends to take legal

action against the purchase ledger controller, terminate their employment or simply obtain a confession with an undertaking to desist;

- obtain purchase ledger records from the entity for examination in a manner that does not arouse suspicion;

- establish which suppliers are suspected of being involved and consider the best way to approach them, which might include:

  - performing confirmation procedures;

  - querying particular transactions;

  - reconciling accounts to establish any unusual patterns of payment, round sum payments or patterns of invoicing;

  - performing analytical procedures on the invoices and payments made;

  - substantively checking the goods or services purportedly received to other accounting records.

It is possible that the requests for information noted above will be directed to those who are involved with the fraud at the supplier and methods of bypassing such persons need to be found.

Computer assisted audit techniques may be helpful.

If an acceptable level of evidence of the fraud can be established, it will then be necessary to estimate the extent of the fraud and, at that point, consider whether the client wishes to interview the purchase ledger controller.

## SECTION 8   ANSWER

(a)   **Overall objectives and balance**

- The overall objective of quality control is to provide reasonable assurance that the auditors' report is appropriate and that auditing and ethical standards and other regulatory requirements have been complied with. Other regulatory requirements include requirements for regulated entities, and stock exchange requirements for listed entities.

- Balances to be achieved include balances between:

  – the responsibilities of the engagement partner and the collective responsibilities of the firm;

  – personal accountability and team-working, particularly with regard to consultation. It is important that the full resources of the firm can be brought to bear on individual engagements;

  – the resources required to build a quality control infrastructure through training and the development of policies and procedures, including monitoring.

- It is essential that the management structure and evaluation, compensation and promotion policies and procedures are designed to prevent commercial considerations taking precedence over quality control. Quality control needs to be built into the reward structure for partners and staff.

(b)   **Particular difficulties faced by smaller firms**

- The independent roles to be taken on by different people that are necessarily combined in smaller firms include the:

  – person(s) with *ultimate responsibility* for quality control within the firm;

  – *engagement partner*;

  – *engagement quality control reviewer*;

  – person(s) responsible for *monitoring*;

  – person(s) responsible for dealing with *complaints and allegations*;

  – person(s) to be *consulted* on technical or ethical matters.

- Some of these roles are mutually exclusive, such as the engagement quality control reviewer and the engagement partner. Others are not but in most cases the individual must have appropriate experience and authority. In many cases, experienced staff can fulfil the roles. Sole practitioners with no staff are likely to be forced to rely on third parties to fulfil some of these roles.

- Other procedures that cause smaller firms problems include the requirements relating to:

  – human resources: the maintenance of *competence* requires training and continuing professional development (CPD). Resources may not be available, and external training consortia and courses are often needed. Training on non-technical matters is required for all staff;

- engagement performance: policies and procedures on **consultation,** which is required for difficult and contentious matters. Consultation is required with persons outside the engagement team, and/or outside the audit firm. Smaller firms, and particularly sole practitioners, may be forced to go outside the firm and have arrangements with other practices, with training consortia or with professional bodies, for example;

- engagement performance: independent **review** procedures may not be possible within small firms due to the small number of staff. External review services are sometimes provided by training consortia and professional bodies;

- **documentation**: smaller firms buy in audit software and methodologies from professional bodies or commercial providers.

(c) **Report to Partners**

**Report to**: the partners of Danco

*Partners' meeting date: XX/YY/20XX*
**Prepared by**: N Partner

**Principal Conclusions and Recommendations:**

The appointment of a partner responsible for quality control is necessary at this stage in Danco's development and demonstrates the firm's commitment to quality control.

Policies and procedures are required in the following areas

- *leadership responsibilities;*
- *ethical requirements;*
- *acceptance and continuance of client relationships;*
- *human resources;*
- *engagement performance;*
- *monitoring.*

1. **Leadership and values**

In all communications, it should be clear that we are committed to quality control and that ultimate responsibility for quality lies with all of the firm's partners. Those to whom we delegate responsibility must have sufficient seniority, authority and experience to assume the responsibility.

Compensation and promotion criteria for partners and staff should demonstrably encourage and reward quality. Management responsibilities should be assigned so that commercial considerations do not override audit quality. Specifically, partners who fail internal quality control reviews (see monitoring, below) should not be promoted and their continued right to sign audit reports should be reviewed. This is generally accepted to be difficult for firms expanding in a competitive market and we must ensure that we are seen to be promoting quality over commercial considerations.

### 2.   Ethical requirements

Policies and procedures for ethical requirements must cover, among other things:

- the evaluation of threats to objectivity and the other fundamental principles and the use of safeguards;
- communicating requirements to staff, and training staff in their application;
- monitoring, including obtaining annual written confirmations of compliance with the firm's policies and procedures;
- processes for dealing with non-compliance.

We have no listed entity clients yet but if they are among our targets, policies and procedures should be developed with a view to this possibility. Policies and procedures for the rotation of engagement partners and other key audit partners including engagement quality control reviewers will be required.

### 3.   Acceptance and continuance of client relationships

It is essential as we grow that we ensure that we only accept and continue with clients where we:

- are competent and have adequate time and resources to service the client, because it may appear to outsiders that the practice is growing beyond its resources;
- can comply with relevant ethical requirements, particularly objectivity;
- have no significant concerns about the client's integrity.

We should review our procedures for changes in professional appointment in the light of the latest requirements.

Danco must ensure that it balances its desire for growth with full knowledge of the risks when taking on new clients.

### 4.   Human resources

We should review our HR policies covering recruitment, performance evaluation, competence, career development and compensation. They must provide us with reasonable assurance that the firm has personnel who comply with ethical requirements and have the competencies and capabilities it needs.

We also need to review our arrangements for:

- continuing professional education (CPD);
- work experience, or 'on-the-job' training;
- coaching and mentoring arrangements.

It is appropriate at this point to consider the possibility of appointing a training manager either from existing staff or from outside the firm.

## 5.    Engagement performance

We have a good quality audit methodology in place, which should ensure consistency in engagement performance provided staff are trained in its use.

We have sufficient staff to ensure that appropriate supervision and review of files takes place but as a matter of priority we must implement engagement quality control review procedures.

In the first instance, we need to develop a policy for which audits, apart from listed entity audits, which we do not yet have, should be subject to an engagement quality control review. It is likely that the policy should include financial services and pension fund clients as well as any others with a 'public interest' element.

There are currently no procedures for consultation either internally or externally on technical matters, for dealing with differences of opinion or for documentation of the quality control system. Arrangements for consultation on technical matters are likely to be increasingly important as we grow. Documentation is important to demonstrate to inspectors that a good quality system is in place. All of these areas require work.

## 6.    Monitoring

At the same time as developing the arrangements referred to above, we need to implement monitoring procedures.

Monitoring is an ongoing evaluation of the firm's system of quality control, including a periodic inspection of a selection of completed engagements, i.e. cold file reviews.

## SECTION 9   ANSWER

Mattco Inc
1, Sycamore Drive
Deale
67193

Danco Partners
2, Hillock Way
Deale
67060

5 March 20XX

Dear Matt

### Audits, Reviews, Agreed-upon Procedures and Compilation Engagements

Thank you very much indeed for coming into the office last week to discuss your requirements. I have pleasure in setting out below the different types of services we are able to offer. I also suggest below which of those services might be appropriate to your specific circumstances.

A summary of the characteristics of the various types of engagement is set out below and further detail provided in the appendix to this letter.

|  | Work performed | Assurance |
|---|---|---|
| Audits | Assessment of the risk of material misstatement and full response, including detailed testing of controls, transactions and balances | **Reasonable:** 'true and fair' or 'fair presentation' audit opinion |
| Reviews | Risk assessment and procedures such as inquiries and analytical procedures to reduce the risk of material misstatement to an acceptable level, but greater than for an audit | **Limited:** nothing has come to practitioners' attention to indicate that the financial statements are not 'true and fair' or 'fairly present' the position and performance |
| Agreed-upon procedures | Procedures agreed with client | **None:** we have performed procedures, these are the findings |
| Compilations | Financial statements are prepared from the information and explanations supplied using the practitioner's expertise | **None:** we have compiled the financial statements from information supplied |

In all cases, we are required to comply with ethical requirements and with international standards on quality control. I should also emphasise that in all cases, any financial information produced by us on your behalf remains your responsibility and we will require you to sign an engagement letter to this effect. This is a requirement of professional standards and not one that we are able to change.

Audit, review and compilation reports are sometimes filed at a public registry with the financial statements or other financial information reported on and are available for public inspection. This is sometimes required by law. It would be unusual for agreed-upon procedures engagements reports to be made public.

I hope you find this useful, please do not hesitate to contact me if you have any further queries and I look forward to hearing from you soon.

Yours sincerely

Ola Miller

## APPENDIX
### Audits, Reviews, Agreed-upon Procedures and Compilation Engagements

(a)   Audit engagements

- **Nature of work performed**

  - Audit engagements involve a full risk analysis and response to the risk of material misstatement. The analysis requires an evaluation of the design and implementation of internal controls and the response often requires testing of controls as well as of transactions, balances and disclosures.

  - Sufficient, appropriate evidence is required to support conclusions and auditors should perform audits with an attitude of professional scepticism, recognising that circumstances may exist that cause the financial statements to be materially misstated.

  - Audits are conducted in accordance with International Standards on Auditing (ISAs) issued by the International Auditing and Assurance Standards Board (IAASB).

  - The financial statements are always the responsibility of the audited entity, and there are robust ethical requirements which require the auditor to be independent of the audited entity.

- **Nature and level of assurance and report**

  - Audit engagements involve reasonable assurance. The risk of material misstatement is reduced to an acceptable level. The audit opinion states that the financial statements give a true and fair view of, or present fairly in all material respects, the financial position, performance and cash flows etc., in accordance with IFRS.

- **Type of information reported on**

  - Audit engagements are generally performed on historical financial statements prepared in accordance with an acceptable financial reporting framework such as IFRS.

(b)   Review engagements

- **Nature of work performed**

  - Review engagements consist principally of analytical procedures and inquiries, based on an assessment of the risk of material misstatement.

  - As with audits, sufficient, appropriate evidence is required to support conclusions drawn and practitioners should perform the review with an attitude of professional scepticism, recognising that circumstances may exist which cause the financial statements to be materially misstated.

  - Practitioners need to have a sufficiently detailed knowledge of the business in order to be able to perform the review effectively, including knowledge of the environment in which it operates and a knowledge of the organisation and its systems, as well as its assets and liabilities.

- Detailed procedures are likely to include inquiries concerning changes in the business, accounting policies, material assertions in the financial statements, the completeness of recorded transactions and subsequent events. Analytical procedures may be applied by comparing current financial statements with previous financial statements, with budgets and industry norms. Formal, written representations signed by management may be necessary, as they are for audits.

- Detailed evaluations of the design and implementation of controls and detailed testing of controls, transactions and balances are not generally performed in review engagements.

- ISRE 2400 on review engagements issued by the IAASB governs the conduct of review engagements.

- Again, the information reviewed is always the responsibility of the entity, and independence requirements apply to review engagements.

- **Nature and level of assurance and report**

  - Limited assurance is obtained in review engagements. The risk of material misstatement is assessed and reduced through analytical procedures and inquiries to a level that is acceptable in the circumstances, but that is greater than for an audit engagement.

  - Limited assurance is sometimes described as 'negative assurance' because the words used to describe it in the review report are generally as follows:

  *Based on the procedures we have performed and the evidence we have obtained, nothing has come to our attention that causes us to believe that the financial statements do not give a true and fair view . . . etc.*

  Review reports normally state that an audit has not been performed, that a review engagement is more limited in scope, that no audit opinion is expressed and that had an audit been performed, other matters might have come to light.

  The engagement letter and review report may restrict circulation of the report provided and may disclaim liability, where appropriate.

- **Type of information reported on**

  - Review engagements may be performed on historical financial statements prepared in accordance with a financial reporting framework such as IFRS. Review engagements are often performed on preliminary financial information and prospective financial information. Additional IAASB and other guidance are applicable to such engagements.

  - Most review engagements are performed at the request of directors, although there are often regulatory or statutory requirements for review-type engagements.

– Review reports are generally addressed to directors of companies. If a review has been commissioned in connection with a particular transaction, the review report may also be addressed to and/or made available to third parties involved with the transaction.

(c)    **Agreed-upon procedures**

- **Nature of work performed**

  – As the name implies, the procedures performed in agreed-upon procedures engagements are agreed by the practitioner and the parties commissioning the report. For example, a practitioner may agree to select a sample of receivables balances for confirmation and to perform detailed testing on a given number of transactions.

  – Those commissioning the report are usually the directors, despite the fact that the report may be for the benefit of a third party, such as an insurance company. The work to be performed may be pre-determined by the third party.

  – The report issued must refer to the procedures agreed. They commonly include inquiry, analysis, re-computation, comparison and other clerical accuracy checks, observation, inspection and obtaining confirmations.

  – Further work is required when matters come to the practitioner's attention indicating that there may be material misstatements or that the assessed level of risk requires adjustment.

  – International Standards on Related Services Engagements (ISRS) deal with agreed-upon procedures engagements.

  – Practitioners are required to be objective in performing agreed-upon procedures engagements.

- **Nature and level of assurance and report**

  – Based on the procedures performed, practitioners report their factual findings. *No* assurance is obtained and users assess the procedures and findings and draw their own conclusions.

  – In all cases, it is important that both directors and third parties understand clearly the nature of the work performed, that assurance has not been obtained and that no audit or review have been conducted. This can be achieved through the engagement letter and the report itself. The engagement letter and report usually restrict circulation of the report provided to those for whom they are intended.

- **Type of information reported on**

  – Agreed-upon procedures engagements may be performed on information that is supplied in application for grants, for insurance claims, and for reports to regulators, on, for example, recorded turnover, recorded assets, working capital and other solvency-type statements.

– These engagements are often performed because of third party commercial, regulatory or statutory requirements. Reports may be addressed to directors and/or third parties.

(d) **Compilation engagements**

• **Nature of work performed**

– Practitioners obtain a general knowledge of the business, the transactions it engages in and its accounting records, and familiarise themselves with the industry and the accounting basis on which the financial information is prepared.

– Documentary evidence of these matters is required. This information is generally obtained by inquiry. Practitioners do not normally assess risk or evaluate the reliability or completeness of the information provided by the entity, the effectiveness of controls, or perform any verification work, although they do read the compiled information and consider whether it appears to be consistent with the practitioner's understanding of the business and free from obvious material misstatements.

– Practitioners are required to be objective in performing compilation procedures engagements, but do not necessarily need to be independent.

• **The report provided**

– The report provided gives no assurance. It generally states that the practitioner has prepared the information from books and records supplied, that the information compiled is the responsibility of the directors, and makes reference to the fact that no audit has been performed.

• **Type of information reported on**

– Compilation reports are prepared where practitioners prepare financial statements or other information on behalf of clients. They use their accounting expertise to collect, classify and summarise financial information. Such reports are often prepared for small clients who do not have the in-house expertise to prepare the required financial statements. The report is generally addressed to the directors who are responsible for the preparation of financial statements.

**Services suitable for Mattco**

• The bank is seeking certification of the next set of financial statements quickly.

• None of the services noted above provide guarantees or absolute assurance. Audits and reviews involve reasonable and limited assurance respectively.

• It will be necessary for the financial statements to be prepared in accordance with IFRS for assurance to be provided. It may be efficient for another team within the firm to prepare Mattco's financial statements in accordance with IFRS. This is permissible under the ethical requirements we are required to comply with but Mattco will remain responsible for the financial statements in any case.

- The procedures performed in a review engagement are not so extensive as those performed in an audit engagement, and do not go into such great depth as an audit engagement, particularly on internal control.

- It may be appropriate to perform a review engagement in the first year but I strongly suggest that you consider an audit engagement in the second and subsequent years because audits involve:

  – a higher level of assurance;

  – more detailed analysis of Mattco's systems;

  – the provision of advice on any weaknesses in systems that come to our attention during the audit including suggestions for improvements.

This is all important because the business is expanding. The larger the business, the greater the expectation by many third parties such as customers, suppliers and lenders that it will be subject to a full audit rather than a lower level review.

## SECTION 10 ANSWER

(a) Five examples: information on which professional accountants can provide assurance

- key performance indicators in greenhouse gas statements;

- prospective financial information such as cash flow forecasts;

- governance, strategy and management processes;

- management information flows and IT security;

- risk management systems and processes;

- information on the design, implementation and effectiveness of internal financial controls;

- regulatory processes and compliance with regulations, such as waste disposal regulations in the manufacture of fertilisers, and food hygiene regulations in food processing;

- compliance with contractual agreements, ethical requirements and behaviour such as employment practices, including child labour.

[NB: more than five examples provided for completeness, students should provide the number required in an exam]

(b) Assurance engagement definition and conditions

- In assurance engagements, practitioners express a conclusion designed to enhance the degree of confidence of the user about the outcome of an evaluation/measurement of information, against specified criteria. For example, in an audit, the audit opinion is the conclusion, the financial statements are the information, and IFRS or another applicable financial reporting framework is the criterion.

- For practitioners to accept an assurance engagement there must be an expectation that relevant ethical requirements including independence and competence will be satisfied and that there is a rational purpose to the engagement. The engagement must exhibit all of the following elements:

  – a three party relationship between the practitioner, a responsible party and intended users;

  – appropriate subject matter;

  – suitable criteria that will be available to intended users;

  – practitioner access to sufficient appropriate evidence to support the conclusion;

  – a written conclusion.

- Appropriate subject matter must be capable of consistent evaluation/measurement against the identified criteria, and of being subjected to assurance procedures to support a reasonable or limited assurance conclusion.

- Suitable criteria are necessary because they provide the framework for a consistent evaluation or measurement of a subject matter. What constitutes suitable criteria depends on circumstances. Criteria may be set out in law or regulation, be developed by industry groupings or designed to meet the needs of specific intended users. Suitable criteria must be relevant, complete, reliable, neutral and understandable.

(c)   **Information in social and environmental reports and associated assurance problems**

Information in social and environmental reports may include information on social, staff and community issues such as:

- employment practices, including child labour, absenteeism, the employment of women and ethnic minorities;

- health and safety records;

- training and education policies, procedures and spending;

- charitable donations and social engagement, including the provision of health and educational facilities for the use of staff and the communities in which entities operate.

Information in social and environmental reports may also cover environmental issues such as:

- the ethical sourcing of raw materials, supply chain materials management and supply chain audits;

- reductions in the use of energy, water and waste materials;

- increases in recycling and the use of recycled materials for fuel and packaging, for example;

- reductions in the use of packaging;

- the use of energy-efficient building materials and consumables such as paper, light bulbs and cleaning materials;

- carbon emissions, targets for their reduction and targets for spills and leaks.

All businesses emit greenhouse gases such as carbon dioxide, nitrous oxide and fluorinated gases. Greenhouse gas emissions can be:

- direct, scope 1 emissions from sources owned or controlled by the entity, such as emissions from factories, vehicles, boilers and incinerators;

- indirect, scope 2 emissions associated with energy from sources owned or controlled by another entity but transferred to and consumed by the reporting entity, such as electricity;

- indirect, scope 3 emissions, such as emissions arising from employee air travel, outsourced activities and the use of the entity's products.

Greenhouse gas statements quantify emissions. They are produced in connection with emissions trading schemes, for regulatory purposes or voluntarily. Government and other bodies provide measurement and reporting guidelines. In some industries, some KPIs involving greenhouse gases have become critical. The weighted average emissions per kilometre have a direct impact on the manufacture and taxation of vehicles in many jurisdictions.

Greenhouse gases are either physically measured at source, or are estimated by multiplying activity data, such as the amount of fuel used, by emissions conversion factors. Gases other than carbon dioxide are often quantified using carbon dioxide equivalents.

Greenhouse gas statements often cover the removal of gases through biological sinks such as trees, and deductions such as purchased offsets. Purchased offsets occur when an entity pays another entity to reduce emissions, increase removals or not increase emissions.

Assurance problems associated with all types of social and environmental reports include:

- the need for practitioners to obtain the relevant technical expertise;

- a lack of well-established reporting frameworks;

- a lack of management experience in producing such statements;

- measurement and estimation uncertainties.

# ABBREVIATIONS

## INTERNATIONAL/GENERAL

| | |
|---|---|
| CAAT | Computer Assisted/Aided Audit Technique |
| CAG | Consultative Advisory Group |
| CPE/CPD | Continuing Professional Education/Development |
| ECGI | European Corporate Governance Institute |
| EQCR | Engagement Quality Control Review |
| GAAP | Generally Accepted Accounting Principles |
| GAAS | Generally Accepted Auditing Standards |
| GCGF | Global Corporate Governance Forum |
| HKICPA | Hong Kong Institute of Certified Public Accountants |
| IAASB | International Auditing and Assurance Standards Board |
| IAESB | International Accounting Education Standards Board |
| IAPN | International Auditing Practice Note |
| IASB | International Accounting Standards Board |
| ICAI | Institute of Chartered Accountants of India |
| ICEQ | Internal Control Evaluation Questionnaire |
| ICGN | International Corporate Governance Network |
| ICQ | Internal Control Questionnaire |
| IDW | Institut der Wirtschaftsprüfer (Germany) |
| IESBA | International Ethics Standards Board for Accountants |
| IFAC | International Federation of Accountants |
| IFIAR | International Forum of Independent Audit Regulators |
| IFRS | International Financial Reporting Standards |
| IIA | Institute of Internal Auditors |
| IIRC | International Integrated Reporting Council |
| IOSCO | International Organisation of Securities Commissions |
| IPSASB | International Public Sector Accounting Standards Board |
| ISA | International Standard on Auditing |
| ISAE | International Standard on Assurance Engagements |
| ISQC | International Standard on Quality Control |
| ISRE | International Standard on Review Engagements |
| ISRS | International Standard on Related Services |
| KPI | Key Performance Indicator |
| OECD | Organisation for Economic Co-operation and Development |
| PAIB | Professional Accountants in Business Committee |
| PAODC | Professional Accountancy Organisation Development Committee |
| PFI | Prospective Financial Information |

| PIAC | Public Interest Activity Committee |
| PIE | Public Interest Entity |
| PII | Professional Indemnity Insurance |
| PIOB | Public Interest Oversight Board |
| SMPC | Small and Medium Practices Committee |
| SPE/SPV | Special Purpose Entity/Vehicle |
| TAC | Transnational Auditors Committee |
| UNCTAD | United Nations Commission on Trade and Development |

## RELATING TO SUSTAINABILITY

| A4S | The Prince's Accounting for Sustainability Project |
| ECX | European Climate Exchange |
| EU ETS | European Union Emissions Trading System/Scheme |
| GRI | Global Reporting Initiative |

## RELATING TO MONEY LAUNDERING

| CDD | Customer Due Diligence |
| DNFBP | Designated Non-financial Businesses and Professions |
| FATF | Financial Action Task Force |
| FIU | Financial Intelligence Unit |
| STR | Suspicious Transaction Report |

## RELATING TO THE UK

| ACCA | Association of Chartered Certified Accountants |
| AGM | Annual General Meeting |
| AQR | Audit Quality Review Team |
| CCAB | Consultative Committee of Accountancy Bodies |
| ES PASE | Ethical Standards Provisions Available to Small Entities |
| FRC | Financial Reporting Council |
| ICAEW | Institute of Chartered Accountants in England and Wales |
| POB | Professional Oversight Board |
| RQB | Recognised Qualifying Body |
| RSB | Recognised Supervisory Body |
| SORP | Statement of Recommended Practice |

## RELATING TO THE USA

| AICPA | American Institute of Certified Public Accountants |
| COSO | Committee of Sponsoring Organizations of the Treadway Commission |
| NYSE | New York Stock Exchange |
| PCAOB | Public Company Accounting Oversight Board |

# INDEX

Printed and bound by CPI Group (UK) Ltd, Croydon, CR0 4YY

18/08/2024

14541741-0001